Artificial Intelligence/ Human Intelligence

An Indissoluble Nexus

Artificial Intelligence/ Human Intelligence

An Indissoluble Nexus

Richard J Wallace
University College Cork, Ireland

NEW JERSEY • LONDON • SINGAPORE • BEIJING • SHANGHAI • HONG KONG • TAIPEI • CHENNAI • TOKYO

Published by

World Scientific Publishing Co. Pte. Ltd.
5 Toh Tuck Link, Singapore 596224
USA office: 27 Warren Street, Suite 401-402, Hackensack, NJ 07601
UK office: 57 Shelton Street, Covent Garden, London WC2H 9HE

British Library Cataloguing-in-Publication Data
A catalogue record for this book is available from the British Library.

ARTIFICIAL INTELLIGENCE/HUMAN INTELLIGENCE
An Indissoluble Nexus

ISBN 978-981-123-287-9 (hardcover)
ISBN 978-981-123-308-1 (paperback)
ISBN 978-981-123-288-6 (ebook for institutions)
ISBN 978-981-123-289-3 (ebook for individuals)

For any available supplementary material, please visit
https://www.worldscientific.com/worldscibooks/10.1142/12177#t=suppl

Typeset by Stallion Press
Email: enquiries@stallionpress.com

Printed in Singapore

What is your aim in philosophy?
To show the fly the way out of the fly bottle.

L. Wittgenstein

Ẹní bá mọ inú rò, a mo ọpẹ́ dá
(Whoever can reason well, will appreciate why he ought to be thankful.)

Yoruba proverb

Preface

Artificial intelligence is an inherently non-serious subject, unlike say, databases or operating systems. This is part of what gives this field its fascination. But at the same time, as an intellectual endeavor it has given rise to a body of results that are of considerable significance for science and engineering. This is why such fascination goes beyond mere intellectual ogling, at least if one is willing to roll up his sleeves and dig into the subject.

One of the distinctive features of AI as a field is that it seems to be intensely interesting to journalists. This, in itself, is reason for caution. It perhaps reflects the presence of certain dramaturgical features, which may in turn indicate a degree of shallowness in the conceptions that inform the field, or even word magic weaving its spell among practitioners as well as observers. But at the same time, as I have already indicated, AI cannot be dismissed on that account.

Here it is worth noting that my relation to the field is that of an insider, but one who has done most of his work in the closely related field of combinatorial search rather than AI per se. Hence, my perspective shares something with that of outsiders, while still being that of someone who has participated from within — and this includes papers in AI conferences (a qualification that many outside commenters cannot claim).

The present book originated as a talk that was given at Covenant University in Ota, Nigeria (as an invited talk at the International Conference on Adaptive Science and Technology — ICAST 2014) and the Obafemi Awolowo Univeristy in Ile-Ife. I wish to express my gratitude for the hospitality of the members of the faculty of engineering and administrators and staff at Covenant and the administrators and members of the Computer Science Department at OAU who helped make my trip to Nigeria a pleasant and memorable one. In particular, I should single out Prof. Sanjay Misra who invited me to give the talk at ICAST, little knowing what would eventually ensue. (So if we take a rigorous, objective view of the matter, it's all your fault, Sanjay!)

I would also like to acknowledge the (implicit) support given by the University College Cork and the Cork Constraint Computation Centre/ Insight Centre for Data Analytics where I have worked for the past 20 years, and in particular the directors of these Centres, Eugene C. Freuder and Barry O'Sullivan. Without the resources made available in this situation, it might not have been possible to carry this project through to completion. And here I should also acknowledge that for much of this time, I was supported, as was the entire Centre, by funding from Science Foundation Ireland.[1]

The idea for the talk actually began with one of the topics discussed in the next-to-last chapter of this book. But when I started to work out what I was going to say, other ideas that had been bouncing around in my head, sometimes for many years, all came tumbling out. At the end, the original idea became something of an add-on, a supplementary topic. Nonetheless, I decided to retain it because of its intrinsic interest and because it does promise to be a means of putting some of the ideas expressed in this book into practice, even if it doesn't quite serve as the consummation (a natural climax if we look at the narrative features of my argument) of what came before.

*

I have tried to make the discussion simple and straightforward, so it can be understood by any intelligent, attentive reader. In keeping with this I have adopted a somewhat personal, colloquial style. One thing that I have not done, however, is to include irrelevant narratives. Lately, this particular mode of presentation seems to have become quite common in popular works with a scientific bent. It is one of the most dreadful intellectual fashions that I have ever encountered. It is simply exasperating to wade through chitchat about a trip one took or a luncheon conversation, which adds nothing to the basic exposition. In fact, it gives such works a genuinely crappy character. The reader can rest assured that he will find no such blemishes in this work.[2*]

On the other hand, there are some journalists, and even some journalist-scientists such as Roger Lewin, who do this kind of thing very well. It would be very interesting to probe more deeply into the reasons for this difference. It may be partly due to the fact that these writers are not writing as experts; they are recording their excursions into an area of knowledge, where they meet experts, who they treat in part as characters in the narrative. So anecdotes are part of the presentation of a character; this means they have a natural place in the narrative, so they do not have the appearance of being thrown in gratuitously.

(Here, I am not talking about concrete examples. These are obviously of critical importance in an expository discussion. On the other hand, when you are introducing a new idea, I don't care whether you first discussed it at lunch with a colleague in a restaurant off Harvard Square. I really don't, and I resent having to read about this in order to get to the actual topic of discussion.)

The lesson is, as Dirty Harry said, know your limits, scientists. Do what you know how to do — and also understand your role in narrative or discourse that you are writing. If you are writing as an expert, then attend to the exposition and try to make that as clear and down-to-earth as possible, without barging in yourself. Don't imagine that your own doings are of interest, unless they have a direct bearing on the point under discussion.

*

I want to touch on one other personal matter before moving on to the book proper. It has to do with the fact that modern computer science, and in particular artificial intelligence, is one of the most extraordinary areas that one could ever hope to work in.

It is easy to forget amidst the clutter of everyday work or the tedium of conferences just how astonishing it all is. We really are dissecting intelligent action and studying systems that we have put together from simpler elements and that exhibit intelligence. This is something that the critics of

AI never seem to properly understand – this extraordinary expansion of human awareness.

And this is yet another reason for trying to understand what we are doing as clearly as we can. So let us begin.

Endnotes

1. At this point I also want to acknowledge the work of Ronan Murray of Murray & McCarthy in preparing the illustrations for this book.
2. Of course, these strictures do not apply to the same extent for frankly autobiographical accounts like James Watson's Double Helix or Feng-hsiung Hsu's Behind Deep Blue. But imagine if Einstein's or Heisenberg's popular books on physics had been larded with irrelevant anecdotes; I think this would have clearly compromised their quality.

Contents

Part I
Introductory

1
Introduction

Human beings have always had an uneasy relation with artificial intelligence. The field has unsettled philosophers and some scientists, as well as journalists and the general public. Even positive accounts of advances in the field tend to resemble the scene in the fifties movie version of *The War of the Worlds* where the earthlings approach a Martian vehicle that has just landed, holding a white flag before them and hoping for a beneficent encounter.

It hasn't helped that the field has been constantly over-hyped. Some of this may be ascribed to journalistic irresponsibility, but part of it has emanated from the field itself. For the very idea of artificial intelligence brings with it a kind of intoxication; creating such artifacts is a genuine Faustian enterprise; and there is something in all this that greatly appeals to a certain vulgar layer (or is it a module?) of the human mind. So, despite the many substantive achievements, some of which are reviewed in succeeding chapters, there is something of the air of the trollop about this field.[1*]

Within the field of computer science itself AI has always had a rather peculiar status. Some would dismiss it altogether. ("AI is bullshit" is the most succinct statement of this attitude that I have come across.) But while most computer scientists take a more indulgent stance, the field has never acquired the solid, good citizen status of a subject like operating systems or computer memory organization or programming semantics.

The situation can be illustrated with quotations from an article that appeared in Life Magazine at the end of the field's early formative phase, carrying the provocative title, "Meet Shaky: The first electronic person".[2] Shakey (the correct name) was a robot built at Stanford University in the 1960s. The author first recounts a demonstration of the robot's prowess in carrying out instructions conveyed to it by a typed message: "PUSH THE BLOCK OFF THE PLATFORM". Shakey was able to do this in the face of obstacles such as a ramp that had been detached from the raised platform and was lying on the floor in the same room, so that it had to be moved into place.

The author then went on to describe the workings of the robot's mind:

> "In defiance of the soothing conventional view that the computer is just a glorified abacus that cannot possibly challenge the human monopoly of reason, Shaky's brain demonstrates that machines can think. Variously defined, thinking includes such processes as "exercising the powers of judgment" and "reflecting for the purpose of reaching a conclusion." In some of these respects — among them powers of recall and mathematical agility — Shaky's brain can think better than the human mind."

In the course of his description, other similar assessments are made:

> "Shaky can usually guess what he's looking at (just as people can) without bothering to fill in all the features on the hidden side of the object. In fact, the art of recognizing patterns is now so far advanced that merely by adding a few equations Shaky's creators could teach him to recognize a familiar human face every time he sees it."
>
> "All these separate systems [in Shakey's 'brain'] merge smoothly in a totality more intricate than many forms of sentient life and they work together with wonderful agility and resourcefulness."
>
> "With very little change in the program and equipment, Shaky now could do work in a number of limited environments: warehouses, libraries, assembly lines."

The author also includes some predictions made by researchers at that time. (Here, he illustrates another distinctive feature of this field of computer science; the obsession of many of its practitioners with future achievements.) This includes a prediction from one of the doyens of the field, expressed with a confidence that can only come from mastering one's social sphere:

> "Marvin Minsky … a 42-year-old polymath who has made major contributions to Artificial Intelligence, recently told me with quiet certitude: "In from three to eight

> years we will have a machine with the general intelligence of an average human being. I mean a machine that will be able to read Shakespeare, grease a car, play office politics, tell a joke, have a fight. At that point the machine will begin to educate itself with fantastic speed. In a few months it will be at genius level and a few months after that its powers will be incalculable.""
>
> "When I checked Minsky's prophecy with other people working on Artificial Intelligence ... many of them said that Minsky's timetable might be somewhat wishful — "give us 15 years," was a common remark — but all agreed that there would be such a machine and that it could precipitate the third Industrial Revolution, wipe out poverty and roll up centuries of growth in science, education, and the arts."

In view of these assessments, it is rather disconcerting to note that at AI conferences almost 50 years later, all the papers are presented by human beings, and human beings still do all the reviewing. This is a strange state of affairs, to say the least, and it cries out for explanation. (Of course, there are implications about human as well as artificial intelligence here, which would, however, take us too far afield. I would go so far as to suggest that some kind of reality distorting influence is in play.)

Returning to the comparison made earlier, can one imagine an article like this on the topic of databases, or even the basic theory of machines?

Having said all this, it is important to emphasize that contemporary AI as a field of science and engineering is both broad and in some places deep, as I hope the chapters in the next section will demonstrate. A substantial field of endeavor falls under the heading of AI, reflected in a stream of scintillating conference papers and journal articles, and a number of imposing texts.[3]

Still, it cannot be denied that from its inception AI has tried to go farther than this, and this is reflected both in its claims and its endeavors. From its inception it has been engaged in a quest to create forms of intelligence that can match human capacities, or even exceed them.

And to some degree it has already done what it set out to do. Systems like Deep Blue and more recently Watson are extraordinary achievements. To build a program that can perform passably against skilled human beings in a specific task is no mean achievement in itself. But these systems have outperformed world champions. (Deep Blue and Watson are discussed at some length in Chapters 2 and 4.)

There are some who have belittled these achievements. The main argument is that while these systems manage to perform impressively in a narrowly prescribed task, this does not represent genuine human-level intelligence. In fact, since it can be questioned whether these systems even understand what they are doing, their achievements may have little to do with the real goals of AI.

But why not at least acknowledge the accomplishments? After all, no one feels badly about the fact that on a flat track no human being can keep up with a Ferrari. (By comparison, the fact that there are people who can seriously compete with a system like Deep Blue is really quite extraordinary, since it appears to be a commensurate achievement.)

And then there are the publications that bob up in the public arena from time to time telling us, sometimes enthusiastically, sometimes apprehensively, that an age of "superintelligence" is just around the corner. But is this really true? Is superintelligence in some form or other nearly upon us? This book will try to answer this question, but not directly. Instead, it is the thesis of this work that the question itself is poorly posed, so that there is a sense in which current and past claims about superintelligence are "not even wrong" because they are based on fundamental misconceptions about the nature of the AI project.

It is a characteristic of such books that little is said about what this "superintelligence" actually consists of. It is all very vague and even phantasmagoric. One of the things I want to do in this book is to 'draw the veil aside' (to the degree that one can) by considering in some depth systems that have achieved remarkable levels of achievement. How do they work? How were they put together? And a question just as important, as this book will make clear: what is the knowledge tradition that gave rise to them, of which they are an indissoluble part?

*

Before beginning a discussion that will take us through several chapters, I want to give some account of what I have in mind when I use the term "intelligence". This can be considered as a working definition; although it will be enlarged upon in some ways, it will be adhered to throughout this volume. Since I wish to be as concrete as possible I will begin with the notion of an intelligent action.

> *An intelligent action is an inference or series of inferences that solves a problem whose solution is not obvious to begin with.*

A problem, in turn, can be defined as a situation in which there is a current state of affairs and a goal state, and the two are not the same. An intelligent action (or series of intelligent actions) takes one from the current state to the goal state.

Intelligence, then, is simply the capacity to carry out intelligent actions as I have defined them.

This definition is intentionally behavioristic in nature. To my mind the central insight of the behaviorists was that no special class of 'mental events' is needed in a full account of psychological processes. This means that it is not necessary to posit some special, metaphysically distinct, mental events (or "subjective states") in any explanation of intelligent acts stated in terms of cause and effect. This general perspective can encompass the information processing and computational views of intelligence and cognition as well as the limited S-R models that the classical behaviorists are generally known for.[4*,5*]

In addition, the present strategy prevents the discussion from wandering off into the intellectual thicket usually referred to as the nature of consciousness, which while not identical often seems to be located in close proximity to the Wood of Error. The point is that there is no need to worry about the deep problems involved in the idea of consciousness in order to discuss intelligence, either artificial or human. (As will be seen later, this can be construed as a kind of render-unto-Caesar strategy.)

As a matter of fact, the definition I have given is more or less the standard definition used in AI.

Of course, the word "intelligence" is often used in different ways in other fields. In particular, psychologists use this term to refer to 'abilities' and to the tests that measure them; here, a major topic of interest is the pattern of differences in such scores across a population of individuals. This is not a concern here. (However, something more will be said about such topics in Chapter 6, where the basic thesis concerning intelligence is laid out.) There have also been discussions about different 'kinds' of intelligence, but these fall under the same abilities rubric. And in some cases, e.g. "emotional intelligence", this kind of thinking is dubious anyway.

I will, however, deal directly with another vexed problem that crops up when thinking about AI, which is the problem of "understanding".

Although this could be confused with the problem of consciousness, I will try to show that the former can be dealt with separately. (In doing this, I do not mean to imply that they are unrelated; but, again, such questions are beyond the scope of the present text.)[6*]

I hope that even at this point the reader has begun to understand that the thrust of the present work is quite different from the usual critiques of AI or most general discussions of the topic.

*

All this does not mean that AI as it develops and matures will not cause social and economic dislocations. There are real problems ahead, especially when one is dealing with a technology 'of the mind', although these are also topics beyond the scope of the present work.

As a result, this book will say nothing about these vital issues. Nonetheless, the ideas put forward in this work are certainly relevant. The main purpose of this work is to clarify the problem of artificial intelligence. And, obviously, this in turn will help to guide our response to the difficulties engendered.

One could go further. Unless we understand the true nature of the problem, the reaction against these difficulties is likely to be benighted and destructive.

However, this work stakes its claims for significance on other grounds. At present many people seem to fall into one or another kind of thralldom when it comes to questions regarding machine intelligence. This book is meant in part to rescue the reader from such "mind-forged manacles". And that strikes me as being of sufficient importance to make a book of this sort worthwhile.

*

The general scheme of the work is as follows.

The next section (Chapters 2–5) carries out an examination in some detail of programs that have accomplished impressive feats of intelligence, in some cases even proving superior to the best human competitors. These are, therefore, our best current examples of "superintelligence". As part of this discussion, I will try to put the systems in their historical contexts, and I will try to give the reader some idea of how they actually work.

In this way the nature of their achievements can be better understood. I will also discuss arguments concerning their limitations.

The third section (Chapters 6-9) deals with the problem of the nature of intelligence. Chapter 6 is in some ways the central chapter of the text. Here, I present a view of artificial intelligence that is somewhat at odds with the typical one. Following this, Chapter 7 considers different kinds of intelligence that can be distinguished, and Chapter 8 considers some perennial AI topics from the new perspective.

Chapter 9 considers what may be the key advance in the study of intelligence in the last 20–30 years, which falls under the general heading of combinatorial search, i.e. the study of solution finding in large spaces of possibilities. At the same time this is a development in which AI is merely one branch. Other participating disciplines are operations research, the field of heuristic search methods, and a field called "global optimization", which is mainly concerned with finding optima for systems that can be described in terms of real-valued functions.

In the fourth section (Chapters 10–12), the focus changes to encompass human intelligence as well as AI. Chapter 10 discusses human responses to the AI, both critical and acclamatory. In Chapter 11, which is entirely about human intelligence (or the lack of it), serious issues are raised concerning limitations of such intelligence in its unaided form. This sets the stage for discussion of a new kind of AI application. Partly as a preparation for this, Chapter 12 presents a new kind of AI challenge, pertaining to aids for discourse and argumentation, in the form of two specific challenges.

In the final section, Chapter 13 summarizes the basic thesis and considers possible further implications. Other important issues are discussed, such as the relation between AI and computer science in general, and remaining open questions.

It may be noted that Chapters 4 and 9 are more technical in nature than the other chapters. If found too daunting on first reading, I think they can be skipped without losing the main thread of the argument.

Finally, it should be noted that when footnote numbers are starred, this indicates that the footnote contains ancillary discussion rather than (or in addition to) citations.[7]

Endnotes

1. In keeping with these observations, it is possible to discern a rather odd symbiosis between journalism and AI. (To my mind, when newspaper reporters and suchlike find an intellectual field continually attractive, this is not a good sign. Remember Marshall McLuhan?)
2. B. Darrach, "Meet Shaky: The first electronic person, *Life Magazine*, May, 1970, 69(21): 58–68.
3. A fine example of the character of AI in the early days is the text by N. J. Nilsson, *Problem-Solving Methods in Artificial Intelligence*, New York: McGraw-Hill, 1971. Much of the key work from this era was collected in two volumes: E. A. Feigenbaum & J. Feldman, editors, *Computers and Thought*, New York: McGraw-Hill, 1963 and M. Minsky, editor, *Semantic Information Processing*, Cambridge, MA & London: MIT, 1968. Of the many contemporary or near-contemporary textbooks one might cite, I will mention three outstanding ones: S. Russell & P. Norvig, *Artificial Intelligence: A Modern Approach* (2nd edition), Upper Saddle River, NJ: Pearson Education, 2003; M. R. Genesereth & N. J. Nilsson, *Logical Foundations of Artificial Intelligence*, Palo Alto, CA: Morgan Kaufmann, 1987; M. Ginsberg, *Essentials of Artificial Intelligence*, San Mateo, CA: Morgan Kaufmann, 1993.
4. In fact, the slant on intelligence that I am taking is usually called "functionalism" within the sphere of cognitive science. In what follows I will use the term "behavioristic" to refer to this physicalistic perspective.
5. To make my position clearer, let me describe a well-known finding from the early days of modern cognitive psychology. This was a reaction time study in which the subject was presented with a pair of letters on each trial, such as one of these:

   A B   a B   a b   A A   b b   A a

   The letters were presented visually in a machine called a tachistoscope. The task was to classify the pairs as either similar or different on the basis of their being the same or different letter of the alphabet. In this case, the three pairs on the left would be classified as different while the three on the right would be classified as the same. The subject indicated his judgment by pressing one of two keys, and he was required to do this as quickly as possible.

   The chief finding involved the similarity judgments. When the two letters were both upper case or lower case (and therefore visually identical), as with the A A and b b pairs, the average reaction time was 80 milliseconds faster than when an upper case and a lower case letter were paired, as with the A a pair. The interpretation was that since in the latter case the visual appearance of the two letters was different, a proper judgment required an extra recoding step. In contrast the other pairs could be matched on their visual appearance alone, so there was no need for recoding to occur before a judgment could be made. This difference was reflected in the difference in average reaction time.

Now, the point of all this is that we have here a causal analysis of an internal mental process that is entirely grounded in physical events, which we can ascertain because of the time required for its execution (and which we can characterize to an extent given the input-output conditions). In other words, this is an analysis of cognition (admittedly of a very simple form) carried out in strictly 'behavioristic', i.e. non-mentalistic, terms.

6. I realize that such a behavioristic perspective seems to overlook or disregard the vast endeavor known as consciousness studies that has grown up in the last 30 or 40 years. (For a recent summary account, see W. Hofman & T. D. Wilson, "Consciousness, introspection, and the adaptive unconscious", In: B. Gawronski & B. K. Payne, editors, *Handbook of Implicit Social Cognition: Measurement, Theory and Applications*, Guilford, 2010.) A leading idea in this work is the "workspace model", which is really just a reference to attention and working memory. In this work, consciousness is sometimes likened to a theater stage, although as D. Dennett has pointed out, this leaves open the question of who the audience is.[6a] I find it odd that use is not made of a more apposite analogy, which is the computer central processing unit, or CPU; after all, this is indeed the 'workspace' of the computer. Moreover, the interrupt system of a digital computer has an obvious resemblance to selective attention in human beings. I suspect it may be because if this metaphor were emphasized, it might draw attention to the fact that in discussing computer operations notions of consciousness are superfluous. And that makes my point.

6a. According to one exposition (B. J. Baars, *In the Theater of Consciousness*, Oxford: Oxford University Press, 1997, p. 45), consciousness "serves to disseminate a small amount of information to a vast unconscious audience in the brain". But either this means that attentional focus serves to tag or filter certain information before it is transmitted to various parts of the brain, a process that must occur by means of physical mechanisms (which can be described without reference to "consciousness"), or the statement doesn't make any sense at all (what on earth is an "unconscious audience"?).

7. This is an idea I took from H. Dreyfus' book on Heidegger, cited later in the text.

Part II

Case Studies

2

Two Impressive Wins for AI

I will begin with two systems that have some reason to be called superintelligent. Each is a game-playing system that was powerful enough to beat world champions — of the human sort — in direct competition.

Deep Blue

Deep Blue was a chess-playing system which in 1997 defeated the world chess champion, Gary Kasparov, in a six-game match. This was the culmination of nearly 50 years of research on programming a computer to play chess competitively, and twelve years since the inception of the series of machines that culminated in Deep Blue.

Why should one be interested in a program or computer system that plays chess? Why is this relevant to the present discussion? One answer was given by Yasser Seirawan in his Forward to Monty Newborn's book on computer chess. Speaking of this program of research in relation to ENIAC, the first electronic computer, he said:

> "Man was creating a machine [ENIAC] that could mimic its creator. The machine was being designed to "think". And what sterner test of "thinking" is there than a game of chess? Chess has agonized its adherents since it evolved centuries ago. A sterner intellectual challenge is hard to find. After all, what on earth are we doing when we play a game of chess if not thinking? Surely, if machines could best man at chess, what more proof need we have that machines indeed can and do think?"[1]

The matches between Deep Blue and Kasparov in 1996 and 1997 were closely watched around the world, and the outcome was reported in many leading papers and other news sources at that time. Here are some examples:

> "In an unexpected victory of machine over man, Deep Blue, the new I.B.M. chess computer, trounced world chess champion, Gary Kasparov, yesterday in the first game of the scheduled six-game match here at the Pennsylvania Convention Center."
>
> N. Y. Times, 1996[2]

> "It was 62 minutes into the match and world champion Gary Kasparov had had enough. … In the most publicized, talked-about and Internet-followed chess event in history, Kasparov's undefeated record came to a stunning halt. The machine, at least for now, had triumphed, and man's relations with computers may never be the same."
>
> MSNBC, 1997[3]

Deep Blue was a specialized machine built at IBM by people skilled in designing special-purpose computer chips. For its time it was extremely fast — it could examine about 200 million positions per second. However, this was considered secondary by the designers. (In Chapter 4 the inner workings of Deep Blue are explored in some detail.)

According to the lead designer, Feng-hsiung Hsu, the basic problem in facing a very talented human player was the latter's adaptability. In Hsu's words, "Human Grandmasters, in serious matches, learn from computers' mistakes, exploit the weaknesses, and drive a truck thru the gaping holes." The solution, therefore, was to build a system that had "very few weaknesses, and only weaknesses that are difficult to exploit"[4]

Deep Blue encoded a vast amount of chess information, so it was far from being a brute force system, although it was sometimes depicted as such in the popular press. It was also constantly being tweaked, even between games in a chess match. Again, from Dr. Hsu, in reference to the match with Kasparov:

> "Our team … put as much chess knowledge as possible onto the chess chip and reduce[d] the number of serious knowledge gaps.

"We … also made it as easy as possible to change the chess chip's playing behavior.

"To deal with previously unknown computer weaknesses showing up in a match, we made the weights associated with the positional features individually adjustable from software."[5]

In doing this Hsu and his team were following in the footsteps of the original chess pioneers. From the earliest work on the problem it was recognized that input from knowledgeable humans would be necessary for building an effective chess-playing system. Thus, Claude Shannon in one of the earliest essays on the subject said, when talking about a move evaluator:

"As a first rough approximation, a position can be evaluated by merely adding up the total forces for each side, measured in terms of the pawn unit. There are, however, numerous other features which must be taken into account: the mobility and placement of pieces, the weakness of king protection, the nature of the pawn formation, and so on. These too can be given numerical weights and combined in the evaluation, and *it is here that the knowledge and experience of chess masters must be enlisted*."[6] (emphasis added)

Hence, from the very inception of the field of automated chess-playing by computer, expert human intelligence was relied upon in the basic coding. Also, as chess programs evolved, a massive amount of human knowledge was funneled into them. As a result, they have some features in common with database systems. This trend reached a climax in Deep Blue. Moves from earlier Grand Master matches were encoded, to be compared with the best move found by Deep Blue's evaluation function. Therefore, nearly all of Deep Blue's decisions were directly informed by human as well as artificial intelligence.

After the Kasparov-Deep Blue match, some AI researchers also weighed in, writing in the mainstream press:

"Deep Blue is unintelligent because it is so narrow. It can win a chess game, but it can't recognize, much less pick up, a chess piece. Since the essence of intelligence would seem to be breadth, …, it's hard to credit Deep Blue with much intelligence.

"However, many commentators are insisting that Deep Blue shows no intelligence whatsoever, because it doesn't actually "understand" a chess position, but only searches through millions of possible move sequences "blindly". The fallacy in this argument is the assumption that intelligent behavior can only be the result of intelligent cognition."

Drew McDermott, N. Y. Times, 1997[7]

In the opinion of the present author, in this passage McDermott effectively counters charges that Deep Blue is "unintelligent". However, he still treats Deep Blue as a kind of stand-alone entity. But is this the proper way to consider Deep Blue and its accomplishments? In considering this question, it is useful to consider the words of Hsu himself, in his book about Deep Blue and the matches with Kasparov a few years later. Here, he writes:

"The "man versus machine" angle apparently sells well for chess books, but it does not capture the true essence of the contest. The contest was really between men in two different roles: man as a performer and man as a toolmaker."[8]

And later in the same book:

"My impression, from what he [Garry Kasparov] said, was that he saw himself as defending the human race against machines. *When I looked at my fellow team members, I saw human faces.* We were simply approaching the problem of playing chess from, shall we say, a non-traditional direction."[9] (emphasis added)

Hsu's remarks serve to introduce the basic thesis of the present work: that AI should never be considered as something 'out there'. Instead it is always part and parcel of a distinctly human enterprise. It is the purpose of the present volume to elaborate on this insight and to spell out the implications in some detail. But first I want to continue the present stage setting exercise by reviewing another notable AI system.

Watson

Watson is a system also created at IBM as part of a project to develop sophisticated question answering systems. Watson was specifically designed to give answers to questions used on the quiz show Jeopardy! The project was so successful that in a contest held in 2011 between Watson and two outstanding championship players, Watson bested its human opponents.

In the game of Jeopardy! there are normally three contestants who compete amongst each other. The competition is carried out over a series of rounds; in each round contestants try to guess what item is being referred to while listening to a series of clues. The material for the contest comes from a variety of topics, such as history, the sciences, and popular culture. On each round there are six categories with five clues of varying worth. The categories and values are presented on a large board, shown in Figure 2.1. The procedure on each round is described in the Wikipedia article on Jeopardy! from which the following is taken (with one alteration):

> The Jeopardy! round begins when the returning champion selects a clue, which may be from any position on the game board. The clue is revealed and read aloud by the host, after which any contestant may ring in using a hand-held signaling device. The first contestant to ring in successfully is prompted to provide a response to the clue, phrased in the form of a question. For example, if a contestant were to select "English Literature for $200", the resulting clue could be "This is thought to be

The Dinosaurs	Notable Women	Oxford Dictionary	Name That Instrument	Belgium	Composers By Country
$200	$200	$200	$200	$200	$200
$400	$400	$400	$400	$400	$400
$600	$600	$600	$600	$600	$600
$800	$800	$800	$800	$800	$800
$1000	$1000	$1000	$1000	$1000	$1000

Figure 2.1. Jeopardy board

Shakespeare's last play.", to which the correct response would be "What is The Tempest?" If the contestant responds correctly, the clue's dollar value is added to the contestant's score, and they may select a new clue from the board. An incorrect response, or a failure to respond within five seconds, deducts the clue's value from the contestant's score and allows the other contestants the opportunity to ring in and respond.[5] If no contestant responds correctly, the host reveals the correct response, and the contestant who selected the clue may choose the next clue.

The question in the passage above is quite straightforward. However, many Jeopardy! questions require more involved forms of inference. Consider the following examples, all of which were used as questions on the actual show.[10] The first is:

Clue: Their grandfather had a number 1 record in 1935; their father, number 1's in 1958 and 1961; and they hit number 1 in 1990.

Answer: What is Gunnar and Matthew Nelson?

Deriving an answer to this question involves putting together multiple lines of evidence. At the same time, multiple clues are presented, any one of which might lead one to the correct answer, although the answer then needs to be checked for consistency with the other clues. Note also that having a number 1 hit in any given year applies to a number of recording artists, so this type of clue does not winnow down the field very much in itself. It is only when the sets of possibilities associated with different years are compared that one can begin to reduce the number of possible answers, in this case to one.

The next example presents a different sort of problem in that the answer is a kind of portmanteau, combining an actor's name with a device based on a common name. Here, there are difficulties in even understanding what question is being asked.

Clue: The "Jerry Maguire" star who automatically maintains your vehicle's speed.

Answer: What is Tom Cruise control?

The next example combines both of the problems found in the previous two. Here, information must be combined, but a criterion for combining information must also be gleaned from the clue, so that one understands the basis for correctly combining such information.

Clue: Unique quality of "First Communion of Anemic Young Girls in the Snow," shown at the 1883 Arts Incoherents Exhibit.

Answer: What is white.

In the next example, a straightforward but somewhat obscure clue is given by "wainscoting"; however, one must make an untypical deduction from it, which again involves combining sources of information derived from the words "standing" and "looking".

Clue: If you're standing, it's the direction you should look to check out the wainscoting.

Answer: What is down.

After some initial setbacks (discussed in Chapter 4), the Watson design team tried an approach that was radically different in some ways from then-existing question answering systems. The system they eventually came up with had a "massively parallel probabilistic evidence-based architecture" using "more than 100 different techniques for analyzing natural language, identifying sources, finding and generating hypotheses, finding and scoring evidence, and merging and ranking hypotheses". The system also used "pervasive confidence estimation". This meant that, "all components produce[d] features and associated confidences".[11] As will become evident in Chapter 4, this feature was essential given the manner of approaching the problem.

It is not too much to say that the techniques developed for Watson have revolutionized this particular field. No system had ever been built that could perform in a complex, open-ended situation like Jeopardy! with any real degree of accuracy. This is shown in Figure 2.2, which compares the performance of a previous state-of-the-art system (solid line) with successful human players (scatterplot at top of graph).[12] Here, "precision" means the proportion answered correctly in relation to the proportion attempted ("%Answered"). In its finished version, the comparable curve for Watson passed through the cloud of dots.

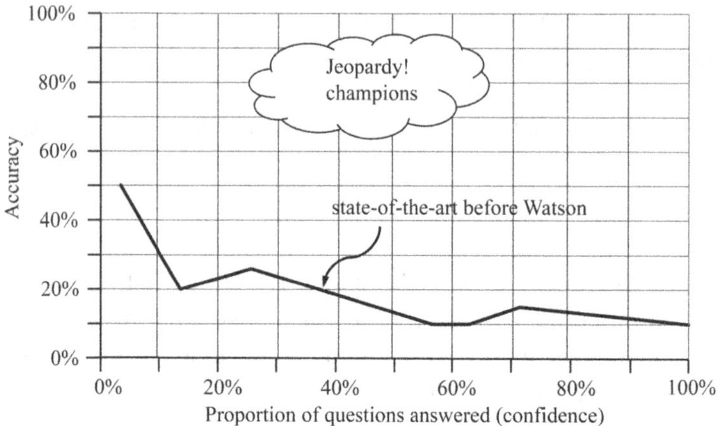

Figure 2.2. Performance of pre-Watson question answering system (solid line) versus champion Jeopardy! players (cloud of individual scores). Percent answered (confidence) versus correctness. (based on Figure 4 of Ferrucci *et al.*, 2010, © 2019 Association for the Advancement of Artificial Intelligence, by permission).

Watson's winning performance elicited the usual reactions. In an interview that appeared in Popular Mechanics entitled, "Why Watson and Siri Are Not Real AI", Douglas Hofstadter said, "Watson is basically a text search algorithm connected to a database just like Google search. It doesn't understand what it's reading." Shortly after this there was a rejoinder in the form of an article entitled, "Why Watson is real artificial intelligence". The authors of the article contended that (i) Watson was deriving responses to questions normally posed to human beings, and this involved both formulating an answer and assessing their likelihood of being correct; plus, all this was being done in real time, (ii) there were in fact similarities between the way Watson worked and the operations of primate brains. They also noted the somewhat deceptive cover involved in 'looking under the hood' where there is only computer code; as they note, this might also be said of human achievements, which in the end are based on the activities of 'unintelligent' nerve cells.[13]

*

Both Deep Blue and Watson were formidable achievements, in some ways like putting a man on the moon. But what was the basis for their achievements, their "superintelligence"?

In the next two chapters, I will try to answer this question by taking cases such as Watson and Deep Blue and 'looking under the hood'. In this way, the reader should get a clearer idea of what these systems are actually doing. At the same time I will show how each system is located within a larger body of work that stretches back long before the computer era. This will serve as a natural lead-in to the main thesis of the book.

In the meantime, it is worth asking about the fate of these systems since their triumphs. What has transpired after the obligatory news articles in the New York Times and elsewhere? Overall, not much — or at least not as much as one might have expected. In fact, the aftermath of each achievement has been a kind of dénouement. This in itself is significant.

This has been clearest in the case of Deep Blue. After gathering dust in some corner of the IBM laboratories for several years, portions of it were donated to the Computer History Museum at Carnegie-Mellon University and the Smithsonian Institute. In the meantime, computer chess has proceeded in other directions. To be sure, the human chess world has been heavily influenced by advances in computer chess. One thing that has happened is that it has lost much of its original mystique. More substantively, most players now use chess programs to analyze positions and for practice. Within the field of computer chess, a number of further improvements have been proposed for making the search problem involved in evaluating positions more efficient. And there are now a plethora of chess programs of high quality that run on ordinary (as opposed to specialized) computer hardware. In addition, people have taken up the question of solving the 'chess problem', i.e. of providing a complete solution to the problem of winning at chess. But it is important to realize that all these activities are almost entirely restricted to the world of chess.

It's worth comparing this situation with the extraordinary expectations that were originally bound up with this enterprise:

> "Chess is the intellectual game par excellence. ... it pits two intellects against each other in a situation so complex that neither can hope to understand it completely, but sufficiently amenable to analysis that each can hope to outthink his opponent. The game is sufficiently deep and subtle to have supported the rise of professional players, and to have allowed a deepening analysis through 200 years of intensive study and play without becoming exhausted or barren. Such characteristics mark chess as a natural arena for attempts at mechanization. If one could devise a successful chess machine, one would seem to have penetrated to the core of human intellectual endeavor."[14]

And now that the task has been accomplished, as far as I can tell it brought none of the revelations that these pioneers had hoped for. Instead, one is reminded of Philip Larkin's "empty attic of fulfillment".

For a while the same fate seemed to loom for Watson, as reflected in a news report in *Businesweek*. Quoting a computer scientist who specializes in medical applications, the author said:

> "The problem with Watson, as he [the scientist] sees it, is that it's essentially a really good search engine that can answer questions posed in natural language. Over time, Watson does learn from its mistakes, but Adlassnig suspects that the sort of knowledge Watson acquires from medical texts and case studies is "very flat and very broad." In a clinical setting, the computer would make a very thorough but cripplingly literal-minded doctor — not necessarily the most valuable addition to the medical staff. There may well come a day when computers can spit out diagnoses and treatment regimens, leaving doctors little to do but enter data and hone their bedside manner, but that day has not yet come."[15]

Speaking more generally, in neither case is there real evidence of conceptual breakthroughs that could lead to important further advances in research and technology. Each system seems to reflect the culmination of many lines of influence rather than being a significant influence in and of itself.[16*]

Perhaps the problem here is the one that Hofstadter pointed to: these systems perform well, but the don't really "understand" what they are doing. But this brings up the whole problem of understanding, viz., what does it mean to "understand"? What are the basic requirements for a system to have this capacity?

With this in mind, in Chapter 5 I will consider two other AI systems. These were not built to compete with people or with other programs, but to embody knowledge of a certain kind. As such, they seem closer to demonstrating the property of understanding, which, according to the critics of Deep Blue and Watson, is lacking in those systems. But as one might expect, their achievements are more difficult to evaluate. However, before continuing this account of major AI systems, I want to delve into the workings of some systems, including the two I have just described. This 'unpacking' exercise will be the subject of the next two chapters.

Endnotes

1. Yasser Seirawan, Forward to M. Newborn, *Kasparov versus Deep Blue. Computer Chess Comes of Age*. New York: Springer-Verlag, 1997, p. xi.
2. B. Weber, "In upset, computer beats chess champion", *New York Times*, February 11, 1996 http://www.nytimes.com/1996/02/11/ us/in-upset-computer-beats-chess-champion.html.
3. J. Fine, "Deep Blue wins in final game of match", *MSNBC*, 1997 http://faculty.georgetown.edu/bassr/511/projects/letham/final/chess.htm.
4. F.-h. Hsu, "Designing a single chip chess grandmaster while knowing nothing about chess", (undated presentation) https://www.hotchips.org/wp_content/uploads/hc_archives/hc10/ 2_Mon/HC10.S4/HC10.4.1.pdf
5. F.-h. Hsu, "IBM's Deep Blue chess grandmaster chips", *IEEE Micro*, March–April, 1999, pp. 70–81, p. 71.
6. C. Shannon, "A chess-playing machine", *Scientific American*, February, 1950, 182(2): 48–51, p. 50.
7. D. McDermott, "How intelligent is Deep Blue?", (original version of article appearing in *New York Times*, May 14, 1997) http://www.nyu.edu/gsas/dept/philo/courses/mindsandmachines/Papers/mcdermott.html
8. F.-h. Hsu, *Behind Deep Blue*, Princeton: Princeton University, 2002, p. ix.
9. *Ibid.*, p. 111.
10. D. A. Ferrucci, "Introduction to "This is Watson"", *IBM Journal of Research and Development*, 2012, 56–1: 1–14, pp. 6–7.
11. D. Ferrucci *et al.*, "Building Watson: An overview of the DeepQA project", *AI Magazine*, Fall 2010, 31(3): 59–79, p. 68.
12. *Ibid.*, Figure 4.
13. W. Herkewitz & D. Hofstadter, "Why Watson and Siri are not real AI", *Popular Mechanics*, 2014, www.popularmechanics.com/ technology/engineering/news/why-watson-and-siri-are-not-real-ai-16477207; M. Brundage & J. Bryson, "Why Watson is real artificial intelligence", *Future Tense*, Feb. 14, 2014.
14. A. Newell, J. C. Shaw & H. A. Simon, "Chess-playing programs and the problem of complexity", *IBM Journal of Research and Development*, 1958, 2, 320–335, p. 320.
15. D. Bennett, "IBM's artificial intelligence problem, or why Watson can't get a job", *Bloomberg Businessweek*, January 10, 2014, www.businessweek.com/articles/177183-ibms-artificial-intelligence-problem-or-why-watson-cant-get-a-job
16. In the case of Watson, these dour conclusions may eventually have to be revised. A great effort continues to apply the ideas and advances in various realms of human endeavor, where such question answering capacities might be put to use. See, for example, D. Ferrucci *et al.*, "Watson: Beyond Jeopardy!", *Artificial Intelligence*, 2013, 199–200: 93–105.

3

Unpacking AI. The Logic Theorist

So what is it about these AI programs that made them capable of intellectual achievements that we would normally think of as examples of human intelligence? Is it possible to explain what they were doing in a simple enough fashion that one can understand the basis for their intelligence and even their 'super-intelligence'?

A Classical AI Program — The Logic Theorist

To begin the process of unpacking, I will start with a much earlier program called the Logic Theorist. This was one of the first well-known AI programs, which helped set the entire AI bandwagon rolling. It is also much simpler than the sophisticated AI programs discussed in the last chapter, so the 'unpacking' process will, I hope, be easier to understand. Following this discussion, in the next chapter, I will carry out a similar exercise with the Deep Blue and Watson systems.

The Logic Theorist was devised by Herbert Simon and Allen Newell with the purpose of proving theorems in a particular domain of mathematical logic. The theorems were from a famous book on mathematical logic, the *Principia Mathematica* of Bertrand Russell and Alfred North Whitehead. Using the axioms that Russell and Whitehead had themselves used, the Logic Theorist was able to generate proofs of some of the theorems. To quote from the article on Logic Theorist in Wikipedia:

> "Logic Theorist soon proved 38 of the first 52 theorems in chapter 2 of the Principia Mathematica. The proof of theorem 2.85 was actually more elegant than the proof produced laboriously by hand by Russell and Whitehead."

Simon himself was more expansive:

> "[We] invented a computer program capable of thinking non-numerically, and thereby solved the venerable mind-body problem, explaining how a system composed of matter can have the properties of mind."[1]

But what did the Logic Theorist program actually do? More specifically, what is meant when one says that the program "proved" these theorems?

The theorems proved by the Logic Theorist are part of what is called the "propositional calculus", which is a system based on propositional logic. Propositional logic is a formalization of certain basic logical relations. For this purpose, certain elementary, irreducible terms are used, called "logical atoms"; they are meant to represent simple propositions, like "The sky is overcast" or "The cat is on the mat". Within the calculus, such propositions are designated by single letters of the alphabet, e.g. p and q. p and q can also be thought of as variables that can take on the "truth values" TRUE or FALSE (or more succinctly T or F). This corresponds to the fact that, generally speaking, a simple proposition can be either true or false. So, for example, if the sky really is overcast the proposition given above is true, but it could also be false.

The relations of the propositional calculus can be expressed in terms of such atoms. With one exception, the basic relations are essentially binary, i.e. they hold between pairs of logical atoms. These relations are expressed by logical operators such as AND, OR, and IMPLIES. (The basic operators used can vary depending on the particular form of the calculus, since some operators can be defined in terms of others; i.e. there are equivalences among these operators.) Just as logical atoms can be true or false, these operators return truth values, which depend entirely on the truth values of the atoms they are applied to.

Taking the three operators just referred to:

(i) AND, often symbolized by ∧, is a conjunctive operator. It takes two terms (such as two atoms) as arguments and returns a value of T only if both of these terms have a value of T. So p ∧ q will return T only if p and q are both T; otherwise it gives a value of F.
(ii) OR, often symbolized by ∨, is a disjunctive operator. Again, it takes two terms and returns a value of T if either of these terms has a value of T. So p ∨ q returns T if either p or q is T or both have a value T. Only if p and q are both F does OR return a value of F.
(iii) IMPLIES, symbolized by →, is a specialized form of implication called "material implication". For a given implication, p → q, this operator returns a value F only if p has the value T and q has the value F; otherwise it returns the value T.

In addition, there is a unary operator, NOT, often symbolized by ¬. NOT takes one argument (one logical atom) and returns a truth value that is the 'opposite' of the value of the atom. Thus, if p has a value T, then ¬p will return the value F.

Using these operators, Russell and Whitehead were able to formulate a set of "logical axioms". With these axioms, they could derive a number of basic logical relations, following very strictly defined rules of inference.

Russell and Whitehead defined three rules that could be used to derive one expression from another[2]:

(i) The RULE OF SUBSTITUTION: If A(p) is any true expression containing the variable p, and B is any expression, then A(B) is also a true expression.
(ii) The RULE OF DETACHMENT: If A is a true expression and A IMPLIES B is also true, then B is a true expression.
(iii) The RULE OF REPLACEMENT: An expression may be replaced by its definition.

In addition, they specified five axioms. These are logical expressions that are assumed to be true *a priori*.

1.2 $(p \vee p) \rightarrow p$
1.3 $p \rightarrow (q \vee p)$
1.4 $(p \vee q) \rightarrow (q \vee p)$
1.5 $((p \vee q) \vee r) \rightarrow (q \vee (p \vee r))$
1.6 $(p \rightarrow q) \rightarrow ((r \vee p) \rightarrow (r \vee q))$

An example will give a sense of how theorems are proved in this calculus. The theorem is:

$$2.01 \quad (p \rightarrow \neg p) \rightarrow \neg p$$

Starting with axiom 1.2,

$$(p \vee p) \rightarrow p$$

we can apply the RULE OF SUBSTITUTION, substituting $\neg p$ for p; this gives the expression:

$$(\neg p \vee \neg p) \rightarrow \neg p$$

Then, using the definition of $p \rightarrow q$ as $\neg p \vee q$, we replace the subexpression $(\neg p \vee \neg p)$ to get

$$(p \rightarrow \neg p) \rightarrow \neg p$$

which is the expression we were looking for.

Constructing a proof in this form, leading from axioms to the theorem to be proved, using only the prescribed rules of inference, is the task that the Logical Theorist carried out. Now, how did it do this?

The fundamental operations used by the program were matching and substitution. For our purposes, it will be sufficient to describe how these were implemented, leaving the other rules of inference aside, since this should be enough to give the reader some concrete sense of how the Logical Theorist carried out its task of proving theorems.

To carry out matching, the logical expressions have to be represented in some way. Essentially this was done by organizing the parts of the expression into a tree-like structure. Consider axiom 1.2 again:

$$(p \vee p) \rightarrow p$$

Notice that the logical operators, or logical connectives (a more suggestive term in this context), form a kind of hierarchy. At the top level is the implication (→), which connects the subexpression (p ∨ p) to the single atom p. Within the subexpression, the connective ∨ joins p with p. We can represent this in the following way:

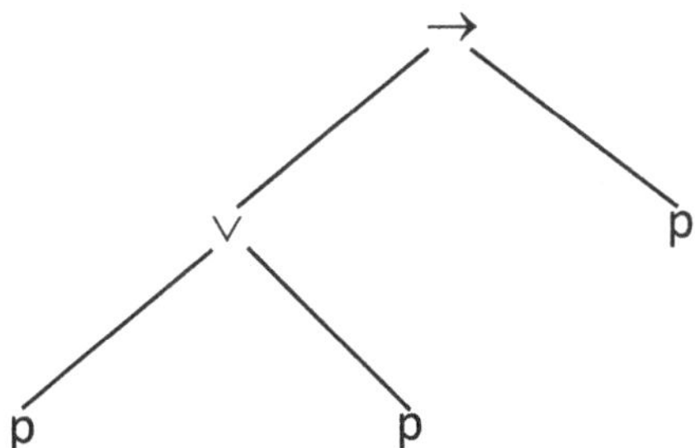

In the actual program, the proposition was stored as a list of elements. Along with each element was a string that represented its position in the tree. So, for example, the p in the lower left-hand part of the tree would be tagged with the string "LL", while the p on the right would be tagged with an "R". So the stored representation for Axiom 1.2 would look something like this:

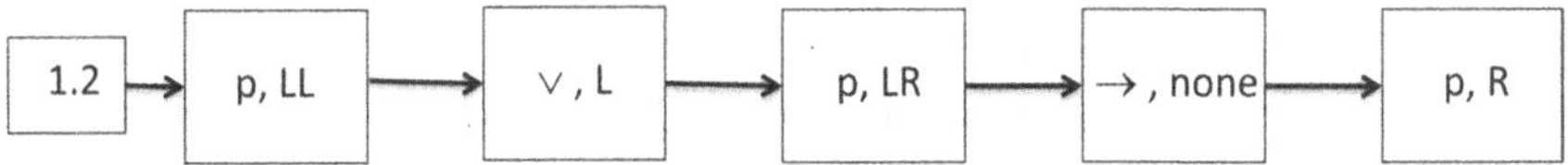

Here, each box represents a location in memory, which can be reached by following the links (arrows) starting from the location that designates the axiom. The axioms (and other propositions derived during the program's operation) are also stored as a list. (The reader can picture vertical arrows, one above pointing to and one below pointing from the box labeled "1.2", which connect this axiom with others in the proposition-list.)

In order for the program to operate on these logical formulas, so that a proof can be derived, it must be able to recognize certain features of the symbols in an expression. Thus, it must be able to determine which symbols are logical variables (like p) and which are operators (like →), which variables are "free", i.e. available for substitution, and which are bound.

This was conveyed through a system of descriptors. Descriptors can be thought of as ID tags, forming a distinct feature set, without which the term, which after all is just a string of bits in computer memory, would be unidentifiable. The position of an element in a particular expression is represented by another set of descriptors, as we have already seen. With such features, code can be written to test for a given feature in association with a term, and perform a specific action if the test is positive (and, possibly, some other action if the test is negative).

With this apparatus, the program could select expressions, substitute terms, and perform term-for-term comparisons (bit-string matching) to determine whether the new expression matched the one to be proved. In order to cut down on search, the program could also transform the expression to be proved, i.e. it could work backwards as well as forwards until it found a pair of expressions that could be matched.

Clearly, there is a sense in which the Logic Theorist discovered proofs of theorems, starting from Russell and Whitehead's axioms. And according to the definition given in the introduction, this qualifies as intelligence. In fact, it is possible that the operations of the Logic Theorist program bear some resemblance to the operations that went on in the brains of Russell and Whitehead when they developed their proofs.[3*]

The next question is: how do we interpret this achievement? To do this, we need to consider the context in which it took place.

One of the outstanding features of modern mathematics in contrast to the mathematics of two or three centuries ago is the greater rigor of its formulations. This has been one of the prevailing themes in the field, particularly since the late nineteenth century with the development of set theory and the renewed interest in giving axiomatic accounts of mathematical systems. In carrying out this program, mathematicians developed formulations of basic ideas that were often mechanical in nature, in that the operations were made more explicit. The *Principia Mathematica* was a major milestone in that project although it depended heavily on the work of Frege and others.[4*]

It should also be noted that the logical axioms in the *Principia* are truisms rather than substantial propositions as in Euclidean geometry or Peano's arithmetic. As a result, it is relatively easy to prove elementary theorems. Hence, the representation given to the Logic Theorist was in some sense complete.

The important point is that the meaning of the axioms proved by the Logic Theorist was completely outside the scope of its endeavors. In fact it would have performed in much the same way if the axioms had been nonsensical as well as the 'theorems', so long as the latter could be derived from the former using the designated rules of inference. Or to put this in a more telling way for our purposes, the Logic Theorist embodied human intelligence and nothing beyond that — other than the fact that unaided human intelligence might not realize all the implications of the axioms that the Logic Theorist could discover. In short, one cannot separate this demonstration of artificial intelligence from the human intelligence that gave rise to it.

In short, I think it is fair to say that the entire AI project would not have succeeded or even gotten off the ground without the prior development of mathematical logic. The latter made it possible to pose problems in a sufficiently explicit way that a well-defined process of problem solving could be envisaged — and solutions could be recognized. There is therefore something peculiarly appropriate in the fact that historically this was the first AI program.

Interestingly, in subsequent years the area of AI that concerned itself with proving logical formulae, and which emerged in the late 1950s, did not follow in the footsteps of this pioneering work of Newell and Simon, which was heavily based on heuristic methods for finding proofs. Instead, the field followed another route and was absorbed into the great stream of research on formalizing logic that began many years before there were any computing machines that could be applied to such tasks. And this is of cardinal importance for the thesis of this book.

Endnotes

1. Quoted in D. Crevier, *AI: The Tumultous Search for Artificial Intelligence*. New York: Basic Books, 1993, p. 46.
2. The terminology used here is from A. Newell & H. A. Simon, "The logic theory machine: A complex information processing system", *IRE Transactions on Information Theory*, 1956, 2: 61–79.

3. In this connection it should not be overlooked that the actual operations carried out by these men undoubtedly involved paper and pencil. Hence, the comparison is really between computer-based computations and some form of "extended cognition". The latter idea, which is somewhat tangential to the concerns of the present work, is discussed in A. Clark, *Supersizing the Mind.* Oxford, 2011.
4. This history could be said to have begun with Aristotle, who first saw that arguments could be described according to general schema, and that the latter could be represented symbolically. But the critical work leading to the mechanization of logic and mathematical proofs in logic began with Frege's work, especially the *Begriffsshrift* of 1879. (Here, the earlier work by Boole should be mentioned, as forming a bridge between classical Aristotelean logic and modern symbolic logic, by demonstrating the mathematical character of certain logical operators.)

4

Unpacking AI, Deep Blue and Watson

In this chapter, we return to the more modern systems whose achievements are much more formidable than those of the Logic Theorist, and carry out a similar analysis. I will start with Deep Blue.

The Game of Chess

In order to discuss some of the same issues in relation to Deep Blue, it is necessary to review some basic ideas in computer chess and then see how Deep Blue built upon those basics.

But even before that, it is necessary to consider the game itself in an historical context. To this end, I will briefly go over the basics of chess and some elements of good play as they have developed over the centuries. Then, in the discussion of computer chess, I will try to show how a stream of formative ideas developed that provided the foundation for the Deep Blue system.

Chess is a game between two players in which the outcome is either that one player wins or that the players draw. The game is played by moving pieces according to prescribed rules on a board marked out in an 8 × 8 pattern of small (identically sized) squares. Both players begin with the same set of 16 chess pieces, arranged in a fixed pattern in the first two rows on either side of the board, as shown in the figure below. One player's pieces are all white, the other's black; hence, the players are referred to as White and Black.

This figure also shows one way of designating the squares on the board. Thus, the piece at the lower left corner is on square a1.

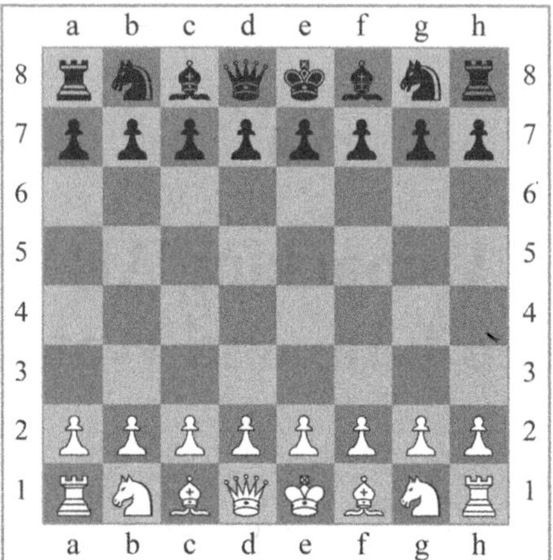

There are six kinds of pieces. In the front row, at the start of the game, there are eight identical pieces called pawns (Row 2 for White and Row 7 for Black in the figure). In the row behind the pawns there are two rooks (in columns a and h); next to each rook is a knight and next to that piece a bishop. At the center of the row is a single queen (column d) and king (column e).

Pawns can move ahead one space (remaining in the same column), and on the first move they can also move two spaces ahead. They can also move to the first diagonal space ahead if an opponent's piece is in that square. Rooks can move either horizontally or vertically on one move, across any number of consecutive open (free) spaces on the board. Bishops can move in a similar fashion along the two diagonals from their current positions. Knights can move two spaces horizontally or vertically and then one space in a direction at right angles to the first. Unlike any other piece, they can move over other pieces to occupy an empty square. The queen (the most powerful piece on the board) can move either horizontally, vertically or diagonally for any number of free spaces. The king can move one space in any direction.

A game always begins with a move by White. After that, the players take turns moving a single piece from one square to another according to the rules of movement for that piece. Each turn is called a "ply", and since players take turns, the game can be thought of as a succession of two-ply moves. In the following example pairs of plies are written on the same line, White first.[1] (Note that each move is indicated by the square the piece moves to. "Q" is for queen, "N" is for knight, "B" is for bishop; in addition "R" is for rook and "K" is for king; and if there is no piece indicated, as in the first two plies, this means that a pawn has moved.)

1. e4 e5
2. Qh5 Nc6
3. Bc4 Nf6
4. Qxf7

At the end of this sequence, the board looks like this:

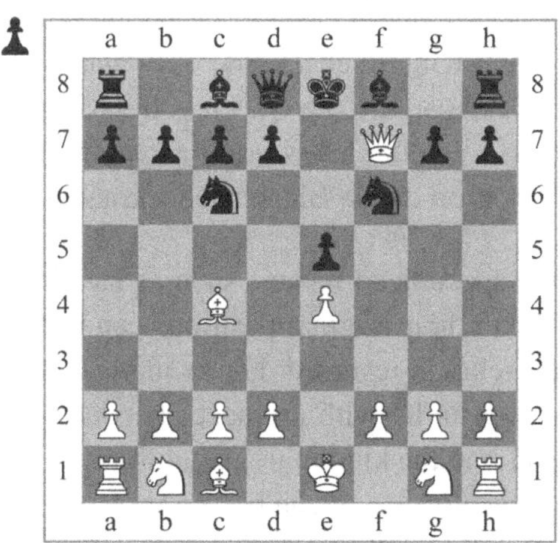

If one player moves a piece to a square occupied by the other player's piece, then the latter has been captured and is taken off the board. (In chess notation, this is indicated by an x; cf. line 4 above.) Since they improve a player's position, such captures are desired subgoals. The ultimate goal of the game is to put the opponent's king in a position where it can be captured on the next move regardless of the defensive move taken by the opponent on the next ply. In other words, a situation is set up in which any move made by the opponent's king or any other piece will also lead to capture of the king on the attacker's next move. This is called a "checkmate", while merely putting the king in a situation where it can be captured in its position on the next move is called a "check". (If a player sees in advance that a checkmate is inevitable, he can resign, and the game is counted as a loss for him.) Returning to the example just given, we have a case in which checkmate is achieved by White on the fourth move, as indicated by the annotation:

1. e4 e5	pawns before Kings each move 2 spaces forward
2. Qh5 Nc6	White moves Queen to right edge of board; Black moves Knight on (his) right ahead of pawns
3. Bc4 Nf6	White moves Bishop to center of board; Black moves other Knight ahead of pawns
4. Qxf7	White's moves Queen to f7, taking pawn, putting King in check; the only black piece that can capture the Queen is the King, but to do so would allow it to be captured by the Bishop on c4, so Black is checkmated

There are some specialized moves, such as castling, in which a king and the closest rook in their original positions can be placed side by side with their left-right relation reversed. For example, if the white king is in square e1 and the rook in h1 with no pieces between them, castling puts the rook in square f1 and the king in g1. In addition, if a pawn reaches the last row on the opponent's side, it can be "promoted" to be a more powerful piece. (Most often this will be a queen.)

Being able to play chess well requires considerable skill, which can only be gained by years of training. For well over a century people have been thinking about how to play this game effectively, and this has resulted in a large body of knowledge. Here, I will only sketch out some of the basics.[2]

In describing strategy, the game of chess is divided into three phases: the opening, the middle game, and the endgame. Each has its own special features, and strategies and tactics that work well in one phase may be irrelevant or even disadvantageous in another.

First and foremost is the fact that, since the ultimate goal is to checkmate, every move is related to that end. Hence, simply capturing pieces is not sufficient. The latter falls under the heading of tactics, but beyond a very primitive level of play, these must be subsumed by larger plans or strategies. In addition, because of the adversarial character of the game, it must entail both offensive and defensive tactics and strategies. As one author put it, "in a well contested game there is always a dovetailing and an integration of purposes".[3]

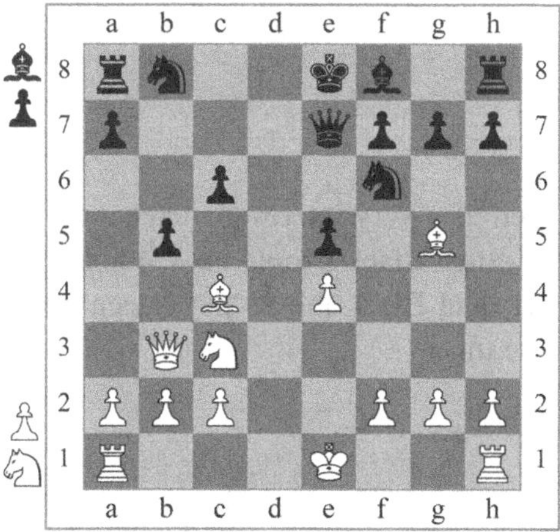

To demonstrate some of these ideas in a concrete manner, I will look briefly at a famous chess match; the game between Paul Morphy and the Duke of Brunswick in Paris in 1858.[4] The figure above shows the board after nine moves. There had been a brief exchange of pieces on the fourth and fifth moves (involving a bishop that Black had advanced into 'White territory') in which Black lost that bishop and White (Morphy) a knight. Note the (subsequent) build-up of White pieces in front of the pawn positions without anything comparable by Black.

The next figure shows the board after twelve moves. Pieces have been exchanged on the left: White's knight took Black's knight's pawn, then Black's bishop's pawn took White's knight and that pawn was taken by White's bishop, which put Black's king in check. This was countered by Black's knight. On the twelfth move White castled and Black moved a rook to d8.

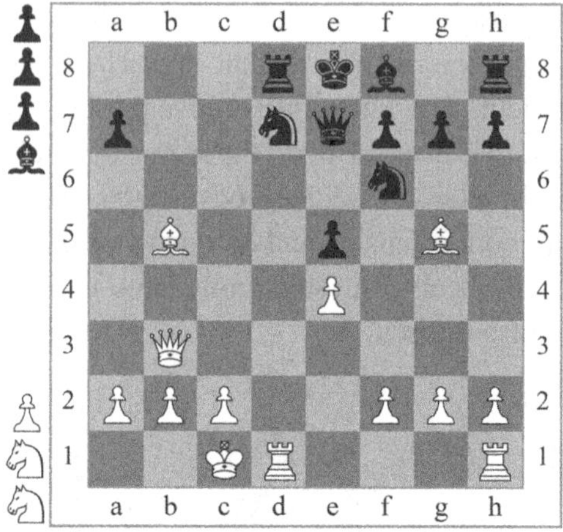

At this point there is a very interesting exchange. White's rook takes Black's knight at d7; then Black's rook takes White's rook. White moves his other rook to d1, and Black moves his Queen one space to e6. The board now looks like this:

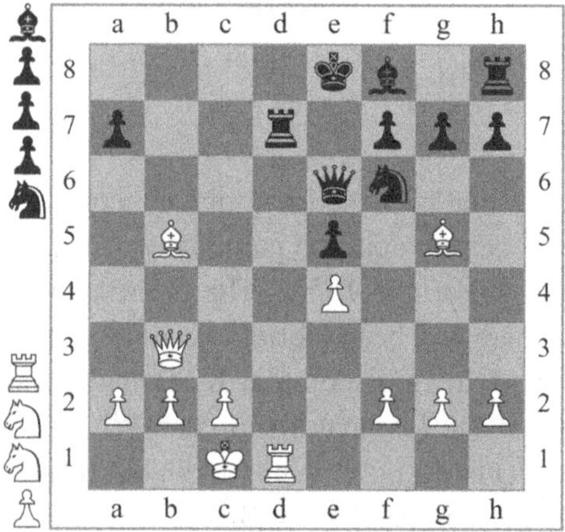

White now takes Black's rook with his bishop; Black takes that bishop with his knight. Then White moves his queen to b8, putting Black's king in check. Black responds by taking White's queen with his knight. Now the board looks like this:

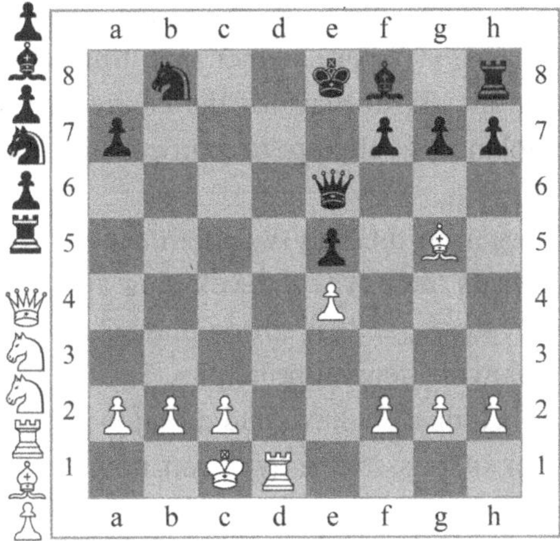

At this point, White moves his rook to d8 for a checkmate.

Note that at the end of the game White is down by two pieces, including a queen. Nonetheless, by sacrificing pieces at crucial points in the game, he (i) maintained the initial advantage that White has by virtue of going first, (ii) forced Black's pieces into positions that left his king open for a checkmate.

There are features of chess that support certain strategies. One is that capture is optional; hence, one can cover one's piece, so that the opponent does not move to capture it. The latter also leads to tit-for-tat strategies, which we saw in the game above. Since checkmating is all-important, this leads to strategies in which one sacrifices pieces to effect a checkmate. This means that above a certain primitive level of play, tactics are always subordinate to strategy. More generally, one is always balancing the importance of immediate gain and achieving a final victory. Finally, putting an opponent in a state of check is a useful tactic, since it limits his options to those involved in getting his king out of check.

It is also interesting to note that the character of the game has changed over the past century and a half. Early nineteenth century players relied largely on intuition. This often led to daring plays, including so-called "gambits" in which a pawn is deliberately sacrificed; some of these have since disappeared simply because they can be answered so effectively that the player loses advantage.

During the next stage chess became "self-consciously strategic". There was an emphasis on "space, rather than time, mobilization rather than attack; then, in attack, to play for the centre and lesser objectives rather than, with violence, to attempt to gain considerable material, or to bring about mate."[5]

Another shift began in the late twentieth century. According to one authority, in these years there was a developing appreciation of specific positions and their features, so that strong players tended to plan on that basis rather than following general principles.[6]

In recent years, computers have had a major impact due to the fact that a large number of possible moves can now be explored starting from a given board position. Computers have therefore emerged as an important training tool, even for grandmasters.[7] One result of this has been that the opening game has been so thoroughly analyzed that it is no longer of real interest to expert players. Another is that famous chess games can now be evaluated to determine whether they were "sound".[8] In other words, given a particular move, is it possible to discover flaws that could have been exploited if the opponent had realized them?

Overall, then, in the field of chess there has been a cumulative growth of 'collective intelligence'. That is, overall there has been a growing appreciation of the logic of chess dispersed over a large number of people.

Foundations of Computer Chess

Automated chess playing systems are highly organized pieces of software or hardware that embody many clever and even profound ideas about game-playing strategies for the game of chess in particular, and in some cases for any well-structured game. Here I will give a brief overview of these concepts.

Perhaps the most basic idea is that of a game tree. This conception applies much more widely than the game of chess. In fact, any game in which a fixed number of players each take turns and where there is a finite set of outcomes can be represented in this way. (However, in what follows we will assume that there are only two players.)

A "tree" in this sense is a structure of nodes and branches, as depicted here:

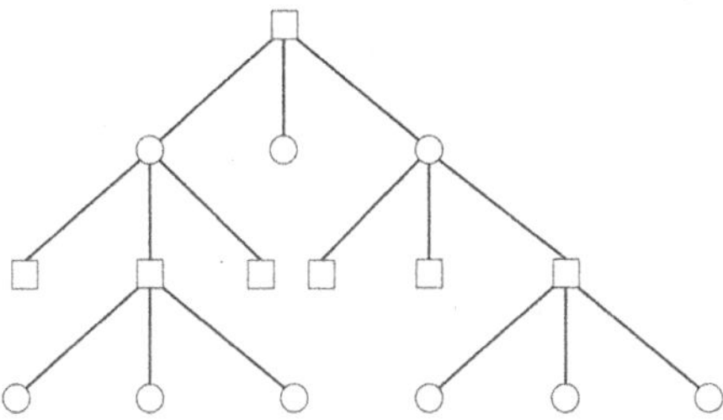

Each node in the tree represents the current state of the board, i.e. the positions of all the pieces, and the branches from that node represent moves that a player might take. Thus, in the case of chess a branch represents one ply. Two kinds of nodes are shown; each represents the current situation for one of the two players.[9*]

The beginning of the game is associated with a single node without an incoming branch, which in this case is at the top of the figure, and which is usually referred to as the "root" (or root-node) of the tree. Since in chess White always moves first, this top node is associated with this player. So in the drawing above, squares always represent states in which White will move, while circles are associated with Black's moves.

The nodes of the tree can also be grouped into levels, where a specific level is given by the number of plies required to reach that node from the root-node. (The connected set of branches leading from one node to another is called a "path" in the tree.) Note that the figure above is drawn so that all branches leading to a specific level end at the same vertical height in the figure. If we number the levels beginning with 0, then White's moves occur at the even levels, 0, 2, 4, and so forth, and Black's at levels 1, 3, 5, etc. With this convention, the number of each level also tells us the length of the path from the root.

Using the game tree conception, we can represent the first game described earlier as a single path in the game tree, which in this case ends on the seventh level. (The path representing the second game ends on the thirty-third level.) The same holds true for every game of chess that has been played to completion, and every game that will ever be played. They are different branches in a single game tree.

With this representation in mind, we can derive a strategy for playing the game that is in some sense provably best. In fact the Minimax Theorem, which describes this best possible strategy, is quite general in that it holds for "every two-person zero-sum game with finitely many strategies".[10]

I will state the theorem and then try to explain what it means and why it is significant in the present context, since on the face of it, it seems to have little or nothing to do with the tactics and strategies for chess that were discussed above.

The theorem says that for every such game there is some value (call it V) and a mixed strategy such that Player 1 (say White) is guaranteed a payoff of V regardless of Player 2's strategy, and Player 2 is guaranteed a payoff of –V regardless of Player 1's strategy.

This strategy is called the minimax strategy because each player minimizes the maximum payoff that the other player can receive. This strategy forms the basis for most of the classical computer chess systems up to and including Deep Blue.

Now what does all this mean?

In the first place one must understand that terms like "strategy" and "payoff value" have specialized meanings in connection with the formalized conception of games that is the subject of game theory. Start with the term, "strategy". In game theory a strategy is a set of instructions that tells the player what move to make in any situation that occurs in the course of a game. (It is therefore a kind of algorithm.) A strategy that specifies a single move in each situation is called a "pure strategy". A "mixed strategy" is based on a set of pure strategies, where the player chooses one of them with a fixed probability. In other words, each strategy has an associated probability, and by definition the probabilities of all the strategies in the set sum to 1. So a mixed strategy involves random choices of a move at each node in the game tree, with biases toward certain moves if there are differences in their underlying probabilities.

We can illustrate these ideas as well as the idea of payoff values from which V is derived, and the minimax strategy itself by considering a simpler game than chess. Here I will use the game of Tic-Tac-Toe (sometimes also called Noughts and Crosses). This is the game where two players begin with a 'playing board', or matrix, with three rows and three columns, usually drawn on paper like this (omitting the outside lines):

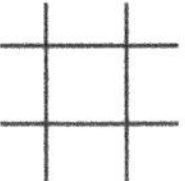

Taking turns, one player puts X's in the spaces while the other draws O's. The player making X's always starts first. The object of the game for both players is to make a row of either three X's or three O's running horizontally, vertically or diagonally across the board. At the same time each player must prevent the other player from doing this.

Despite the simplicity of this game, there are a large number of possible outcomes. Since on the first move an X can be placed in any square on the board, there are nine possible moves that X can make. Given any of these, there are eight possible moves for O, then seven for X, and so forth. This gives 9! = 362,880. However, since not all paths in the game tree are nine branches long, the actual number of possible games is 26,830.[11*] Since this is far too much to draw, or comprehend, I will illustrate the minimax strategy by considering partial games, in which six squares are already filled in.

In Figure 4.1, the game has reached the point depicted on the board in the upper right hand corner. Also shown is a simple scheme for labeling the spaces on the board, inspired by the chess board labeling scheme. Player X has the next move, and he can choose to put an X in one of the three open spaces.

The portion of the game tree (a subtree) that begins with this situation is also shown. For example, if X chooses a2, then player O can win by putting an O at b1 (the middle space at the top), or he can 'throw away' the game by putting his O at c2; in this case, the game is a draw. In the tree diagram each final state (also called a leaf node) is labeled with a value representing the outcome from X's perspective. A +1 is a win for X, and –1 is a win for O, and a 0 is a draw.

Figure 4.2, which shows the same subtree, also shows the minimax scores. Let's begin with the leaves at the lowest levels. In each case there is only one branch from the node above, so the single minimax score is

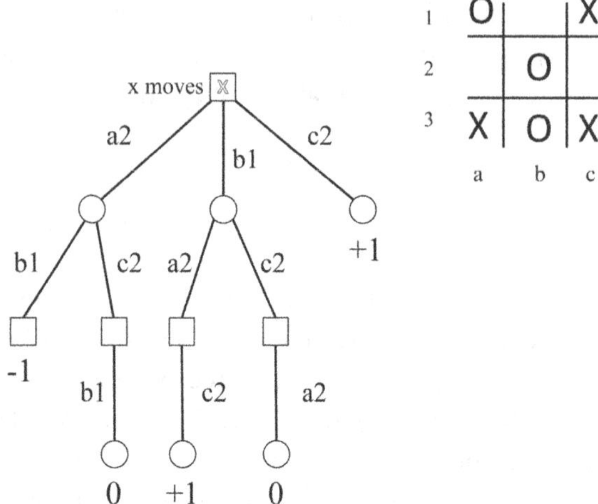

Figure 4.1. Tree-graph depiction of a game of tic-tac-toe, up to the current state of the game (shown to the right).

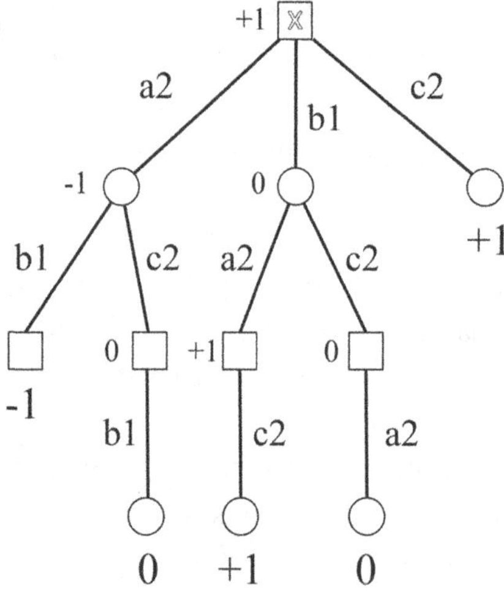

Figure 4.2. Game tree for same tic-tac-toe game showing minimax scores.

carried up to the parent node. Now, at the next-to-last level, each node has a sibling connected to the same node above. These branches represent moves by O, and in order to maximize from X's perspective, O must choose the node with the lowest value (i.e. a –1 is a win for O and a loss for X).

Therefore, since an O in space b1 gives a win for O, while an O in space c2 will lead to a draw, it is the –1 that is carried up to the parent node. The same reasoning gives a 0 for the node leading to moves a2 and c2.

Now for the final carry, since this is X's move, the largest value will be chosen. Move a2 is now associated with a –1, b1 with a 0 and c2 with a +1, so a +1 is carried up to the parent. Since this is associated with c2, it can be deduced that this is the move to make under the minimax strategy.

In this case, when we can work out the complete game tree, we can always determine the best strategy to use — without paying any attention to the internal structure of the game. Instead we are simply considering a list of possible moves at each step in the game, labeling them in relation to the possible outcomes given the situation that results from that move. We can do this because we are considering the game exhaustively; in this case we do not need to have any insight, i.e. perception of the relation between moves and the structural features of the game. So in the game above, we do not have to see that since an X in space c2 wins the game, this is the move to make, and we don't need to look (search) any farther. Nor do we need to consider general strategic features of the game such as the strength of the middle position. And when an exhaustive analysis can be carried out, we obtain a strategy that will always win or draw if that is possible. This is the import of the Minimax Theorem, which applies to all games with the requisite features.

At first blush the present analysis seems to reduce any game of this sort, even chess, to the level of a trivial exercise. And this would be true if one could analyze the entire game tree. However, there are about 30 possible moves at each point in a game of chess, which gives a conservative estimate for the size of the game tree of 10^{120}. In addition, the number of possible board positions is 10^{43}. When the number of possibilities is this large, it is impossible to exhaustively search the game tree or to maintain a dictionary of all possible positions with the best move for each.

In cases like this it is customary to rely on proxy scores based on various assessments of board quality. In this way one can carry out a partial search of the (remaining) game tree beginning at the current position. Different moves are explored for so many plies, and scores for the boards that result are computed. Then the same type of minimax search that was proven to give optimal strategies when the complete game tree could be analyzed, can be carried out using these proxy scores.

System	Turing	Kister et al.	Bernstein et al.	Newell et al.
Date	1951	1956	1957	1958
Board	8 X 8	6 X 6	8 X 8	8 X 8
Alternatives	all	all	7 plausible	variable
Depth	until dead	2	2	until dead
Static evaluation	numerical many factors	numerical material, mobility	numerical material, mobility area of control king defense	non-numerical value vector goals
Combining values	minimax material	minimax best value	minimax best value	minimax first acceptable

Figure 4.3. Some key features of early chess-playing programs.

In devising these scores, computer scientists relied on heuristics devised earlier by students of the game, the chief of which is simply the number of remaining pieces on the board. Different pieces are given different values, and the most basic measure of board quality is the sum of those values, or, from the perspective of a player, the sum of his pieces minus the sum of the other player's pieces. Other values can be added, such as "doubled, backward and isolated … pawns" and mobility, measured by the number of possible moves. This gives an equation such as the following:

$$f(P) = 200(K - K') + 9(Q - Q') + 5(R - R') + 3(B - B' + N - N') \\ + (P - P') - 5(D - D' + S - S' + I - I') + (M - M')$$

where K, Q, R, B, N, P stand for the player's own king, queens, rooks, bishops, knights and pawns, respectively, while K', Q', etc. are the corresponding values for the other player. D, S, and I are the numbers of doubled, backward and isolated pawns, and M is the mobility score.[12]

As shown by the data in the table above (Figure 4.3), all of the early chess-playing systems used some version of the minimax strategy to determine the next move to make.[13] (Note: Turing worked by hand and considered only exchanges of pieces. The other "systems" were actual computer programs.)

Once this approach to computer chess had been established, further methods were devised to make the original brute-force search more efficient. Chief among these was the introduction of alpha-beta pruning. This is a method of tracking the minimax values still possible by calculating bounds on the acceptable values (called alpha and beta), using information received so far during search. For our purposes, it is important to note that it is a basic component of all classical computer chess systems.

To get an idea of how this method works, I will use a simple game tree, shown in Figure 4.4. In this tree there are four levels, where processes indicated by squares always select the maximum value they receive (from processes below) and circle-processes choose the smallest value. Execution starts at the top and works its way down, at each level going from left to right. (This is an example of what is called depth-first search.) Whenever a leaf node (circles in the bottom row) is reached, it merely returns its value (shown inside the circle) to the parent node above. At the beginning of search, alpha is set to a very small value (here minus infinity), and beta is set to a very large value (here plus infinity). This ensures that these original values will be replaced by some values in the leaf nodes.

At the beginning of minimax search, the initial values of alpha and beta are passed down from level to level, as shown on the far left. When the first leaf node is reached, it passes back its value, 6. Since the parent process maximizes, it substitutes this value for the minus infinity that it began with (6 is bigger than minus infinity). It passes this down to the next leaf node (second from the left), and that node returns its value, 7. Since

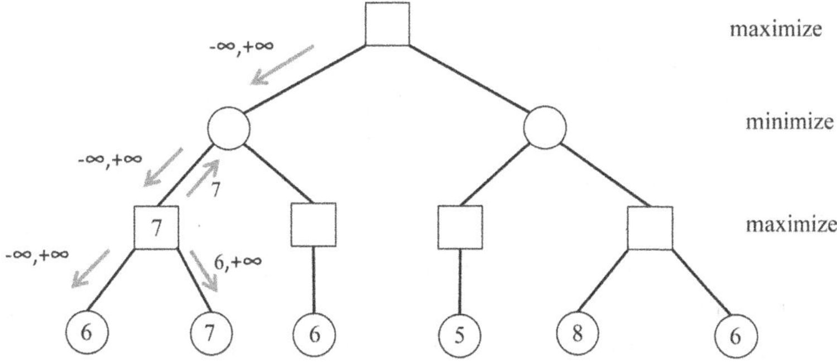

Figure 4.4. Game tree to illustrate first stage of minimax calculations.

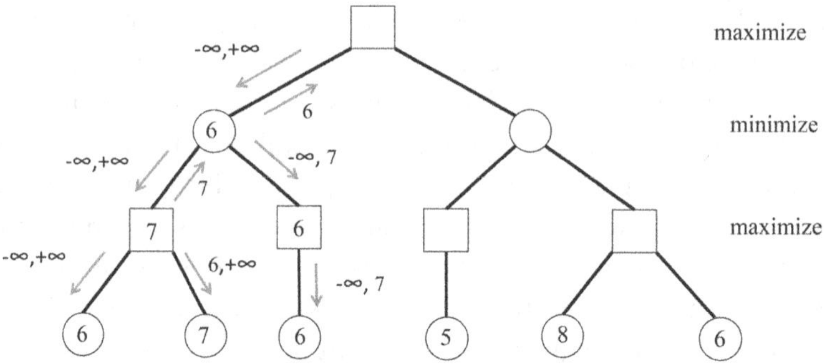

Figure 4.5. Next stage in minimax calculations.

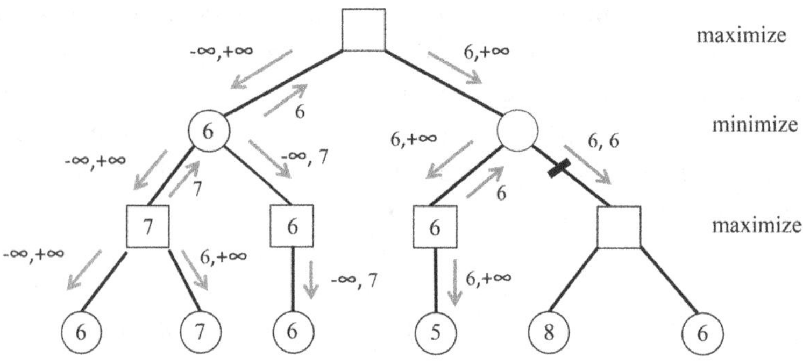

Figure 4.6. Final stage of minimax calculation.

7 is bigger than 6, the maximizer substitutes this new value; since it has no more children, this is its final value, which is passed up to its parent, as shown.

Figure 4.5 shows the next part of the procedure. The process on the next higher (second) level is a minimizer; moreover, it treats the numbers it receives as beta-values. So, since 7 is less than plus infinity, the minimizer substitutes the 7 and passes it down to the next child, as shown. This branch of the tree ends in a 6, which is passed back up to the minimizer (not shown), and since this is less than 7, the minimizer resets its beta value to 6 and also passes this final value to its parent above.

Now, as shown in Figure 4.6, the process at the top is a maximizer; moreover, it treats the values it receives as alpha values. Since 6 is bigger than minus infinity, the maximizer makes this the value of alpha, and also sends the new alpha value down to its second child (on the right). That child then sends it to its child, and so forth until the first leaf on this side is reached.

Since the value of that leaf node is 5, this doesn't change the original value of its parent, which sends back the value 6 that it received originally. Then, since the process at the next (second) level is minimizing, and since it treats the values it receives as beta values, it substitutes the 6 for the original value of beta it received, which was plus infinity. As a result beta is now no greater than alpha. This means, first, that nothing larger than 6 will pass through the minimizer to the maximizer above. But this means that nothing in the final branch can change the value of that maximizer. So the branch below the cutoff point shown in the figure doesn't have to be searched. (Note that any bigger value down below will not change the level 2 minimizer's value, and anything smaller will not change the value of the maximizer above it. In the present tree, the maximizer below the cutoff will return an 8, but this will be ignored since the minimizer above already has a lower value (6) for beta. The reader can try other values for the two leaves on the right to see what happens.)[14*]

Another important innovation with a similar aim is the use of transposition tables. In many instances a series of moves leads to identical board positions, and of course each evaluation of a position will give identical results. Search costs could be reduced if positions that have already been evaluated are not re-evaluated when rediscovered. Of even greater importance is the opportunity to avoid searching subtrees, just as with alpha-beta pruning.

It was also noted early on that many of these search algorithms could be "parallelized". That is, portions of minimax search involving different parts of the game tree could be done in parallel, for much greater real-time efficiency.

In all of this, notice how far we've moved away from the specifics of the game of chess, including specific tactics and strategies. And how by transforming certain aspects of the game into general formal representations, human reasoning can be applied to very general problems such as making minimax search more efficient, and the results of this effort can then be applied to chess as well as any other game.

*

But where did these ideas come from?

The mathematical analysis of games began early in the twentieth century. The minimax theorem goes back to a paper by John von Neumann published in 1928.[15*] However, the study of games did not become a vigorous area of research until after the publication of von Neumann and Morgenstern's book on economics and game theory in the 1940s.[16]

Alpha-beta pruning is also a fairly early idea that evidently occurred to several people independently in the 1950s.[17] Transposition tables were introduced in the late 1960s.[18] Since then several further refinements of game-tree search have been suggested and incorporated into chess playing programs, including transposition tables and similar devices.[19]

For our purposes it is important to appreciate how everything rests on the correctness of von Neumann's original theorem. This means that the entire field of computer chess has a formal underpinning that from the very outset placed it outside a simple empirical investigation of chess playing. (The same of course holds for other game-playing programs.) In fact, a chess program can be thought of as embodying certain truths about the world, which in this case were established by human beings. An important question is whether something like this can be said about human intelligence.

Another interesting historical fact is that computer chess and AI research underwent a partial bifurcation during the 1970's and 80's.[20] After that, computer chess became an area given over in large degree to specialized knowledge bases and hardware, and it no longer received anything like the degree of attention from the AI community that it had in earlier years. (Note that this predates the advent of Deep Blue or even its immediate predecessors.) And this certainly has some bearing on the question of what Deep Blue's victory means when assessing the status and nature of artificial intelligence.

One thing that should be obvious at this point is that to consider Deep Blue outside the stream of ideas and programs that eventually gave rise to the system is to commit a serious intellectual blunder.

*

In addition to being located within the large historical framework just sketched out, Deep Blue is part of a specialized stream of work whose focus is building hardware, or chip-based, implementations of chess-playing programs. The Deep Blue system thus reflects a confluence of two research streams, one concerned with chess playing, the other with integrated circuit design, that originated in the late 1970s.

It should be noted that the overriding concern in all of this work was to increase speed in terms of positions examined per second. In Chapter 2 I pointed out that Deep Blue consulted grandmaster moves in deciding what move to make. However, this was basically 'icing on the cake' and was one more hedge against very strong players like Kasparov. The basic chess engine was a system for performing brute-force search, and the key idea was to speed up the operations so that the game-tree could be explored to greater depths, starting from the current position. In fact, it has been shown that there is close relation between the ratings that are normally used to rank chess players (based on competitions) and the depth that a program can search in the game tree; for an important range of depths ratings increase by 200 points with each additional level of search.[21]

Recall that game tree search involves both selecting a next move (i.e. opening a new node in the game tree) and evaluating 'final' positions (in this case positions at some cutoff). In the 1970s people began to think about how this could be done with specialized hardware, based on a single chip. Although there is some earlier history to this idea, the first fully competitive system to use such hardware was the Belle computer. This was the reigning champion in computer chess in the early 1980s.[22]

Belle began life as a software system that could search at a rate of about 200 positions per second. In its hardware manifestation it could search 160,000 positions per second, an 800-fold speed-up. (Interestingly, even later in the same decade this was considered rather slow.)

For move generation, a key idea was to build a generator in the form of an 8 × 8 array of combinatorial circuits, each representing a square on the chessboard (cf. Figure 4.7). Each of these circuits included a transmitter (XMITTER in the figure below) and a receiver (RECVR). Connecting wires (arrows in figure) originating from the transmitter led to each of its possible neighbors (e.g. the knight line would transmit to up to eight neighbors, depending on the square). Similarly, the receiver received input signals from all of its neighbors. The receiver output lines led to a priority network (not shown in Figure 4.7).

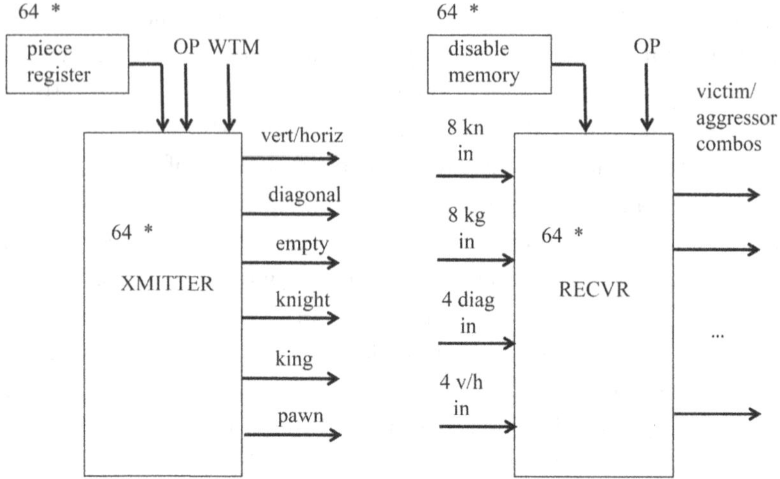

Figure 4.7. Diagram of BELLE chip layout. (Based on Condon & Thompson, 1983; from Levy, 1988 by permission).

Following a proposal that had originated earlier, moves were ordered by two operations (cf. OP in the figure), called find-victim and find-aggressor. During the find-victim cycle, the system located the most valuable piece under attack. During the find-aggressor cycle, the system found the lowest-value aggressor attacking the victim. In both cases the final selection was made by the priority network. After this, the selected move was disabled so that the same move would not be found again during the search. In this way the system cycled through successive moves to explore the game tree.

Hsu and his co-workers entered the picture in the mid-1980s, with the advent of ChipTest, which quickly evolved into Deep Thought. Hsu brought a number of ideas to the table,[23*] but first and foremost he was able to devise circuit designs that allowed both the generator (discussed above) and later the move evaluator to be put on a single chip. This opened the door to systems that could explore much more of the game tree and thus challenge world champion chess players.

The mature version of Deep Thought could search 700,000 positions per second, well beyond any other system at that time. A later three-processor version was able to search 2,000,000 positions per second.[24] This enabled the system to play at the level of a Grand Master.[25]

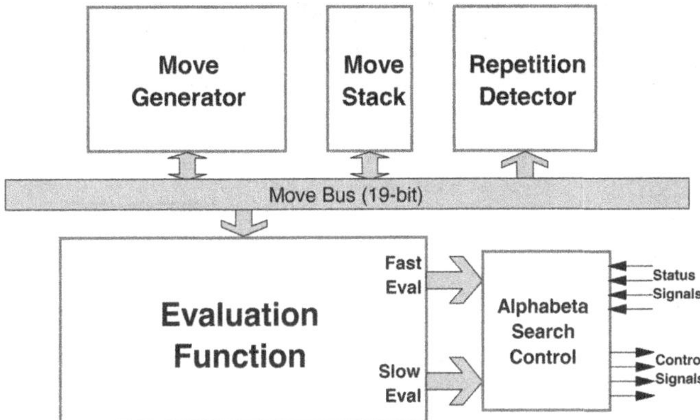

Figure 4.8. Schematic diagram of Deep Blue operation. All these functions were located on one chip, as shown in Figure 4.9.

To get a sense of Hsu's approach to the problem at this time, here are some quotations from his account of the development of Deep Thought:

> "... there were two major problems. The first was that the Belle chess move generator had too many transistors. The circuit size was simply too big."[26]
>
> "... I had made a wrong assumption. I assumed that the Belle designers ... must have explored ways to reduce the number of transistors. I forgot that the Belle designers ... were not trying to fit their design onto a single chip. They designed Belle with discrete off-the-shelf chips, and the chips used for the disable-stack were fairly easy to come by. For them, the disable-stack was perhaps the most elegant solution. It just was not the best solution for a single chip design."[27]
>
> "Another reason why I did not like the external disable-stack solution was that it was really a nine-chip design. Eight memory chips would be needed for the 64-bit wide external disable-stack. The widest memory chip in those days was only 8-bit wide.
>
> "At this point, an idea hit me. The new idea rid the whole design of the disable-stack, not just the chip itself."[28]
>
> "My final implementation of the complete move generator used about five-hundred and fifty transistors on average for each square. Without the design change, the number would have been over two-thousand transistors per square, and the chip would have been too large by a factor of four."[29]

The reader should note how far we are in all of this from the game of chess itself, at least as human beings would view it. But given all the

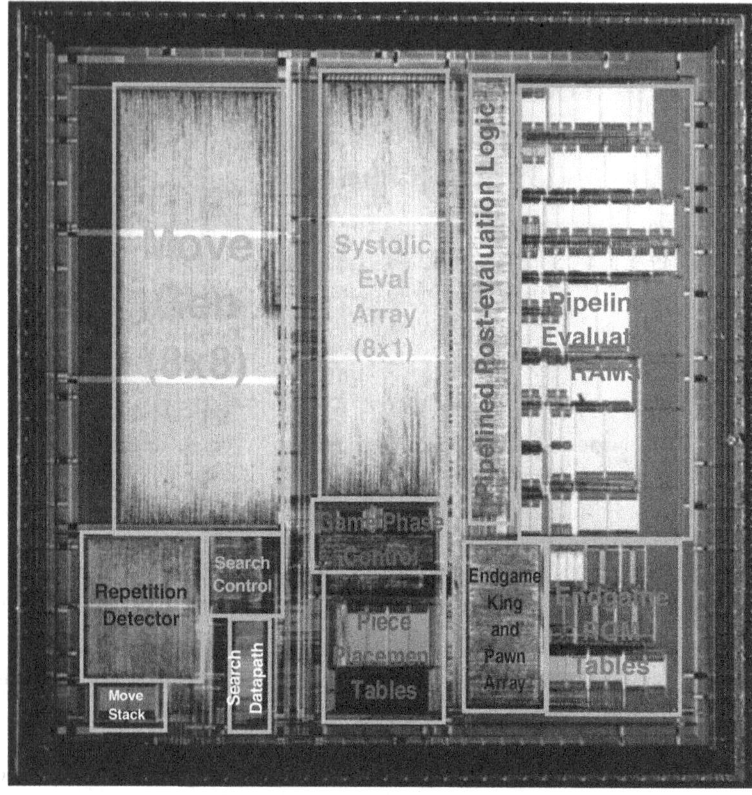

Figure 4.9. Picture of the actual Deep Blue chip.

- Scalable parallel system
- 30 node IBM RS/6000 SP supercomputer
- 16 chess accelerator chips per node
- 200 million chess positions per second average

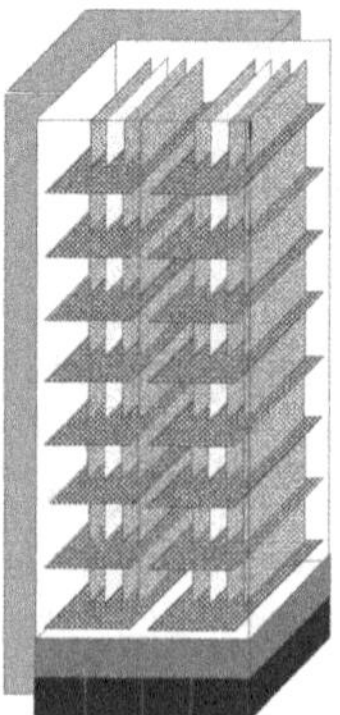

Figure 4.10. The Deep Blue system.

earlier advances beginning with minimax search that Hsu took for granted, he could direct his thinking toward the task of building a more efficient special-purpose circuit.

This is not to say, however, that Hsu and his collaborators ignored chess issues, although my impression is that contributions in this arena came somewhat later.[30*] In fact, their work in this area contributed to the shift away from simple brute-force search (that had been abetted by the advent of special-purpose hardware) to more selective search strategies that took place during the late 1980s. These advances helped overcome the "horizon effect" that limited earlier systems. In these cases a system chooses on the basis of evaluations k levels deep without taking account of the fact it may be giving its opponent the opportunity to inflict greater losses. However, all these new techniques were framed in terms of the basic alpha-beta search and its evaluations of positions, as indicated in Figure 4.8.

For example, a technique introduced by Hsu and his collaborators, called singular extensions, was based on the magnitude of difference in the evaluation returned for one branch from a node in the game tree compared to other branches from that node. So, again, the thinking that led to these advances was nested within the earlier formal analysis of game tree search.

Interestingly, this strategy often uncovers the lines of attack (called "forcing lines") considered by master players. So in this case the formalized thinking does in fact address real issues of chess tactics.

A third critical advance was the parallelization of minimax search with alpha-beta pruning. This means that independent branches of the search tree can be analyzed in parallel.[31*] Effort along these lines had begun with Deep Thought and was used for the three-processor version mentioned above. It was to reach a high state of development in the successor system, Deep Blue.

Other enhancements involved the evaluation function. One was the use of both a fast, partial evaluator and a slow, full evaluator. If the former could bound the search, evaluation was cut off at that point; otherwise full evaluation was carried out. In fact, the fast evaluator was sufficient for the endgame, so the slow evaluator was only needed for the opening and middle game.

A very important further advance was that the weighting of different features for evaluation could be tuned through the controller. Sometimes this was done automatically using heuristic search (a method discussed in Chapter 9). More often it was done manually. As a result, weights could be tuned between games during a match, as was done when Deep Blue played Kasparov. It was also at this point that the database of grandmaster moves was used to compare Deep Blue's choices for a move with those made by grandmasters.

Each chip in Deep Blue can evaluate 2.5 million positions per second. Figure 4.9 shows its configuration.[32] Note that the move generator and evaluator are both on the same chip.

The next Figure (4.10) shows the complete Deep Blue system used in the match against Kasparov.[33] In this configuration there were 480 chips like the one shown above. This system was able to search up to 200 million nodes per second, which allowed it to search a tree of depth 12 (in addition to special extensions).

In all of this Hsu and his team were following in the footsteps of the original chess pioneers. Recall that a critical problem for game-tree

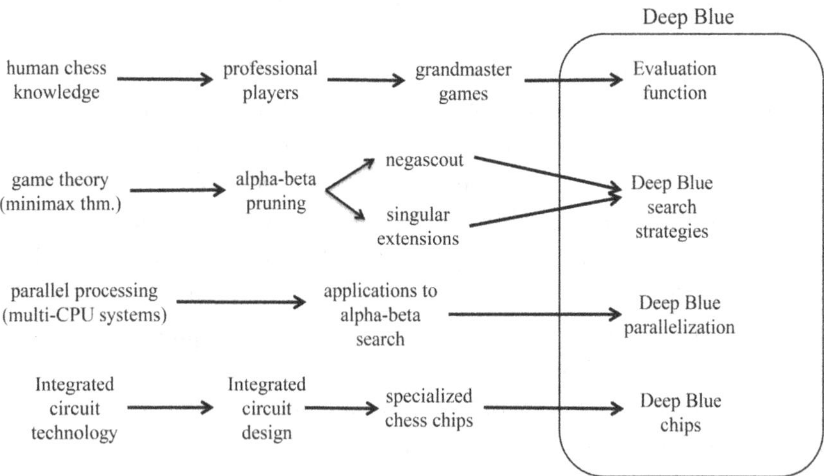

Figure 4.11. World graph showing the many influences that led to different features of the Deep Blue system, shown on the right.

analyses of chess is that the game tree is too large to be explored completely. This means that minimax search can only be partial, and to be effective it must rely on reasonable assessments of board positions that represent a current state of play. Deep Thought and Deep Blue were demonstrations of how much can be done within these basic constraints, worked out by earlier researchers.

The many relations between Deep Blue and its antecedents can be shown by means of a world graph such as in Figure 4.11. This shows how Deep Blue represents a confluence of developments in several areas of research, technology and other kinds of human endeavor. In a very real sense, this serves to give us a better sense of what Deep Blue actually is.

Watson

Like Deep Blue, Watson is part of a research tradition, in this case one concerned with developing systems that are able to answer questions about a particular topic or topics. Like so many other areas of AI, this line of research got its start in the early 1960s or slightly before. Although it can be considered a subtopic of natural language processing, question answering also has connections with the field of information retrieval and more recently with search engines for the World Wide Web. Retrieval systems, however, return documents or Web links to documents containing information that may be relevant to a query; they do not try to answer a question directly. This is reflected in the fact that queries for documents often take the form of strings of keywords rather than fully formulated questions.

The most significant early question-answering programs dealt with restricted topics such as baseball games or lunar rock samples and allowed focused questions to be asked about the topic. Almost at the inception of the field, two different approaches emerged. The first used complex indexes and was therefore closely related to information retrieval systems. The second used an approach based on parsing the question and deriving a symbolic structure of its meaning. In some cases this amounted to a representation in symbolic logic, where predicates (relational symbols) were applied to terms. So, for example, the question, "Who was the catcher for the Mets in 1956?" might be translated as:

THEREEXISTS x (sport-played(x, baseball), player-position(x, catcher), team-member(x, Mets), year-playing(x, 1956)).

"THEREEXISTS x" means that there is something in the world designated by the variable x, and the following list of predicates apply to this x. Each predicate such as "sport-played" holds for the arguments within the following pair of parentheses; so "sport-played(x, baseball)" means that for some discrete entity to qualify as x, it must play baseball. Commas between predicates are logical ANDs — which means that for the entire expression to be true all of the predicates must hold simultaneously.

To give the reader a more concrete sense of how these systems worked, I will briefly cover one of the earliest successful systems, called BASEBALL.[34] BASEBALL answered questions about baseball games played in a certain year, including information about which teams played which, and whether a team won or lost a particular game. A possible question that BASEBALL could answer successfully is:

Who did the Red Sox lose to on July 5?

The information required to answer such questions was stored in a database that took the form of attribute-value pairs such as "TEAM = Red Sox" or "Place = Boston" or "Game No. = 96". Pairs could be organized hierarchically, e.g. under "Month" and "Place" or they could simply be a list of pairs defining a particular game.

Since this was the early 1960s, questions were entered on punched cards. After a question was read in, the system used a simple parsing procedure that labeled each word with its part of speech, then scanned the sentence to locate noun, prepositional and adverbial phrases. It also converted passive verbs to the equivalent active form. So a question like,

Who did the Red Sox lose to on July 5?

became

(To [who]) [the Red Sox] lose (on [July 5])

In the next stage of processing, with the help of a dictionary, a list of attribute-value pairs was set up that represented the question plus an attribute with a missing value, which indicates the information wanted. Continuing with our example, this list would appear as follows:

Team(winning) = ?
Team(losing) = Red Sox
Month = July
Day = 5

With this information, the database was searched for the list of pairs that matched the complete attribute-value pairs, and then the missing value was extracted and given as the answer.

Over the next few decades, this area of inquiry gave rise to a distinct research stream, closely allied of course to the more general area of natural language processing. The use of such systems as natural language front-ends for databases, already implicit in BASEBALL and other early systems became the major focus of the area. During this time much of the emphasis was on natural language processing, including improved algorithms for syntax analysis and methods for dealing with semantic issues such as handling quantifiers (e.g. "some" and "all"). Methods for handling questions requiring numerical answers and other special problems were also developed, usually by calling subroutines associated with the basic natural language parser. All of this was tightly coupled to databases and their formal structures as well as to specific domains of application, such as lunar geology or aircraft maintenance parts.[35*,36]

At the same time that these efforts were proceeding, AI researchers concerned with natural language continued to work on the topic of question answering. This work served to uncover many interesting and problematic issues that arise in real-world situations in regard to question answering that are still of current interest.[37] These include recognizing goals and intentions, which may determine the way that the question is answered. For example:

Q: What's the combination of the printer room lock?

A: The door's open.

Another related topic is the problem of representing possibilities, which is required for answering what-if questions. Finally, there is the problem of recognizing misconceptions implied by a question and answering accordingly, as in the following example:

Q: What's the interest rate on this stock?

A: Stocks don't have an interest rate. They may pay a dividend periodically.

These several problems also raise important issues concerning how to evaluate the quality of an answer, rather than simply judging it as correct or incorrect. (As we will see, these various issues and problems could be sidestepped by Watson in the context of the Jeopardy! game.)

In the late 80s and early 90s, the field of information extraction emerged as a distinct entity.[38] This development was facilitated by the establishment of a tailored venue, the Message Understanding Conferences or MUCs. Unlike the typical science or engineering conference, these conferences were built around a competition, and groups were required to submit a system to be evaluated in order to attend the conference. As part of this endeavor, testbeds were established along with systematic methods for evaluating systems. The main task that had to be performed was filling out a description in the form of a template with required fields, by extracting requisite pieces of information from a given set of messages. In addition, templates for entities had to be combined into a larger scenario template.

To do all this, a system first had to automatically annotate the text messages so that relevant information could be identified, including persons, organizations and number amounts. Here is an example, where the annotation is done with Web mark-up language tags[39]:

Mr. <ENAMEX TYPE="PERSON">Dooner</ENAMEX> met with <ENAMEX TYPE= "PERSON">Martin Puris</ENAMEX>, president and chief executive officer of <ENAMEX TYPE="ORGANIZATION">Amnirati & Puris</ENAMEX>, about <ENAMEX TYPE="ORGANIZATION">McCann</ENAMEX>'s acquiring the agency with billings of <NUMEX TYPE="MONEY">$400 million </NUMEX>, but nothing has materialized.

The tag ENAMEX (for "entity name expression") designates people or organizations, while the tag NUMEX ("numeric expression") in this case designates a monetary value.

And here is an example where an organization template was filled in after annotating the following text[40]:

> "We are striving to have a strong renewed creative partnership with Coca-Cola," Mr. Dooner says. However, odds of that happening are slim since word from Coke headquarters in Altlanta is that ...

<ORGANIZATION-9402240133-5> :=
ORG_NAME: "Coca-Cola"
ORG_ALIAS: "Coke"
ORG_TYPE: COMPANY
ORG_LOCALE: CITY Atlanta
ORG_COUNTRY: United States

The number in the ORGANIZATION header identifies the original message and indicates that this is the fifth template derived from this message.

A schematic picture of the information extraction process is shown in Figure 4.12. This is meant to give a generic view, ignoring the considerable differences among individual systems, which might elaborate a particular step or even omit it. In fact, during this period dozens of specific techniques for these different tasks were proposed and tested, each of which had its own strengths and limitations, and this is important for understanding Watson and putting it in its proper context.

In the preprocessing stage various text items such as dates are changed to a canonical form. Then keywords such as "bomb" are identified using a dictionary. Sentences that do not contain any keywords may be filtered out. Syntactic analysis usually involves indentifying parts of speech, noun and verb phrases, conjunctions, etc. Some systems then carry out a deeper semantic analysis which also allowed them to predict that allied concepts would be found. This could be based on frame-and-slot representations of concepts as well as concept hierachies (such as animal -> bird -> robin or human -> terrorist). Finally, the information obtained in these analyses is merged to form a set of filled templates.

An interesting development that took place in the course of this work, which bears on the Watson project, was that initial efforts that involved a fairly deep analysis of the syntax and semantics of messages gave way to simpler strategies that achieved nearly the same results. The key motivator was time: thus it was reported by one group that their earlier system that

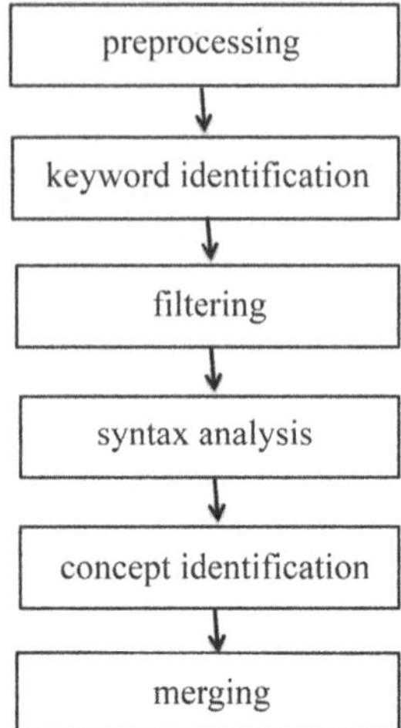

Figure 4.12. Steps in process of information extraction.

did elaborate parsing and interpretation took 36 hours to analyze 100 messages, while a later system that only carried out 'shallow' processing took 11 minutes.[41] From the examples I have read, one factor that made it possible to adopt such strategies was that each competition covered a specific domain such as "naval sightings and engagements", "electronic circuit fabrications" or terrorist attacks in Latin America.[42] This meant that a small number of patterns could be used such as <Perpetrator> attacked <HumanTarget>, where the terms in brackets are matched to words before and after the specified word.

The relevance of this work for our concerns is that a number of the techniques devised for these tasks were then used in question answering systems. This occurred as part of new developments that changed the character of this area.

Around the turn of the century, there was renewed interest in question answering within the field of information retrieval. As in the information extraction field, an attempt was made to facilitate this endeavor through a conference. In this case, a track on question answering was added to an existing venue, the annual Text Retrieval Conference (or TREC). For a while this was the major platform for presenting new developments in this field. As in the earlier message understanding conferences, TREC organizers established testbeds and set up competitions.[43] Participants included a group at IBM who later formed part of the Watson team.

A spur for this upsurge of interest was the desire to extend question answering to more open-ended domains, based on a corpus of texts, rather than well-organized databases related to a circumscribed body of knowledge. Additional impetus came with the emergence of the World Wide Web in the late 1990s, since people immediately saw the benefits of systems that could trawl the Web for exact answers rather than simply returning links to possibly relevant Web pages.

For its competitions the TREC organizers put together a corpus of documents that contestants were to use in finding answers. Reflecting the information retrieval background, contestants in the TREC competitions were not required to produce a well-formed answer in English. Instead they had to return passages culled from documents (50 or 250 bytes in length depending on the test run)[44*] that contained the answer to the question. Each system rated the passages it found and returned those with the five highest ratings.

Naturally many of the question answering systems submitted to TREC carried over techniques from the mother area of information retrieval (IR). Recall that in IR the task is to retrieve documents that contain information that a user is seeking, and that the user indicates his or her interest by a set of terms or keywords. Classical IR techniques require that a set of documents be indexed. Indexes are based on document features; usually these features are terms found in the document, terms such as "Julius Caesar" or "ribonucleic acid". In order to distinguish different documents, term-weighting procedures are used; the classic ones are weighting a term by the frequency in which it appears within a document and weighting it by the inverse frequency with which a document contains that term (so that terms receive higher weights if very few documents contain them). Both can be combined. Taken together, the set of weighted terms forms a vector: $(w_1t_1, w_2t_2, \ldots, w_nt_n)$. Since the t's are 0's or 1's, this amounts to a vector of non-negative weights. User queries, which are also sets of terms, can be turned into vectors of the same type, and various similarity measures can be used to match documents to queries. In addition, a host of techniques for more effective weight setting have been devised and tested, including incorporation of morphological variants into

		documents			
		doc 1	doc 2	doc 3	doc 4
	house	0	0	1	1
terms	car	1	0	0	1
	dog	0	1	0	0

Figure 4.13. Example of word-document feature set for finding appropriate information in documents.

the frequencies, assessing co-occurrence of related terms in a text, and statistical assessments of document and corpus frequencies for a given term.

In addition to vector-of-weights methods, there are Boolean similarity methods. These are also based on sets of features, which again are normally terms found in the documents. In this case if a document contains that term the document-term combination is scored as a 1. In effect, this creates a large two-dimensional matrix where the rows of the matrix are terms and the columns are documents. Then when a document contains a term the corresponding matrix entry is 1, otherwise it is 0, as in the example, shown in Figure 4.13.

Queries take the form of Boolean expressions involving terms joined by Boolean operators, e.g. "Julius Caesar" AND ("Brutus" OR "Cassius") AND NOT "Cleopatra". In addition a NEAR operator can specify that certain terms should occur in close proximity to each other. In this case similarity measures are based on the union and intersection of sets of terms rather than geometrical relations between weight vectors.[45]

Another classical IR technique is query expansion. Instead of simply using the words in the query to search for documents, other terms are derived including morphologically related terms, synonyms, and even words that are semantically related.

To see how these various techniques were applied to question answering, along with various extensions, it is useful to have a general schematic to refer to. This is provided by the diagram in Figure 4.14, taken from a summary article written in the early 2000's.[46] This diagram outlines the basic steps that any question answering system must follow. It also

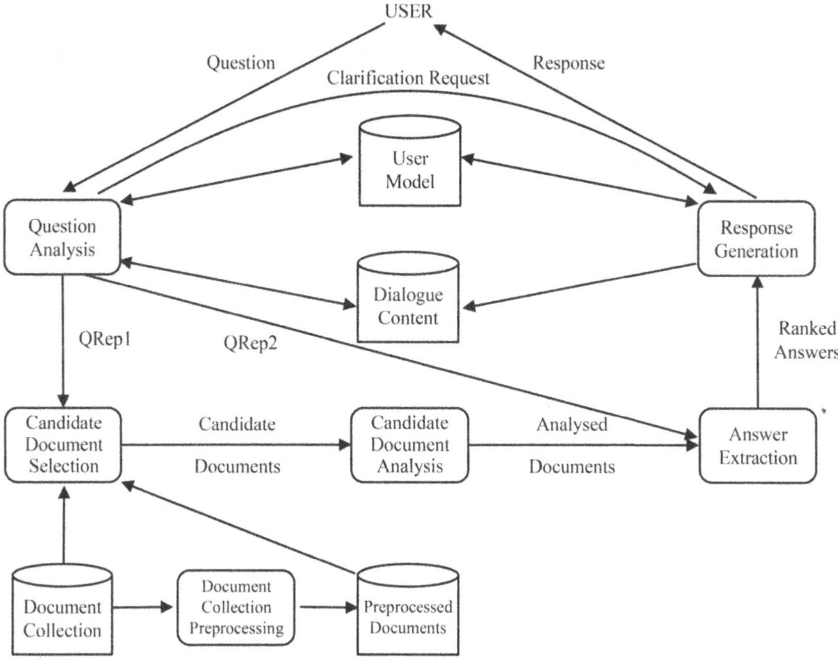

Figure 4.14. Generic architecture for a question answering system (reprinted from Hirschman & Gaizauskas, 2001, Figure 1, by permission).

distinguishes the different information flows and their targets, e.g. that the contextual information used in response generation can be separated from document selection and answer extraction.

As indicated by the diagram, many question answering systems perform document selection and answer extraction in successive stages. The first naturally makes use of information retrieval strategies, while the second is heavily influenced by techniques devised for information extraction.

In trying to carry out the task of question answering it quickly became clear that a major problem is determining what is being sought by way of an answer; in fact, this is obviously prior to the task of composing items of information to provide an answer. This insight led to elaborate schemes for question — and answer — classification (all part of the "question analysis" step in the diagram). Question classification begins with question-words (who, what, how, etc), if they are present, which suggest natural differences in the type of answer required. In many cases one can make further distinctions, as between how-much (quantity) and how-long (duration).

An important idea that emerged in the course of this work was the notion of a focus or asking point. This is a word or phrase in the question that indicates the kind of answer required. In other words, it is a key feature that can be used for answer classification. In the simplest cases the focus is the question-word; for example "who" indicates that the answer must be a person. On the other hand what-questions normally include a noun that indicates the kind of answer sought, as in:

What is the tallest mountain in the Alps?

Here, "mountain" is the focus, and from this the system can deduce that the answer must be a member of the class <mountain>. (The "the" before the noun indicates that the answer is a specific mountain, while "Alps" and "in" indicate that it must be in a particular mountain range.) On the other hand, for the question:

What kind of an animal is a squirrel?

"animal" would be the focus, while "what kind" indicates the type of question being asked. From this it can be deduced that some sort of class term is required, and that it is a subclass of "animal".[47]

In order to determine the kind of answer sought, most systems use a predefined set of answer types. Initially, these consisted of about a dozen categories such as <person>, <location>, <date>, <time>, <money>. As time went on these taxonomies became much more elaborate with over one hundred categories arranged into hierarchies.

To deduce the appropriate category for a given question, researchers made use of tools and methods from natural language processing. A common technique (called lexical chaining) was to use WordNet to find either higher categories or associated words starting with the words in the question. In the second example above, the system would look up "squirrel" and quickly find that it was subordinate to "mammal", to "vertebrate", etc. and finally to "animal". Hence, the system has found a chain in the WordNet noun hierarchy from "squirrel" to "animal". (Note that in this case, the WordNet search also returns answers to the question in the form of terms in the path between "squirrel" and "animal".)[48]

An example where some sort of semantic analysis is required is the question:

What year did Hitler die?

The answer to this question can be found in sentences like, "The Nazi leader committed suicide on April 30, 1945" or "Hitler killed himself in 1945". But in order to determine this, the system must be able to deduce that "suicide" and "killed himself" refer to the death of the person in question.[49]

Other techniques for answer classification involve statistical models. In all cases these methods calculate the most likely member of a set of possibilities, here, the set of possible answer types. In order to do this the system must be trained to be able to recognize feature-category relations in order to make reasonable inferences; to this end, techniques from machine learning have been brought to bear.

On the document side, it is fairly obvious that techniques from information extraction such as tagging named entities can be used to characterize documents for question answering. Again, these techniques can be amplified using ideas from natural language processing (NLP indexing). An example is tagging subject-verb-object patterns. Another is to search for concepts (along with keywords) that match concepts deduced from the question. This can be carried further, by translating both question and answer into logical forms in order to try to deduce the latter from the former.[50] In some cases systems of weights were also added to the mix.

On the other hand, for questions like those used in the early TREC competitions that required simple facts for answers, it is often possible to avoid complex linguistic analysis. One alternative is to find specific patterns of text strings that are associated with certain kinds of information. For example, the question,

What year was Mozart born?

requires a date for an answer. One pattern with this information that often appears in texts is a name followed by the dates of birth and death in parentheses, e.g. "Mozart (1756–1791)". Therefore, if the system looks for the pattern <name, left parenthesis, four digit number, dash, four digit number, right parenthesis> where the name matches the party involved, then it can find the answer to this question. With many such patterns it may be able to answer a number of questions without having to analyze them linguistically.[51]

The usual method for locating relevant passages was to scan the text using a window of a certain size, e.g. 20 or 30 consecutive words. Then windows that contained the appropriate target patterns could be returned. Passages could be further evaluated using confidence estimates, that is estimates of the probability of being correct given the question and answer. Again, this involved training the system with examples where the correctness was known in order to test features that could be used in connection with the question-answer comparison. For example, suppose that the feature is the number of content words (i.e. ignoring articles, conjunctions and prepositions) in the passage (aside from the answer/target) that are also found in the question. If the number in the question is, say, 4, then the probability that the passage contains the correct answer is found to increase as the number of identical content words in the passage increases from 0 to 4. So this feature can be used for confidence estimation.[52]

During the first decade of the century some researchers began to experiment with multi-strategy techniques; this included a group at IBM.[53] In these systems different approaches, say a semantic analysis and a statistical approach based on predictive features, were run in parallel. Different strategies also incorporated different knowledge sources: while some scanned documents, others interrogated databases containing specialized, often quantitative knowledge. The answers produced by these different strategies had to be compared in some fashion to obtain a final answer; this was done by an "answer resolution" component that combined answers from different sources and also computed a "confidence value" for the answer derived.

In trying to adapt IR and IE techniques to question answering, researchers could build upon some general empirical observations. The most important was:

> "... that when a document successfully answers a question, all of the components of the question are to be found together, usually within a passage of a sentence or two."[54]

The same investigators also found that "the number of other occurrences of query terms elsewhere in the document does not seem to be an indicator of the passage's worth".

Another observation is that:

> "when a document and a query match on several words, the individual matching words will have the same word sense"[55]

This means that word sense disambiguation is often not necessary for locating answers to queries within passages of text.

Both these rules of thumb reflect the fact that connected text has certain regularities that can be used to determine whether a passage contains the information that will answer a query. So a system that can assess these properties may be able to perform the task even if it does not 'understand' what is being asked. (And who is to say that these features of connected discourse have no bearing on the problem of understanding?)

Another significant observation has to do with the number of passages in the corpus that contain the information being sought. In the words of one group of investigators:

> "Given a source ... that contains only a relatively small number of formulations of answers to a query, we may be faced with the difficult task of mapping questions to answers by way of uncovering complex lexical, syntactic, or semantic relationships between question string and answer string. ... However, the greater the answer redundancy in the source, the more likely it is that we can find an answer that occurs in a simple relation to the question, and therefore, the less likely that we will need to resort to solving the aforementioned difficulties facing natural language systems"[56]

Various methods have also been devised for the last step in the process, answer construction. Two different approaches have been used. The first involves extraction, i.e. cutting and pasting from existing text(s). The second involves "generation", i.e. returning a well-formed statement or single word or phrase that is a proper answer to the question. An interesting example of the first type of strategy is called "answer tiling". In this procedure sets of words of various size, called n-grams, that were collected during retrieval are combined to form larger n-grams. So two trigrams {A, B, C} and {B, C, D} might be tiled to produce {A, B, C, D}.

Such tiling is guided by a system of weights associated with each term and proceeds so as to retain the terms with maximum weight.[57]

During the first decade of this century, as part of its research in IR and question answering systems, IBM carried out an important infrastructure project that was to underpin the Watson effort. The system that resulted was called the Unstructured Information Management Architecture or UIMA. It was meant to serve as a common framework for many researchers working on document analysis and information retrieval. (The Watson project came later.)

The most important feature of this framework was that it allowed multiple subsystems, each performing some kind of textual analysis, to work in concert. The diagram in Figure 4.15 gives a schematic view.[58] Each subsystem, or "analysis engine" receives information about a document, represented in a common form (the Common Analysis Structure or CAS, written in XML), and returns its results in the same form. Coordination is effected by the systems referred to in the figure as the Analysis Sequencer and the Analysis Structure Broker. The former, as its name indicates, determines the order in which analysis engines receive information to begin working on. The latter delivers the information to the appropriate engine. A single engine can be built from 'smaller' engines (each with its own Analysis Broker), so that the system has a recursive

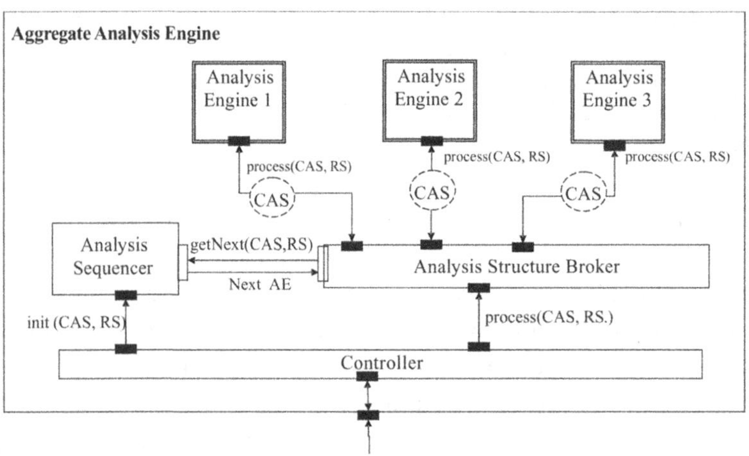

Figure 4.15. The UIMA Aggregate Analysis Engine (reprinted from Ferrucci & Lally, 2004, Figure 5, by permission). Further details in text.

structure. (In fact, the figure shows an "aggregate" engine; Also, unlike other parts of the figure, the "controller" is actually part of the general framework.)

In this way, the many strategies already discussed in this section could be incorporated into a single system. As already noted, multi-strategy approaches were gaining in popularity at the same time, but these still involved only a few agents. One of the aims of the Unstructured Information Management Architecture was to allow a large number of agents or engines to coordinate their activities and for such a system to be built without an enormous investment in time and effort. This was to prove crucial for the success of the Watson project.

Supporting all these research efforts were developments in the hardware that should not be overlooked. During all this time there was continuous improvement in computer speed and storage capacity; in addition, the 1990s witnessed the emergence of computer networks. Because of these advances it became possible to process enormous amounts of data, including connected text, in a reasonably short time. This meant that entire documents could be processed instead of only titles and abstracts, which is of course essential for question answering with open domains. One effect of this was that the corpuses used in competitions grew progressively larger over the years. (Another advance was the evolution of parallel computing, which played a crucial role in the Watson system.)

Finally, it is important to remember that the success of these systems is determined by human judges. Thus, there are always human beings in the loop, even after such systems are up and running.

*

This discussion of earlier work should be enough to give the reader a sense of the rich assortment of techniques that had been devised in several allied fields concerned with finding information in text sources prior to the building of Watson. This background is essential for understanding what Watson actually is. This includes what was 'added to the mix' to enable it to perform successfully and what problems were avoided or finessed. Some of the latter will now be considered.

In most cases question-answer systems give discrete, "factoid" answers to questions like, "What is the capital of Romania?" As an elaboration of this, when querying technical databases the answer might be in the form of a table or graph that includes a large number of related facts. Since the late 1990s there has been a growing interest in questions with non-factoid answers such as requests for definitions or explanations. But since Watson falls under the former heading, we need not concern ourselves with these lines of investigation.

Another interesting restriction is that Watson avoids extensive semantic analysis of a question. In particular, it does not use elaborate representations of concepts, i.e. a world model. On the other hand, it must be able to figure out the sort of thing that the questioner is looking for. Moreover, it must search through material that represents extensive realms of knowledge, since although there are specified topics for questions, the range of possibilities is still enormous and the boundaries poorly defined. And as already noted, the creators of Watson, following in the paths laid out by earlier researchers in the fields of information retrieval, did not concern themselves with the question of whether it was necessary for the system to "understand" the material involved in the answer.

The Watson project began in 2007, as a continuation of a large research effort on text analysis and question answering systems that had been going on at IBM since the 1990s, some of which was discussed above. But despite all this accumulated knowledge and expertise, when the IBM team first attempted to apply existing techniques to the game of Jeopardy!, they were stymied. As the authors put it:

> "Our investigations ran the gamut from deep logical form analysis to shallow machine-translation approaches. … Our efforts failed to have significant impact on Jeopardy or even on prior baseline studies using TREC [Text Retrieval Conference] data."[59]

In other words, these methods were simply not up to the challenge. But why was this? What made coming up with the right answers for Jeopardy! so difficult given 45 years of research on question answering, including a decade of research on so-called open domain questions?

Perhaps the most important reason lies in the fact that the situation in Jeopardy! is quite unlike the standard question-answering task. In the latter case the user who poses the question is interested in using the system for his or her benefit, and therefore trying to be as helpful as possible, which means asking the question in a way that will guide the search to the correct answer. But in Jeopardy! the form of the question is part of the challenge put to the answerer. As such, it may be posed in a way that is allusive, so that understanding what is wanted by way of an answer becomes an important part of the task.

To deal with this problem, Watson first carries out an extensive syntactic analysis of the sentence. Suppose it is given the question:

> The Nobel Prize was awarded to Albert Einstein for his work on this phenomenon. (answer: photoelectric effect)

The sentence is first parsed using a specialized grammar called a slot grammar.[60] The key feature of such grammars is that when a part of speech is identified, then certain other parts of speech are expected; these are the "slots" that need to be filled in using other words in the sentence. For example, once "award" is identified as the main verb (designated "top"), then slots for subject and object are expected. In the present case, this leads to the following parse tree:

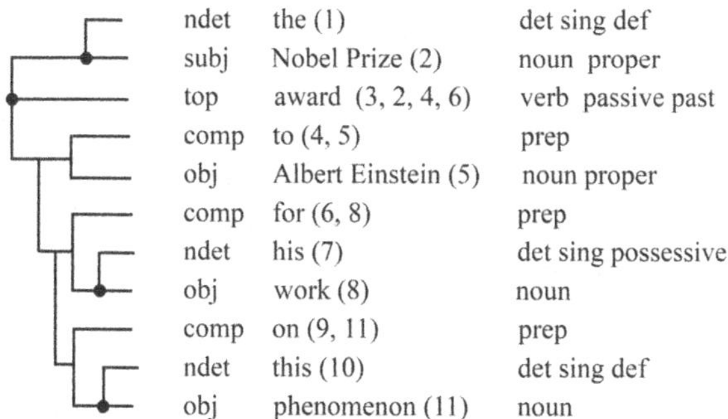

In the next step, this syntactic structure is transformed into a semi-logical form called the predicate-argument structure. The latter basically highlights the basic dependencies shown in parentheses in the output from the original parse (indicated after the words in the figure above), while discarding more 'superficial' structures. Continuing with our example, the parse above could be transformed into the labeled, directed graph below.

After this, relations can be deduced that aid in answer classification (deriving the answer type), as well as allowing further inferences. They can also facilitate scoring the various pieces of text possibly containing

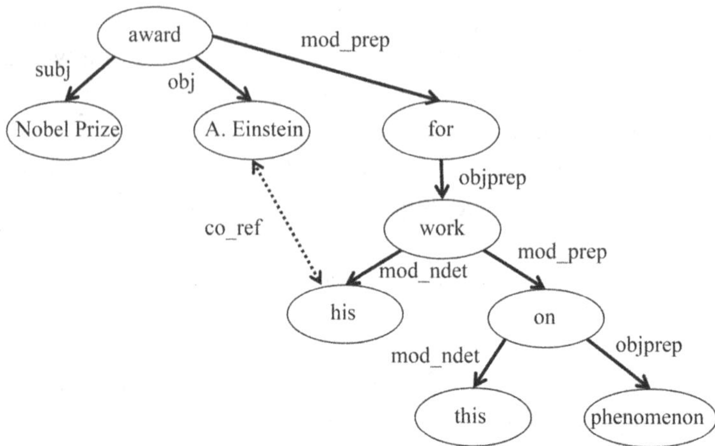

Figure 4.16. Graphical representation of grammatical relations of sentence on previous page (reprinted with some alterations from Fan *et al.*, 2012, Figure 1, courtesy of International Business Machines Corp., © 2012 IBM).

the answer that must be matched against the question. In the present example, some relations that could be derived from this predicate-argument structure are research(scientist, subject) and award(prize, recipient).

In order to find potential answers to the query, Watson interrogates various prepared knowledge stores. The major resource consists of encyclopedia (Wikipedia) articles. In addition, specific material on subjects like Shakespeare and the Bible were collected. Other sources included specialized lists such as the kings of England and movie databases.

An important observation made by the creators of Watson was that in many cases, answers to Jeopardy! questions can be found in the titles of encyclopedia articles. Moreover, in these cases the words of the article are likely to match words in the question. On the other hand, if words in the title match clue-words in the question, then the answer is likely to be found in the body of the article. These discoveries were turned into simple heuristics for searching for answers, e.g. choose articles where there are matches between title words and question words, and these were added to standard passage selection strategies drawn from the question answer literature (including earlier work done at IBM).

To further capitalize on these strategies, documents that did not conform to the title-based encyclopedia style were altered to follow the same format; these were called title-oriented pseudo-documents. In addition, 'artificial' documents were composed that contained additional relevant knowledge about a topic. This was done by starting with a "seed document", collecting Web documents with matching terms, extracting paragraphs with common terms that met other criteria such as the existence of some independent information, and from these forming new pseudo-documents that were then added to the corpus.

Yet another approach to storing knowledge (the PRISMATIC system) involved extracting knowledge in the form of what the authors refer to as frames and slots. Frames are record-like structures whose entries are called slots. (In the programming language or data structure literatures they would be called the fields of the record.)

For example, suppose the system encounters the sentence:

> "In 1921, Einstein received the Nobel Prize for his original work on the photoelectric effect."

This gives rise to two frame-representations. The first, FRAME01, is shown below:

SLOT	VALUE
verb	receive
subj	Einstein
type	<person>/<scientist>
obj	Nobel prize
mod_vprep	in
objprep	1921
type	<year>
mod_vprep	for
objprep	FRAME02

The slot-types are derived from the constituents of the grammar used in the syntactic analysis already referred to. A few other slot types were included, based on well-known semantic relations like set-superset relations (called isa relations, e.g. robin isa bird). In addition, proper names like Einstein are flagged as such.

When information is encoded in this form, it is possible to derive other relations from patterns common to many frames, an operation called "frame projection". These are based on common grammatical relations such as subject-verb-object (SVO) or noun-isa-modifier. So, for example, if a number of frames are found in which the proper nouns, "Einstein" and "Nobel Prize" occur along with the stem verb "receive", then the SVO frame (Einstein, receive, Nobel Prize) can be extracted. And since "Einstein" has an isa relation to "scientist", the system may also be able to derive this noun-modifier combination.[61*]

In addition to generating candidate answers, Watson uses the PRISMATIC knowledge base to identify types for answers in order to match those deduced from the question. The projection feature allows Watson to derive semantic links that might otherwise have remained undiscovered; this was instrumental in answering Jeopardy! questions that required fusing two apparently disparate entities.

Using these sources of information, Watson carries out an elaborate process of generating candidate answers, which its creators call hypothesis generation. At each stage of the process, several strategies are used in parallel, as shown in Figure 4.17.[62] In each case, search is guided by elements (focus words, relations) found in the query generation phase. For example, the term "Einstein" can be used to select documents for TOD generation (i.e. generation of candidate answers from document titles). At the same time, the research and award relations can be used to select encyclopedia articles where relevant terms appear in the title (TIC or Title-in-Clue search). At the same time, both kinds of clue can be used to select frames in the PRISMATIC knowledge base, in particular, those involving isa relations. Simultaneously, these and other clues are passed to the Indri and Lucene search systems, which use standard question answering strategies such as the text-window passage search described earlier to find candidate answers. (The latter are passage search systems created by other groups and available online that were incorporated into Watson.[63*]) In addition (not shown in the figure), there are direct answer lookup procedures used with lists and specialized databases (e.g. for movie titles).[64*]

Together, these procedures were very successful in finding good candidates. In one test with over three thousand questions that were new to

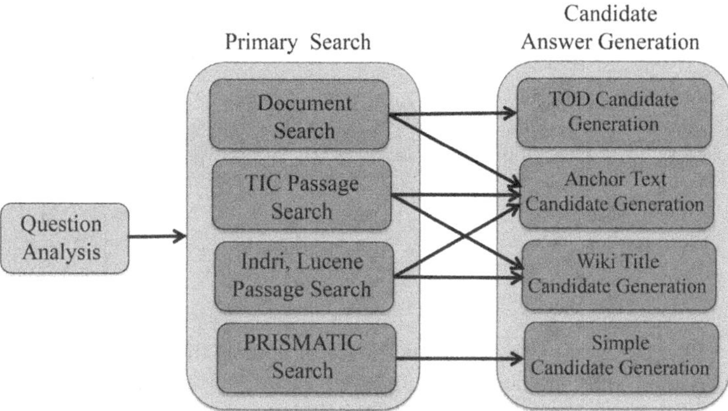

Figure 4.17. Components of PRISMATIC knowledge base including links between them (adapted from a portion of Chu-Carroll *et al.*, 2012, Figure 2, courtesy of International Business Machines Corp., © 2012 IBM).

Watson, the correct answer appeared in the set of candidates 87% of the time.[65*]

As shown in Figure 4.18, after the hypothesis generation stage, which may produce several hundred candidates, Watson carries out a complicated process of winnowing down the candidate set, scoring the remaining candidates, and ranking them for likelihood before making the final decision to provide an answer. The main stages of this process are represented by the three boxes with black borders on the right side of the figure. (The steps that we have just discussed are represented by the boxes without borders.)

In the soft filtering stage the candidate answers are typed, and an attempt is made to match these types with the lexical answer types (LATs) deduced from the original question, a process called type coercion. This is carried out with several different algorithms, working with a variety of sources. All follow a basic four-part scheme:

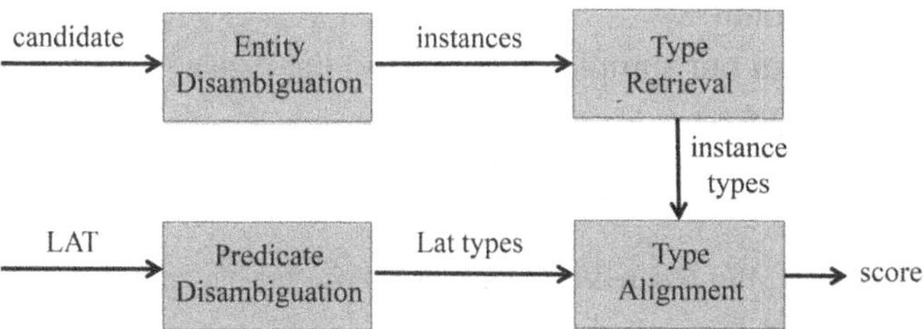

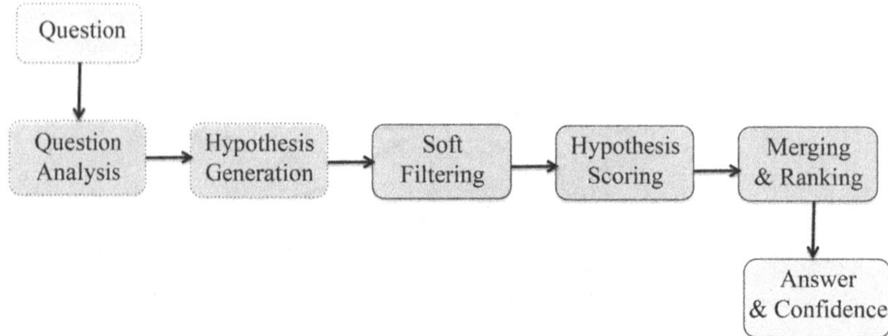

Figure 4.18. Diagram of basic Watson's basic operations from Jeopardy! question to answer (adapted from portion of Chu-Carroll *et al.*, 2012, Figure 2, courtesy of International Business Machines Corp., © 2012 IBM).

For example, suppose that one candidate is "special relativity" and the LAT, taken directly from the question, is "phenomenon". The entity disambiguation process might return "physics theory" and "relativistic effect", and "effect" alone. In this case the predicate disambiguation process may well just pass along the LAT. Then the type alignment algorithm that uses WordNet might discover that "phenomenon" can be linked to "effect". So in this case "special relativity" would receive a positive score, as would "photoelectric effect" if that was also one of the candidates.

Passage scoring relies on four different approaches to compare passages with the original question:

- Word match
- Word pair structural match
- Text alignment, based on words and word order
- Logical form match

By using multiple strategies, Watson avoids some of the limitations of structural matching based on common syntax. At the same time it can take relations into account.

Consider again our sample question and the passage quoted above:

> (question) The Nobel Prize was awarded to Albert Einstein for his work on this phenomenon.
>
> (passage) In 1921, Einstein received the Nobel Prize for his original work on the photoelectric effect.

Note that the word match would give a positive score based on the common appearance of "Nobel Prize" and "Einstein". The text alignment algorithm would pick up the similarity between "for his work on" and "for his original work on". Similary, the logical form match might be able to detect the common predicate award(prize, recipient). All this would lead Watson to give this passage a relatively high score.

An important technique used in the hypothesis scoring stage is called supporting evidence retrieval.[66] The main technique is to substitute a candidate answer for the focus in the original question. Then the parsing and search processes are carried out in the same way as before to obtain new passages, followed by passage scoring. So in our example, "photoelectric effect" and "special relativity" would be substituted for "phenomenon". Note that in the first case, the sentence above would be retrieved as before — and given an even higher score.

The final merging and ranking stage makes use of a number of strategies and techniques drawn from other areas, with special emphasis on the fields of statistics and machine learning. Sophisticated techniques capable of making fine discriminations (in the form of "confidence estimations") are necessary due to the plethora of candidate answers, only 1% of which are correct in many cases.[67] Here, it will only be possible to give a brief sketch of the process, alluding to a few of the most important techniques that are brought to bear at this stage.

In some cases several candidate answers refer to the same entity (e.g. "JFK", "Jack Kennedy", "John F. Kennedy"). These must be recognized as equivalent; in addition, a canonical form is chosen to represent them. In addition to recognizing equivalence, Watson can derive instance_of relations, so it is able to relate a category to specific examples (e.g. "Excalibur" is an instance of "sword").

Answer merging entails merging the features associated with each answer as well as their scores. The latter is done through various kinds of averaging, in particular a form of weighted averaging where successively lower scores are discounted even further by dividing them by increasing powers of 2 (called a "decaying sum").

Finally, a single score is associated with each answer by combining the feature scores. To do this effectively, models are derived which are essentially weighted sums, where the weights are derived by training on numerous instances in which the correct answer is known. (This is where machine learning techniques are critical.) For illustration, a simplified sum is shown below[68*]:

$$f(x) = \text{SUM } m = 1..M\ (beta_m * x_m)$$

Here, f(x) designates the combined score for answer x, x_m is a single feature and $beta_m$ is the weight for that feature. Machine learning is used to learn the weights.

Different models (of the same form) are used for different types of questions and answers. For example, specific models (i.e. specific sets of weights) were derived for puzzle questions, for dates and numbers, for questions with no focus, questions with "useless LATS" ("it" or "this"), etc.

These various procedures are carried out in a succession of phases. There is an initial phase in which identical answers are merged and their scores computed and normalized. Then all but the top 100 answers are discarded. Later phases involve merging of answers deduced to be equivalent (cf. the Kennedy example above), sharing of evidence depending on the relations between answers (e.g. features may be transferred from a location to a country if the candidate is a location and the LAT is a country), and further pruning away of lower-scoring answers.

Last but not least, in order to compete in an actual Jeopardy! contest, Watson had to perform all these computations in a few seconds. This in itself was a challenge that had never been faced before. In fact, the initial version of Watson running on a single processor required one to two hours to answer a question.[69] For Watson to be competetive, this time had to be reduced to a few seconds.

This reduction in time was achieved using massive parallelization. This was done using the modular UIMA framework described earlier. To support parallelization, special UIMA Analysis Engines were used (called CAS Multipliers) that, given one input (in the form of a Common Analysis Structure, or CAS) produced multiple child CASes. These could then be distributed to multiple processors so that tasks such as candidate generation and evidence scoring could be done in parallel. In addition, information sources such as PRISMATIC were replicated on multiple servers so that this information could be accessed in parallel. In the final system there were thousands of processes running on dozens of different machines.[70]

*

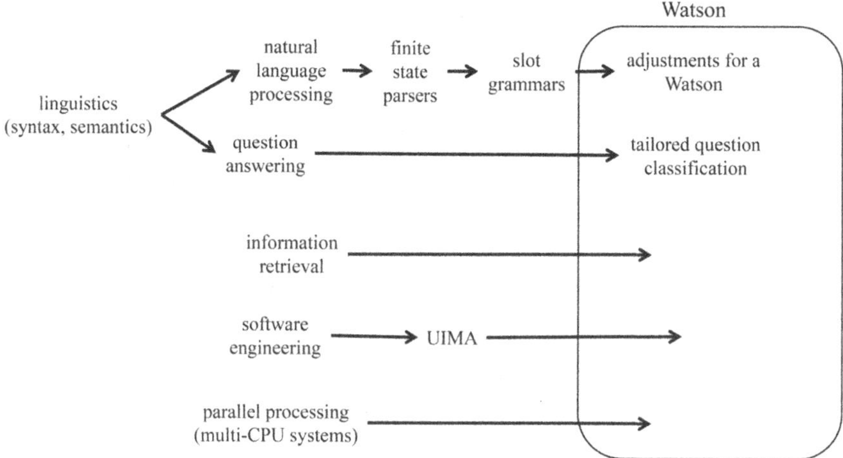

Figure 4.19. World graph of ideas and influences eventually incorporated into Watson.

Just as with Deep Blue, Watson must be viewed as part of a much larger network of information, and it was this network that gave rise to the world-class performance in the Jeopardy! contest. In order to better understand this aspect of Watson and to appreciate the many lines of inquiry that have gone into building this system, I have prepared another world graph, shown in Figure 4.19. As in the previous world graph, this figure shows the kinds of information incorporated into the Watson system, and their origins.

In addition to these general sources of ideas, human intelligence was used at numerous junctures to tailor the system to handle the peculiarities of Jeopardy! clues. These included the use of a pronoun as the focus, as in "Astronaut Dave Bowman is brought back to life in his recent novel 3001: The Final Odyssey", where the focus "his" indicates that the answer is a person. Note how different this is from the more usual question form such as, "Who was the author of the novel, 3001: The Final Odyssey?", where "author" is the focus.

Thus, all sorts of information about the peculiar features of Jeopardy! questions went into designing Watson, especially in selecting and organizing its information sources. In many cases, this amounted to tailoring the system so that it could perform well in this particular game. This is reflected in the following quotation:

"In spite of these adaptations, care was taken not to degrade parsing of normal English. This is done in part by use of switches for the parser that are turned on only when parsing Jeopardy! questions."[71]

These summary paragraphs from a 2010 progress report on the Watson project also serve to show the real character of a system such as this[72]:

"After many nonstarters, by the fourth quarter of 2007 we finally adopted the DeepQA architecture. At that point we had all moved out of our private offices and into a "war room" setting to dramatically facilitate team communication and tight collaboration. We instituted a host of disciplined engineering and experimental methodologies supported by metrics and tools to ensure we were investing in techniques that promised significant impact on end-to-end metrics. Since then, modulo some early jumps in performance, the progress has been incremental but steady. It is slowing in recent months as the remaining challenges prove either very difficult or highly specialized and covering small phenomena in the data."

"After approximately 3 years of effort by a core algorithmic team composed of 20 researchers and software engineers with a range of backgrounds in natural language processing, information retrieval, machine learning, computational linguistics, and knowledge representation and reasoning, we have driven the performance of DeepQA to operate within the winner's cloud on the Jeopardy task"

"By the end of 2008 we were performing reasonably well — about 70 percent precision at 70 percent attempted over the 12,000 question blind data, but it was taking 2 hours to answer a single question on a single CPU. We brought on a team specializing in UIMA and UIMA-AS to scale up DeepQA on a massively parallel high-performance computing platform. We are currently answering more than 85 percent of the questions in 5 seconds or less — fast enough to provide competitive performance, and with continued algorithmic development are performing with about 85 percent precision at 70 percent attempted."

*

Both Deep Blue and Watson were formidable achievements, in some ways like putting a man on the moon. But how should we characterize their "superintelligence"?

Just as with the Logic Theorist (and every other AI program that mimics some form of human intellectual achievement), in these systems it is ultimately impossible to separate the AI from the human intelligence that went into it. From the earliest to the latest AI systems, this situation hasn't changed in the slightest.

Deep Blue, as we have seen, depended on a long period development of knowledge about the game of chess. This was followed by intense research over several decades in which people learned how to build computer programs that could incorporate this knowledge in order to analyze the chessboard and select good moves reliably and efficiently.

Similarly, Watson has its own historical antecedents, without which its organization and performance really don't make sense. The question-answering problem originated in AI as one facet of the study of natural language understanding and world knowledge. But during the ensuing decades, more specialized lines of inquiry emerged that were heavily influenced by fields concerned with data engineering, especially information retrieval. At the same time, other streams of research continued in directions that were more closely related to the original focus. When Watson was conceived its roots lay more in the IR-IE line of inquiry, which gave it its basic character.

In addition, Watson's sources of information are all based on documents prepared by people (Wikipedia, IMDB), in which knowledge has already been systematized to a very high degree; it is simply able to scan them for specific information better than any individual human being. In this respect, Watson's performance is entirely derivative. Like Deep Blue, it is inconceivable outside the human framework — in contrast to a Paramecium or bumblebee.

As noted earlier, many critics of AI allude to a different problem. They claim that, while these systems perform very well, they don't really "understand" what they are doing. But this brings up the whole problem of understanding.

Certainly, it can be maintained that QA systems are in some ways performing sleights-of-hand. Here is an example:

> Question: What is the name of the rare neurological disease with symptoms such as: involuntary movements (tics), swearing, and incoherent vocalizations (grunts, shouts, etc)?
>
> Answer (short passage): "Who said she had both Tourette's Syndrome and"[73]

Note that there is no indication as to why this is the correct answer, since the entire exercise is based on matching words from the question or derived from it with terms (e.g. noun phrases) in the passage.

This is why on rare occasion Watson's answers were wildly off. Thus, when given a question involving: "the inspiration for this title object in a novel and a 1957 movie [which] actually spanned the Mae Khlung", instead of deducing the correct answer, "The Bridge on the River Kwai", or passing on the question, the answer that Watson gave was, "What is Kafka."[74] How it could have come up with such a response is a mystery hidden in the coils of unconscious inference, which is Watson.

With these thoughts in mind, I now want to review two other AI systems. These were not built to compete with people or with other programs on a specific problem, but to embody knowledge of a certain kind. As such, they seem closer to demonstrating the property of understanding, which, according to the critics of Deep Blue and Watson, is lacking in those systems. But as one might expect, their achievements are more difficult to evaluate.

Endnotes

1. This example is called the "Scholar's Mate". See G. Abrahams, *Chess* (revised), Kent: Hodder & Stoughton, 1953, p. 43.
2. It should be noted for the record that the author is not a skilled player. Hence, this section is based on my reading of experts' discussions of the game.
3. Abrahams, op.cit., p. 31.
4. *Ibid.*, pp. 235–236.
5. *Ibid.*, pp. 178–179.
6. J. Nunn, *Understanding Chess Move by Move*, London: Gambit, 2001, p. 6.
7. See "World chess champion Magnus Carlsen: 'The computer never has been an opponent'", http://www.dw.com/en/world-chess-champion-magnus-carlsen-the-computer-never-has-been-an-opponent/a-19186058.
8. Nunn, op. cit., p. 7. See also the Wikipedia article, "Software for handling chess problems".
9. The resulting structure is called a tree because there are no cycles. (Although theoretically both players could reverse their last moves and return to a previous state, thus producing an effective cycle, this can be represented as a new node in the game tree. Anyway, this sort of 'pathology' does not usually occur in practice.)
10. The quote is from the entry on minimax in Wikipedia.
11. Many of these games are equivalent under rotation or reflection; removing all but one of each of these leaves 765 unique games. This number and others in the text are taken from the Wikipedia entry on Tic-tac-toe.

12. Most of this discussion, including the specific equation is from C. E. Shannon, "Programming a computer for playing chess", *Philosophical Magazine*, 1950, 41: 256–275.
13. The information in the table is taken from A. Newell, J. C. Shaw & H. A. Simon, "Chess-playing programs and the problem of complexity", *IBM Journal of Research and Development*, 1958, 2: 320–335, Table 1.
14. This is a nice example of how devilishly clever algorithms can be. Note how the alpha and beta values are always locally appropriate for making a cutoff decision by virtue of the basic tree structure and the rules for passing information from node to node in the tree.
15. For the early history of game theory, see U. Schwalbe & P. Walker, "Zermelo and the early history of game theory", Department of Economics, Canterbury University, 1997 and references therein. I'm not certain whether trees as such were discussed in this early work. At this time there was no field of graph theory, but trees had been identified as an interesting type of structure in some areas such as chemistry.
16. J. von Neumann & O. Morgenstern, *The Theory of Games and Economic Behavior*, Princeton, NJ: Princeton University, 1944 (edit. 2, 1947; edit. 3, 1953).
17. Wikipedia entry on "Alpha-beta pruning", citing an article by Newell and Simon.
18. M. Newborn, *Kasparov versus Deep Blue*, New York: Springer-Verlag, 1997, Chapter 4.
19. Ibid., See also B. Abramson, "Control strategies for two-player games", *ACM Computing Surveys*, 1989, 21: 137–161.
20. Newborn, op. cit., p. 3.
21. D. Levy & M. Newborn, *How Computers Play Chess*, New York & Tokyo: Ishi, 2009 (reprint of 1991 edition), p. 192.
22. J. H. Condon & K. Thompson. "BELLE: Chess hardware". In: M. R. B. Clarke, editor, *Advances in Computer Chess 3*, Oxford: Pergamon, 1983, pp. 45–54. Reprinted in D. Levy, *Computer Chess Compendium*, New York & Tokyo: ISHI, 1988. Figure 4.7 is based on the two figures shown on pages 287 and 288.
23. Other innovations included a superior configuration for prioritizing moves, which drastically reduced the number of wires that had to be added to the chip for this purpose, and a pipelined version as well as important improvements to the alpha-beta algorithm, some of which are outlined in the following paragraphs. See, for example, T. Anantharaman, M. S. Campbell & F.-h. Hsu, "Singular extensions: Adding selectivity to brute-force searching", *Artificial Intelligence*, 1990, 43: 99–109.
24. Levy & Newborn op. cit., pp. 201, 204. By this time, in the late 1980s, Deep Thought was the World Chess Champion.
25. *Ibid.*, table on p. 192.
26. F.-h. Hsu, *Behind Deep Blue*, Princeton: Princeton University, 2002, p. 26.
27. *Ibid.*, p. 27.
28. *Ibid.*, p. 28.

29. *Ibid.*, p. 29.
30. I say this because published accounts in Artificial Intelligence and Scientific American appeared in 1990, some years after the first advances in chip design.
31. In fact, parallelization of alpha-beta search is very tricky and inevitably involves searching more nodes than one would with a single sequential search. This can be forestalled by communication between parallel processes, but communication has overhead that affects overall runtime. Deep Blue uses specialized procedures to distinguish inner nodes in the search tree where communication was allowed from leaf nodes where there was no communication. See S. Hamilton & L. Garber, "Deep Blue's hardware-software synergy", *IEEE Computer*, October 1997, 30(10): 29–35.
32. Taken from a slide presentation by F.-h. Hsu, "Designing a single chip chess grandmaster while knowing nothing about chess", (undated presentation) https://www.hotchips.org/wp_content/uploads/hc_archives/ hc10/ 2_Mon/HC10.S4/HC10.4.1.pdf
33. Taken from the source cited in footnote 31.
34. B. Green, Jr., A. K. Wolf, C. Chomsky & K. Laughery, "BASEBALL: An automatic question-answerer", *Proceedings of the Western Computer Conference*, 1961, pp. 219–224.
35. W. A. Woods, "Transition network grammars for natural language analysis", *Communications of the ACM*, 1970, 13: 591–606; N. Sager & R. Grishman, "The restriction language for computer grammars of natural language", *Communications of the ACM*, 1975, 18: 390–400. The former is historically perhaps the most influential parsing method for natural language (called "augmented transition networks"); it is interesting that it was developed in connection with a question answering system. In this case, the system was designed as a front-end for a database of information about geological material brought back from the moon landings. See also, W. A. Woods, "Progress in natural language understanding — An application to lunar geology", In: *Proceedings of the American Federation of Information Processing Societies (AFIPS)*, 1973, 42: 441–450.
36. Much of this work is summarized in A. Copestack & K. Sparck Jones, "Natural language interfaces to databases", *Knowledge Engineering Review*, 1990, 5: 225–249.
37. B. L. Webber, "Questions, answers and responses: Interacting with knowledge-based systems". In: M. L. Brodie & J. Mylopoulos, *On Knowledge Base Management Systems*, New York: Springer-Verlag, 1986, pp. 365–402. B. L. Webber, "Question answering". In: S. C. Shapiro, *Encyclopedia of Artificial Intelligence, Volume 2*, New York: John Wiley, 1990, pp. 814–822.
38. This part of the discussion relies heavily on R. Gaizauskas & Y. Wilks, "Information extraction: Beyond document retrieval", *Journal of Documentation*, 1998, 54: 70–105 as well as papers from Message Understanding Conferences (MUC 3–6).
39. From R. Grishman & B. Sundhelm, "Message Understanding Conference — 6: A brief history", *Proceedings of the Sixteenth International Conference on Computational Linguistics — COLING'96*, Copenhagen: Center for Sprogteknologi, pp. 466–471.

40. *Ibid.*, p. 468.
41. J. R. Hobbs, D. Appelt, M. Tyson, J. Bear & D. Israel, "SRI International: Description of the FASTUS system used for MUC-4", *Fourth Message Understanding Conference*, 1992, pp. 268–275.
42. Grishman & Sundheim op. cit., pp. 466–7.
43. E. Voorhees, "The TREC question answering track", *Natural Language Engineering*, 2001, 7: 361–378.
44. Since in the code used at the time a single character could be represented in one byte of information, this meant that passages could include 50 or 250 characters including spaces and punctuation marks.
45. These and other methods are described in texts on information retrieval such as R. Baeza-Yates & B. Ribero-Neto, *Modern Information Retrieval*, 2nd edition, Boston: Addison-Wesley, 2011.
46. L. Hirschman & R. Gaizauskas, "Natural language question answering: the view from here", *Natural Language Engineering*, 2001, 7: 275–300.
47. D. Moldavan *et al.*, "LASSO: A tool for surfing the answer net", In: E. M. Voorhees & D. Harmon (Eds.) *Eighth Text Retrieval Conference (TREC 8)*. NIST Special Publication 500–246, 2000, pp. 175–183. See also D. Roth *et al.*, "Learning components for a question-answering system", In: E. M. Voorhees & D. Harmon (Eds.) *Tenth Text Retrieval Conference (TREC 2001)*. NIST Special Publication 500–250, 2001, pp. 539–548.
48. D. Moldovan & E. Novischi, "Lexical chains for question answering" In: S.-C. Tseng, T.-E. Chen & Y.-F. Liu (Eds.) *Proceedings of the Nineteenth International Conference on Computational Linguistics — COLING 2002*, San Francisco: Morgan Kaufmann, 2002, pp. 674–680.
49. Example taken from K. L. Kwok, L. Grunfeld, N. Dinstl & M. Chan, "TREC-9 cross language, Web and question-answering track experiments using PIRCS", In: E. M. Voorhees & D. Harmon (Eds.) *Ninth Text Retrieval Conference (TREC 9)*. NIST Special Publication 500–249, 2001, pp. 419–428.
50. S. M. Harabagiu & S. J. Maiorano, "Finding answers in large collections of texts: Paragraph indexing + abductive inference", In: *AAAI Fall Symposium on Question Answering Systems*. AAAI Technical Report FS-99–02. Menlo Park, CA: AAAI, 1999, pp. 63–71; S. Harabagiu *et al.*, "FALCON: Boosting knowledge for answer engines" In: E. M. Voorhees & D. Harmon (Eds.) *Ninth Text Retrieval Conference (TREC 9)*. NIST Special Publication 500–249, 2001, pp. 479–488.
51. M. M. Doubbotin, "Patterns of potential answer expressions as clues to the right answers", In: E. M. Voorhees & D. Harmon (Eds.) *Tenth Text Retrieval Conference (TREC 2001)*. NIST Special Publication 500–250, 2001, pp. 293–302. See also: Roth *et al.* op. cit.
52. J. Xu, A. Licuanan, J. May, S. Miller & R. Weishedel, "TREC2002 QA at BBN: Answer selection and confidence estimation", In: E. M. Voorhees (Ed.) *Eleventh Text Retrieval Conference (TREC 2002)*, NIST Special Publication 500–251, 2002.

53. One of the first systems that embodied multiple strategies was the PIQUANT system developed at IBM: J. Chu-Carroll, J. Prager, C. Welty, K. Czuba & D. Ferrucci, "A multi-strategy and multi-source approach to question answering", In: E. M. Voorhees (Ed.) *Eleventh Text Retrieval Conference (TREC 2002)*, NIST Special Publication 500–251, 2002, pp. 281–288. Later developments are described in J. Chu-Carroll, K. Czuba, P. Duboue & J. Prager, "IBM's PIQUANT II in TREC2005", In: E. M. Voorhees (Ed.) *Fourteenth Text Retrieval Conference (TREC 2005)*, NIST Special Publication 500–266, 2005.
54. J. Prager *et al.*, "The use of predictive annotation for question answering in TREC8", In: E. M. Voorhees & D. Harmon (Eds.) *Eighth Text Retrieval Conference (TREC 8)*. NIST Special Publication 500–246, 2000, pp. 399–411.
55. D. D. Lewis & K. Sparck Jones, "Natural language processing for information retrieval", *Communications of the ACM*, 1996, 39: 92–101.
56. E. Brill, J. Lin, M. Banko, S. Dumais & A. Ng, "Data-intensive question answering" In: E. M. Voorhees & D. Harmon (Eds.) *Tenth Text Retrieval Conference (TREC 2001)*. NIST Special Publication 500–250, 2001, pp. 393–400, p. 394.
57. *Ibid.*, pp. 396–7.
58. Taken from Figure 5 in D. Ferrucci & A. Lally, "UIMA: An architectural approach to unstructured information processing in the corporate research environment", *Natural Language Engineering*, 2004, 10: 327–348.
59. D. Ferrucci *et al.*, "Building Watson: An overview of the DeepQA project", *AI Magazine*, Fall 2010, 31(3): 59–79, p. 67.
60. J. Fan, A. Kalyanpur, D. C. Gondek & D. A. Ferrucci, "Automatic knowledge extraction from documents", *IBM Journal of Research and Development*, 2012, 56–5: 1–10.
61. To get some idea of the size of the enterprise, at the time of writing the original corpus amounted to 30 gigabytes of text, from which 995 million frames were extracted, an average of 1.4 per sentence.
62. Based on Figure 1 of J. Chu-Carroll, J. Fan, B. K. Boguraev, D. Sheinwald & C. Welty, "Finding needles in the haystack: Search and candidate generation", *IBM Journal of Research and Development*, 2012, 56–6: 1–12.
63. When they incorporated the Lucene system into Watson, the authors made some important modifications: (i) sentence offset from the beginning of the article was factored into the scoring of passages, because the authors had noticed that answers were often found at the beginning of an article, (ii) elements in longer sentences were scored higher than elements in shorter ones, (iii) sentences with named entities were scored higher because they were "more likely to be relevant, since most Jeopardy! answers are named entities" (Ibid., p. 5). These are telling examples of how human intelligence is inserted into a software system, so that the latter becomes an expression of the former.
64. Watson is an extremely successful example of what has come to be known as the portfolio approach to solving hard combinatorial problems. This has also been used to solve combinatorial search problems of the sort discussed in Chapter 9. It reflects

the fact that in these domains there does not seem to be an algorithm or strategy that is superior to other methods in all cases. Hence, applying multiple strategies simultaneously gives better results overall than using any one strategy.

65. It's also worth noting that these methods were subjected to extensive empirical testing to evaluate their separate and combined contributions. Again, we see that human intelligence was being applied in numerous ways at every step in the development process. This is unsurprising, but its significance seems often to be overlooked.
66. J. W. Murdock *et al.*, "Textual evidence gathering and analysis", *IBM Journal of Research and Development*, 2012, 56–8: 1–14.
67. D. C. Gondek *et al.*, "A framework for merging and ranking of answers in DeepQA", *IBM Journal of Research and Development*, 2012, 56–14: 1–12, p. 7.
68. Several different approaches were tested before the logistic regression model was selected as the one giving the best results overall. In this model the sum is actually part of an exponent, and the exponential term (e raised to the sum) is a reciprocal in the denominator of the expression. See *Ibid.*, p. 5.
69. E. A. Epstein *et al.*, "Making Watson fast", *IBM Journal of Research and Development*, 2012, 56–15: 1–12, p. 1.
70. Ibid., p. 5. Also D. A. Ferrucci, "Introduction to "This is Watson"", *IBM Journal of Research and Development*, 2012, 56–1: 1–14, p. 10.
71. A. Lally *et al.*, "Question analysis: How Watson reads a clue", *IBM Journal of Research and Development*, 2012, 56–2: 1–14 p. 3.
72. D. Ferrucci *et al.* 2010, op. cit., p. 75.
73. Moldovan *et al.* 2000, op. cit., Table 3, p. 180.
74. Stephen Baker. *Final Jeopardy. The Story of Watson, the Computer that will Transform the World.* New York: Houghton Mifflin, 2011, p. 5.

5

Two More Cases: Programs that 'Understand'

The AI systems reviewed in the previous three chapters were built to achieve fairly specific goals (although Watson goes beyond this to some extent). But systems can be built whose activities are more open-ended. These systems involve discovery and learning. It can be argued that one of the requirements for a 'genuinely' intelligent system is that it is able to acquire new knowledge, which it can then use in further operations. For this reason, these systems may be better contenders for that label than the ones we have considered so far.

In this chapter I will describe two such systems. One of them (AM) is an old system first developed in the 1970s, which generated a great deal of interest at the time. Although it is now considered to be largely of historical interest, I will argue that it is one of the most important AI systems ever constructed. The other (NELL) is a contemporary system first described about ten years ago, and it remains an ongoing project up to the present time.

Because they deal with more general human-like capacities, both systems are also relevant to the general problem of "understanding". The question is, does the activity of these programs constitute a form of "understanding" — in any sense of the word — with respect to the area to which they are applied? This vexed issue, which is never well defined, is often brought forward in criticisms of AI programs. Here, I will only touch on it in passing. For the present, the main goal is still to examine programs with impressive capacities and to give a close account of what they are actually doing. (The whole business of understanding is discussed at greater length in chapter 10 in the section on critiques of the AI program.)

AM

AM was created by Douglas Lenat in the mid-1970s[1]. Rather than solving a particular kind of problem, AM's goal was to discover new concepts while working in a substantial field of inquiry. The field chosen for the initial study was mathematics, in particular, number theory.

The system was based on "plausible strategies" for finding new ideas. For example, there was a strategy that was crucial for discovering concepts such as prime number:

> "If f is a function which transforms elements of A into elements of B, and B is ordered, then consider just those members of A which are transformed into extremal elements of B. This set is an interesting subset of A."[2]

The system began "with a large corpus of primitive mathematical concepts, each with a few associated heuristics." Lenat characterized it thusly:

> "Currently, AM begins with nothing but a scanty knowledge of concepts which Piaget might describe as prenumerical: Sets, substitution, operations, equality, and so on."[3]
>
> "The concepts AM starts with are meant to be those possessed by young children (age 4, say)."[4,5*]

AM's task was to discover new concepts in the field of number theory by deriving them from the ones it was given, using its heuristics to do so.

To illustrate the process, here is an excerpt from a run (taken verbatim from Lenat, 1982, p. 21, including comments added by the author, which are in italics). The reader should be aware that AM's output consists of strings of pre-set form; the system was not designed to perform natural language processing. So, the "reasons" that are printed are essentially for the user rather than the system, since they are merely text attached to elements in its database (specifically, the heuristic rules; see below). At the same time, however, they are associated with actual features of the system that determine its decisions[6*].

TASK 65
Filling in examples of the following concept: "Divisors-of." 3 reasons:

(1) No known examples for Divisors-of so far.
(2) Times, which is related to Divisors-of, is now very interesting.
(3) Focus of attention: AM recently defined Divisors-of.

20 examples found, in 9.2 seconds. e.g.: Divisors-of(6) = {1 2 3 6}

TASK 66
Considering numbers which have very small sets of Divisors-of(i.e., very few divisors). 2 reasons:

(1) Worthwhile to look for extreme cases.
(2) Focus of attention: AM recently worked on Divisors-of.

Filling in examples of numbers with 0 divisors. 0 examples found, in 4.0 seconds. Conjecture: no numbers have 0 divisors.

Filling in examples of numbers with 1 divisors. 1 examples found, in 4.0 seconds. e.g.: Divisors-of(1) = {1}. Conjecture: 1 is the only number with 1 divisor.

Filling in examples of numbers with 2 divisors. 24 examples found, in 4.0 seconds. e.g.: Divisors-of(13) = {1 13}. No obvious conjecture. This kind of number merits more study. Creating a new concept: "Numbers-with-2-divisors."

> AM had previously derived the notion of singleton, doubleton, etc. Above, AM was actually defining the set of numbers which gets mapped into a doubleton of numbers by the operation Divisors-of. I took the liberty of translating this into the above form, which uses the numeral "2."

Filling in examples of numbers with 3 divisors. 11 examples found, in 4.0 seconds. e.g.: Divisors-of(49) = {1 7 49}. All numbers with 3 divisors are also Squares. This kind of number merits more study. Creating a new concept: "Numbers-with-3-divisors."

> How did AM notice that conjecture? It took a random sample of Numbers-with-3-divisors, say, 49. Then it asked what other known concepts "49" was an example of. The two answers were: Odd-numbers and Perfect-squares. AM then tested these conjectures on the other ten examples just found. The only surviving conjecture was that all numbers-with-3-divisors are also perfect-squares.

During the first flush of success in the late 1970s, Lenat described AM's achievements in the following way:

> "AM began its investigations with scanty knowledge of a hundred elementary concepts of finite set theory. Most of the obvious set-theoretic concepts and relationships were quickly found ... AM discovered natural numbers and went off exploring elementary number theory. Arithmetic operations were soon found (as analogs to set-theoretic operations) and AM made rapid progress to divisibility theory. Prime pairs, Diophantine equations, the unique factorization of numbers into primes, ... these were some of the nice discoveries made by AM."[7]

Once again, I will try to 'unpack' the system to the extent that the reader can form some conception of how it actually worked. Then I will evaluate its achievements.

AM was designed to generate new "concepts". But what is a concept in its terms? A concept in AM was represented by a "frame-like data structure". Basically, frames are like records in an ordinary programming language like C or Pascal. A record is a compound data structure composed of heterogeneous pieces of information. In C or Pascal such entries are called fields. In these as in most programming languages, each field is of a distinct data type. So one field might hold only integers, another might be an array of fixed size, while another might be an entire record structure of a different type. Frames adopt these general ideas while extending the notion of field to more abstract entries (often called "slots"; Lenat usually calls them facets, and I will use his terminology), which may also include calls to subroutines (often called "demons", although Lenat simply calls them functions, since they are subroutines that return a value).

Among the facets in AM's concept-frames were entries such as Examples, Definitions, Generalizations, Specializations, Domain/Range,[8*] Interestingness, and Suggestions. The concepts were organized as a hierarchy, which was in fact critical for the operation of the program.

The top-level concepts are shown in the diagram in Figure 5.1.

The two most elaborated concepts shown at the bottom of the diagram were <operation>[9*] and <structure>. Under <operation>, there were forty-seven more specialized concepts, such as <inverted-operation>, <difference>, <intersect>, <delete>, <insert>, and <composition>, and

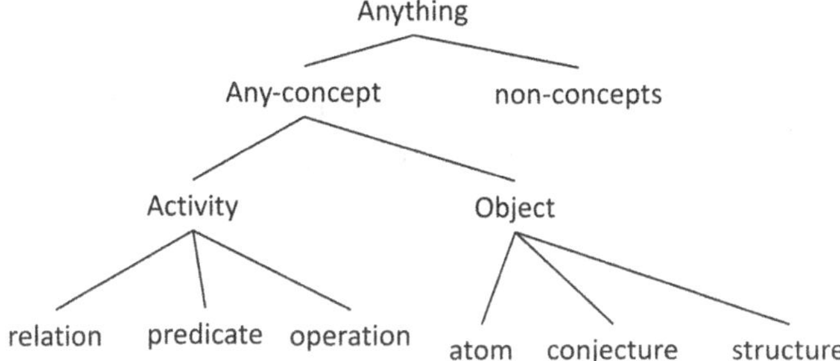

Figure 5.1. The top level of AM's concept hierarchy.

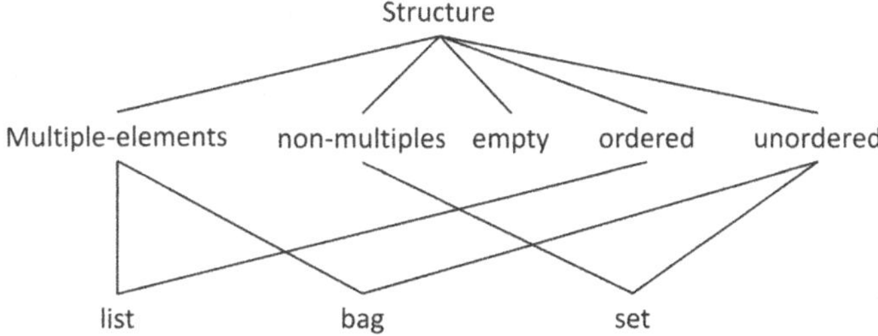

Figure 5.2. Some of the concepts found below <structure> in AM's concept hierarchy.

further specializations of these such as <set-intersect>, <list-intersect>, <set-insert>, <list-insert>, <set-delete>, and <list-delete>. The main concepts under <structure> are shown in Figure 5.2.

AM's activities involved three separate components, called tasks, actions and heuristic rules. In the following discussion, I will use the term "operation" instead of Lenat's term "action". Heuristic rules involved heuristics with their usual meaning, which is rules-of-thumb to follow in making decisions. As such they were meant to embody the "plausible strategies" referred to earlier. However, in AM they took a particular form that is described below.

A task specified an operation and the concept and facet to which it was to be applied. Tasks to be performed were kept in a list called the agenda. For example, a task could be:

Fill-in examples of <set>

The whole of AM's activities consisted in choosing a task on the agenda according to its priority (see below) and performing it. In the course of performing that task, other tasks might be added to the agenda. So AM could theoretically continue forever, although in practice it was given a fixed time to run or it stopped when nothing on the agenda was above some minimum threshold of 'interest' (cf. below).

The actual operations that composed a task were derived from the heuristic rules. Heuristic rules were stored in concept facets. In fact, almost all of the rules were stored with the high-level concept <any-concept>, where they could be obtained for use by more specialized concepts. So, in order to perform the task shown above, the system would work its way up the concept hierarchy (by following links which were actually values in the generalization facet) until it reached <any-concept>, where it would pick up the relevant heuristics and execute them.

In addition, object concepts often had "definitions", which were the names of functions that could be called to check the examples of that concept produced by a fill-in task. These were accessed via tasks of the form:

Check examples of <set>

Again, this task was part of a heuristic. A similar kind of procedure was used to create concepts, based on a different set of facets (involving interest and specialization) and functions.

The tasks on the agenda had "priority ratings", which served to guide the flow of control. These ratings were based on 'interestingness' values given to each concept, facet and operation. In addition, a set of reasons associated with a task were given values that were also included in the formula for the priority rating.

Continuing the example of prime numbers, the tasks might be:

Fill-in examples of <divisors-of>
Create specializations of <number> with few <divisors-of>

Given these tasks, AM creates the concepts numbers-with-2-divisors and numbers-with-3-divisors. At the user's behest, AM then gave the former the name "prime numbers".

*

The AM project may have been the first to introduce search concepts, especially the idea of a search space, into the study of creativity and discovery. It also represents a pioneering attempt to characterize the ill-defined process of discovery in terms of transformations that can then be broken down into sequences of simpler operations.

Nevertheless, it must be acknowledged that this is a primitive first try at the problem, and as such it is riddled with kludges. In a study of AM published in 1984,[10] the authors showed that information important for the operation of the system was embodied in "procedures and statements in the program" and not made explicit. This was even suggested by certain phrases in Lenat's text, e.g.

(Rule 50) "… ensure that every scrap of C.Defn has been used"

There were also indications that structures had been tailored to affect control, e.g.

> "The secret is that each heuristic rule is stored somewhere a propos to its 'domain of applicability' .."

Hence, the control structures were not as simple and uniform as had been claimed.

In fact, a careful examination of the system shows that much of its success depended on code 'buried' in the facets of certain specialized concepts, in particular <canonize> and concepts associated with basic ideas associated with mathematical functions, such as <invert-an-operation>.

Tellingly, in a serious attempt to create a version of AM using a different programing language called Prolog,[11] those authors were unable to reproduce the functionality of these critical concepts.[12*] This seems to be because this functionality depended on properties of the programming language used by Lenat. This particular language allows one to manipulate code, since the code is in the form of lists, which can also be manipulated with other functions in the same language. Using this capacity, the code associated with the <canonize> concept produced a function that returned the length of a list under some specializations of the <canonize> concept. This led to canonical lists of the form (T), (T T), (T T T), etc. With these the system could then perform operations that conjoined the lists or separated them, which the human user recognized as arithmetic operations (here, addition and subtraction) on numbers. It was in this sense that AM 'discovered' numbers.[13] A similar sequence of steps using the inverse-operation concepts led to the 'discovery' of prime numbers referred to above.

On the other hand (and I often find myself using this phrase in writing about these systems), AM's use of list lengths could be considered as a kind of intuitive a priori that may turn out to be necessary in this arena. Might we not discover that the same holds true for human beings if we could view the inner workings of their creative efforts?

In the same way, one could criticize AM and its creator for its crude attempts at aping human cognition, including a simple-minded definition of a concept as a frame, and the realization of the notion of "exploring" a concept by filling in pre-defined facets. But this line of argument, in addition to being tellingly vague, misses the essential point. In fact, something of this sort or something equivalent must exist as a substrate for human concept formation and elaboration. Moreover, since the goal here is a general theory of intelligence and intelligent performance, if AM is a genuine example of this, then whether or not it is 'built like a human' is immaterial.

However, there are other givens that AM employed such as inverse functions, and more generally, functional transformations, where this argument seems strained. These are themselves highly abstracted concepts that only emerged in their present form after centuries of mathematical investigation. In this case, their inclusion in the givens of the system is problematical.

More generally, in his discussion of AM, Lenat never seems to ponder the fact that the "scanty" "prenumerical" knowledge that AM is given was much harder for humans to acquire — as concepts — than numerical concepts like prime numbers. So, when compared with human endeavors, AM is actually working in a reverse, top-down, fashion.[14*] This is clear from another heuristic that was used to derive the concept of the square of a number:

> If a newly-interesting operation F(x,y) takes a pair of N's as arguments,
> then create a new concept, a specialization of F, called F-itself, taking just one N as argument, defined as F(x,x), with initial worth Worth(F).[15]

Referring back to Lenat's ideas about a strategy for finding prime numbers — why would anyone use the (more abstract) notion of a funtion to do this? (And is it even possible to do it in this way?) What undoubtedly happened in practice is that, once the principle of division as applied to integers had been discovered, people then noticed that there were certain numbers that could only be divided by themselves (and by 1, which, since it divides every other integer isn't terribly interesting in this respect). Finding more and more of these numbers, they eventually gave them a name.

This in itself, however, doesn't mean that AM is irrelevant for studying how a system might make discoveries. After all, it is entirely possible for there to be more than one way to do this. Moreover, even if people didn't originally have the more abstract notions as realized concepts, these ideas may have been imbedded in human thinking, so that they could serve to guide the process of discovering a concept such as prime numbers in a manner that was similar in some basic respects to AM's use of heuristics.

On the other hand, it doesn't seem possible for AM to use its methods to discover the more abstract concepts for itself. This is because the entire AM process appears to consist of deducing various specializations of the concepts embedded in its heuristics.

There are other issues. For one thing, since AM was a software system with a given organization, why should the criterion for success be the rediscovery of mathematical concepts deemed important by human mathematicians? In fact, we don't really know whether this criterion is truly applicable to the system as it was built. (This is in fact a deep issue bearing on the definition of intelligence itself.)

Thus, in many ways the AM project was hopelessly gimcrack, although this does not necessarily apply to the software system itself. Throughout there is a certain vulgarity of intention, which was a common feature of artificial intelligence in its pioneering days, and which it has not yet shed completely even today.

But to reiterate (and extend) my contention: AM was one of the most important AI systems ever built. In part this was due to the boldness of Lenat's attempt. The fact that his assessment of AM was partly delusional doesn't contradict this; nor does the fact that it was not great science (or even that AM is something of a sleight of hand — cf. the top-down versus bottom-up comment above). It was important because it raised issues that are central to the interpretation of AI systems and of AI itself.

AM was 'doomed to fail' simply because so little was known at the time about the topics it was designed to simulate, i.e. the psychology and sociology of human discovery. And there is still not enough known. Nonetheless, it has helped us to move forward toward that end — by making the problem more concrete, by forcing people to think more clearly about the basic problems involved.

In particular, one thing that many critics of AI often lose sight of is that, as we know from centuries of scientific investigation into brain function, cognition requires a substrate — it must be based on a physical system of some form. And, of course, it involves something we call information. It is a reasonable presumption that this holds true for discovering new ideas as much as for following a recipe (i.e. algorithm) for doing sums, as children learn to do in school. Moreover, as Kant argued, cognitive systems must begin with some form of a priori or 'hard-wired' knowledge. The great open question, of course, is the nature of that requisite knowledge. It may be quite different in character from the information encapsulated in the AM program. But even so, the fact that AM followed the more general requirement, which is to begin with some a priori information and use it to develop new forms of information, ensures that it has some significance.

In thinking about claims for AI systems making significant, or even modest, discoveries, it is worth examining some cases of human discovery. I will recount two examples from my own field of constraint satisfaction. In doing this, I am aware that I have not yet introduced the subject properly; this is in fact done in Chapter 9. Nonetheless, it should be possible for the reader to understand the thrust of these examples even without fully understanding the ideas involved. (I, therefore, recommend going over this account again after reading Chapter 9.)

The field of constraint satisfaction involves finding solutions to problems such as scheduling nurses in a hospital or configuring an automobile with the requisite parts. Problems like these involve combining elements so that they go together properly in some overall pattern. For example, nurses have to be scheduled so that everyone gets their required hours, manpower requirements are met, days-off requirements are observed, etc. Generally speaking, these problems can be very, very hard, so that only small problems can be solved to completion. Nonetheless, certain configurations of requirements turn out to be provably easy. This was first demonstrated by Freuder in the early 1980s. He called this phenomenon "tractability" and these problems were designated as tractable problems. Although it was a few years before the significance of this work was really appreciated, the idea of tractability eventually became a lynchpin of the field. In later years, new forms of tractability were discovered that both clarified the original idea and extended its range of application.[16]

The point is that the discovery process was spread over a period of two or three decades. In large part, this was because it involved appreciating the significance and the implications of an idea, so that it was not just a one-shot "discovery". This involved conceptual development, i.e. refining and elaborating the original conceptions. Such development is probably unavoidable, because the phenomena of Nature don't come to us as pre-packaged products that are clearly labeled and arranged on some celestial supermarket shelf.[17*] They can only be revealed through painstaking analysis, either empirical or, in the case above, analytical. And really basic ideas are never seen clearly at first.

Here is another example from the same field. A basic strategy for solving problems in the field of constraint satisfaction is to look for "local consistencies" throughout the problem, e.g. of the form, "given X is there any Y that goes with it?" The idea is that if there isn't, then X need not be considered when looking for a solution to the entire problem — since it doesn't even work locally. (For example, in an automobile if a certain trunk size isn't consistent with the possible wheelbases, then it can't form part of any reasonable design.)[18]

Now, more than 20 years after the original idea was proposed, someone had a further idea. Continuing our automobile example, suppose we settle on a certain value for a variable such as trunk size. Then we check the entire problem to see if all the local consistencies can hold under this condition. If this isn't possible, then this value can be discarded. Now, we can repeat this for every possible value and every possible variable. This simple extension turns out to be a very powerful method for eliminating unworkable values and thereby simplifying a problem.[19]

Then, after about 20 more years, a further idea was proposed. While going through the problem in the same way, checking that each value can support a consistent network, instead of considering the entire problem at each step, consider only a small, localized region of the network adjacent to the value being considered, to see if it can be made consistent. This, in fact, is where the effects of reducing the number of options for one element will have the greatest effect. And for some problems, one can remove almost as many values, and therefore simplify the problem as much as when one examines the entire problem at each step.[20]

In connection with this, it is surely significant that in the field of constraint satisfaction there has been no advance that was not due to human beings, even though many of the advances are as simple as the ones just described. So, as of today, no one has developed an effective technology for making scientific discoveries, even very modest ones. I suspect this is because no one even knows what it is that we need to do in order to develop such a technology. In other words, in some deep sense, we don't even know how to characterize the problem. So one shouldn't look too harshly upon the shortcomings of AM, since the problem that it was supposed to solve was so ill-posed in the first place.[21*]

And this takes us back to the central contention of this book, which is that much, perhaps all, of the work in AI is limited in its orientation and compass because of fundamental misconceptions about the nature of intelligence. The latter topic will be taken up in the next chapter. But first we will take a look at another AI system. Like AM, it also bears on the question of understanding and, therefore, the meaning of intelligence.

NELL

NELL, which stands for Never-Ending Language Learner, is a system that learns a large miscellany of facts about the world on the basis of information that it gathers from pages on the Web.[22] Like Deep Blue and Watson, when descriptions of NELL began to appear it was picked up by journalists and written up in the popular press. So readers were regaled with titles such as, "Aiming to Learn as We Do, a Machine Teaches Itself" and "Read the Internet, Speak English" and "Is NELL The New HAL?". Here is a typical account:

> "In a basement at Carnegie Mellon University a computer is reading the web. It's been doing so for nearly nine months, teaching itself the complexities and nuances of the English language. And the smarter it gets, the faster it learns.
>
> "That computer is NELL, the Never-Ending Language Learning system, and it's the star of a project involving researchers from Carnegie Mellon, supercomputers from Yahoo!, and grants from Google and DARPA. The project's aim is an elusive but important one: to design a machine that can figure out the subtleties of language all on its own. As Tom Mitchell, chairman of the school's machine learning department explains, "We still don't have a computer that can learn as humans do, cumulatively, over the long term." NELL would be the first that does so.
>
> "The system trawls hundreds of millions of web pages, collecting facts and sorting them into one of 280 categories, classifications like cities, plants or actors. It has learned nearly 400,000 such facts to date, with 87 per cent accuracy. NELL also currently knows some 280 relations, pieces of language that connect two facts together. NELL probably knows that James Franco (actor) lives in (relation) New York City (city). And the more NELL learns, the faster and more efficient it gets at teaching itself."[23]

The "complexities and nuances" that NELL learns are in fact largely restricted to instances of concepts and binary relations, that is, relations between a pair of concepts. For example, if the concepts <AmericanState> and <city> are in the knowledge base along with the relation <city-in-AmericanState>, then if the system encounters the phrases "city of Boise" and "Boise, Idaho", it may be able to infer that Boise is an instance of <city> and that Idaho is an instance of <AmericanState>. From this it can also infer the fact that Boise is a city in Idaho, i.e. that the two concept-instances together form an instance of the relation <city-in-AmericanState>.

NELL learns by analyzing the textual and verbal contexts in which a word appears, relating them back to the concepts and relations that are already in its knowledge base. In this way, given a concept and some initial word patterns where instances of that concept might appear, NELL is able to detect new instances involving other words from the Web page texts that it scans. From this information it can also detect new patterns where concepts appear. And with these new patterns it can detect instances of the concept that it would otherwise have overlooked. In this way NELL "bootstraps" itself, so that it becomes a more powerful learning system while it at the same time it amasses more and more facts about the world. Since it learns instances of many concepts and relations at the same time, it is able to use rules regarding coordination among concepts, such as mutual exclusion rules, in order to avoid erroneous inferences about concepts in relations (more on this below).

(Nonetheless, it is still necessary to correct the system periodically to weed out improper interpretations. One case, taken up and repeated in several news stories, involved the noun phrase "Internet cookies". Since <cookie> was already classified as a type of <baked-good>, NELL deduced from the sentences, "I deleted my Internet cookies" and "I deleted my files" the fact that <computer-file> was also a type of <baked-good>.)

In contrast to the typical machine learning system, NELL is run continuously, 24/7, so that over time it can build up a massive store of knowledge. One version of the program began running in 2010; by 2015 it had amassed a corpus of almost 100 million facts together with estimates of the likelihood that they were correct.

The table In Figure 5.3 shows some of the facts learned by NELL. These are examples of instance learning. So for example, NELL learned that Cubans are a kind of <ethnicGroup>, that spruce beetles are a kind of <arthropod>, that legal assistant is a kind of <profession>, etc. It also learned that Troy is a city in the state of Michigan, that balls are used in the sport soccer, that Will Smith is an <actor> who starred in the <movie> Seven Pounds.

Predicate	Instance
Ethnic group	Cubans
Arthropod	spruce beetles
Sport	BMX bicycling
Profession	legal assistants
MediaType	chemistry books
cityInState	(Troy, Michigan)
tvStationInCity	(WLS-TV, Chicago)
sportUsesEquipment	(soccer, balls)
athleteInLeague	(Dan Fouts, NFL)
starredIn	(Will Smith, Seven Pounds)
cityInCountry	(Dublin Airport, Ireland)

Figure 5.3. A sample of beliefs learned by NELL using information found on the Web. (Taken from Table 1 in Carlson *et al.* 2010[24]).

What is especially interesting about NELL from the perspective of the present work, and which is not obvious from a mere description of its activities and accomplishments, is that this system is nested within an enormous body of work done in the field of machine learning and other parts of AI over the past forty years, including major theoretical developments. This is perhaps the main feature that sets NELL (and Watson) apart from early AI systems like the Logic Theorist and AM. (Deep Blue, which is based on very specialized knowledge about chess, is a special case, although it also relies on significant theoretical analysis, in this case pertaining to the general structure of games.)

For example, there is at present a considerable amount of fairly deep theory about learning hypotheses that match the state of the world to a suitable degree. This comes down to learning functional mappings between input and output, the latter being the set of hypotheses.

One useful distinction in this domain is between inductive and analytic learning. Inductive learners learn a hypothesis from a set of examples they are given. As such they are restricted by their original input; there are also certain theoretical limits on what they can learn in a reasonable amount of time. Analytic learning systems begin with a domain theory, i.e.

a set of a priori statements about a domain. They are also given a series of examples from which they can derive hypotheses, but if they can match features of the examples with statements in the body of knowledge, they are able to learn hypotheses much more efficiently than inductive learners.

Another important distinction is between "supervised" and "unsupervised" learning. In the former case, explicit examples are given along with feedback as to whether they fit a given hypothesis or not. In the latter case, the system uses general a priori principles of a statistical nature, such as proximity relations and recurrent patterns, to derive classifications, structural features, etc. NELL is based on a hybrid approach called semi-supervised learning. Systems of this type are given some examples, while they also learn other examples without supervision. Because NELL is given its supervised examples in the form of an initial knowledge base, in some respects it resembles the analytical learning systems just described; it can therefore be expected to acquire new knowledge with great efficiency, while at the same time it will be limited by its rather restricted 'domain theory'.

In addition, NELL builds on a decade or more of work on information extraction from the Web, not all of which comes under the heading of AI or natural language processing. During this time, researchers in computer science developed some very general algorithms for extracting semantic information based on text "wrappers" that tend to appear before and after a given word — treated merely as a character string — when it appears in Web documents. The best ones were incorporated into NELL, specifically in the CSEAL component shown in Figure 5.5.

Finally, NELL also incorporates various advances in data mining, natural language processing, and Web applications. For example, an important learning component (CPL in Figure 5.5) works on text that has been preprocessed with an open source natural language processor that tags words with their parts of speech. With this input, CPL is able to detect noun phrases, and consequently to find patterns associated with noun-concepts, such as "mayor of x".

NELL also depends heavily on accurate statistics. These are obtained by large-scale searches, which is done using a framework called MapReduce that has become popular for a variety of tasks involving massive amounts of data and multiple programs, often on many machines, running in parallel.

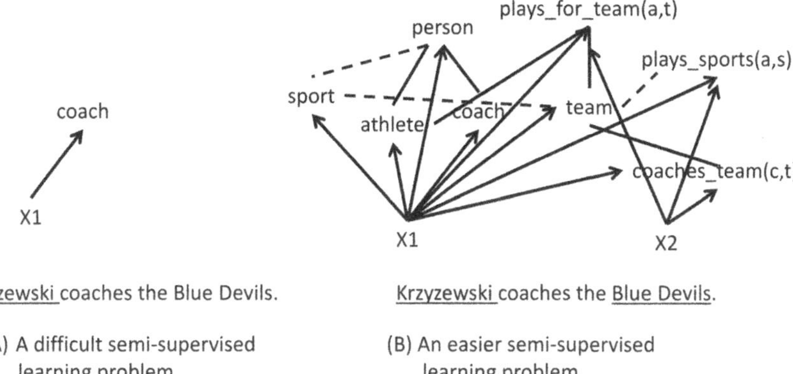

Figure 5.4. Sparse versus dense network of relations. Learning is easier in the latter case. (From Carlson *et al.*, 2010,[25] Figure 1, by permission.)

NELL's main contribution to the work that it built upon was to learn many facts at the same time. By assuming various constraints between certain concept instances, it was able to make stronger inferences from the data it collected as well as filter out false hypotheses. The most common type of constraint was mutual exclusion; an example of this is <person> and <sport> (cf. diagram B in Figure 5.4). So, in the network shown in Figure 5.4, if it can be established that Krzyewski is an instance of <person>, then this means that Krzyewski cannot be an instance of <sport>.

NELL uses four components to extract knowledge from Web pages. These are shown in Figure 5.5. As already noted, CPL (for Coupled Pattern Learner) extracts patterns based on noun phrases from preprocessed text. The next component CSEAL (for Coupled SEAL, where SEAL stands for Set Expander for Any Language) extracts "wrappers", which are strings that appear before and after a target string. An example of a wrapper is the string,

.html" CLASS="shopcp">*arg1* Parts</A>

that surrounds the concept instance denoted by the italicized arg1. This wrapper was associated with the Web page advertising car parts. In this case arg1 is always the name of a car, i.e. acura, audi, buick, cadillac, etc. Hence, one the wrapper is identified, it can be used to find other instances of the concept <car> that appear on this page. The next component,

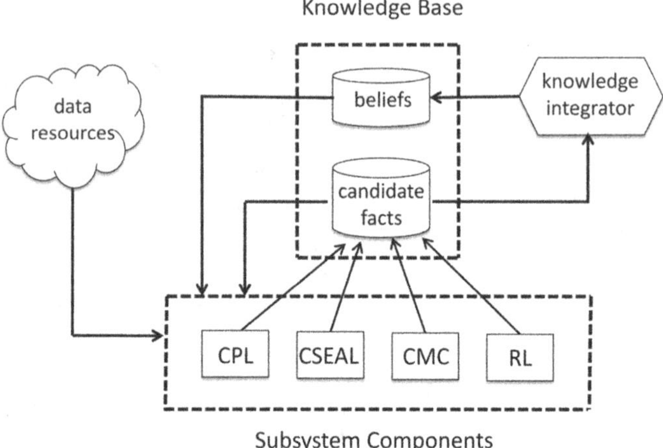

Figure 5.5. NELL's architecture (from Figure 1 in Carlson *et al.*, 2010[26] © 2019 AAAI (www.aaai.org), by permission).

CMC (Coupled Morphological Classifier), classifies noun phrases on the basis of various morphological features, while RL (Rule Learner) learns a restricted class of if-then rules.

It is interesting that a careful account of NELL's accomplishments shows that they are much more modest in scope than the initial claims for AM. (The contrast with the vague and rather overblown statements in the newspaper reports should also be noted.) Nonetheless, the system does learn a substantial body of facts about the world. Although the details of how it actually does this are very intricate (and have only been touched upon here), its achievement is also more well-defined.

The use of constraints combined with bootstrapping is perhaps the most interesting aspect of NELL with respect to the question of general intelligence. In particular, this seems like a potentially powerful means of leveraging a priori knowledge to gain more knowledge effectively and even to expand one's set of assumptions in a disciplined way. (The basic notions of constraint networks and "constraint satisfaction" are discussed at greater length in Chapter 9.)

I hope that by now the reader appreciates that, just as with the other systems that have been described, NELL only exists (and, indeed, only makes sense) within a much larger framework of human endeavor. If anything, this aspect of AI systems has become more pronounced in recent years with the development of applications that can perform many of the tasks that are necessary in a complex system reliably and efficiently. It's also worth noting that the plug-in capability of these applications, which allows them to be used as modules in systems like NELL and Watson, represents yet another major advance in software technology that has occurred in the past several decades. The point is that all of these advances were necessary before a system like NELL was even possible.

There is another, double-edged implication of this particular AI project that may be of general significance. As we have seen, NELL is a nice demonstration of how successful contemporary AI methods have become in generating interesting and impressive results. I think this shows the power of logic and combinatorial search in producing results that qualify as intelligent. But at the same time, NELL (at least in its present state) is a kind of reductio ad absurdum of the thesis that by this approach in and of itself one can create "general intelligence". The argument is as follows.

NELL uses text as its basic input. But text qua text is derivative; it doesn't mean anything in and of itself. It's significance is derived from its connections with the world-at-large, involving our perceptions. To put this another way, it is not clear that one can build a true a priori out of text. In other words, NELL is a typical demonstration of artificial intelligence in a case where the existence or emergence of general intelligence probably doesn't make any sense.

Hence, the fact that NELL seems to achieve a form of general intelligence on this basis must be an illusion. But in this case all such demonstrations of general intelligence in AI systems are problematic — because they all use similar methods.

On the other hand, as I've already indicated, there is no reason not to consider NELL's achievement as a form of genuine intelligence. Perhaps the argument just given depends on looking at the problem from too narrow a perspective, one that is too oriented to the requirements for human intelligence. But if the perspective and the criteria are altered to something that is less human-centric, then what is NELL showing us? In other words, what is the significance of this demonstration?

Overview

Consider again the systems that outperformed the most accomplished humans: Deep Blue and Watson. What is the basis of their "super-intelligence"?

Essentially, it seems to be this. Each system involves the co-location of a considerable amount of information, organized so as to be readily accessible. In this respect, its capacities go far beyond what even the most accomplished human being seems capable of. To a large degree then, in these cases "super-intelligence" means having a superior memory.

This may be one reason why the two most successful systems, both of which exhibit features of super-intelligence, are in some ways less interesting than AM and NELL. This is because the goals of latter were quite open-ended, while the former are on the face of it impressive dead-ends.[27*]

On the other hand, the most important single fact about the work described in this chapter is that none of it seems to have led anywhere either. This is in striking contrast to the discoveries in constraint satisfaction that were described above. Therefore, any discussion that takes the claims for any of these systems at face value whether one agrees or not, is missing a vital point: genuine discoveries are not made by autonomous systems acting outside of various social contexts. This leads to a deeper inquiry into the actual nature of intelligence, which is the subject of the next chapter.

Also, in contrast to AM, when we inquire into an actual pattern of discovery, we find that the evaluation of an idea depends on further discoveries, which are then linked back to the original one and which enlarge its significance. (In fact, this line of thought may lead to a reductio ad absurdum in regard to systems like AM as models of genuine discovery.)

In AM we also have an example of the vexed problem of incorporating the solution surreptitiously, that arises again and again in considerations of the achievements of these systems. As will become apparent in later chapters, the present work speaks directly to this issue.

It also should be emphasized that systems such as NELL and Watson may very well lead to further interesting research because they embody some extremely significant discoveries. But it is human beings who will take the next step. This brings up the whole issue of fundamental advances in knowledge — a level of activity and information exchange where at this date machines play no part.

I must hasten to add at this point that the intent of this discussion of cases is not to impugn AI or to dismiss or disparage some of its greatest achievements. (It may, however, impugn some AI investigators.) More bluntly, I'm not interested in defending the Human Race against The Machines; in fact, I find such activities more deeply vulgar than any excesses that AI researchers have committed (cf. Chapter 10).

At the same time, I am not interested in defending the Church of AI against the Indelibly Benighted. The point is to understand what AI is, i.e. what is going on when we build systems like these that seem to be doing something interesting that bears some resemblance to human cognition? How should these artifacts be characterized?

It's also important to bear in mind that the basic idea of computation is the key to understanding intelligence. This is the core insight behind AI. Once again, the goal here is to better understand the nature of the computations underlying the output of an AI artifact.

Let us turn back now to the "But does it think?" issue. Taking Deep Blue as a concrete example, it clearly accomplishes a task that involves what we human beings call "thinking". Therefore, the answer is, "Yes!" And the same argument holds for Watson and NELL. NELL in particular seems to pass the "understanding" test raised by so many critics of these systems.

With AM there are some difficulties in interpreting its output. Here, the problem is deciding what it's actually thinking about.

In short, AI has enabled us to think more clearly about what thinking actually is. We can consider AI systems as systems that "think by design". (Note to the reader: do you see how useful it is to think 'behavioristically'?)

There is another aspect to all this. Consider AM again, and Lenat's reassessment of its capacities in the mid-80s. If Lenat's original understanding of AM was seriously deficient, as his admissions seem to indicate, what does this say about human understanding? Among other things, is "understanding" really the vital quality that critics of AI systems make it out to be? Are we even talking about a process that can be delineated in a straightforward way? Or, in line with Wittgenstein, on analysis does it devolve into numerous language games?

As a parenthetical note, I would like to raise another issue in regard to Watson, as well as other IR and IE technology. Are they providing us with new kinds of understanding? In addition, it is worth keeping in mind that there may be convergences here between whatever means the brain uses to answer questions and the methods used by these systems.

The take-home message from the chapters in this section is that, in examining an AI artifact we must always consider how human intelligence has been involved. The two are always intertwined, as these examples show. These considerations lead to a particular conception of intelligence.

Endnotes

1. The system is described in R. Davis and D. B. Lenat. (1982). *Knowledge-Based Systems in Artificial Intelligence*. McGraw-Hill. In writing this essay I also made extensive use of a Prolog version of AM written by Bruce Porter and various co-workers that I downloaded from the Website at https://github.com/akkartik/am-utexas.
2. *Ibid.*, p. 4.
3. *Ibid.*, p. 5.
4. *Ibid.*, p. 101.
5. To support his contention that the *a priori* concepts in AM are rudimentary, Lenat cites Piaget's book, *Language and Thought in the Child* (3rd edition, London: Routledge, 1997; original, 1959). However, there is nothing in this book to justify the citation, since it is mostly about a transition from egocentric to social orientation in using language. However, in another book by Piaget, titled *The Child's Concept of Number* (London: Routledge, 1952; original 1941), there is some relevant discussion of this point, especially with respect to the child's comprehension of one-to-one correspondence and its implications regarding identity in quantity. But even here, I find nothing that demonstrates comprehension of the general concepts of sets, bags, inverse operations, etc. And, try as I might, I cannot get my head around the idea that a concept like <canonize> (which is one of AM's initial concepts) is part of the repertoire of a four-year old. This significance of this will be brought out further along in this chapter.
6. I would not assume that we are not reading 'touched up' language in some places. Some of it seems to go beyond pre-formatting. For example, why isn't the "All numbers with 3 divisors …" conjecture prefaced by that word, as another conjecture was earlier?

7. D. B. Lenat, "Automated theory formation in mathematics", *Proceedings of the Fifth International Joint Conference in Artificial Intelligence*. MIT, 1977, pp. 833–842.
8. Domain and range are mathematical concepts that refer to sets of elements associated with a function. Take, for example, the function $y = x^2$. Suppose that in our example x can be any positive or negative integer (whole numbers like 1, 2, 3, etc.) or zero. This set of numbers is the domain of the function. The range of the function is the set of all values that y can take, given these values of x. For example, if $x = 0$ then $y = 0$, if $x = 2$ then $y = 4$, if $x = -2$ then $y = 4$, etc. In other words the range of y consists of all positive integers that are perfect squares and also zero. One can also use these ideas for non-numeric functions. Consider, for example, all the questions that can be answered "yes" or "no". We can represent this as a function whose domain is the set of all these questions, and the range is the two words, "yes" and "no". In each case, the function maps a value in the domain of that function into a (single) value in the range.
9. In this discussion, I use angle brackets to denote AM's concepts.
10. G. D. Ritchie & F. K. Hanna. (1984). "AM: A case study in AI methodology", *Artificial Intelligence*, 23: 249–268.
11. This is the system referred to in Footnote 1.
12. In the case of <canonize>, only a few facets are listed without any indication of serious development, and some of them are commented out. When I searched for the implementation (via a Definition facet) of the invert-operation concepts such as <invert-an-operation>, I found the following:

    /* I don't get these — marcos */

    followed by a piece of code that was commented out and another function that appeared only to produce a definition name.

    In this version of AM, new concepts were formed by deleting facets of old concepts. As a result, many new concepts were "worthless"; the user determined which were discarded and which were added to AM's knowledge base.
13. This is discussed in D. B. Lenat & J. S. Brown. (1984). "Why AM and EURISKO appear to work", *Artificial Intelligence*, 23: 269–294.
14. As a matter of fact, I find it odd that Lenat doesn't discuss these issues himself.
15. Lenat, 1982, *op. cit.*, p. 46.
16. E. C. Freuder, "A sufficient condition for backtrack-free search, *Journal of the ACM*, 1982, 29: 24–32.
17. This metaphor is derived from an article once read in a popular magazine that I have not been able to locate. In discussing the obvious deficiencies of a supposed test of ESP that was done by having people call in to a radio show, the author made the remark, "Science is not like going to the supermarket." Although it didn't resonate when I first read it, I now think that this statement contains a profound insight, to wit, that Nature doesn't come in neat packages, so that it takes both fortitude and endless

attention to details as well as mother wit to capture her secrets. Because of the enormous success of the scientific enterprise (as well as certain deficiencies of human cognition), this is now often lost sight of.

18. D. Waltz, "Understanding line drawings of scenes with shadows", In: P. H. Winston, editor, *The Psychology of Computer Vision*, New York: McGraw-Hill, 1975, pp. 19–91.
19. R. Debruyne & C. Bessière, "Some practicable filtering techniques for the constraint satisfaction problem", In: *Proceedings of the Fifteenth International Joint Conference on Artificial Intelligence-IJCAI'97. Vol. 1*, San Francisco: Morgan Kaufmann, 1997, pp. 412–417.
20. R. J. Wallace, "SAC and neighbourhood SAC", *AI Communications*, 2015, 28: 345–364.
21. I have to admit that at the end of the day I cannot entirely shake off the idea that Lenat may be the Carlos Casteneda of artificial intelligence. So I may have made too much of this program, although it is clear that Lenat managed to make his version produce results that were intriguing. (In this connection, it should be noted that people other than Lenat, including one very prominent computer scientist, used Lenat's version of AM.)
22. A general description of NELL is given in A. Carlson, J. Betteridge, B. Kisiel, B. Settles, E. R. Hruschka, Jr. and T. Mitchell. (2010). "Toward an architecture for never-ending language learning", *Proceedings of the 24th AAAI Conference on Artificial Intelligence — AAAI-2010*. AAAI Press, pp. 1306–1313.
23. K. Vanhemert. "Right now a computer is reading online, teaching itself language", http://www.gizmodo.com.au/2010/10/right-now-a-computer-is-reading-online-teaching-itself-language/
24. Carlson *et al.*, *op. cit.* (ref. 21), Table 1.
25. Figure taken from A. Carlson *et al.*, "Coupled semi-supervised learning for information extraction", *Third ACM Conference on Web Search and Data Mining-WSDM 2010*, Figure 1.
26. Reference 22, Figure 1.
27. As noted in Chapter 2, while this is basically true of Deep Blue, it isn't entirely fair to Watson since its creators are still casting about for applications. In fact, I think it is likely that some of the ideas that went into the Watson system will find use elsewhere. Nonetheless, because this was a project whose main goal was to mimic some human achievement, once this was accomplished, it had no obvious raison d'etre, unlike a more straightforward software application designed for a task that has continuing relevance.

Part III

Intelligence and Artificial Intelligence

6

The Nature of Intelligence

In this chapter I will present a simple thesis and try to develop some of its implications.

The basic idea is that intelligence is always agent-like in nature. An immediate implication of this is that it is always misleading to view an intelligent agent in isolation. This is especially true for a program or system that is said to exhibit artificial intelligence.

The term "agent" is borrowed from the literature on multi-agent systems. This was a 'hot topic' in AI in the 90's, and during that decade there were possibly more conferences and workshops on this topic than any other in the field of AI. During this time several lengthy papers were published that were devoted to the question of just what an agent is, since it wasn't clear how to distinguish an agent from, say, a program or a subroutine. What follows is my take on what an agent is, based partly on these and other readings.[1,2] In my view there are two key features that characterize agents and multi-agent systems (as will become clear, the two ideas cannot be separated).

1) The first is that there must be a distributed system of intelligence.

What this means, essentially, is that the computational system is not a single integrated structure, such an ordinary digital computer or a single program running on such a device; instead, it is distributed in space and perhaps in time. This in turn implies that the problem-solving process is performed across a network of distinct components, which therefore must communicate information amongst themselves. The idea of a network of computing elements is in fact basic to the idea of distributed computing.

Here, it should be emphasized that I am not assuming that such a system involves explicit AI methods, only that tasks are carried out that could be called intelligent. (There is blurring here between intelligence and the notion of computation that might as well be admitted up front, and will be explored in more detail in the final chapter.)

Such networks are usually depicted as graphs, as in the figure below. This is a simple and perspicuous means of doing this, since it makes the basic distinction between computing elements (the nodes of the graph) and lines of communication between them (the arcs of the graph) explicit.[3*]

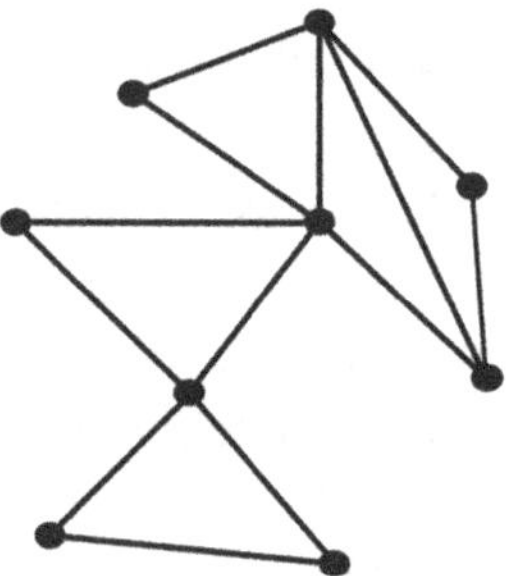

An example of a distributed system in computer science would be a set of communicating programs that run on the same or different machines. An email system, for example, must be based on distributed computing to be useful; obviously, however, a basic email system performs simple functions that do not require problem solving at that time, so it wouldn't usually be considered an example of distributed intelligence. Another example would be a business application system in which payroll, order entry and process control are handled by programs on different machines, but these machines are networked so that data produced by one program can be used by another.[4] These are all examples of distributed processing. They are, therefore, not cases of distributed intelligence, i.e. distributed problem solving. In fact, according to Davis and Smith, in most distributed processing systems, "The word distributed is usually taken to mean spatial distribution of data — distribution of function or control is not generally considered."[5]

If the network also changes over time then it can be called an evolutionary system. Note that the term "evolutionary" does not refer to computations per se, which always take time, but to the components of the system that carries out the computations. Thus, to say a system is evolutionary in this sense means that components are added and removed over the course of time — or that the components themselves change over time, so that at different times they behave differently.

2) The second defining feature is that there are distinct components within the system that have a degree of autonomy with respect to their actions and decisions. An individual component of this type is called an agent; if there is more than one agent, then we have a multi-agent system.

Here, it is important to note that the definition of an agent requires the existence of a distributed system in which it is embedded. In other words, if an entity is not a node in such a system then it cannot be called an agent under the present definition.

As noted, the key feature that distinguishes agents from other elements in a distributed computing system is the autonomy of the agents. But what does this mean? What are the distinguishing characteristics of an entity that makes it autonomous? The crucial characteristic is the ability to make choices, or decisions, where the choices made are not prescribed by the system designer. In other words, an agent's actions are not 'hard-wired'; they are not determined by the inputs to the agent. Another way of looking at this is that each agent has an individual frame of reference, which gives it a basis for making decisions, along with its assessment of the situation (i.e. the inputs that it receives).

An absolutely fundamental feature of intelligence networks is that they use some form of communication, which in turn rests on a system of recognizable signals that agents can send as well as recognize. In other words, messages must be sent between agents, and there must be some means of properly encoding and decoding them. Usually we say that agents share a common language, although, depending on the task and the means of decoding, it isn't clear that they must share a common code as long as messages can be decoded properly.

To clarify these ideas, as well as to introduce the reader to the computational view of intelligence networks, I will describe some specific examples in more detail. They are drawn from the world of computing artifacts, since these are fairly easy to concoct and understand. But it should not be lost sight of that they are meant to illustrate ideas of much greater generality, which can be applied to both human and artificial intelligence. (This thread will be picked up in the next section.)

First I will describe a system that demonstrates distributed intelligence, but does not involve agents, as I have defined them. This system solves a specific type of problem where values must be chosen that are subject to constraints. It could involve full-fledged agents as I have defined them, but, as the example shows, in this case this isn't required.

In this example, each node in the network can perform certain computations independently of the others, but it makes no decisions about what it should compute. Here, a node is programmed to minimize a value that represents energy use in an associated real-world system, perhaps a component of a physical plant. At the same time values have to be chosen so that they match up with the values calculated by the other nodes. This means that an acceptable solution can only be obtained if nodes communicate with each other in order to compare their values.

To make the description more concrete, let's assume that there are three nodes, called "X", "Y" and "Z". We will also assume that for each node, only values in a certain interval are physically possible. (They might be the only values allowed by the associated physical component.) To further simplify the example, we only consider values that are whole numbers, so the interval is really a sequence. Then the restrictions pertaining to other nodes can be described as mathematical relations based on the sets of values. (Restrictions like these might occur because the physical components must be synchronized, or because they share resources, or whatever.)

A situation of this sort is shown in Figure 6.1. The values that a node can select are shown in brackets next to that node, e.g. X must select either 5, 6, 7 or 8 as its value. That restrictions hold between values selected by different nodes is indicated by the arcs in the graph. Next to each arc is an equation that expresses the actual relation that the values must satisfy. So there is a restriction holding between X and Z such that the value selected by node Z must be 3 greater than the value selected by X. Similarly, the value selected by node Y must be greater than the one selected by Z. (Note

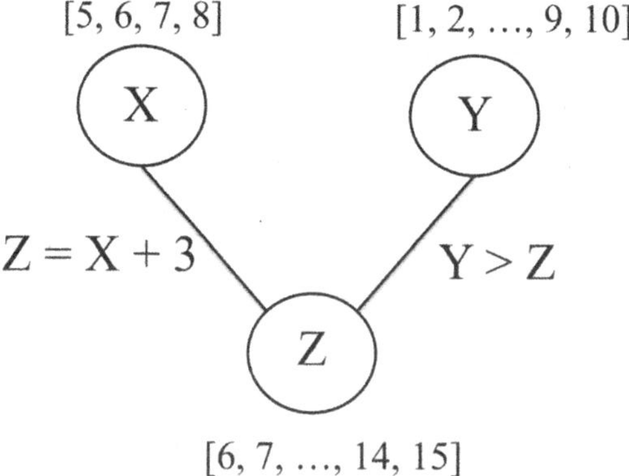

Figure 6.1. Network to select values for X, Y and Z that satisfy stipulated relations that must hold between them (shown beside the two edges). Further explanation in text.

that Z must therefore satisfy two restrictions, while the other nodes need only consider one.)

Recall that each node must select the smallest value possible given the various restrictions placed upon it. Because no node has all the information required to do this globally, the problem must be solved in a distributed manner. This can be done with a distributed algorithm, and in this case the behavior of the nodes, and therefore the state of the system, can be determined at each step. (This is the reason for not calling the nodes agents.) Part of the algorithm involves message passing, which must therefore follow some fixed script, or protocol.

In the first place, we assume that messages are only passed between nodes which are involved together in a relation that must be satisfied (i.e. only between nodes joined by an arc in the figure). In addition, we impose a kind of priority ordering, so that nodes with labels that come before other nodes will initiate message passing. In the example here, this means that Z will not pass any messages unless it receives a message from X or Y.

So, to begin with, each node selects the lowest value, i.e. 5 for X, 1 for Y, and 6 for Z. X and Y send messages to Z, which indicate their selection. Because Z's value must be 3 greater than X's, the lowest value it can select is now 8. At the same time, there is no value that Z can select that is less than Y's value. So Z sends an "OK" message to X and a "NOT-OK" message to Y, along with its own value. Y then selects the lowest value compatible with Z's selection, which is 9, and sends the message back to Z. At this point every node has a value and the restrictions have all been met. So the system has solved the problem.[6*]

It should be obvious that the type of problem just specified could be solved by this network regardless of the values that each node is given to work with. So this is a genuine, albeit rudimentary, form of distributed intelligence — focused on one specific type of problem.[7*]

Now I want to consider a network that is a genuine multi-agent system. The system I will describe is an actual software system developed in the nineties.[8] As far as I know it was not put to use as a real-world application; instead, it was run on a "simulation testbed" designed for the transportation domain. Since my purpose here is pedagogical, to explain a basic conception through examples, this is not a critical limitation.

As with the previous example, the network was built to perform a specific task. The task was to schedule pick-up and delivery trucks for a company or a related group of companies.

The problem faced by the system was to organize truck deliveries so that these were made in a timely fashion while minimizing company costs. There were two kinds of agents in the system: shipping company agents (roughly corresponding to human dispatchers or managers) and truck agents (each one corresponding to the driver of a truck). Shipping agents took orders from customers and sent them out to the truck agents, who then bid competitively for all or part of the order. To do this, a truck agent had to compose a route that would include the new deliveries in such a way as to minimize costs;[9*] this was necessary for it to calculate a bid that could actually be met. The shipping agent then collected the bids and computed a bid that was sent to the customer. If the customer accepted the bid, then the truck agents were notified.

Figure 6.2 gives a schematic depiction of the system. Figure 6.3 shows the kind of problems that have to be solved in order to carry out the task. It is important to note that because this was a multi-agent system, these problems were solved in a distributed fashion: each truck computed a best route for itself, while clustering of orders (the order allocation problem) was solved implicitly by a bidding procedure in which a shipping agent broadcast an order to a set of truck agents who then placed bids

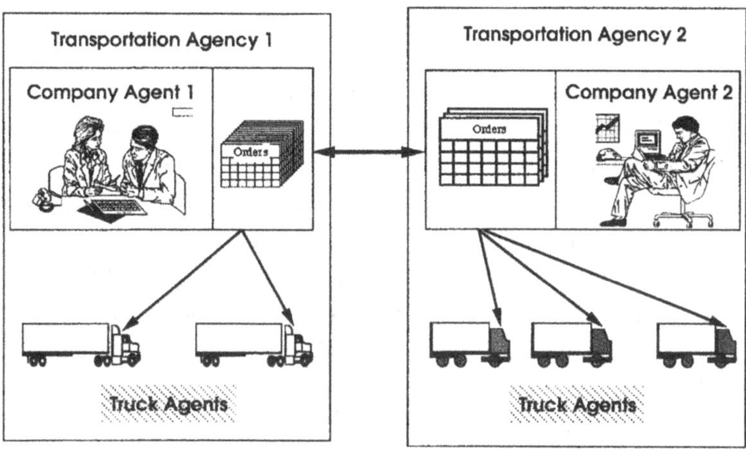

Figure 6.2. Diagrammatic scheme of shipping and trucking system (reprinted from K. Fischer *et al.*, 1999, Figure 3, by permission).

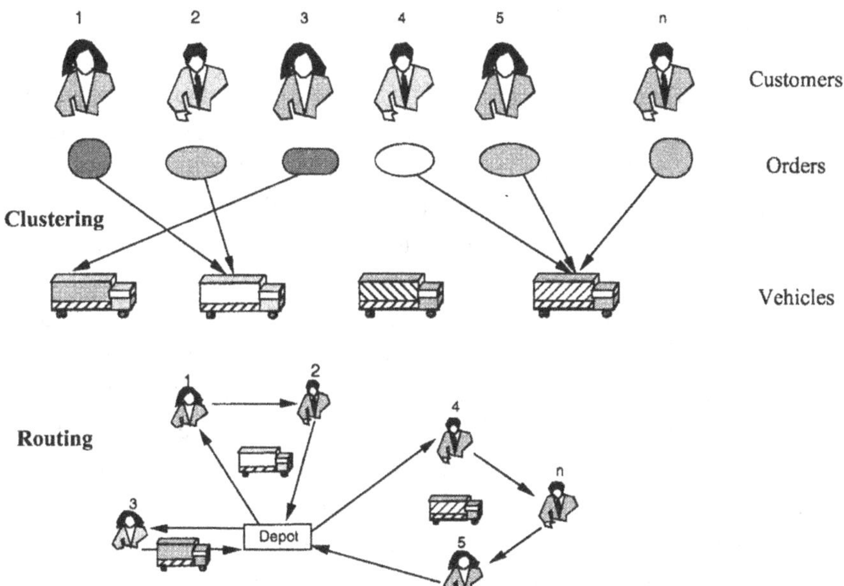

Figure 6.3. Two facets of shipping problem: allocating orders to trucks and finding a cost-effective route for each truck (reprinted from K. Fischer *et al.*, 1999, Figure 7, by permission).

depending on whether they could fit the new order into the existing orders that they had to deliver.

Interactions among software agents were carried out according to a prescribed format, an elaboration of a well-known bidding protocol devised during the previous decade called the "contract net protocol".[10] For our purposes, the details are not important (they simply specify more precisely the behaviors described above). What is important is that these 'agents' followed rather specific plans of action imposed by the designers.

At the same time, as part of their plans, agents had to collect information and make decisions. There were also subtle, indirect interactions among the agents that could not be specified in advance. For example, a shipping agent's response to a particular truck agent, granting or rejecting its bid, depended on information gathered from it as well as other truck agents that were bidding. Moreover, whether an agent actually made a bid depended on whether the new task could be fit into its existing schedule in a cost-effective way; so for a given bid it wasn't clear to begin with which agents would even tender bids (or what the values of the bids would be). So this little system does exhibit, to a degree, the features of a set of autonomous entities in a network laid out in the definition.

Another significant feature of this network is that different agents took on different roles. In this case there were two roles, designated by the terms shipping and trucking. Basically, this means that the operations of the network could be separated into two functional types.

I have presented these examples to give the reader a more concrete sense of what an agent-based intelligence network is. Because of their simplicity and because these are constructed systems, they highlight some of the basic features of such systems. In addition, they serve to introduce a computational perspective that in fact is the major subtext of this work.

The major limitation of these examples is that they are non-historical, in contrast to the intelligence systems that are of greatest interest for the present discussion. The latter, in contrast, always have an evolutionary character. This should be kept in mind in the discussion that follows.

Another interesting issue raised by these examples is the degree to which an agent is aware of other agents as agents and of the network as a whole. In the multi-agent system just described it could be argued that there is some implicit representation of other agents that is reflected in the form of the communications. But there is certainly no understanding of other agents' roles.

*

Now, to return to the main argument — that all intelligence is agent-like, and therefore network-like, in character. (Recall that according to the definition I have given, the very notion of an agent requires that it be part of a multi-agent network.) But what does it mean to say that all intelligence has this character? What about Watson and Deep Blue for example?

In a larger sense, and this is central to the present thesis, an AI system like Deep Blue is always part of a larger intelligence network that involves humans agents. This includes both the people who created the system in the first place and those who use it afterwards. Within this larger network each of these software/hardware systems represents a solution to a problem, such as the problem of how to send messages between users over a computer network or the problem of how to play champion-level chess. But in each case, the problem itself was formulated — and the solution confirmed — by human agents. So in each case there is a network of intelligent agents.[11*]

In this context, it is interesting to consider the first example described above (a system that coordinates energy minimization) and to reflect on who the human agents are in this case. In the first place, there is the agent who devised the particular network described, i.e. the present writer. However, in imagining this system, the author relied on the work of other people who have done research on distributed constraint satisfaction. In turn, these people made use of the work of earlier investigators in AI as well as in the general area of computer science. So in fact this simple example really resides within a vast network of intelligent agents.

*

The arguments just given apply to AI and to other computer-based systems. But the thesis can be extended further, to systems in which all of the agents are human. That is, the claim I am making is not merely that AI systems always have an agent-in-a-network character, but that this is true of human intelligence as well.

The agent-in-a-network character of human intelligence has been recognized in the past, perhaps most famously by Newton in the following remark written in a letter to Robert Hooke[12]:

> If I have seen further it is by standing
> on the shoulders of giants.

Returning to our first case study, and looking over at the other side of the table, we might ask, is a Garry Kasparov conceivable without a well-developed tradition of chess-playing? Is he not part of a large intelligence network of historical proportions, stretching back at least several centuries?

As another example, consider the case of William Shakespeare. Shakespeare is generally considered not only a great writer but a colossus of human thought and expression, one of the architects of modern Western Civilization. Not only did he write upwards of 40 plays as well as 150 sonnets and two long poems, he also changed the English language. (Shakespeare's works are perhaps one reason for the Latinate character of English.[13]) He was also the greatest coiner of new words and phrases in English (and probably human) history. His vocabulary was prodigious; a standard estimate is 20,000 words in Shakespeare's works vs. 8,000 in Milton's.[14]

> "when Francis Drake, Henry Hudson, and Captain John Smith were expanding the boundaries of the world, ... Shakespeare, Rembrandt, ... were revolutionizing human thought and expression."[15]

At the same time, Shakespeare borrowed slavishly from modern and ancient sources[16]:

- The Comedy of Errors is based on a comedy by Plautus.
- In the historical plays, Shakespeare sometimes transcribed whole passages from Hall or Hollingshed.
- The Tempest may be based on a particular form of the Comedia D'Italia, the pastoral comedy.

Consider the plot of The Tempest as summarized by Bate and Rasmussen for the Royal Shakespeare Company at Stratford[17]:

> Twelve years ago Prospero, the Duke of Milan, was usurped by his brother, Antonio, with the help of Alonso ... Prospero and his baby daughter Miranda were put to sea and landed on a distant island where ever since, by the use of his magic art, he has ruled over the spirit Ariel and the savage Caliban.
>
> He uses his power to raise a storm which shipwrecks his enemies on the island. Alonso searches for his son, Ferdinand ... Sebastian plots to kill Alonso and steal the crown. The drunken butler, Stephano, and the jester, Trinculo, encounter Caliban and are persuaded by him to kill Prospero so that they can rule the island. Ferdinand meets Miranda and falls in love. ... As Prospero's plan draws to its climax, he confronts his enemies and forgives them. Prospero grants Ariel his freedom and prepares to leave the island for Milan.

Now, compare this description with the following examples of the Comedia D'Italia pastoral comedy[18]:

- Il Mago — "deals with The Magician who inhabits a remote island where a group of buffoons are shipwrecked. After various tricks, plots and amorous adventures, all is happily resolved."
- La Nave — "deals with a shipwreck on a remote island where a magician holds sway over some spirits. After various tricks, plots and amorous adventures, all is happily resolved."
- Li Tre Satiri — "deals with three satyrs who are used by a magician on a remote island to torment a group of shipwrecked buffoons. After various tricks, plots and amorous adventures, all is happily resolved."

So yes, Shakespeare is a towering literary and intellectual figure. But his achievement was also agent-like in nature. It would not have been possible if he could not draw on the prior work of many other people.

*

Looking at all this from a somewhat different perspective, we could ask, to what degree is AI — or HI — as it is normally presented a sleight of hand? Consider again the Kasparov/Deep Blue match. Implicit in all of the notices cited in Chapter 2 was the assumption that two intelligent entities were competing with each other. We have now made clear the fallacy in considering Deep Blue a stand-alone intelligence. But isn't the same true of Kasparov? For, as shown in Chapter 4, he is also embedded in a vast evolutionary intelligence network that is concerned with the game of chess and how to play it well. And just like Deep Blue, a grand master like Gary Kasparov could not exist without that network. Thus, from the perspective of the framework I am laying out, a match-up like this has a strong element of smoke-and-mirrors on both sides.

In all these cases a basic error is being made, an error of omission or oversight, which I will call the Fallacy of Omniscient Intelligence, or FOI. Here I will make a few speculative remarks as to why this might this be so. One might title these remarks, "Towards an evolutionary psychology of FOI".

An important aspect of human intelligence as it plays out in the social realm is convincing others (other human agents) of one's intellectual competence. This may be the basis of FOI, which in turn has been unwittingly transferred to AI. Interesting variants (extreme forms) of this process, which is well-nigh universal, can be observed:

- The guru syndrome
- Theories of everything (the "Casaubon syndrome")

Clearly, all this is tied in with important psychological phenomena such as leadership, sexual selection (cf. groupies and other types of 'followers'), etc.

*

It should be emphasized that in laying out the present argument, I am not concerned with developing a Theory of Intelligence in any complete sense. Instead, I am attempting to delineate a property of intelligence as it occurs in the world-at-large, one that is basic to intelligence in practice, and the comprehension of which is essential for a proper understanding of AI and our relations to it. As a result, there are many issues and topics related to ideas of intelligence that will be left out of the discussion.

In particular, since ours is a task- or application-oriented perspective, we will assume that the agents involved can at least cope with the task. In psychology notions of intelligence have most often been bound up with the study of individual differences in capacity, which bears on the question of coping. Since this problem is more or less orthogonal to present concerns we will not consider it here. Nor will we have much to say about possible 'components of intelligence' or 'kinds' of intelligence as they have been studied in psychology (although some general questions concerning human versus machine capabilities will be dealt with in Chapter 10).[19*]

More pertinent, at least on the surface, is the study of social networks, which has become an area of great interest in the Age of the Internet. Eventually, I can't see how this area will not be relevant to the ideas proposed here. And I am certain that it will be needed if these ideas are to be properly systematized. For example, in a theory of intelligence networks, it will be important to ask questions about issues such as the minimal connectivity of a network, or network size and growth. However, at this time it is more important to establish certain critical ideas and to tease out important relationships. Under these circumstances, to delve into various quantitative aspects of such networks will probably yield only trivial results, being a mere academic exercise, and may even draw attention away from issues of real importance.[20*]

One significant limitation of the usual network representation is that the nodes and links do not directly represent the information required in intelligence networks as they are conceived of here; at best they can only indicate channels of communication. This is why the diagrams presented earlier in this chapter are not to be taken as true models. They are simply meant to represent the entities that embody intelligence, along with their critical 'social' connections. Moreover, these are only toy, non-historical networks. Their purpose was to support the argument by giving some kinds of concrete examples.

*

It is worth dwelling a bit more on the differences between intelligence networks that involve human beings and those, like the illustrative examples given above that involve only computer programs. Take for example, networks dedicated to dispatching and routing a fleet of trucks.

A key difference between HI- and AI-based dispatching and routing systems is that for human beings the role of truck driver or dispatcher is just a day job. This highlights a critical point: that human agents are general-purpose systems that through learning and instruction can be specialized for a particular task. Along with this, human agents often have some awareness of — and comprehension of — the network in which they function. They can view the network as a network, something that most software agents cannot do.

At the same time, in both cases agents are limited in their larger understanding of the situation in which they are embedded; to a great degree their knowledge is confined to specific tasks within the network. Thus, it is highly unlikely that a human dispatcher will know much (if anything) about the historical development behind the role of dispatcher or its relation to the field of logistics as an area of application.

A related difference is that generally it is humans who accommodate to software, including intelligent systems, not vice versa. In other words, an HI system is more flexible and extendible. (At the same time, it should be noted that when this occurs, both humans and software become part of a larger intelligence network.)

Humans are also very flexible in regard to the variety of channels through which communication occurs, as well as the conventions used in communicating information of various types. This includes information transmission between humans and artifacts. A software system is markedly deficient in comparison.

In humans, with complex skills and knowledge, transfer is often a kind of re-creation rather than a simple transmission. This can apply to day-to-day operation in a limited task-oriented network, but it is even more striking when we consider knowledge traditions that evolve through time. In this connection, consider again the case of William Shakespeare and his re-use of older narratives. One well-known example is his use of an old story recorded in a compendium of tales by the sixteenth century French writer Belleforest, called *Les Histoires Tragiques*, in writing the plot for the play Hamlet. The original story, which can be found on the Web in an English translation, is a rather primitive story of murder and revenge; although many of the plot elements in Shakespeare's play can be found in it, the characters are only rudimentary, cardboard figures in comparison with the persons in the play.[21*] So in this case we cannot talk about transmission without also talking about transformation as well.

The evolutionary character of human intelligence networks is implicit or explicit in many discussions of culture and tradition. A nice example of the latter is found in Hobhouse's *Mind in Evolution*:

> "What is peculiar to human intelligence, is the rise of tradition as a third force impinging upon the other two [the others being heredity and individual experience]. The instinct of each individual human being is in contact throughout his life with the body of beliefs, moral judgments, social institutions, rules of art or craft that make up the tradition of the society into which he is born. These enter into his character, interpenetrate his hereditary impulses, not only encouraging and restraining, but with more subtle power, prescribing to each impulse the sphere within which it is to move, and the object on which it may exercise itself. And the character so formed is all the while in interaction with the results of experience in the narrower sense of that which the individual finds out for himself, as opposed to that of which he is told."[22]

Another significant feature of human beings is the ease with which they set up new intelligence networks — trade networks, spy networks, scientific teams and larger associations, etc. In each of these associations there is some over-arching goal or interest that can be identified. In addition, of course, there are many human associations whose main goal is simply association with like-minded people, but this does not contradict the point being made here.

In contrast, in software multi-agent systems, agents are not capable of forming associations by themselves, submitting to rules, and adopting required roles. Vital interests are still established externally.[23*]

In this connection, it is worth noting that multi-agent systems of the sort described above are always (as far as I know) reflections of human organizations. And this harks back to the central theme of this work, the idea that AI systems are always embedded in larger networks. The take-home lesson is this: one cannot really understand a computer system of this sort without embedding it in a larger, historical network.

Finally, I want to make one more related point, which pertains to AI systems specifically. It should be borne in mind when trying to characterize these systems that they, like biological systems, are evolutionary in nature. In this case, their evolution is embodied in a succession of computer programs. One simple example: the evolutionary development from the Logic Theorist to the General Problem Solver, or GPS. Both involve a kind of means-end analysis. (In LT this took the form of reasoning backwards.) Of course, evolution in this form occurs only because these systems are embedded in larger networks based on human intelligence; in fact, this has to be seen as a special case of the formation of traditions that was just discussed.[24*]

Along with the network character of intelligence, this is an aspect of the field that is insufficiently emphasized. Among other things, this shows the necessity of historical analysis for understanding intelligence of any sort.

*

The present perspective on intelligence is not meant to deprecate the idea of autonomy. Instead, to the degree that it is correct it should clarify this idea, as well as indicating why it is important that certain basic components in an intelligence network have a degree of autonomy.

Turning back to the matter at hand, when should we regard AI systems as achieving autonomy? This, of course, is another way of asking when we should regard AI as having achieved something on par with human intelligence. Now, given the basic thesis of this chapter, our decision must be based on the functioning of such artifacts within some general human intelligence network. In fact, there are already numerous cases of computer-based systems that support intelligent activity within such networks. In some cases, such as aircraft control, they even achieve a degree of autonomy. But at the same time they are clearly subordinate and certainly not on par with the humans in the network.

The example just mentioned concerning aircraft control suggests an important distinction that should be made — between autonomous control and independent initiation of interactions. Any judgment of 'real' artificial intelligence would seem to involve the latter.

One criterion that could be suggested is that this will occur when they achieve a certain parity in their interactions with human. One way of putting this is to suppose that there are "conversational thresholds" that can be defined (at least roughly). AI systems would be considered autonomous parts of human intelligence networks when they reach certain conversational thresholds.

*

The thesis outlined in this chapter leads to an obvious question: why should intelligence be agent-like in character? I think the answer is that the basis for intelligent action develops slowly over time, and only networks can support this kind of historical development. Individual agents after all have limited lifespans, so until now at least a single agent could not suffice.

There are other possible reasons: it may be that only with a population of agents can information be gathered effectively — because a population supports a variety of experiences. Also, multi-agent systems can better support specializations — and a broader range of knowledge.

But in order for this idea to be taken seriously, it must have some basis in the natural world. And it must square with what we know about living organisms. In short, we should see some evidence of it elsewhere.

In fact, throughout the living world there are instances of organization within and between organisms that seem to have the characteristics of intelligence networks as I have defined them.

A striking example of an apparent task-oriented biological intelligence network is found in the behavior of cellular slime molds.[25] These are organisms that can exist either as single cells or as multi-cellular systems, depending on the conditions in which they find themselves. In the words of one author:

> "In their vegetative growth these organisms are animal-like and feed and grow as do small amoebae generally; but subsequently through their unique behavior they give rise to fruiting structures that are definitely plant-like in pattern and in construction."[26]
>
> "In the presence of food they [the single-celled organisms] promptly begin feeding by the ingestion and digestion of bacterial cells, grow, and increase rapidly in numbers by repeated divisions. During this period each myxamoeba pursues a wholly independent course. But with the exhaustion of the available food supply, and marking the initiation of the fruiting phase, the myxamoeba collect into aggregates which, since no fusion of individuals occurs, are termed pseudoplasmodia.

> Subsequently these pseudoplasmodia give rise to fruiting structures, or sorocarps. This is accomplished in the simpler forms by the heaping up and encystment of myxamoeba, and in the higher forms by the orderly differentiation of comparable individuals into sterile supporting tissue and spores."[27]

Later in the process, the spores residing within the cap are released. This multi-cellular adaptation therefore serves as a dispersal mechanism allowing the cells to travel much greater distances than they could in the single-cell state. Pictures of several different species of slime mold in their multi-cellular state are shown in Figure 6.4:[28]

For our purposes, the most important point is that the entire process of aggregation and differentiation is guided by a massive system of communication between individual cells. Chemical signals, presumably released because of lack of food, lead to aggregation by triggering taxes (directed movements) guided by chemical gradients. Other signals lead to changes in DNA transcription and cell differentiation.[29] For our purposes,

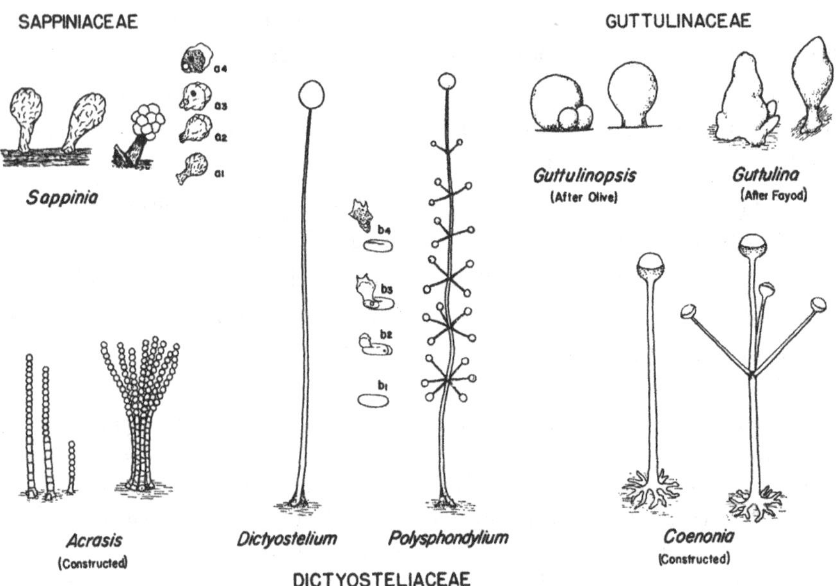

Figure 6.4. Structures formed by different species of cellular slime molds (reprinted from Raper, 1940, Figure 1, by permission).

it is enough to note that a system of signaling processes enable members of this species to carry out functions that individual cells could not do alone.

Other slime mold networks demonstrate other capacities. A particularly apposite example for our purposes is the ability to form paths across terrains that minimize the distances required to connect different points. This was demonstrated in one species, Physarum polycephalum, by placing food sources in various locations near the plasmodium.[30] The plasmodium first spreads out and encounters the sources. Subsequently, much of the cell mass is retracted until there are only narrow corridors of protein tubules connecting the different food sources, as shown in the Figure 6.5. [31]

When we consider the animal kingdom, many other examples of intelligence networks can be cited below the human level. These include recruitment for foraging in ants via pheromones, foraging recruitment in honey bees via the "bee dance", hunting packs in canines such as wolves and hyenas, mobbing of a predator by birds and other animals, and numerous other social activities. All of these appear to be examples of agents communicating with one another in order to accomplish a particular task; i.e. they are intelligence networks as defined here.

The key factor in all this is communication. That is, once entities have evolved the capacity to communicate (or in the case of cellular slime molds, the capacity to respond in common to a signal), then the way is open for possible development of intelligence networks. Obviously, there are varying levels of complexity possible based on the sophistication of the communication system, but this topic is outside the scope of the present discussion.

Viewed from this perspective, what is a multi-cellular organism? Should it be thought of as an intelligence network in a compact form? In fact, I think it would be a mistake to make this identification. For one thing, a multi-cellular organism is not designed for one specific task or even a collection of similar tasks. Instead, it is more accurate to characterize it as a framework in which (largely cellular) intelligence networks can function. The same can be said for the cell itself (most strikingly, the eukaryotic cell) as well as symbiotic systems such as lichens.

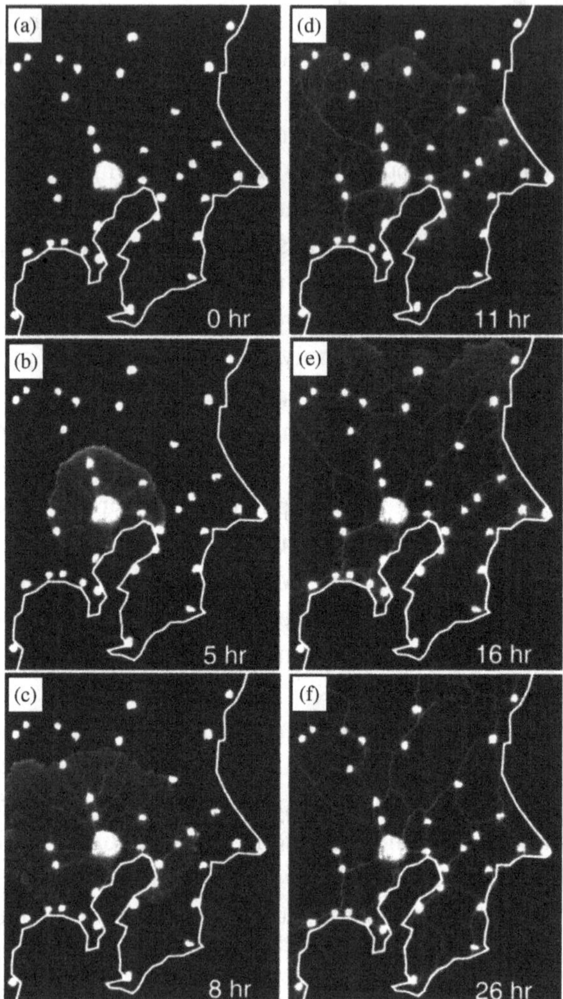

Figure 6.5. A cellular slime mold determines shortest routes between food sources. Pictures A-C show the cell mass spreading out from its original location; pictures D-F show the progressive restriction to direct routes between food sources. (Adapted from Tero *et al.*, 2010, Figure 1, by permission).

Thus, there is nothing in evolutionary or developmental biology that contradicts the ideas presented in this chapter. On the contrary, the existence of intelligence networks — in the form of communicating agents — appears to be a fundamental phenomenon in the living world, and a significant outcome of biological evolution. It is even possible that the formation of intelligence networks can be taken as a third principle of biological evolution on par with the principles of anagenesis and cladogenesis, which refer, respectively, to evolution within a species and to division via speciation into separated groups resulting in divergent forms. This third principle could be called cosmogenesis, defined as the tendency of biological organisms to form intelligence networks based on common signals or systems of communication. Because of requirements of common inheritance, in most cases this will only occur within a species, although this is not a question that needs to be resolved here.[32*]

All this raises many further questions concerning the evolution of such capacities, as well as the interplay — and perhaps conflict — between natural selection of individuals and intelligence networks that these individuals may form and support. There is also the question, hinted at by the paragraph above on the relation of multi-cellularity to intelligence networks, of how systems can evolve that can serve as foundations for intelligence networks. But since these questions are outside the scope of the present work, whose purpose is to present a basic idea and to demonstrate its validity and its relevance to AI as well as to some HI problems, they will not be dealt with here.[33*]

Endnotes

1. Distributed artificial intelligence (DAI) and its allied field of distributed computing appeared sometime before the field of multi-agent systems. The latter sprang up in the 1990s and became a dominant area of AI for much of the decade and beyond. During this time there was a melding of DAI and MAS (cf. Chaib-Draa *et al.*, cited below).

   Among various works on DAI, a very useful volume is G. M. P. O'Hare & N. R. Jennings, editors, *Foundations of Distributed Artificial Intelligence*, New York: John Wiley, 1996. A classic reference for distributed computing is G. Tel, *Introduction to Distributed Algorithms*, 2nd edition, Cambridge: Cambridge University Press, 2000. Among the many, many works on agents and multi-agent systems there is M. Woolridge, *An Introduction to MultiAgent Systems*, New York: John Wiley, 2002. See also H. J. Levesque & F. Pirri, *Logical Foundations for Cognitive Agents*, Berlin: Springer, 1999. Some important papers that I found useful are: R. Davis & R. G. Smith, "Negotiation as a metaphor for distributed problem solving", *Artificial Intelligence*, 1983, 20: 63–109; L. Gasser, "Social conceptions of knowledge and action: DAI foundations and open systems semantics", *Artificial Intelligence*, 1991, 47: 107–138.; B. Chaib-Draa, B. Moulin, R. Mandiau & P. Millot, "Trends in distributed artificial intelligence", *Artificial Intelligence Review*, 1992, 6: 35–66.

2. C. Hewitt, "Viewing control structures as patterns of passing messages", *Artificial Intelligence*, 1977, 8: 323–364.
3. Graphs of this sort are highly qualitative in nature, so that not all of the features of a figure like this have representational significance. For example, differences in length of different arcs in the figure have no meaning. (Sometimes arcs are labeled with numbers called weights, but these then form an added feature of the representation.) The important point, representationally, is that certain nodes are connected to other nodes. In addition, although in this figure no edges cross, this is neither basic nor necessary to this form of representation (although graphs where this is the case are designated as a special class, called planar graphs). On the other hand, proper graphs do not have more than one arc between nodes, and there are no arcs from a node to itself. (A network with these properties is called a multi-graph.) Finally, graphs like the one shown here are called undirected graphs. If edges have direction, then the resulting object is a directed graph (and in this case two nodes may be connected by a pair of edges having opposite directions).
4. These examples were suggested by a passage in Davis and Smith, *op. cit.*, p. 65.
5. *Ibid.*, p. 66.
6. It can be proved that this procedure will find an optimal solution to this problem. But it is not necessary to go into details here.
7. A simple procedure like this will not work with all network configurations. However, there are more general algorithms that can. A useful resource here is M. Yokoo, *Distributed Constraint Satisfaction*, Berlin: Springer, 2001.
8. A description of the system first appeared in K. Fischer, J. P. Müller, M. Pischel & D. Schier. "A model for cooperative transportation scheduling". In: V. Lesser, editor, *Proceedings, First International Conference on Multi-Agent Systems: ICMAS-95*. AAAI Press/MIT Press, 1995, pp. 109–116. A later reference, from which Figures 6.2 and 6.3 are taken, is K. Fischer, B. Chaib-draa, J. P. Müller, M. Pischel & C. Gerber, "A simulation approach based on negotiation and cooperation between agents: A case study", IEEE Transactions on Systems, Man, and Cybernetics, 1999, 29: 531–545.
9. This, like the distributed intelligence problem described above, is an example of a constraint satisfaction problem (CSP). In the present case, each truck agent used a constraint solver to find solutions to its problem.
10. The contract net protocol was first described in R. G. Smith, "The contract net protocol: High level communication and control in a distributed problem solver", *IEEE Transactions on Computers*, 1980, C-29: 1104–1113.
11. This is of course reflected in the world graphs presented in Chapter 4.
12. See Wikipedia article, "Standing on the shoulders of giants".
13. cf. E. F. Clafin, "The Latinisms in Shakespeare's diction", *Classical Journal*, 1921, 16: 346–359.

14. The estimates of 20,000 and 8,000 for Shakespeare and Milton are apparently due to O. Jesperson in *Growth and Structure of the English Language*, New York: Teubner, 1905. More recently, various scholars have expressed some skepticism regarding the relative size of Shakespeare's vocabulary in comparison with other writers. (E.g. H. Craig, "Shakespeare's vocabulary: Myth and reality", *Shakespeare Quarterly*, 2011, 62(1): 53–74. Nonetheless, especially for the 16th century it seems to have been quite large.
15. R. Shorto, *The Island at the Center of the World*, New York: Doubleday, 2004.
16. A true appreciation of the extent of Shakespeare's erudition did not occur until the late 19th century. The study of sources culminated in an eight volume reference: G. Bullough, *Narrative and Dramatic Sources of Shakespeare*, London: Routledge and Kegan Paul, 1957–1975.
17. I cannot find the original source for this summary. Something very close (and clearly derived from this source) can be found at http://www.playbillder.com/show/vip/Hamden_HS_Mainstage_Ensemble/2015/The_Tempest_20165/page/3.
18. Quotations are from a paper by K. Gilvary presented at the Shakespeare in Italy Conference in 2007.
19. In this connection, a few words may be said about the notion of "extended minds" (cf. R. Menary, editor, *The Extended Mind*, Cambridge, MA & London: MIT, 2010, or A. Clark. *Supersizing the Mind*, Oxford: Oxford University, 2008). In the first place, I largely agree with the thrust of the extended mind idea. From a computational perspective, an implement used in an intelligent activity is part of the system which gives rise to the output that defines that activity as intelligent. So if one wants to use the word "mind" to designate the overall activity, then indeed its reference should include those implements. On the other hand, elements like a pen or pencil and paper should still be designated as implements or aids since they don't have computational powers in and of themselves. So I would say that the issues dealt with under the rubric of extended mind are somewhat tangential to the present discussion.
20. The present conceptions may have some relation to the "actor-network theory" (ANT) of Latour and others, although I am not certain about this. This is because people working within this framework seem content to traipse about among topics related to meaning and interpretation especially in relation to scientific concepts (As in J. Law & J. Hassard, *Actor Network Theory and After*, Oxford: Blackwell, 1999) without conveying anything concrete or distinct. So maybe it is just a matter of similar sounding terminology.

    Moreover, engaging with Latour's writing on this subject is like engaging in a fencing match, since his main concern seems to be to defend himself against actual analysis or evaluation, lest the inquirer realize that any substance the 'theory' has is rather trivial, as well as being ineptly stated. This leads to a particular style of discourse in which the writer darts from topic to topic, cites an example and then drops it, says one thing and then claims that the opposite is true as well, or goes into why his conceptions are not this, or this, or this. In his writing one also comes across sentences like, "Microbes, neutrinos of DNA are at the same time natural, social and discourse." Obviously, Latour chose the phrase "neutrinos of DNA" not because it means anything (are microbes nothing but DNA? Have they essentially no mass?), but for much the same reasons that Andre Breton put discordant ideas together in a line of verse — because the result has a certain aesthetic bounce while conveying a vague sense of deeper significance. Hence, I don't see much point in exploring the relations between the present ideas and ANT in any detail.

21. Belleforest based his narrative on one that appeared much earlier. The tale of Amlethus was first written down by Saxo Grammaticus in the late twelfth century. A version in English was printed in *The Gentleman's Magazine* in 1845 and can be found on the Web.
22. L. T. Hobhouse, *Mind in Evolution*, London: Macmillan, 1901, p. 319.
23. As an aside I might note that all these considerations serve to indicate the inanity of the meme idea in coming to terms with cultural evolution. For example, making connections between ideas (memes) requires intelligent agents; it's not a matter of ideas hopping from place to place like independent genetic elements. Consideration of this and other similar arguments suggests to me that the meme idea may be a reductio ad absurdum of the whole Dawkinsian perspective
24. Taking the present perspective, one can begin to understand why the agents area in AI has not had its anticipated impact. Because if everything is agent-like and embedded in larger networks, then setting up a limited system of toy agents that are not strongly linked to the intelligence networks of the larger world is not likely to result in anything especially profound or interesting. The problem is that these agents do not reflect that world in anything except their basic structures, which they share with any other piece of software. (This does not mean that such exercises are valueless; at the very least, they have helped to refine the notion of an agent itself. And of course the field is still young and ongoing.)
25. As usual, good introductions to this topic can be found in the Wikipedia articles, "Slime mold" and "Dictyostelium". See also J. T. Bonner, *The Social Amoebae. The Biology of Cellular Slime Molds*, Princeton: Princeton University, 2009.
26. K. B. Raper, "The communal nature of the fruiting process in the Acrasieae", *American Journal of Botany*, 1940, 27: 436–448, p. 436.
27. *Loc. cit.*
28. *Ibid.*, p. 437, Figure 1.
29. Bonner, *op. cit.* reviews these processes and the research that led to their discovery.
30. A. Tero *et al.*, "Rules for biologically inspired adaptive network design", *Science*, 2010, 327: 439–442. Unlike the examples just mentioned, this species of slime mold exists in aggregate form as a single cell. A related work is T. Nakagaki *et al.*, "Minimum-risk path finding by an adaptive amoebal network", *Physical Review Letters*, 2007, 99: 068104–1-4.
31. *Ibid.*, Figure 1, p. 440.

32. There is one other feature of human intelligence systems that has an analogy of sorts in biological systems. This is the lateral transfer of information. At the human level this takes the form of particular ideas being transferred from one context to another, which may be completely unrelated with respect to specific function. This topic was explored at length in the television series *Connections*. In biological systems, the lateral transfer of genes, sometimes in the form of transposons, which can even take place between two separate species, seems similar, although here the transfer does not involve intelligence systems as directly.
33. It is intriguing that one can discern a degree of resemblance between the ideas presented in this chapter and certain features of Bantu thought as described in P. Tempels, *Bantu Philosophy*, Paris: Presence Africaine, 1959 (orig. Dutch, 1945). In particular the present view of intelligence networks seems to have a genuine affinity with the conception of individual human beings as part of a larger web of 'forces', in this case, however, based largely on kinship. Note that the similarity of interest here is not the content of the beliefs (I have only a vague notion of what is meant by "forces", and there is no hint of a computational conception), but the kind of perspective taken in both cases.

    I have no idea whether my African colleagues in Engineering and Computer Science would agree with this assessment or even whether they as denizens of the 21st century are even familiar with such ideas. In fact, they might argue that it is an example of the folk knowledge that is found in all cultures, now superseded by more sophisticated kinds of knowledge and knowledge gathering. And of course they would be largely correct. However, in this case I find a distinct perspective that seems akin to the thesis of the present volume, and for this reason it is worth noting and perhaps examining further.

7

Varieties of Intelligence

In this chapter I explore some of the ramifications of the perspective on intelligence presented in earlier chapters. Most of the examples involve human agents basically, although in many cases — and this is significant — artifacts can be added to the intelligence network. The basic message is that the principles of intelligence described in Chapter 6 can be realized in a variety of different ways, and, therefore, that a classification of sorts is warranted.

This discussion is deeply informed by the computational perspective.

*

Up until this point (and disregarding the biological examples discussed briefly in Chapter 6), two types of intelligence have been distinguished: human and artificial (HI and AI). In this chapter, the scope of the discussion will be extended to include new categories.

The first category of intelligence to be discussed I will call "human artificial intelligence" (HAI). This can be defined as an AI artifact that includes a human being as a necessary part of the apparatus. The meaning will become clearer when we consider examples.

But before doing this I should explain why I want to discuss this topic at all. In the first place, the idea is introduced in order to further elucidate the question: What exactly is artificial intelligence? But it also bears on the more general question of the nature of intelligence as well as demonstrating the power of the computational view.

The first example of this form of intelligence comes from the field of decision analysis. In my view what is called "prescriptive decision analysis" can be viewed as an instance of HAI. But first I must say something about the field in general and how this topic fits into the present discussion.

Historically, the field of decision analysis has comprised two sorts of endeavor. One, called normative decision analysis, is concerned with spelling out the properties of good decisions as precisely as possible, using formal methods. For example, good decisions should conform to the principle of transitivity: if A is preferred to B and B to C, then A should be preferred to C and not vice versa. This can be expressed in the language of mathematical relations. Here, the relation R is a preference relation, and ARB means that A is preferred to B.

Much of the work on normative decision analysis uses the idea of a utility function, which is a way of representing ideas such as transitivity in a compact form. Simply put, if we have such a function (or at least know that such a function exists), then we know that if outcome A is preferred to outcome B, then the function will give a higher value for A than for B (in decision-theory-speak, the "utility of A is greater than the utility of B").[1] The importance of all this is that it can be shown (by some very interesting theorems) that if certain properties such as transitivity hold for any possible outcomes in the situation, then there is such a function. So we can go directly from overt preferences (e.g. "I prefer A to B") to statements about relative utility.

The other classical area of decision analysis is descriptive decision analysis. This is simply the empirical study of the actual behavior of decision makers. So, regarding the issue of transitivity, descriptive decision analysis asks whether (or the degree to which) real decision makers exhibit this property in their decisions.

Beginning in the 1980's, decision analysts began to distinguish a third category, which they called prescriptive decision analysis.[2] This consists of methods for aiding decision makers, especially when a decision involves complex tradeoffs that are difficult to represent and handle effectively. Typically, the decision analyst uses some kind of formal model to guide the process.

Over the years there has been much discussion about how to characterize the preference orderings derived from prescriptive methods.

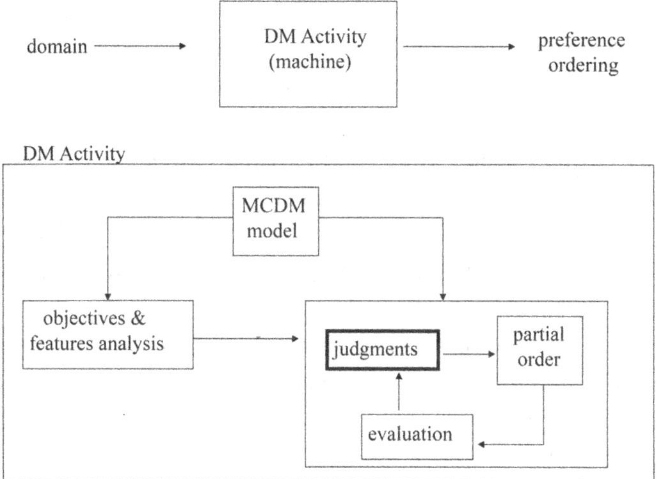

Figure 7.1. Diagram of a prescriptive decision maker, i.e. a machine for producing consistent preference orderings according to some model of decision making. The box that represents the human component is indicated by heavy lines.

Although the naïve position is that prescriptive methods are methods for eliciting preferences from the user, I share the view first espoused by Roy that these methods produce artificial orderings, which combine whatever partial preferences the decision maker might have in a way that ensures that the final ordering will have the features of good decisions, according to normative theory. Roy called the methods used for this "decision aids". Here, I take the view that when prescriptive decision methods are used together, they comprise a kind of abstract machine. The decision maker (DM) is a component of this machine who makes elementary judgments that are then combined in a systematic way according to some model of preferences (a multi-criteria decision model or MCDM). Since a consistent preference ordering among complex, multi-dimensional objects is a solution to the decision maker's problem, this abstract decision making machine is therefore an example of artificial intelligence. But it has the property that a human being is a necessary component; hence, its designation as human artificial intelligence.

A schematic diagram of a prescriptive decision maker (PDM) is shown in Figure 7.1. At the top of the figure, there is a basic input-output diagram, which shows the overall transformation effected by the PDM. At the bottom, the components of the PDM are shown, with information flow indicated by arrows between components. The process begins with an initial stage (indicated by the small box on the left) in which the objectives are decided upon and the various features of the problem are delineated and put in a form in which simple comparisons can be made. Then a series of decisions are made by the human decision maker, following whatever scheme is set out (prescribed) by the MCDM. This continues until the various scenarios are ordered in a systematic way, again according to criteria prescribed by the model.

Another example of HAI involves scientific investigation itself. Insofar as this requires a specific methodology (which it does in any particular instance), this is a kind of human artificial intelligence. One way of putting this is that scientists voluntarily submit to a particular methodology in order to properly carry out the production of scientific knowledge. (Since any science involves the output of a collection of investigators working simultaneously or in historical time, this is also a kind of group HAI, or GHAI (cf. below).)

It should be emphasized that one cannot extend this idea to all knowledge gathering or knowledge generating activities, such as the employment of writing tools. The latter are implements; they don't form systems for producing intelligent results in and of themselves. While it is true that any HAI system can be considered a kind of prosthetic device (like a pencil or a piece of experimental apparatus), it is because its direct function is intelligent action, i.e. it operates to solve a particular problem, that it is classified as a form of intelligence.

Of course, there are many differences between this example of HAI and the last. Perhaps the most important is that embedding a person in a decision making machine can be done with a modicum of training; in fact prescriptive decision making is meant to be a ready aid, and judgments are not expected to require new information nor special expertise. In contrast, a human being can only be properly embedded in a given science machine (aka specialized field of study) after a long period of training and only after mastering a sizeable body of related knowledge.

Scientific investigation has, of course, been analyzed in various ways in the past. Two major lines of thinking are what I will call classical philosophy of science, which was essentially ahistorical, and more modern history-based accounts of the nature of scientific progress, which also often claim epistemological import.

Classical philosophy of science is concerned with characterizing science in terms of its logical foundations.[3] The object is to establish grounds for the validity of scientific principles (e.g. scientific laws and theories) as well as the properties that distinguish scientific from non-scientific concepts. Within this arena, important issues are the logical problems posed by induction (i.e. generalizing from specific instances), how to establish the truth of a hypothesis, and so forth.

However, especially during the latter half of the twentieth century, there was a counter-movement of sorts. This was based (in part) on examination of the way that science was actually carried out, using historical documents and in some cases personal experience. It is associated with names such as Ludwik Fleck and Thomas Kuhn.[4] A major claim that came out of this line of investigation is that science in practice does not operate according to the logical-empirical account given by philosophers of science — or even by scientists themselves. Instead, scientists tend to work within a set of assumptions of which they are only partly aware, which Kuhn called a "paradigm". This continues until a sufficient number of inconsistencies arise. Under these conditions at some point there is a "scientific revolution" in which a new paradigm develops that incorporates both the original findings and the experimental results that did not fit the old paradigm. As the new paradigm is established, practitioners undergo a kind of conversion, including a perceptual-cognitive reorganization of their thought, which affects the way they actually 'see' the field in which they are working. (An alternative, and perhaps more realistic view is that old practitioners never really give up their cognitive schemas, which are based on the old paradigm. But over time they are replaced by new practitioners who learn the new paradigm as they enter the field, so that their cognitive schemas correspond to it.)

In the first place, it must be admitted many of Kuhn's pronouncements, in particular the central idea of scientific paradigms, have proven to be problematic at best and may even border on the vacuous.[5,6*] Nonetheless, I think there was some genuine truth in Kuhn's original account. I suspect that the problem was that he made the ascent into the theoretical realm prematurely, and the result was a poorly delineated and rather grandiose idea floating in conceptual cloudland. To borrow a turn of thought from D. H. Lawrence, this may be a case where one should trust the insight even if you can't trust the exposition.

The idea that historically science does not always follow a path that is in accord with the precepts of classical philosophy of science is certainly true. A well-known example is the concerted effort by some physicists in the 'old guard' to derail the efforts of promoters of the wave theory of light in the early nineteenth century, which, however, was ultimately unsuccessful. An equally telling example is the failure to notice (i.e. to 'see') counter-examples to intelligent design, such as fully terrestrial species of ducks that still had adaptations for aquatic existence like webbed feet — until Darwinian evolutionary theory made them intelligible.[7] Nonetheless, it is hard to see these as refuting all accounts of the logic of empirical investigation.

I think this controversy can be resolved at least in part by using the same three categories that were introduced above in connection with decision analysis. Classical philosophy of science is basically normative (and prescriptive) in character, setting out the properties that scientific inference should follow if it is to be sound. In contrast, the history of science 'counter movement' is essentially descriptive. Among other things, this suggests that the normative-prescriptive-descriptive distinctions have wider scope than just decision analysis.

I will make one further claim about science-in-practice from the perspective I am developing, one that in some ways bridges the gap between the normative and descriptive accounts described above. This is that a science machine requires continuous input in the form of empirical results in order to function effectively.[8*] New data are constantly needed to correct misconceptions and to refute wrong hypotheses, as well as to refine concepts. As such, the science machine serves to overcome fundamental vagaries of human thought, especially a proclivity for making plausible inferences, which appears to be ineluctable. We know from history that it is also a means of overcoming corruption and fraud. From this perspective, the science machine acts as a kind of servo-mechanism. By operating within this kind of system, human intelligence becomes enhanced and amplified.

While this is essentially meant to be a descriptive account, it might also give rise to normative principles, especially ones having to do with evidence and belief. Or even, for want of a better term, normative-mechanical principles. As such, it might lead to philosophical discussions of science that are less ethereal in character than those in the classical literature because the latter only treat the logic of propositions and not the data stream that guides the discourse.

At this point I suspect that some readers are feeling uneasy about the present discussion. They may be wondering whether any of this really pertains to "artificial intelligence" as they understand it. Well, the whole point of this book is to bring such understanding into question. And part of this effort involves overturning assumptions about what AI is. In fact, what this entire section implies is that AI is not something that has to do specifically with computers — that once one takes the proper computational perspective (which the computer revolution has allowed us to do for the first time), one can see that many innovations devised in the course of human history involve artificial intelligence in one way or another. That is, they involve the basic agents-in-a-network organization amplified with various artifacts and 'artificial' methodologies.

*

A related topic that I want to touch on briefly is the use of computer programs in mathematics as an aid in proving theorems. The most famous example is the proof of the four-color problem in graph theory: that, given a "map", i.e. a surface divided into subareas of any shape and size, four colors are sufficient to color it so that no two areas with a common border have the same color.[9*] The basic strategy of the proof was to generate an "unavoidable set" of configurations, meaning that at least one of them had to appear in any map, and then to show that each of these configurations was "reducible", meaning that it could not appear in a "smallest-sized counterexample".[10] (If this could be done, this would show that there was no such counterexample, so all maps could be colored with four colors.) Proving reducibility involved checking all possible colorings, a lengthy but fairly routine procedure. Moreover, the set used in the first version of the proof was quite large, comprising 1,936 configurations.[11*] Because of these conditions, this part of the proof could only be worked out with the help of a computer program. The program, therefore, formed an integral part of the overall proof.

More recently, some important proofs in the field of combinatorics have involved SAT solvers, i.e. programs that determine whether a Boolean formula such as

$$(p \vee q) \wedge (\neg p \vee r) \wedge (p \vee q \vee \neg r)$$

has a solution, i.e. an assignment of TRUE and FALSE to the logical variables in the formula (here, p, q and r) that makes the formula true overall. (If it does have a solution, it is called "satisfiable"; otherwise it is "unsatisfiable".) This can be done because at certain points in the basic proof, the proposition in question can be translated into a Boolean formula, and if this formula is satisfiable then that proposition is true. To establish whether the formula is satisfiable, which is very difficult for human beings to do except for very simple formulae, the formula is encoded (automatically) and given to a SAT solver. So SAT solving by a computer program becomes an integral part of the overall proof.

Now, the point of bringing these examples into the discussion is that I would not call them genuine examples of HAI — and it is interesting to consider why they are not. The reason is that they don't in and of themselves constitute intelligent machines, or artifacts, in which human beings are embedded as a kind of computing element. Instead, they function as aids for human intelligence, so under the present conception of intelligence they are essentially examples of HI. However, there is the added twist that in this case HI uses computational tools, which because they form part of the inference process deserve to be called AI, to find a solution.

Software put to use in this fashion can also be contrasted with automatic theorem provers, which of course are examples of AI. That is, the latter systems, while constructed by human beings and existing (like all forms of intelligence) within an extended network of agents, operate as autonomous agents to produce specific outputs, which are valid proofs of mathematical theorems.

*

The next category to be considered has sometimes been referred to as "collective intelligence" or "Group Minds", although these terms have been used in connection with other phenomena as well.[12]

In line with the present discussion, here I will use the term "Group Intelligence". Of course, from what has been said already it can be inferred that there is a sense in which all intelligence is really group intelligence. But a distinction can still be made — related to performance at a specific point in time. For example, both Kasparov and Deep Blue acted as single agents during a match between them, even if each of them was also part of a large network of agents. In these cases, the problem-solving activity is agent-centered.

In contrast to this, the key feature of group intelligence as defined here is that the output of the network, which constitutes the material basis of its "intelligence", is not expressed by any single agent. Instead, it is expressed by the network as a whole.

As already indicated, the present conception is more precise and delimited than the usual conceptions of group minds, group cognition, etc. Past discussions of this subject often conflate group intelligence (as defined here) with social organization per se as well as with individuals functioning within groups.

So, for example, group intelligence as I am describing it does not include notions like "collective IQ", when this refers to an overall increase in IQ as a function of being in a group.[13] In fact, this idea is essentially the same as the concept of human intelligence presented in Chapter 6. Within the scheme presented in this book, the examples discussed by these authors represent a potential amplification of HI as it has existed ever since the dawn of human culture, rather than a new and distinct form of intelligence.

Nor am I referring to social groups, in particular those whose members identify themselves as belonging to a certain group. Although such groups may provide a framework for group intelligence in the present sense, a social group as such does not constitute an instance of this category of intelligence in and of itself. Moreover, in many cases, these organizations may be better thought of as amplifying individual HI (for instance, a chess club) — so we are again in the realm of HI as described in Chapter 6.

Turning to actual examples, perhaps the best-known (and in some ways the most striking) case of group intelligence is a market-based economic system. This was clearly pointed out by F. A. Hayek who was also among the first to understand that a free market is a kind of computational system.[14] Here, each agent acts as a component of the system, i.e. he or she performs actions within a distributed network of agents. Hence in this capacity an agent is analogous to a transistor or circuit inside a computer. In this case, the output of the network-as-a-whole is the efficient allocation of resources and the balance of supply and demand.

The example just given has basically to do with the distribution of goods and services. A related example is product production. Here, I will draw on a famous essay that illustrates the point very well: "I, Pencil" by Leonard Read.[15]

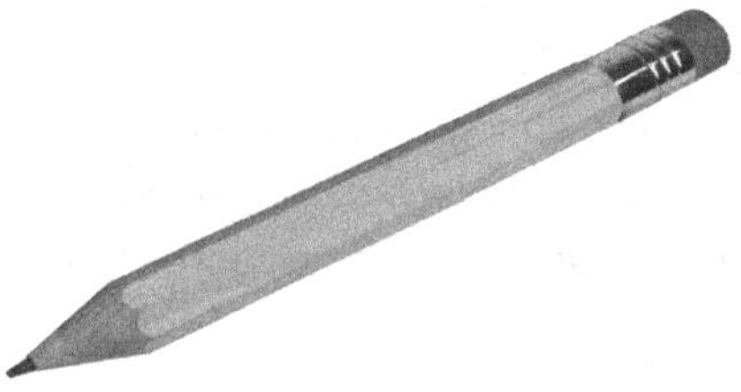

The product that Read deals with is the ordinary lead pencil, like the one depicted above. In Read's words,

> "… I am seemingly so simple. … Yet not a single person on the face of the earth knows how to make me." Yet "there are about one and one-half billion of my kind produced in the U.S.A. every year."

The author takes the reader through the many steps involved in the production of this item. He also shows how each step represents a confluence of knowledge. (In fact, there is a remarkable similarity here to the situation of Kasparov and Deep Blue, who also represent confluences of knowledge.) Here, I will list the basic steps with some commentary about them from Read's essay.

In the first step, cedar is harvested.

> "contemplate all the saws and trucks and rope and countless other gear used in harvesting and carting — and all the knowledge that went into these instruments"

Then the logs are shipped to a mill.

> “imagine the individuals who make flat cars and rails and railroad engines and who construct and install the communication systems incidental thereto”

Then there is the millwork, where the logs are cut “into small pencil-length slats”, and the slats are “kiln dried and tinted”, “waxed and kiln dried again”.

> “How many skills went into the making of the tint and the kilns, into supplying the heat, the light and power, the belts, the motors ... ?”

Then there is the leading. The “graphite [used in this step] is mined in Ceylon [Sri Lanka]”.

> “Consider these miners and those who make their many tools and the makers of the paper sacks in which the graphite is shipped and those who make the string that ties the sacks and those who put them aboard ships and those who make the ships”
>
> “And we haven’t yet considered the lacquer (“do you know all the ingredients of lacquer?”) and the brass band and the labeling.”

Clearly this is a case where many kinds of intelligent agents work together to create a final product. But that output comes from the group action rather than a single agent, so it is quite properly called group intelligence.

Another example, which I find less interesting in this context, is collective decision making, such as decisions made by voting. Basically, this is a statistical summary of individual decisions rather than group computation as exhibited by the previous examples. So while it qualifies by definition as an example of group intelligence, it represents a rudimentary form at best.

Returning for a moment to HI and the subject of knowledge traditions, I am claiming this is HI rather than G(H)I — because it manifests itself as intelligence in individual agents. Admittedly, however, the lines are blurred. In particular, there is often an element of collaboration. Moreover, the maintenance and extension of knowledge traditions requires the training of agents, often extensive training, and this must be carried out by other agents.

*

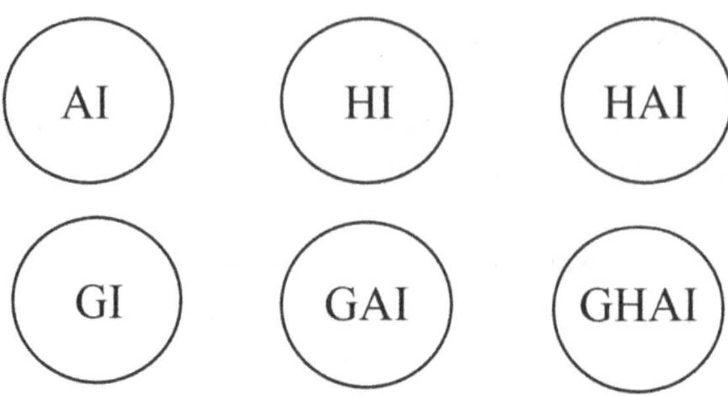

Figure 7.2. Various forms of intelligence as indicated by the present discussion.

An even more interesting example is the evolution of language, which is clearly the product of a network of agents, and not any particular individual, as the following passage (from LeBon) points out:

> "What, for instance, can be more complicated, more logical, more marvellous than a language? Yet whence can this admirably organised production have arisen, except it be the outcome of the unconscious genius of crowds? The most learned academics, the most esteemed grammarians can do no more than note down the laws that govern languages; they would be utterly incapable of creating them."[16]

In this case, also, there is no real question of intentionality involved. LeBon seems to have it right when he refers to the "unconscious genius" of what I am referring to as the group mind.

This example also shows, once again, the power of thinking about such phenomena in computational terms. Only by looking at these various phenomena in these terms can we see the similarities in the partly conscious rise and growth of scientific research and the largely unconscious development of language.

*

To summarize the discussion in this chapter, we seem to have the beginnings of a classification, which could be diagrammed as shown in Figure 7.2. (Some of these categories have not been named specifically, but the meaning should be clear; "A" always stands for artificial, "H" for human, "G" for group, and "I" for intelligence.)

This diagram does not give any indication of relations between the groupings. For now, it does not strike me as necessary to speculate about this. The important point is that each instance in each category is also an instance of agents operating within a network.

*

A final point concerns the existence of "web intelligence". How does this fit in here? Is this a separate kind of intelligence, a special kind of group intelligence? I would say that the Web is better described as a communication medium or framework for creating intelligence networks. (So it has the same status as the biological frameworks, such as multi-celled organisms, mentioned in Chapter 6.) Therefore, I don't think it entails a different kind of intelligence on par with the ones described in this chapter or included in the diagram above. But it certainly raises interesting issues, which, however, will not be delved into at this point.

In this chapter, we have encountered many forms of intelligence, all of which can be comprehended within a computational framework. — The computer has clarified many facets of the world and especially of life — from genomics to jurisprudence.

I hope by now the reader will have grasped that artificial intelligence is really nothing new. In fact, we have been creating artificial intelligence for centuries — in the form of economic, legal and political systems.

Endnotes

1. There are numerous good introductions to the field of decision analysis. A classic text is R. D. Luce & H. Raiffa, *Games and Decisions*, New York: Dover, 1985 (original 1957). More recently the first author has penned another volume: R. D. Luce, *Utility of Gains and Losses*, Mahwah, NJ: Lawrence Earlbaum, 2000. A major compendium of utility theory is S. Barbera, P. J. Hammond & C. Seidl, *Handbook of Utility Theory* (2 volumes), Dordrecht: Kluwer, 1998.
2. See, for example, D. E. Bell, H. Raiffa & A. Tversky, "Descriptive, normative, and prescriptive interactions in decision making", In: D. E. Bell, H. Raiffa & A. Tversky, *Decision Making: Descriptive, Normative, and Prescriptive Interactions*, Cambridge: Cambridge University, 1988, pp. 9–30.
3. For examples of 'classical' philosophy of science see H. Reichenbach, *The Rise of Scientific Philosophy*, Berkeley: University of California, 1951 and Ernest Nagel, *The Structure of Science*, New York: Harcourt, Brace & World, 1961.

4. Ludwik Fleck, *Genesis and Development of a Scientific Fact*. University of Chicago, 1979 (original, 1935); Thomas Kuhn, *The Structure of Scientific Revolutions*. 1st edition. University of Chicago, 1962)
5. A nice summary account of the problematic character of Kuhn's ideas can be found in a review of a longer work of criticism, (*Criticism and the Growth of Knowledge*, I. Lakatos and A. Musgrave, editors, Cambridge: Cambridge University, 1970), that appeared in the journal Science: D. Shapere, "The paradigm concept", *Science*, 1971, 172: 706–709.
6. Here, I will say something about what to me is the chief oddity of the Kuhnian view of scientific discovery. Kuhn makes much of the difference between "normal" and "revolutionary" science. He refers to the former as essentially "puzzle solving". (In the 1970 work just cited he also takes Popper to task for not recognizing that the latter's account of scientific discovery applies largely or wholly to revolutionary or paradigm-changing efforts.) Now, based on my reading and my experience as an experimental scientist, Kuhn's depiction of normal versus revolutionary science seems hopelessly misguided. This is because all basic scientific research involves discovery in one form or another (just as Popper assumed). That's what separates it from applied areas like engineering, where one indeed engages in puzzle-solving within an assumed framework such as Newtonian physics or relational database theory. Take, for example Herschel's discovery of infrared radiation. By itself it didn't threaten any paradigm; but it certainly wasn't "puzzle-solving" (what, exactly, was the puzzle to be solved here?). Instead, the result was an important extension of our knowledge about the world. Also, Stephen Gray's discovery of electrical conduction using the simplest of materials or Dufay's demonstration that electrification was a general property of matter were not examples of puzzle-solving.

   For another example, consider all the work in molecular biology over the past 30 years. Consider the discovery of a new signaling molecule, e.g. RAS signaling. Was this just "puzzle-solving"? Wasn't this an important, nay, fundamental, extension into the unknown? Well, in my book that's hardly a matter of mere "puzzle-solving" — although I can't see that it was paradigm-shattering either. And even when someone is simply trying to extend basic ideas, for example in extending ideas about adaptation and speciation by studying a form of grass that can live on soil heavily polluted with lead or copper, the basic process is still one of discovery. After all, this line of research necessarily began with a discovery — that a given variety of grass could live in soil that other species and even other members of the same species could not survive in. No one foresaw this particular situation; hence it certainly didn't begin with a puzzle to be solved. After the initial discovery, came attempts to elucidate the phenomenon. This subsequent process of elucidating the basis of the capacity could be considered a kind of "puzzle-solving", but it still involved reaching into the unknown. And the point is that this is a cardinal feature of basic research, whether it is 'paradigm changing' or not. The whole thrust of basic scientific research is not to solve puzzles but to extend knowledge and to firm up the evidential base.

Moreover, the banality that appears within this enterprise — and there is pedestrian research to be sure — is not so much due to puzzle-solving as asking questions and producing findings that are not terribly interesting because they don't make significant discoveries. An example that comes to mind is the mass of research in quantitative genetics, including behavior genetics, on heritability. So a given study might show that a certain species-typical behavior in rats has a 50% heritability. In addition to being of limited interest in itself (what if it had been 65%?), this tells us nothing about the causal factors underlying the behavior. In other cases the studies are of limited value because the methodology is inadequate; for example, prior to Mendel many studies of heredity based on crosses between strains gave confusing and contradictory results because the investigators were unaware of the need to have pure lines to begin with.

I have the impression that Kuhn himself did not have much actual experience in empirical investigation. Moreover, he seems to have been mesmerized to an extent by the cuteness of his formulation. (Of course, there are definite grades of importance and degrees of originality within or between streams of research, as well as research that simply extends our ideas versus that which causes major upheavals. But I see no clear dichotomy of the sort posited by Kuhn.) At any rate, I don't think that the Kuhnian formulation really does justice to the cumulative growth of genuine scientific knowledge. Instead, it partakes of the cocktail party aspect of discussions of the nature of science that go on apart from the progress of actual research.

7. A. Lightman & O. Gingerich, "When do anomalies begin?" *Science*, 1991, 255: 690–695.
8. These remarks apply to sciences that examine the physical world rather than sciences of the artificial such as computer science, where many of the results can be derived deductively.
9. The border requirement avoids situations where two areas meet at one point; in such cases both can receive the same color. Without this restriction, maps could be constructed that require any number of colors.
10. There are many accounts of the four-color problem, among them the *Scientific American* article by K. Appel and W. Haken, the authors of the first correct proof (October, 1977, vol. 236, no. 4, pp. 108–121) and R. Wilson's *Four Colors Suffice* (Princeton, 2002).
11. A later version of the proof managed to reduce the size of the unavoidable set to 633 reducible configurations.
12. Classical discussions of the 'group mind' idea are Gustav Le Bon's *The Crowd* (1895; Eng. transl., T. Fisher Unwin, 1896) and William McDougall's *The Group Mind* (Cambridge; Cambridge University, 1920). More recently there has been (as so often happens these days) a raft of books and articles on this and related subjects. A useful summary work is C. List & P. Pettit, *Group Agency*, Oxford: Oxford University, 2011).

13. P. Lévy, *Collective Intelligence: Mankind's Emerging World in Cyberspace*, New York: Basic Books, 1999; H. Jenkins, *Convergence Culture: Where Old and New Media Collide*, New York: New York University, 2006.
14. F. A. Hayek, "The use of knowledge in society", *American Economic Review*, 1945, 35: 519–530.
15. Leonard Read, "I, Pencil", *The Freeman*, December 1958, pp. 32–37.
16. LeBon, op. cit., p. v–vi.

8

Implications for Some Perennial AI Themes

The conception of intelligence that was presented in the previous chapter has implications for some perennial topics and themes in AI, which will be discussed in this chapter. The first is well known to anyone who has read anything about AI. The others are less well known, but, in my view, some are far more significant.

Some of the discussion in this chapter does not speak directly to the ideas presented in Chapter 6. However, I have included it because it should give the reader a better understanding of the field as a whole. (And in this case, it must ultimately be relevant to any general discussion of the nature of intelligence as well as the endeavor to create artifacts that exhibit intelligent behavior.)

The Turing Test

At the beginning of the computer era, the mathematician Alan Turing wrote a paper on the question of whether we will ever be able to ascribe the capacity for thinking to computers.[1] After dismissing the original question, "Can machines think?" as too vague to admit a proper answer (actually he called the question "meaningless"), he proposed a game (that he called an "imitation game") that could be played in lieu of a direct assault on the problem. In the usual version of the game, a person and a computer communicate with an interrogator through some medium that prevents the latter from perceiving the contestants directly.[2*] The interrogator must pose questions so as to evoke answers from each contestant that he can use to deduce which contestant is human and which is a machine. If a sufficient number of interrogators fail to choose correctly, then we can conclude that the machine is operating at a commensurate level as human beings in the same situation.

As Turing noted, this "question and answer method seems to be suitable for introducing almost any one of the fields of human endeavour that we wish to include."[3] Thus, it allows the same wide-ranging given-and-take that is possible with human beings.

In addition to engendering a seemingly endless stream of commentary from philosophers and computer scientists, Turing's ideas have inspired an actual contest known as the Loebner competition, after its founder and sponsor. More recently, dissatisfaction with the original test and its concrete realization in the Loebner competitions has led to an alternative proposal for testing machine intelligence called the Winograd test.[4*]

The reader will probably have noted the resemblence of the Turing Test to the idea of conversational thresholds that was mentioned briefly in Chapter 6. To the extent that that idea has real merit, it suggests that Turing was strangely perspicacious in introducing his game as a means of probing the question of machine intelligence. However, there is one important difference. The Turing Test as it is usually described does not involve independent initiation of conversations by the artifact; instead it just reacts. And to my mind this difference is critical.[5*]

In addition, the situation proposed is so artificial (!) in comparison with practical applications of intelligence, that it seems to me unlikely that endeavors along these lines will ever bear fruit. Especially in its concrete manifestations, the Test seems essentially irrelevant and may even be an obfuscation of the genuine issues raised by developments in this area. In some ways, it is therefore a red herring.[6*] But at the same time, given its connection with some fundamental issues such as autonomy, it may be possible to derive something of genuine value from the lead Turing has given us.

There are, it seems to me, two lines of argument to be considered. The first concerns the adequacy of this particular approach to assessing computer intelligence. After all, why should human beings be particularly good at making such decisions? Evidently, there are vague notions of human social skills in assessing personal qualities through interaction, but whether such skills should extend to the present case is not at all clear. The second, and to my mind more important question, is whether this kind of assessment is useful in some ultimate sense. Isn't it more important to understand what is involved in various forms of intelligent behavior? From a scientific or objective point of view, it is then immaterial whether behavior that is judged to be intelligent is carried out by human Agent X or computer Agent Y. And since the present perspective doesn't admit the existence of agents outside a network of such agents, this would seem to render the entire exercise meaningless.

Another problem is that the challenge of passing the Turing Test can devolve into yet another circumscribed goal, much like beating a human being at chess. Hence, Hsu's comment about the nature of the chess contest is also apposite in the present context. Supposing that challenge can be met successfully, what will be the ultimate outcome? Will it lead anywhere, or will it be just another intriguing dead end?

In addition, a compelling argument can be made that the Turing Test is best viewed as a test of human rather than artificial intelligence. That is, a human being observes a kind of charade, a simulacrum of human intelligence. The question is, can he detect this? From this perspective, it becomes clear that the test has more to do with social psychology than computer science.[7]

This aspect of the Turing Test has been commented on before, notably by Hayes and Ford in a 1995 essay entitled, "Turing Test Considered Harmful".[8] They note that the outcome of the "imitation game" "depends crucially on how clever, knowledgeable, and insightful the judge is". Moreover, they argue that a successful player of this game would probably need to 'psych out' the judge, cast doubt on the other player's humanness, etc. But in this case, the game-playing elements have undermined the original purpose of the test. They also note that what counts as 'being humanlike' changes over time.

All this is borne out by the experience of the Loebner competition, which began in 1991. This competition was established at the behest of an industrialist, in order to realize the Turing test in practice. It was organized by a group of academics and professionals, who spent about two years hammering out the procedures to be followed. One of the organizers had this to say about their efforts:

> "The intricacies of setting up a real Turing Test that would ultimately yield a legitimate winner were enormous. Small points were occasionally debated for months without clear resolution."[9]
>
> "Turing's brilliant paper had not gone far enough to yield practical procedures. In fact, we realized only slowly that his paper hadn't even specified an outcome that could be interpreted meaningfully."[10]

It is interesting and to my mind extremely significant that realizing Turing's proposal in practice was so fraught with difficulty. This is typically what happens when one transitions from arguments and discourse on a topic to trying to examine it properly in the actual, physical world, and it should reinforce one's skepticism regarding the power of mere argumentation to settle any question that pertains to the latter.

It is also significant that the first winner of the competition was a program that engaged in "whimsical conversation", as the following example shows:[11]

> Judge: Hello! You seem to be feeling quite witty today.
>
> Program: Hello, judge, what is your mood today? happy? sad? ready for some fun? Hello — how's the weather up there today? Let's talk about psychology!
>
> Judge: It has been a long day! Now I think I'm ready for some fun. The weather isn't very pleasant today. Do you have any jokes that could lift the clouds?
>
> Program: Everybody talks about the weather, but nobody seems to do much about it. Why do you need to tell me now you think you're ready for some fun? Groannnnnn..................
>
> Judge: Well you did ask me!
>
> Program: Now you really have outdone yourself in asking stupid things! Woof.... wooof.. .. woof.... Why do you think I did ask you?
>
> Judge: Do you find insults to be humorous? I think maybe you asked me because you don't really know me and are trying to break the ice.
>
> Program: Is that the real reason? Was that whimsical enough for you? Oh, I find insults to be humorous?

Five of the ten judges ranked this program as human (although neither this nor the other programs outranked the two human respondents overall). The key was that by entering it under the category of whimsical conversation, the program didn't need to stay on topic or even be completely coherent in order to appear able to carry on a conversation and therefore pass the test. This certainly seems to bear out what was said earlier about the nature of the Turing test in actual practice.

Another significant problem is that in practice detecting a 'charade' of this sort (and, more importantly, determining its nature) typically requires extensive examination of the system (i.e. the kind of unpacking that I have tried to do in earlier chapters). Examining the output is not enough — one must dig into the system itself. This is because such 'detection' involves understanding the system at greater depth. Two examples from the 1980's show this clearly:

- Clancey's investigation of MYCIN in the 1980's in association with the GUIDON program[12]
- Woods' examination of properties of semantic networks, particularly in his well know paper, "What's in a link?"[13]

MYCIN was an important early example of production (rule-based) systems. Its purpose was to diagnose diseases from symptoms and prescribe antibiotics, and according to various tests it did this quite well.

Now, the original goal of Clancey's GUIDON program was to make "use of MYCIN's explanation facility for a tutorial setting". In the course of his work, Clancey came up against the fact that the rule representation used in MYCIN was 'overloaded' with respect to the functions it was performing. In addition, various orderings, especially of the hypotheses in a rule's premise greatly affected the system's output. Thus, various strategies were introduced into the system although they weren't an explicit part of the representation.

Speaking more generally, Clancey discovered that some rules were true inference rules, while others were what he called "task rules". In addition, he found that "procedural knowledge appears in almost every rule". Here is an example of what Clancey called a task rule[14]:

RULE092
IF (1) gather information about cultures taken from the patient and therapy he is receiving
(2) determine if the organisms growing on cultures require therapy
(3) consider circumstantial evidence for additional organisms that therapy should cover
THEN determine the best therapy recommendation

As Clancey said, "this is a procedure, not a logical conjunction". An example of an inference rule is[15]:

RULE535 ("alcoholic rule")
IF (1) the infection which requires therapy is meningitis
(2) only circumstantial evidence is available for this case
(3) the type of meningitis is bacterial
(4) the age of the patient is greater than 17 years, and
(5) the patient is an alcoholic
THEN
there is evidence that the organisms which might be causing the infection are diplococcus-pneumoniae or e. coli

However, even here the rule is not functioning in a strictly logical fashion (as advertised). In Clancey's words, in this case the "first three clauses … the context clauses, really control the order in which goals are pursued, just as in a task rule".[16]

In hindsight, it is clear that the careful analyses of early AI systems by people like Woods and Clancey, together with the analysis (and polemics) of Hayes and other champions of first-order logic as a representation language (see below), effected a fundamental change in the character of AI research. It led to what I will call the ascendency of the Neats.[17*]

Neats and Scruffies

> There are two types of people in this world,
> the simple-minded and the muddle-headed.
>
> A. N. Whitehead[18]

This is an old distinction, which is probably unfamiliar to most contemporary readers, and which will seem dated to those who do recognize it, being part of the parlance of the 70's and 80's. I will argue that it is still very much with us, and in fact it will always be with us.

Basically, the distinction refers to certain differences in the kinds of activities done within the field of AI, reflecting differences in ultimate concerns. Scruffies are more hands-on, less concerned with formalization than creating systems that produce interesting output. Neats, on the other hand, are the formalizers who strive to formulate clear definitions of critical concepts in AI, and who are concerned with developing systems with well-defined forms of representation, or "semantics". (An example of a system with ill-defined semantics is the MYCIN system discussed in the previous section. There, the rule syntax was found to be associated with a medley of different actions or operations.)

We can see why it may be necessary to have both Neats and Scruffies by considering the limitations of each in turn. First, what's wrong with Scruffies?

Simply put, Scruffies often work on poorly defined problems, leading to flawed conclusions, and thence to inflated claims and even self-delusion. In addition, the systems that they build use representations that are problematic (without a well-formed semantics), systems such as AM and MYCIN. We have just seen some very good examples of this in Clancey's analysis of the latter program, and earlier we saw much the same thing in the case of AM.

And what's wrong with Neats?

I would argue that the biggest danger is 'missing the big picture', i.e. failing to get hold of the real problem. This is seen most clearly in a tendency to formalize trivial problems or properties. More insidious is the tendency to trivialize significant problems, which are then adroitly formalized. In this case one comes up against the Illusion of Completeness, where the completeness of the representation blinds one to the gaps and omissions. One could even say that Neats are a special species of Flatlanders, unable to see beyond the frameworks they devise.

This is related to the problem that Wittgenstein saw as central to philosophy — of "showing the fly the way out of the fly bottle". Note that given the Illusion of Completeness, in this case the fly doesn't even know it's in a bottle. So it's difficult to see how such a task can be done except in a scruffy fashion.

So how does all this fit within the framework described in the last chapter? In fact, it fits very nicely; with the ascendency of the Neats, people fit into a larger framework. Such a collective framework may be necessary if general principles are to emerge and not just intriguing pieces of software.

As I have said, the problematical character of systems like AM is one of the main reasons for the ascendency of the Neats. In some ways, though, this has amounted to 'taking the easy way out'. As a result, contemporary AI has a somewhat schizoid character. One the one hand there are hordes of Neats doing their own Neat stuff. On the other there is still the occasional grandiose AI system built in the same spirit as classical AI systems. But this is likely just another stage of a long historical process.

The ascendency just mentioned was, I think, inevitable and is not to be decried. It reflected the growing maturity of the field. Because of their inadequacies, the Scruffies are always doomed to eventually occupy a somewhat marginal position.

So it is likely that the Scruffy role as a full-fledged occupation is indeed a thing of the past. Nowadays Scruffies have to work within certain boundaries that have been largely established by the Neats. Nonetheless, as I have argued above, there will always be a need for some degree of scruffiness. AI (and science in general) must always include a certain amount of trial-and-error.

I think it's safe to say that the distinction between Neats and Scruffies really does reflect issues that are fundamental. As a result, Neats and Scruffies are embroiled in a kind of eternal conflict,

> but reconciled among the stars
>
> T. S. Eliot[19]

The Great Logic Debate

Early in its development, AI faced a basic question: Should logic be considered as the basic form of representation in artificial intelligence? Is logic sufficient for this task?

As always there were a variety of opinions. Roughly speaking, one got a different answer to these questions depending on whether the researcher was a Neat or a Scruffy:

The Neats said, "Yes!"

The Scruffies said, "No!"

In the 1960s and 70s, when the Scruffies were predominant, there was a general belittlement of logic in the AI community. Along with this came the development of other forms of representation that were meant to be alternatives. These included frames, where entities in the world were represented as record-like structures with "slots" for the various features, production rules, which are sets of if-then statements, which can be triggered to perform sequences of inferences, and semantic nets, which are node-and-arc systems where nodes generally represent concepts and arcs represent relations.

In all cases these systems had a network character, although they differed in the way that this entered the representation — for production rules it was implicit in the content of the rules, which could then be connected on the basis of similarity in content; for semantic nets, it was explicit in the edges or "links" between concept-nodes. It was perhaps this network character that made it seem, for a while, that these forms of representation had features that 'went beyond' ordinary logic.

During the 1970s, however, the tide began to turn. Patrick Hayes and others argued that:

- The alternative formulations could all be expressed in first-order logic,
- Some kind of first-order logic was fully adequate in all cases studied.[20,21*,22*]

In addition, analyses such as those by Clancey and Woods discussed above convinced many people that AI systems needed to be based on well-defined formalisms, i.e. formalisms with elements and combinations of elements whose meaning was clear and consistent. In ideal cases at least, this would allow researchers to construct rigorous tests of validity in order to evaluate these systems properly.

Moreover, as Hayes took pains to point out, in promoting alternative systems, many researchers failed to distinguish between the means of implementing knowledge-based systems and formal representations.

For my money, Hayes won the debate over representation. However, I don't think he or anyone else fully resolved the debate over the adequacy of logic in AI. Because I think that the real problems concerning adequacy (or inadequacy) lie in a different direction.

Hays and others said: You can use logic as a general representation; it covers all the other kinds of representation. The critical phrase here is "you can use". Loosely speaking (which in this context is oddly appropriate), this is where the Neats slip up and the Scruffies slip in.

A critical assumption made by logicists is that for any AI system there is a well-defined system that is functionally equivalent. And in many cases, including perhaps most of the classical AI systems, this is indeed true. But it seems to me that all this depends critically on being able to specify the problem to be solved in very precise terms. And in fact, to a very large degree the activity of researchers in AI and related fields involves specifying problems to which they engineer solutions. But this is not something that is ever done by the systems themselves (although, interestingly, despite all its deficiencies AM truly was a baby-step in that direction). And it certainly appears that as long as we remain in the Realm of the Neats, this will be the situation.

A related issue is the distinction between declarative and procedural forms of representation. Basically, "declarative" in this context refers to knowledge in the form of specifications in some language. "Procedural" refers to knowledge that is implicit in certain procedures. So for example, knowing how to ride a bicycle involves some form of implicit representation of the various forces that come into play in this situation so that one can maintain his balance on the bike while going forward. If knowledge of this sort was written down in formulas, this would be a declarative representation.

This distinction is characterized in a well-known text on artificial intelligence in this way:

> "There are two major ways we can think about a machine having knowledge about its world. Although our ideas about the distinction between these two points of view are still being clarified, it seems that, in some of our machines, the knowledge is implicit; in other machines, it is represented explicitly."[23]

According to the authors, a program that does matrix inversion is an example of procedural knowledge, while a "tabular database of salary data" is an example of declarative knowledge. Regarding the latter, they say:

> "... explicit representations of knowledge are those that *can be interpreted* as making declarative statements. We call knowledge represented in this way declarative knowledge because it is contained in declarations about the world. Such statements typically are stored in symbol structures that are accessed by the procedures that use this knowledge."[24] (emphasis added)

Since logical expressions are clearly declarative in nature, the argument that logic is a sufficient form of representation in AI is therefore also an argument that declarative knowledge is sufficient.

Although it originated in computer science, the distinction between declarative and procedural knowledge has been taken up by people in cognitive psychology and neuropsychology, particularly in connection with learning and memory.[25] A key empirical finding is that patients with neurological damage, resulting in failures to recall or recognize stimuli that they have been presented with earlier, can still learn certain sensory-motor tasks including some that involve the same stimuli. For example, these people can learn to read words written in reverse although they cannot recognize whether or not these words were presented earlier. Subsequently, similar dissociations have been demonstrated in normal, intact subjects during the course of learning. For example, people can learn to anticipate the next position that a stimulus will appear even when they cannot recognize or describe the pattern of presentation.

Now, we know from Wittgenstein's arguments about meaning and language that in this case the procedural/declarative distinction is quite problematic. Among other things, his discussion shows that the 'declarativeness' of human language is in many ways illusory. Indeed, the whole point of introducing the notion of language games was to explore the idea of meaning as part of language-in-use, and this, in turn, implies that there is a significant procedural side to meaning expressed through language.[26*]

So what does this imply in regard to the problem at hand? In the first place, it seems pretty clear that psychologists and neuroscientists are using the terms "declarative" and "procedural" in a somewhat different way than AI researchers. In the former case the terms refer to what appear to be distinct memory systems, one of which involves language and reproduction of specific items of information. Of course, the fact that there are two systems instead of one is very interesting and does bear on the overall interpretation of the difference between two kinds of knowledge, but it doesn't necessarily imply that there is any deficiency in logic that would prevent it from representing both — and this is the question that AI researchers are grappling with.

The distinction we are grappling with here may be that of an account of how an information system actually works as opposed to the use of logic to represent the information in the system. In this case then, logic is not necessarily restricted to those forms of information that have been called declarative, but can be used across the board. In fact, there is a stream of work in AI concerned with modeling actions and processes, and as part of this work forms of "procedural logic" have been proposed, i.e. formalized systems of inference that deal with processes.[27]

All this brings into question the idea that the declarative-procedural distinction has to do with fundamentally different kinds of information as opposed to differences in how information is to be used — or that only certain kinds of information are amenable to some form of logical representation. In this vein, I will suggest an alternative hypothesis. This is that the distinction in question has to do with requirements for communication. In order for information to be communicated effectively, it has to be packaged in a way that it can be transmitted and received on the other end. One method for doing this is to discretize the information. This may be necessary if items of information are to be combined in various ways. Moreover, it is likely that the requisite information processing will need to be done by specialized modules.

In the case of human language, it comes as no surprise that the discretization is one that we can easily comprehend — since that was its purpose in the first place. And it is also not surprising that in this case there are specialized memory systems associated with language, and that their substrates are different from the substrates for, say, motor learning.

This argument may also bear on a related controversy that pits connectionism (in the form of "neural networks") against symbolic representation. In fact, in some ways this seems like a variant of the procedural-declarative controversy. Thus, the main problem with a 'purely' connectionist system — as it is presently conceived — may be that it will have difficulty communicating. (There may also be problems of self-reflection.)

This argument also bears on philosophical issues concerning the adequacy of logic, including logical accounts of epistemology such as logical atomism. It is the discretization of declarative knowledge in the form of language that allowed people to devise systems of logic in the first place. This may be due to the fact that the systems involved (in the human brain) had a suitably discretized structure, which allowed further applications such as logical formalisms. So perhaps it all comes down to flexibility of application.

These issues can be further clarified if we relate them to the ideas of the last chapter. To do this, I will return to the work of Clancey and Woods that was discussed earlier and say something more about what it was that they were doing. This is particularly relevant because, as noted earlier, their work was one of the motivations for more formal approaches to AI. Essentially, they were trying to explicate certain AI systems and even general forms of representation that were then in use. As noted, they found that in these systems, the meaning of the basic elements was often ill-defined, since the same elements (e.g. rule antecedents) had different meanings in different contexts. Overcoming these difficulties means developing 'cleaner' forms of representation, and one approach is to use the method of formal semantics already developed in logic, so that each term has a single referent.

Now, putting aside questions of adequacy of this logicist program for developing a proper science of AI, what is the purpose of all this? Is it not ease of explication — by human beings? In other words, the main aim of the logicist program is to ensure that human developers know what they have done when they have built an AI system, and to be able to communicate this to others. Hence, once again, we see that one cannot separate the evolution of a logicist program from the inextricable relationship between human and artificial intelligence.

Finally, there is one respect in which the 'insufficiency of logic' has always been recognized. This is simply because problem solving requires a multiple deductive process know as "search". Because in most situations of real interest, the number of possibilities (i.e. the combinatorics of the situation) is so great that logical inferences need to be guided. To take an apposite example, automatic theorem proving generally involves "proof plans", i.e. plans for how to search the space of possibilities in order to find the appropriate propositions from which a correct proof can be constructed.[28] And search plays a somewhat similar role in every other area of AI.

This has led to the current perspective where logic shares the stage with search. And this is also the present embodiment of the declarative/procedural debate. In this way, AI researchers have managed to formalize the procedural side of intelligence along with the declarative, at least with respect to certain kinds of problem solving.

Physical Symbol Systems and the Knowledge Level

In the 1970s and early 80s Newell and Simon attempted to lay down some general definitional principles for intelligent systems. A central plank of their proposal was that any intelligent system must be based on physical symbols organized into symbolic structures.[29] These structures had two basic features:

- They designated objects in the environment.
- They were interpretable within the system itself.

Generally speaking, the process of "interpretation" involves discriminating among symbolic expressions in order to behave appropriately (where "behavior" includes any kind of processing). These processes, along with the symbolic structures, made up what they called a "symbol system".

In one paper, Newell listed what he thought were the major requirements for an entity to be said to have a "mind" (i.e. have a requisite degree of intelligence).[30] These included the following functionalities (others involved origins and specific tie-ins with biology):

1. Behave as an (almost) arbitrary function of the environment (universality).
2. Operate in real time.
3. Exhibit rational, i.e., effective adaptive behavior.
4. Use vast amounts of knowledge about the environment.

5. Behave robustly in the face of error, the unexpected, and the unknown.
6. Use symbols (and abstractions).
7. Use (natural) language.
8. Exhibit self-awareness and a sense of self.
9. Learn from its environment.

An added stipulation was that these capacities should "be realizable as a physical system". Newell argued at some length that symbol systems as he and Simon had defined them were a necessary part of any system with mind-like properties.

Whether 'true' intelligence requires manipulation of symbols in ways envisaged by Newell and Simon is an interesting question, which we will come back to later in Chapter 10 in the discussion of various critics of AI. But for now I want to restrict the discussion to how all this is related to the present thesis.

Now, under the present interpretation of intelligence, one must include in the list above a capacity to communicate in a way that allows the transfer of knowledge between agents. This is, of course, implicit in the requirement for the use of a natural language, but I think the basic requirement is more general and at the same time limited in important ways with regard to what must be transferred. Thus, in many cases a combination of (symbolic) communication and individual learning is required for the transfer of what we would call knowledge.

Note that under the present hypothesis, communication is an essential requirement for intelligence. Thus, if intelligence resides within a network of agents, there must be means of communication, as noted in an earlier chapter. This requires some system of communication, and that in turn requires discretization of some sort. Hence, the present thesis seems to require (and if true to buttress) the symbol system hypothesis.

Although it doesn't bear directly on the concerns of this chapter, there is one other component of Newell's thesis that I will discuss briefly because of its intrinsic interest. This is the claim that some kind of working memory is necessary for such a system to function. This is certainly consistent with current views of human cognition, since one of the major developments in cognitive psychology over the past half-century has been the concept of working memory. Interestingly, there is also compelling evidence for such capacities in standard laboratory animals such as the domestic rats and pigeons. Considered in the light of the present argument, this suggests that these animals are working with a symbol system of some sort — despite the fact that they can't tell us about it.

A few years after the work on symbol structures first appeared, Newell introduced the idea of a "knowledge level" in computer organization, tying it to the prerequisites for artificial intelligence.[31] He began with the well-known fact that computer systems are organized hierarchically, according to a scheme like the one shown below.

He then proposed that AI systems should have a knowledge level located at the same level as computer configurations. This 'level' was characterized by having goals and 'knowledge' and acting in accordance with these. The 'knowledge' was actually stored in the symbol system located at the level just below.

As the article goes on to explain, the knowledge level and knowledge itself are not physically based levels in the sense of those shown in Figure 8.1. I think it would not be amiss to call it a virtual level, in which certain features located at the configuration level in the figure (which Newell does not specify very clearly) organize information in relation to the functioning of the agent-as-a-whole. The information utilized to this end is mostly at the symbol level, but it could conceivably include some information at other levels as well.

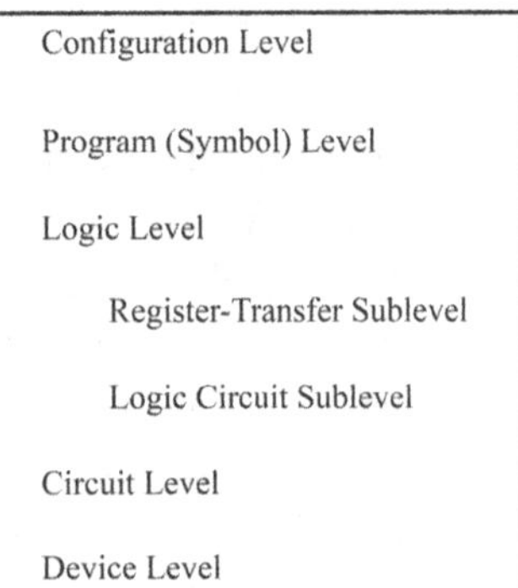

Configuration Level
Program (Symbol) Level
Logic Level
Register-Transfer Sublevel
Logic Circuit Sublevel
Circuit Level
Device Level

Figure 8.1. Hierarchical organization of a computer system. (After Newell, 1982, Figure 2).

One important contribution of this work was to introduce the notion of an agent as a basic form of organization for AI (although the study of agents as an distinct stream of research in AI did not emerge for another ten years). So, like the symbol system ideas, these ideas seem to dovetail very nicely with the present proposals. In fact, the ideas set forth in this article are really very close to the major thesis of this book. The big difference is that the present conception of intelligence refers it to agents operating within a network, while Newell's conception remains at the level of the individual agent. The former can, therefore, be thought of as placing the knowledge level in a larger context as well as positing further requirements for an intelligent system.

One implication of the newer conception involves the Great Debate between the symbolists (under the banner of Good Old-Fashioned AI) and the connectionist-neural-network people, which I have not yet alluded to, and which continues to this day. Although this debate is critical for evaluating the importance of the symbol systems idea (note that connectionist systems do not meet the second requirement above, that of interpretability), it is rather tangential to the thrust of the present thesis, which doesn't depend on how information is stored in a given agent. On the other hand, by emphasizing the necessity of communication among agents, it implies that some sort of symbol processing is necessary; otherwise, it is impossible to understand how knowledge can be communicated.

To close this section, I want to briefly discuss two phenomena that show the necessity for communication between agents as well as some form of symbol processing to support knowledge and intelligent action.

The first pertains to the growth of mathematics and logic. Now, it is a fact of overwhelming importance that major developments in mathematics and logic, by which I mean the emergence of new areas or systems, is always accomplished through the development of new notation. In other words, in these areas where exactness of thinking is paramount, new symbols always seem to be required, symbols that can be written down. For example, the basic notion of mathematical quantity could not be understood until continuous quantities could be represented discretely — by real numbers. Among many other advances, this allowed geometrical ideas to be expressed algebraically by translating mathematical "points" into lists of coordinate values.

The second pertains to the processes that underlie heredity. Here, it should be noted that transfer of information from parent to offspring in the form of genes (as well as epigenetic effects) can be viewed as an instance of communication. And, obviously, this communication involves a kind of symbol system. Moreover, work over the last fifty years has elucidated the way in which the symbol system is interpreted — in the form of genetic transcription and translation. This includes (in eukaryotic cells) complex systems of enhancers that seem to be a kind of logic network that can determine the conditions under which a given transcription will occur.

AI and the Commerce of Ideas

There is an old saw in this field that says, "AI exports its successes". What this means is that ideas that are really effective can usually, perhaps always, be extracted from their original context in an AI system and used in general computer science applications.

A classic example is the data structure known as the stack. In computer science a stack is a sequence of elements that can change dynamically with the addition or deletion of elements. At the same time, such changes always occur in well-defined ways, i.e. they follow strict rules. Suppose we start with a stack of one element.

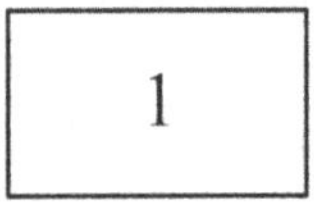

1

Then the first rule is that additional elements must be added on one end of the sequence (here, this will be end on the left side of the diagram). This is called the "top" of the stack. So if element 2 is added to our stack, and then element 5, the stack will look like this:

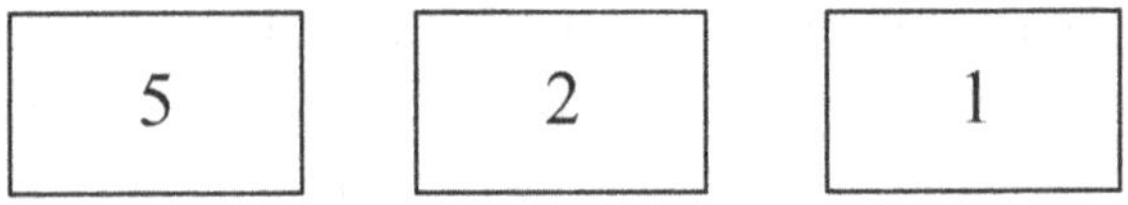

5	2	1

(This operation is called "pushing".) Now, in order to remove elements, we take them off the same end, i.e. off the top (an operation called "popping"). So if we wanted to remove element 2 and retain 5, we would have to pop two elements off the stack, and then push one back on, to give:

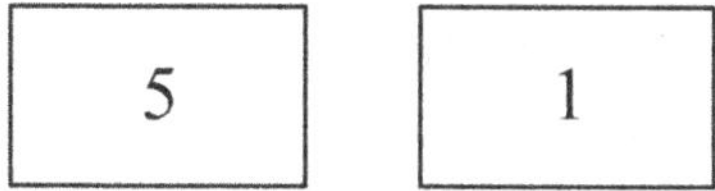

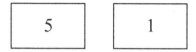

In case the reader is wondering why anyone would make these changes in such an inefficient way, it turns out that certain operations such as parsing sentences can be done very efficiently with a stack. (This is because certain basic structural features of sentences are reflected in stack operations.) Moreover, it has certain well-defined computational properties, which make it of great significance in practical and theoretical computer science.

However, the point that I want to make here is that this basic data structure, that is taught in every introductory computer science course on the subject of data structures, originated in the early work of Newell and Simon on the Logic Theorist, where lists of elements needed to be handled in an efficient, coherent manner in the course of proving theorems. So what was once part of AI is now basic computer science.

In a number of cases, algorithms originally devised within AI can be used in other contexts. An important example is the wide array of algorithms that fall under the heading of machine learning, including neural networks, decision trees, support vector machines and many others. Another is the discovery of a particular form of combinatorial optimization, captured by a representation called the constraint satisfaction problem. Since this is the major topic of the next chapter, I merely mention it here. But in the 1980s this idea, which had first been formulated in the 1970s began to be applied outside of AI proper in order to solve certain types of industrial problems that heretofore had either been tackled by hand by domain experts or with certain techniques devised by people working in an entirely separate field called operations research.

On the other hand, AI has often borrowed techniques from other fields. Perhaps the most important example of this involves notions about uncertainty and its representation. In particular, certain kinds of probabilistic inference (such as Bayesian reasoning[24]) with origins in mathematics and statistics have become integral to many AI systems. And of course, logic itself had a lengthy history and had reached an advanced state of development long before it was used in AI.

Some nice examples of such borrowing can be found in the field of case-based reasoning (CBR).[32] This is a popular AI method in which a store of cases with solutions put together from earlier experiences is consulted when a new problem of the same type is encountered. In this approach, a case is retrieved from the store that according to some metric is most similar to the present case. Then the solution procedure is applied; during this problem solving process, the old solution is like to be tuned, i.e. adjusted, to fit the present case. If the procedure is successful, the new case is added to the store.

Now, CBR is quite promiscuous in adapting methods from other domains in order to carry out the procedure just outlined. For example, various forms of "nearest neighbor" analysis, which is a well-known family of statistical techniques, can be used to rate the similarity of cases in the store to the present case. Or in some cases fuzzy logic (coming from a field of this name) has been used in the case selection process. Finally, methods from other areas of AI such as machine learning have also been used. (The store itself is often built using database methods as well as existing database software.)

There are also a number of instances where ideas considered to be part of the subject matter of artificial intelligence have been elaborated more or less independently in other areas. Thus, some of the logical formalisms used in AI have also been the basis of advances in the field of data base systems in the form of logic databases. Knowledge representation issues similar to those studied by AI researchers have also been incorporated (independently) in semantic databases as well as conceptual modeling for databases.

Similar developments have occurred in the area of programming languages. For example, object-oriented programming (and object-oriented databases) involves ideas such as inheritance networks that are also important in AI. And, of course, there is logic programming, in which an important fragment of the predicate calculus has been used to create bona fide programming languages, the best-known being Prolog. This example is of particular interest in this connection because Prolog has in turn been used for building AI systems. It is hard to think of a better example of how AI fits into a more extensive commerce of ideas.

Other interesting examples of interplay between AI and other separate fields can be found in connection with applied mathematics. This includes the area known as symbolic mathematical computation (or algebraic computation).[33] This field of research began to take form in the 1950s when certain well known techniques (i.e. algorithms) for performing algebraic and symbolic integration were first programmed. An important stimulus for further work was the finding that many of the classical algorithms were in fact very inefficient. A few years later, symbolic techniques for performing integration became an important research area in AI.[34*] Some of this work led eventually to commercialized systems such as MACSYMA. However, by now many of these systems are not viewed as AI systems at all. Moreover, after a period in which AI and symbolic computation were closely intertwined, the fields separated, as the latter became both more specialized and more algorithmic.

Another example of such interplay involves the use of search techniques originating in AI and related areas to assist in the proof of theorems in pure mathematics. In some instances, it was possible to reduce certain facets of the original problem to a set of cases that could be represented as logical formulas. Each of these could then be solved with the methods referred to above (and discussed in the next chapter).[35] In some cases, there has been an interesting iterative process — carried out by human mathematicians — in which the proof was simplified while the computer's contribution was characterized in more formal terms. The impetus for this was to gain assurance that the overall proof was valid. But the fact remains that it would not have been possible to prove these theorems without the help of the computer programs.

In summary, over the years a broad swath of intellectual activity has grown up around the field of artificial intelligence. Goods in the form of ideas are constantly being shuttled in and out of the core field. New areas of investigation appear as spin-offs, new intellectual 'markets' are opened up, and researchers rush in to exploit them. All this goes on with the same verve and bustle that one finds in a system of commercial endeavor — or, for that matter, in a living organism.

All this has definite implications for our understanding of the nature of AI. In the first place, it means that the boundaries of what we call AI are necessarily fuzzy and can change over time. In fact, it raises the question of whether AI is anything more than a set of social conventions. Or, perhaps more accurately, is what we call AI basically the institutionalization of certain human activities that are not distinguishable as such from other human activities except for the rubric under which they are carried out?

Endnotes

1. A. M. Turing, "Computing machinery and intelligence", *Mind*, 1950, 59: 433–460.
2. In fact, the original proposal carried an interesting twist. In this version of the game, a man and a woman communicate with the interrogator, who has to decide which is the man and which is the woman. Now, some authors have interpreted this more elaborate construction as somehow reflecting Turing's homosexuality and concerns about gender identity, etc., etc. To my mind such interpretations have more to do with our current obsessions or hang-ups than with the development of the argument; I can't believe that Turing was that shallow or frivolous. Remember that this is a mathematician-logician writing. The extra 'twist' serves to make the entire construction more precise. It begins with a game of deception between two human beings. Having accepted that is a reasonable challenge for an interrogator, we are then asked to consider what would happen if one of the players was replaced by a machine. This seems to me to be the purpose of the original gender game, which Turing disregards thereafter (see Section 2 of the paper), speaking about an imitation game involving a machine in the form that it is usually described.
3. Turing, *op. cit.*, p. 435.
4. Possibly the most interesting question about the Turing Test is why people continue to discuss it. Why does it appeal to a certain kind of intellectual? And more generally, what does this say about human beings?
5. As an aside, it is also worth noting that the present network view of intelligence allows for an essentially infinite Turing machine 'tape', so that biological intelligence no longer needs to be qualified in this respect.
6. It may be, as D. Dennett has suggested, that Turing never meant his idea of a behavioral test to get this far out of hand, and that his 'test' was more a philosophical exercise designed to forestall unproductive debate than a suggestion to be realized in practice. If so, he might be quite dismayed at the result.
7. This kind of argument has been put forward by various authors. See J. Weizenbaum, "ELIZA — A computer program for the study of natural language communication between man and machine", *Communications of the ACM*, 1966, 9: 36–45; N. Block,

"Psychologism and behaviourism", Philosophical Review, 1981, 40: 5–43; S. Watt, "Naïve psychology and the inverted Turing Test", *Psycoloquy*, 1996, 7(14); and the next citation.

8. P. Hayes & K. Ford, "Turing Test considered harmful", Proceedings of the *Fourteenth International Joint Conference on Artificial Intelligence-IJCAI-95*, Morgan Kaufmann, 1995, pp. 972–977. See also, K. M. Ford & P. J. Hayes, "The Turing Test is just as bad when inverted", *Psycoloquy*, 1996, 7(43).
9. R. Epstein, "The quest for the thinking computer", *AI Magazine*, Summer 1992, 81–95. Quoted passage on p. 81.
10. *Ibid.*, p. 83.
11. *Ibid.*, p. 83. That things haven't changed all that much in the past 20 years is indicated by a report on the 2012 contest: R. Fisher, "Chatbots fail to convince despite Loebner Prize win", *New Scientist*, May 2012.
12. W. J. Clancey, "The epistemology of a rule-based expert system — a framework for explanation", *Artificial Intelligence*, 1983, 20: 215–251.
13. W. A. Woods, "What's in a link: Foundations for semantic networks", In: D. G. Bobrow & A. Collins, *Representation and Understanding*, New York: Academic, 1975, pp. 35–82.
14. Clancey, *op. cit.,* p. 236.
15. *Loc. cit.*
16. *Loc. cit.*
17. There is a curious resemblance between the initial acceptance of the intelligence of systems such as MYCIN and later doubts about what their actual accomplishments were and the Turing Test itself, that I don't think anyone has drawn attention to. In a sense, AI researchers were faced with a similar situation as the one envisioned by Turing. Their mode of solution is, therefore, quite relevant to the discussion about the status of the Test.

    There is another interesting question in connection with rule-based systems. Why did it take so long for people to ask where rules come from — and perhaps equally important, what makes for a good rule?
18. I was once told that this remark appeared in a letter, but I haven't been able to verify this. At any rate, it does sound like something Whitehead might have said.
19. T. S. Eliot, Burnt Norton, *Four Quartets*, Harcourt, 1943.
20. See P. J. Hayes, "In defense of logic", *Proceedings of the Fifth International Joint Conference on Artificial Intelligence — IJCAI'77.* Vol. 1. Morgan Kaufmann, 1977, pp. 559–565; P. J. Hayes, "Computation and deduction", *Proceedings of the Second Mathematical Foundations of Computer Science Conference*, Prague: Czechoslovakian Academy of Sciences, 1973, 105–118.
21. "First order logic" or predicate logic refers to a logic in which inferences can take into account the properties of relations. This is not possible in the simpler "propositional logic", which is a logic of statements taken as a whole. In the latter, a fact like <the cat is on the mat> is treated as a logical atom, and is either true or false. The rules of

the logic deal with the ways that such atoms can be combined so as yield compound propositions that are either true or false. So, for example, if <the cat is on the mat> and <France has many grape vines> are both (assumed to be) true, then propositional logic allows one to infer that both propositions together are also true. But if one of them is assumed to be false, then the logic allows one to infer that the combination of both propositions is false. (For further examples, as well as a more formal representation of propositional logic, see Chapter 3.) In contrast, predicate logic allows us to represent the relations expressed by propositions. So the statement <the cat is on the mat>, which contains a single relation, can be expressed as On(cat, mat). Here, the term "On" is a predicate that stands for the general relation of being on top of; it has two arguments, here "cat" and "mat". We can also "quantify" the statement and say either that For-All cats, On(cat, mat), or There-Exists a cat such that the relation On(cat, mat) holds. With this means of representation, we can express inferences between predicates, such as For-All X, Y: Wet(X) And On(X,Y) => Wet(Y). This proposition expresses the fact that this inference holds for any X and Y. (Here, arguments beginning with a capital letter are variables, while arguments entirely in lower case are constants. The "=>" means implies.) Given this general fact, then, by following well-defined rules of instantiation, we can deduce from Wet(cat) that Wet(mat) also holds.

22. In fact, there had been a "logicist" stream of thought in AI, begun in large part by John McCarthy in the late 1950s and early 60s that called for the use of logical languages in building and describing AI systems. But this did not become a major force until the 1980s.
23. M. R. Genesereth and N. J. Nilsson, *Logical Foundations of Artificial Intelligence*, Palo Alto, CA: Morgan Kaufmann, 1988, pp. 2–3.
24. *Ibid*., p. 3.
25. Among the many references on this topic are L. R. Squire, B. Knowlton & G. Musen, "The structure and organization of memory", *Annual Review of Psychology*, 1993, 44: 453–495; L. Squire, "Memory systems of the brain", *Neurobiology of Learning and Memory*, 2004, 82: 171–177; For one attempt to apply this distinction to animals, see A. Dickinson, *Contemporary Animal Learning Theory*, Cambridge: Cambridge University, 1980.
26. To quote the man himself, "For a large class of cases of the employment of the word 'meaning' — though not for all — this word can be explained in this way: the meaning of a word is its use in the language" L. Wittgenstein, *Philosophical Investigations*, New York: Macmillan, 1953, #43 (p. 20). And to quote from the Stanford Encyclopedia of Philosophy, "when investigating meaning, the philosopher must "look and see" the variety of uses to which the word is put". http://plato.stanford.edu/Wittgenstein/.
27. See M. P. Georgeff, A. L. Lansky & P. Bessiere, "A procedural logic", *Proceedings of the Ninth International Joint Conference on Artificial Intelligence — IJCAI'85*, pp. 516–523.

28. See A. Bundy, "A science of reasoning", In: J.-L. Lassez & G. Plotkin, editors, *Computational Logic: Essays in Honor of Alan Robinson*, Cambridge, MA & London: MIT, 1991, pp. 178–198.; A. Bundy, "Planning and patching proof", B. Buchberger & J. A. Campbell, editors, *Artificial Intelligence and Symbolic Computation — AISC-04*, LNAI No. 3249, Berlin: Springer, 2004, pp. 26–37.
29. A. Newell & H. A. Simon. Computer science as empirical inquiry: Symbols and search. *Communications of the ACM*, 1976, 19: 113–126.
30. A. Newell. Physical symbol systems, *Cognitive Science*, 1980, 4: 135–183.
31. A. Newell. The knowledge level. *Artificial Intelligence*, 1982, 18: 87–127.
32. The illustrations in this and the next paragraph are based on I. Watson, "Case-based reasoning is a methodology not a technology", *Knowledge-Based Systems*, 1999, 12: 303–308.
33. See J. Cohen, *Computer Algebra and Symbolic Computation*, Natick, MA: A. K. Peters, 2003. A nice review, although by now dated, is J. Calmet & J. A. Campbell, "Artificial intelligence and symbolic mathematical computation", In J. Calmet & J. A. Campbel (eds.) *Artificial Intelligence and Symbolic Mathematical Computation* (AISMC-1, Karlsruhe, 1992). Lecture Notes in Computer Science 737. Berlin: Springer-Verlag, 1993, pp. 1–19.
34. Early symbolic integration systems such as SAINT (for Symbolic Automatic Integrator) employed a search process based on a set of transformations. Thus $\int \tan^4 y \, dy$ might be transformed into $\int z^4/(1 + z^2) \, dz$. If more than one transformation could be made, the program evaluated the simplicity of the resulting expressions and selected the simplest transformation to work on. It continued in this fashion, making transformations, and perhaps backtracking if the latest transformation was judged more complicated than one that was rejected earlier, until the integral could be resolved.
35. The particular case referred to here is, B. Konev & A. Lisitsa, "Computer-aided proof of Erdös discrepancy properties", *Artificial Intelligence*, 2015, 224, 103–118. See also: A. Bundy, "Automated theorem provers: a practical tool for the working mathematician?", *Annals of Mathematics and Artificial Intelligence*, 2011, 61:3–14.

9

A 'Big Win': AI and Algorithms for Combinatorial Search

Artificial Intelligence and Search

I want to begin this chapter by considering another problem studied by early AI researchers, called the 9-puzzle.[1*] The object of the game is to rearrange the tiles on a board so that the numbers on the faces are in order, and (in some versions) the empty space is in the lower right-hand corner. Tiles can be only be moved by shifting them into the empty space. So in the puzzle shown in Figure 9.1 there are four first moves; for example, the 1-tile can be moved 1 space down, so the empty space is in the top row between the 4 and the 8. In this case, there are only two possible moves in the next step; for example the 4-tile can be moved to the right, which leaves the empty space in the top-left corner. In this way the tiles can be slowly rearranged until eventually they are all placed in appropriate places.

Why am I discussing this topic? Because one cannot understand AI and its successes without understanding this aspect of the endeavor. To this day, search remains a central topic in the field. This can be expressed in the following formula (which of course is meant only to be suggestive):

$$\text{AI} = \text{logic} + \text{search}$$

In fact, a substantial portion of the major successes in AI have been due to the discovery of efficient methods for carrying out combinatorial search, as I will now show.

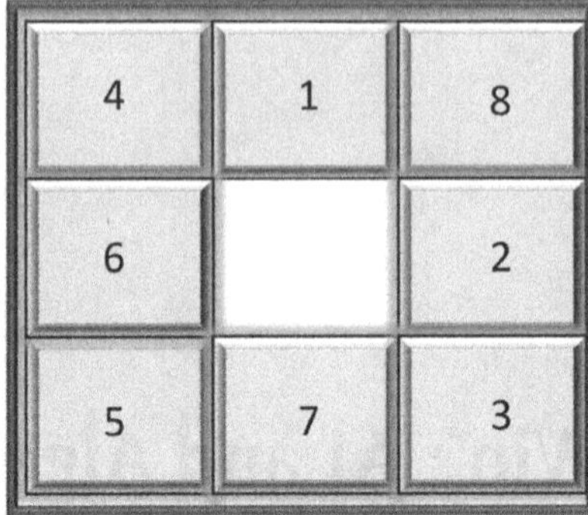

Figure 9.1. The nine-puzzle problem. The object is to move the tiles so the numbers are in order: 1, 2, 3 in the top row from left to right, 4 and 5 in the middle row, and 6, 7, 8 in the bottom row. Tiles can only be moved into an empty space.

Constraint Satisfaction Problems

In the 70's and 80's, AI re-discovered or, better, discovered for itself, the idea of optimization (or feasibility) under constraints. This was an extension of its focus on search as an important aspect of intelligence, something that had emerged in the earliest years of AI history, from research on automated chess playing and theorem proving.

The initial discovery occurred in the early 1970s in the context of machine vision. At that time researchers at the Massachusetts Institute of Technology were working on a long-term project called Blocks World whose goal was to build machines that could perceive simple three-dimensional layouts composed of blocks resting on a plane surface.[2*] An example is shown in Figure 9.2.

Perception involved interpreting a scene by detecting changes in brightness and linking these points to form edges.[3] Once edges were detected, then corners could also be determined, since these were points where different edges converged. Then the task was to combine the edges and corners into a coherent representation of the scene. For example, if the scene were the one depicted in Figure 9.2, the system would have to determine that there is a simple arch in the center of the scene composed of a block lying horizontally on top of two other vertical blocks.

In studying this problem, researchers had discovered that for rectangular blocks there is a restricted number of ways that edges can meet, i.e. a

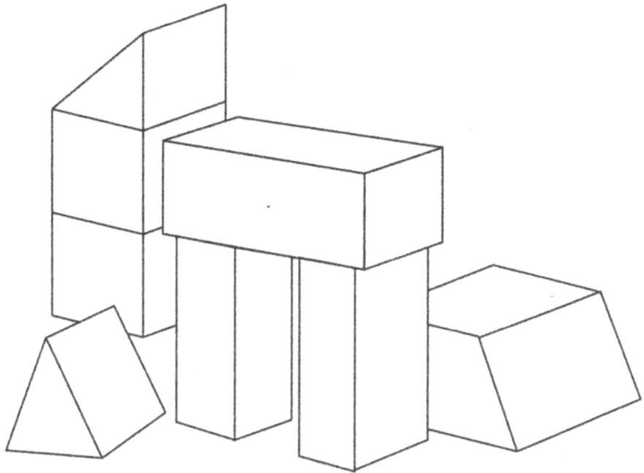

Figure 9.2. A Blocks World layout.

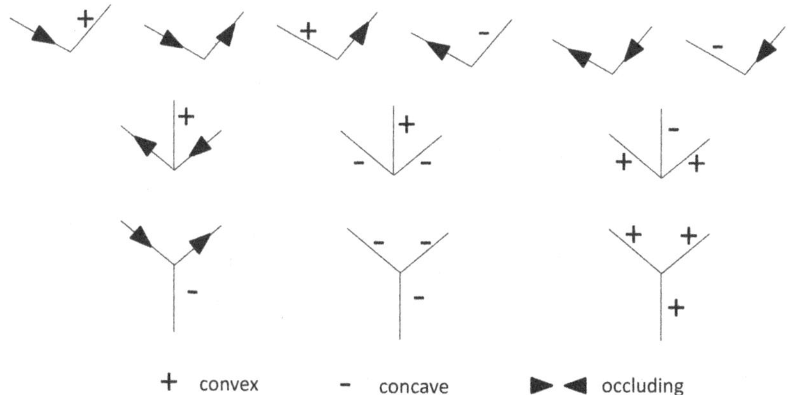

Figure 9.3. Legal labels for junctions, after Huffman, 1971.

limited number of possible configurations that produced corners.[4] The twelve possibilities are shown in Figure 9.3. (For occluding edges, the occluding body is assumed to be on the right of the direction of the arrow. Hence, either of two arrow head labels can be associated with a given line.)

In Figure 9.2, the horizontal block on top of the arch has seven corners, which should be labeled as in Figure 9.4.

Now, given this basic vocabulary of corner labels, suppose that the system can determine where the corners are and whether a corner has two or three edges, and whether two corners are connected by an edge.

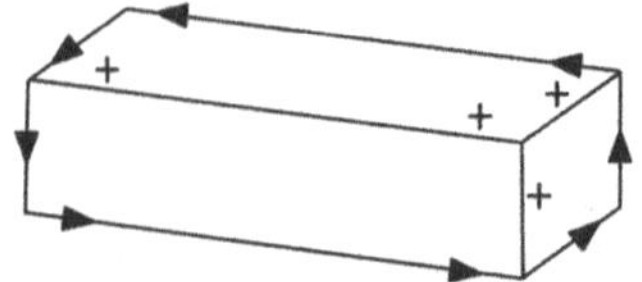

Figure 9.4. A properly labeled block.

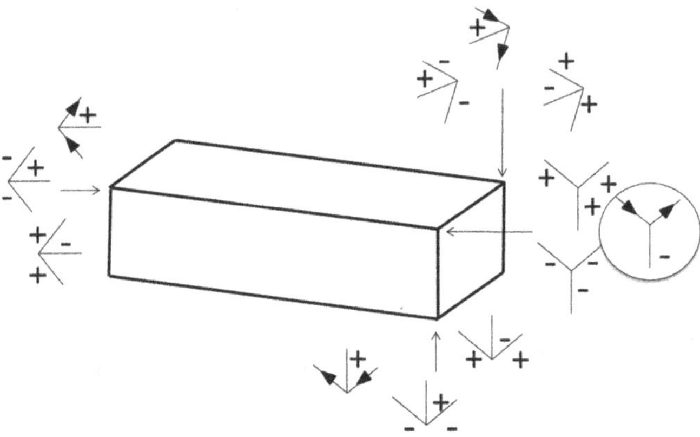

Figure 9.5. Showing the possible labelings for each corner with three incoming edges.

This means that for each corner it discovers, it has a set of possible labels that it could apply. Using the same horizontal block as an example, we can diagram the situation as shown in Figures 9.5 and 9.6. (Figure 9.5 shows possible labels for the corners with three edges, Figure 9.6 for the corners with two edges. In all cases these are taken from the set of twelve labels shown above.) Incidentally, with these sets of possible labels there are $3^4 * 6^3 = 17{,}496$ ways to label the block.

Now consider the labeling in Figure 9.5 that is circled. Notice that if this were the correct label, then the upper left edge of this corner is an occluding edge. In this case, the labeling of the corner on the far left must have a middle edge that is also occluding. But for this corner there is no such labeling. This means we can 'discard' the circled label since there is no labeling in the other set that can go with it. By the same token, in the diagram shown in Figure 9.6 we can discard the three labels of the upper left corner that are circled because their labels can't be matched with labels on one or the other adjacent, three-sided corners. But if we discard

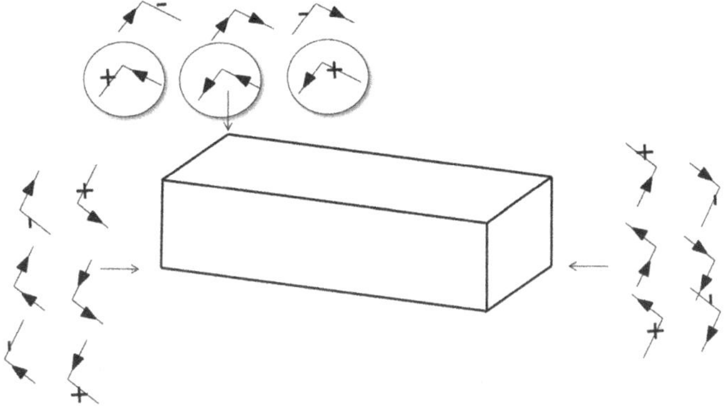

Figure 9.6. Possible labelings for each corner with two incoming edges.

these, notice that we can now discard one of the three-corner labels on the left, namely,

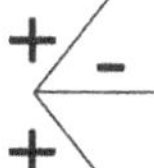

because none of the remaining upper (two-sided) left corner labels can match it. If we continue in this way, we can reduce the sets of possible labels to those shown in Figure 9.7. This gives $3^3 * 2^3 * 1 = 216$ possible ways to label this block, making this a much easier problem to solve. (In this case there are three ways to label the corners in a way that is consistent. Normally, when other blocks must be labeled as well, only one labeling that is consistent everywhere can be found.)[5]

It was several years before it was realized (at least in print) that the procedure just described is an example of a general strategy that can be applied to many kinds of combinatorial problem. All of them can be construed as labeling problems in which a set of entities must be given labels, and the entities are 'connected' in ways that require the labels to be mutually consistent among them. (The entities are called "variables"; in addition, the labels are often referred to as "values".)[6]

In the early days of this developing field, "connections" were always between pairs of entities, just as each corner in the block above is

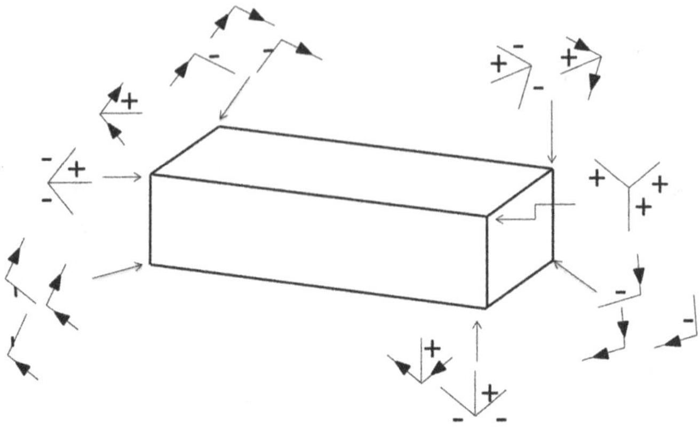

Figure 9.7. Labels that are still possible after eliminating those that are inconsistent with (can't go with) labels at the opposite end of an edge.

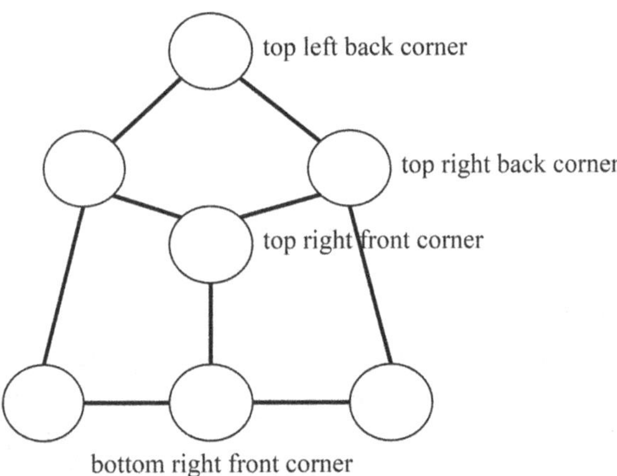

Figure 9.8. A block represented as a graph; nodes represent corners and arcs edges.

connected to another corner by a single edge. If this is the case, then we can represent the problem as a system of nodes and arcs, as shown in Figure 9.8. Here, I have labeled four of the nodes to indicate the corners that they correspond to in the original two-dimensional drawing. Note that just as in the drawing, the top left back corner is connected to the top right back corner, as well as the (unidentified) top left front corner, and both of

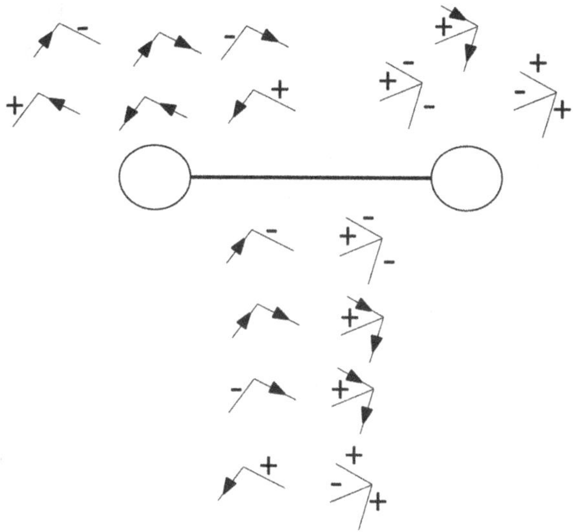

Figure 9.9. Showing, first the possible labels for each of two nodes (those associated with the edge at the top and back of the block), and second the pairs of labels that can 'go together' to make an acceptable labeling for the corners of that edge.

these are connected to the top right front corner. More generally, every node in the graph corresponds to a corner in the drawings shown in the earlier figures, and every arc (or edge) between two nodes corresponds to an edge in the original block.

Now, since adding labels to all the nodes of this graph will make a messy picture, I will take a single pair of nodes joined by arc, and show how it is labeled in this representation of a blocks world labeling problem. These are nodes that represent the top left and top right back corners. In Figure 9.9, the possible labels for each node are shown just above it (six for the top left corner with its two edges and three for the top right corner with its three edges). Below the arc is shown the possible ways that labels for each node can go together. (Recall that labels can go together only if the labels on the edge connecting the corners are the same, i.e. both – or both + or both ▶ or both ◀.)

At this point, we can see that two of the labels for the node on the left cannot be paired with any labels of the right hand node; this means they can be disregarded, since they can't appear in any complete labeling of the figure.

Now, I will go one step further, and introduce a simpler representation than these complicated corner figures. For each kind of label I will use a separate letter, for example:

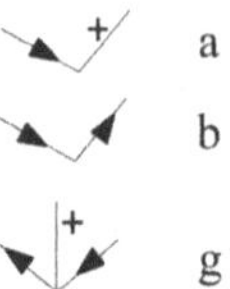

(My rule for assigning letters to labels is simple; starting with "a", I gave letters to the labels in Figure 9.3 above that shows the complete vocabulary, going from left to right and top to bottom.)

With these simpler labels, we can represent the full problem in a much more compact way. The diagram in Figure 9.10 illustrates the same problem of labeling the edges and corners of the block, where each node is shown with a set of possible labels and each arc has its associated set of possible label-pairs shown beside it.

Now suppose we go through the problem, node by node, and for each possible label we check to see if there is a label in each adjacent node that

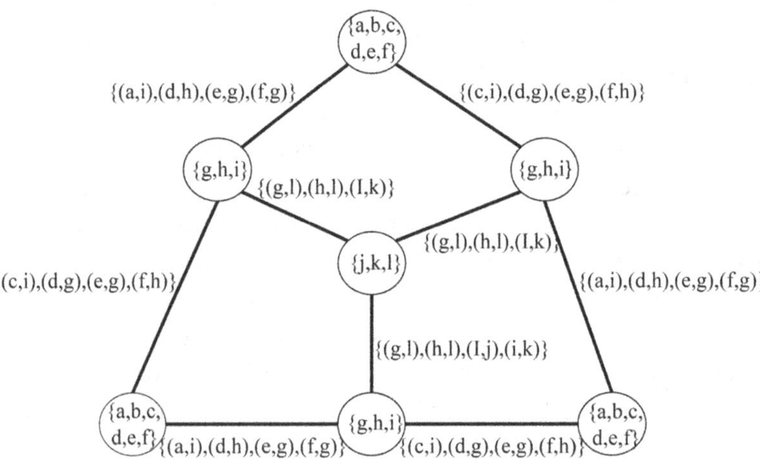

Figure 9.10. Graph representation of block, showing all possible labels for each node (inside the node) and possible label pairs associated with each edge. (For example (c, i) is a possible pair for the top right edge, requiring that the topmost node in the figure is labeled with a c and that the node below it on the right is labeled with an i.)

goes with this label. For example, taking the node at the top, we can immediately see that only labels a, d, e and f can go with a label in the node below and on the left, and only labels c, d, e and f can go with a label in the node below on the right. This means that the only viable labels are d, e, and f. (This same fact was pointed out earlier using the original corner and edge labels.)

Over the years, a number of systematic procedures have been devised to ensure that all labels that are inconsistent with labels in adjacent nodes are discarded, as well as ensuring that no other labels are discarded. These are called arc consistency algorithms, since they ensure that every remaining label for a given node can go with at least one label at the other end of each connecting arc. Devising and testing such algorithms is an important part of the field of constraint satisfaction or constraint programming.

One area where arc consistency reasoning (and more generally, local consistency reasoning, i.e. reasoning about small portions of the overall problem) proves to be quite powerful is solving logic puzzles and other puzzles of inference. This includes the well-known Sudoku puzzle, an example of which is shown in Figure 9.11. Recall that the goal of the puzzle is to fill in the blank squares with integral numbers between 1 and 9 so

4		5			7			1
	8		1	6			3	
		9		5		7	4	
		7		4		1		2
9	1		5				6	
	2		8		6			5
5			4		3	2		
	7	3			1		5	
8				2		6		3

Figure 9.11. A Sudoku puzzle.

that all nine digits appear in each of the nine rows and each of the nine columns as well as in each of the nine 3 × 3 mini-blocks (separated in the figure by double lines). In doing this, we are not allowed to change any of the numbers in the original puzzle.

Again, we have a kind of constraint satisfaction problem. In this problem, each of the requirements that we have just stipulated is represented as a separate constraint. We can also consider each square to be filled as an individual variable, or node in the constraint graph. Each variable then takes one of nine values, i.e. the digits 1 through 9. For each square that has a number (label) in the original problem, we assign that label to that variable, essentially reducing the set of possible values to a single one.

Now, we can draw the constraint graph in different ways, depending on how we wish to represent the constraints. For example, the fact that in each mini-block all the numbers have to be different can be expressed with inequality constraints. The diagram in Figure 9.12 depicts the variables associated with the upper left mini-block in the Sudoku board, including the three variables already assigned a value. Only the constraints for the variable that represents the square in row 1, column 2 are shown. Simply put, the diagram shows that whatever value is assigned to

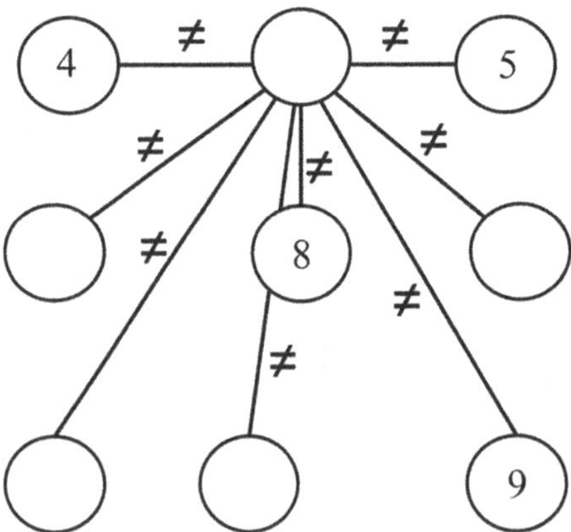

Figure 9.12. Representing the inequality relations between the square in row 1, column 2 of the Sudoko puzzle shown in Figure 9.11 and each of the other squares in the same 3 × 3 mini-block of the puzzle.

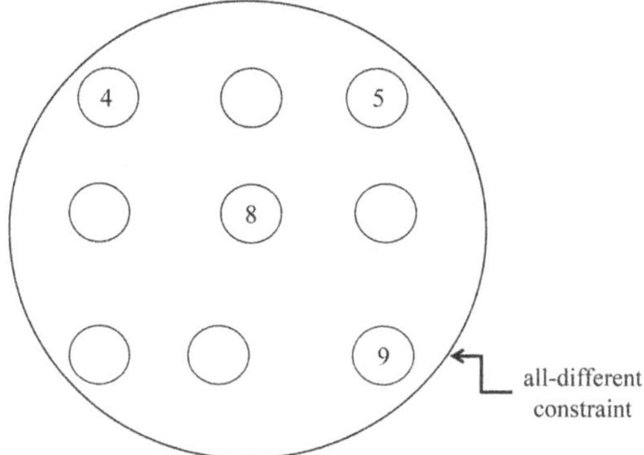

Figure 9.13. The same mini-block shown in Figure 9.12, represented by a single "all-different" constraint (instead of 18 inequality constraints).

that variable, it must be different from each of the other variables in this subgraph. Now, in the full depiction of the problem, each of the other nodes would have arcs connecting it to all of the other variables in this set, each expressing an inequality relation. But since this would produce a graph that would be hard to read (having 36 constraints in all), these other arcs are not shown in the diagram.

We can express the situation in a much simpler way, by using non-binary constraints, i.e. constraints that include more than two variables. The diagram in Figure 9.13 depicts an entire set of relations for the same mini-block in the upper left corner, using a single "all-different" constraint, represented by the large, enclosing circle. This constraint says that all of the variables in that constraint must be different from each other. (It should be appreciated that this is equivalent to having inequality constraints between each pair of variables in this set.)

Now in the full representation of the problem, there would be eight other sets of inequality constraints (or, equivalently, eight other all-different constraints), one for each of the other mini-squares. In addition there would be nine sets of inequality constraints (or nine all-different constraints) to represent the fact that for each row all the squares must have different values, and nine sets of inequality constraints for the nine columns. (Incidentally, if inequality constraints were used, this would give a total of 810 inequality constraints.)

Now notice that by using arc consistency for each inequality constraint with one of the variables that already has an assignment, we can remove the value assigned from the domain of the other variable in the constraint. Consider again the mini-block in the upper left corner of the board, and the empty square in row 1, column 2. Common sense, here in the guise of arc consistency reasoning, tells us that this square cannot have any of the following values: {4, 5, 7, 1}, since they are already used in the top row, {8, 1, 2, 7} since they are already used in the second column, and {4, 5, 8, 9} since they are already used in this mini-square. If we take the common values in these sets ({1, 2, 4, 5, 7, 8, 9}), we see that the only values that this square can take are 3 and 6. Similarly, the only values available for the square in row 2, column 1 are 2 and 7, for the square below it, 1, 2, 3 and 6, for the square in row 3, column 2, 3 and 6. Finally, for the square in row 2, column 3 there is only one value, 2, so we can go ahead and give it that value. But as soon as we have, we can discard this value from the sets for the empty squares in column 1. But when we do this, we have only one value left for the square in row 2, column 1 (7), so we can give the square that value.

This is as far as we can get reasoning with inequality constraints. However, if we reason based on the all-different constraint we can also deduce that 1 is the only possible value that can be assigned to the square in row 3, column 1, using an extended form of arc consistency. (How this is done is beyond the scope of the present discussion.) Anyway, the point is that this form of reasoning about constraints that are local to a part of the problem can take us a long way toward a full solution, although in most cases some form of search is required in the end. And since the procedure used is algorithmic in character, it can be coded up in a program, in this case one that solves Sudoku puzzles.

The third example I want to consider is part of a larger area of endeavor, in which the aim is to derive schedules for tasks or events, which again are subject to constraints. This includes scheduling tasks in building and manufacturing (called project scheduling), scheduling work flow on a factory floor (called shop scheduling), and many other forms. Within this constellation of problems, I want to consider the special class of sports scheduling, and within this sub-domain, the problem of scheduling games for major league baseball teams across a playing season.

The first thing to notice is that producing a complete schedule for a full season of major league baseball is a big problem, much more imposing than the previous two examples. Currently there are 30 major league baseball teams, and each plays 162 games in the regular season, for a total of 2430 games. In this case, also, coming up with schedules that satisfy special constraints, such as those related to the occurrence of holidays or that reflect the wishes of advertisers, may have a significant impact on a team's income, running into hundreds of thousands of dollars.

Since this is such a different problem than the previous ones, it isn't immediately obvious that any of the techniques that have been described so far can be applied here. On the other hand, there are some obvious constraints that are built into the way major league baseball is played. For instance, on a given day for each scheduled game, two teams play. And this means that neither team will play any other team on that day. For any game, in addition, one team plays on its own home field, while for the other team this is an "away" game.

There is also an obvious constraint in that the schedule on a given year begins in April and ends in October. This gives about 175 days, which means that each team must play nearly every day. (Normally, a team plays only one game in a day; an occasional "double-header" may be played to make up a game that was cancelled, but this would not be in the original schedule.) Two teams play each other for a series of three or four (very occasionally two) consecutive games, which is called a "round". There is also a rule that no more than three consecutive rounds will be played at home or away.

In major league baseball there are two leagues, the American and the National. Each league is divided into three divisions, East, West and Central. Each division now has five teams. In contemporary schedules in addition to playing nineteen games against each of the other teams in its own division, a team plays six to seven games with each team in the two other divisions of the league (intra-league games) as well as a total of twenty games with teams in the corresponding division in the other league (inter-league games). Six of the inter-league games are with its "rival" team and three to four are with each of the other teams in that division.

Schedules must be arranged so that each type of match (intra-division, intra-league and inter-league) is spread fairly evenly across the entire season. On the other hand, a team cannot be expected to shuttle back and forth across the country round after round; to avoid this, away games against teams in a different division may be scheduled together in one road trip.

In fact, once one begins to think about it, it becomes obvious that all sorts of constraints are implicit in an ordinary sports schedule. And this is typical of the many problems to which constraint technology can be applied. To repeat the mantra of the field, "Constraints are everywhere!"

The programs used to create contemporary major league baseball schedules are proprietary, so I cannot say how, exactly, they work. In the literature on sports scheduling, attention has been mostly focused on simplified schedules (some of which, however, are directly applicable to other sports such as European soccer league schedules).

An important example of this is called round-robin tournament scheduling. In a round-robin tournament there is a set of players (possibly teams), and each player must play against every other player a fixed number of times. To take a simple example, suppose there are six teams, call them A, B, C, D, E, F, and each team must play every other team once. This means that each team must play five games, each one with a different opponent. Supposing that games are played in synchrony, then there must be three games in each time period, or slot. The following diagram shows one solution.

		games		
		1	2	3
	1	A-B	C-D	E-F
	2	A-C	B-F	E-D
slots	3	A-D	C-F	E-B
	4	A-E	B-C	D-F
	5	A-F	B-D	E-C

Here, in the first slot A plays B, C plays D and E plays F.

Scanning a major league baseball schedule, one can see that it doesn't quite fit this pattern. Nonetheless, the teams remain roughly on par

KC	MIN	CLE	CWS
	+3		
		-3	
			+3
		+6	
	-6		
-4			
			-6
+7			
	+9		
			-9
		+9	
		-12	
			+13
	-13		
+10			
-13			
-16			
		+15	
		-19	
	-16		
+19			
			+16
	+19		
			-19

Figure 9.14. Pattern of games played by the Detroit Tigers against other teams in the same division in the 2015 baseball season. Explanation in text.

throughout the season with respect to number of games played. This also holds for intra-divisional games. The table in Figure 9.14 shows the pattern of intra-divisional games for the Detroit Tigers in the 2015 season.

Each row in the table shows a successive round, and each entry shows the total games played so far in the season against the opponent listed in the column header (as indicated earlier, the final totals must all be 19). The black line between rows 14 and 15 indicates the All-Star break. A "+" before the number means that this round was played at home; a "–" means it was played away.

The table shows that the totals for each opponent remain roughly on par, although the difference between the minimum and maximum total can sometimes be as high as six. In addition, there seems to be some effort made to limit the number of successive rounds played at home or away. In particular, there are never any more than two successive rounds against a particular opponent that are the same in this respect.

Still another feature of real schedules is the pattern of day and night games. In particular, if a team travels from one stadium to another, it never plays a day game in the latter stadium unless there is a day's break between games. So the patterns on successive days in different stadiums are either day-night or night-night, never night-day and very rarely day-day.

Patterns like these are constraints, and as such they can be represented by the methods already discussed. A very simple example involves a home-away constraint, which ensures that whenever two teams play each other, one is at home and the other is away. Suppose we have a large set of variables of the form:

home[i, t]

which are set to 1 if team i plays at home in time-slot t and 0 otherwise. Another set of variables has the form:

plays[i, j, t]

which is set to 1 only if team i plays team j in time-slot t (and takes the value 0 otherwise). Then one way to express this constraint is the following:

plays[i, j, t] = 1 ➔ home[i, t] + home[j, t] = 1

where the arrow means "implies". In words, this says that if team i plays team j then only one team can be the home team, i.e. one and only one home[i, t] variable can be set to 1.

The day-night constraint with regard to stadium changes could be handled by using variables of the form:

daygame[i, t] = 1

which is set to 1 if team i plays a day game in time-slot t. Then, under conditions that are a little hard to specify in terms of these variables, e.g.

plays[i, j, t] $\neq$ plays[i, j, t+1] and (at the same time) home[i, t] + home[i, t+1] $\leq$ 1, the following relation should hold:

$$\text{daygame}[i, t] \geq \text{daygame}[i, t+1]$$

Anyway, this should give one a sense of how a complicated problem like this can be approached by representing it as a constraint satisfaction problem.[7]

Notice how in this discussion we have gone from scene labeling to solving a logic puzzle, to scheduling baseball games, and in each case we were able to describe the problem in the same general fashion — as one of assigning values (labels) to a set of variables in such a way that the constraints of the problem are satisfied. This gives some indication of the power of the constraint satisfaction formalism. In fact, during the 1990s some of the most impressive practical achievements in AI involved casting large real-world problems into the format of constraint satisfaction, and then using efficient search algorithms to solve them.

The last decade was the first time that an automated schedule was chosen for a major league baseball season. However, for this kind of problem the most successful search techniques often went beyond the specific field of constraint programming to employ methods from the related fields of mathematical programming and heuristic search. In the next subsection, I will briefly touch on these other fields before giving one final example, where these alternative methods are often used, and which will bring us back to the theme of intelligence and search.

There is also a human story behind this particular advance in technology. Prior to the development of a computer program powerful enough to produce a satisfactory solution for this problem, major league baseball schedules were produced by a husband-and-wife team who were masters of this abstruse craft. The leader of the team who produced the successful scheduling program had this to say:

> "It was fascinating to hear the story of the Stephensons, and a little heart-breaking to hear them finally losing a job they obviously loved. I have never met Henry or Holly, and they have no reason to think good thoughts about me. But I think an awful lot of them.

> "I began working on baseball scheduling in 1994, and it took ten years of hard work ... before MLB selected our schedule for play.
>
> "Why were we successful in 2004 and not in 1994? At the core, technology changed. The computers we used in 2004 were 1000 times faster than the 1994 computers. And the underlying optimization software was at least 1000 times faster. So technology made us at least a million times faster. And that made all the difference. Since then, computers and algorithms have made us 1000 times faster still. And, in addition, we learned quite a bit about how to best do complicated sports scheduling problems.
>
> "Another way to see this is that in 1994, despite my doctorate and my experience and my techniques, I was 1 millionth of the scheduler that the Stephensons were. Henry and Holly Stephenson are truly scheduling savants, able to see patterns that no other human can see. But eventually technological advances overtook them."[8]

The reader will note the striking similarity to our earlier account of the Deep Blue/Kasparov competition. As Feng-Hsiung Hsu put it, in both cases there was a contest between the toolmaker and the performer. In both cases, a key problem was the sheer combinatorial complexity (number of possibilities), which in the end could be better handled by massive computation, but only if this was guided by human intelligence. Again, there is an indissoluble nexus.

Optimization Under Constraints

As already mentioned, with the emergence of the field of constraint satisfaction, AI rediscovered, or discovered for itself, the fundamental idea of optimization under constraints. I think it is fair to say that the development of this idea, together with models and methods for handling such situations, is one of the great achievements of 20th century science. Considered from an algorithmic perspective, this idea has been studied and elucidated within four broad areas of research:

- Artificial intelligence (and related areas), as represented by the constraint satisfaction problem (CSP), and the satisfiability (or SAT) problem[9*,10*]
- Operations Research (OR), where it is realized in various forms of mathematical programming

- Heuristic search methods, or metaheuristics — here a miscellany of topics including algorithms for the traveling salesman problem, genetic algorithms, and algorithms for certain operations research problems with discrete variables coalesced into a distinct area of research based on a certain style of search
- Global optimization of complex mathematical functions (i.e. finding the values of the independent variables which give the maximum or minimum value for the function), in those cases when this is carried out under restrictions (constraints) regarding the values that the variables can take (insofar as this employs non-analytic methods specialized for this field, which are in fact forms of heuristic search)[11*]

Interestingly, the last-mentioned category can lay claim to be the oldest, since some of the major techniques in this area were first proposed in the 18th and 19th centuries. However, at that time the notion of constraints had not yet been incorporated; instead, the aim was to find optima for complicated functions that could not be solved analytically. With rare exception, a concerted interest in optimization under constraints only began in the late 1950s and 1960s. Operations research arose in the 1940s and early 1950s, motivated by organizational and logistics problems encountered during World War II (although some of the problems that now fall under its purview were first described in the 1930s). Some important ideas for heuristic search go back to the 1950s, although the field did not begin to coalesce until the 1980s; however, its history is further complicated by the fact that some of its techniques resemble those in the area of global optimization. Finally, constraint satisfaction search began in the 1970s, stemming from a consideration of certain problems in machine vision, as already indicated.

In this chapter's discussion I am limiting myself largely to methods in the first and third categories, since these have been associated with AI. (For the interested reader a brief account of the other two categories can be found in footnote 12.)

So how does one actually solve a constraint satisfaction problem, once it has been properly encoded as a set of variables, values and constraints? In this discussion, I will return to the Sudoku problem and show how a complete solution can be found.

There are two basic classes of methods. One class consists of complete methods, by which I mean that a method of this type will always produce a correct solution if there is one — and if there is no solution, it will always report that fact correctly. The other class is the class of incomplete methods; these, in fact comprise the field of heuristic search. The big difference between these and complete methods is that while the solutions produced are guaranteed to be correct in both cases, heuristic search methods cannot guarantee that they will find a solution if there is one (hence the name "incomplete"). Moreover, because they cannot make that guarantee, they cannot report the lack of a solution with assurance; they can only report that no solution was found in the time given.

These differences are due to the fact that complete search methods explore the space of possible solutions systematically. They cover all possibilities, although most are enumerated implicitly.

In this connection it is important to appreciate just how large these problems are. Recall that in the blocks-world problem discussed earlier, a single block had 17,496 possible variable assignments (only three of which were correct solutions). In the Sudoku puzzle, there are 45 empty squares, each with nine possible values; so the total number of possible assignments is 9^{45}. This is approximately equal to 8.7×10^{42}, which, according to the Wikipedia article on big numbers, is nearly 9 tredecillion. And I hesitate even to estimate the number of possible ways there are of assigning values to variables in the major league baseball scheduling problem.

As these calculations show, unless the "search space" (i.e. the number of possible full assignments) is reduced drastically either before or during search, complete methods have almost no chance of actually running to completion. So, although in theory the complete methods that I will describe are guaranteed to always return a correct solution (or report that no correct solution exists), in practice one must often rely on incomplete methods, which can "scale up" much more effectively. That is, they continue to find solutions in reasonable times as problem size increases.

Happily, as we have already seen, many of the total number of possibilities can be eliminated before search even begins, by using local consistency reasoning. So in our blocks world problem, by using arc

	1	2	3	4	5	6	7	8	9
1	4		5			7			1
2		8		1	6			3	
3			9		5		7	4	
4			7		4		1		2
5	9	1		5				6	
6		2		8		6			5
7	5			4		3	2		
8		7	3			1		5	
9	8				2		6		3

Figure 9.15. Sudoku puzzle of Figure 9.11 with row and column numbers indicated.

consistency, we were able to reduce the number of possible solutions to 216, a number small enough that we could enumerate all of them, checking each one in turn for correctness.

To give the reader some idea of how search is actually carried out automatically, and some of the ways that it can be made more effective, I will use the Sudoku puzzle introduced earlier (shown again in Figure 9.15 with rows and columns numbered). The complete method I will describe is called backtrack search. This method of search attempts to build a solution step by step, by assigning one variable at a time, each time ensuring that the growing partial solution satisfies all constraints among variables given a value so far. For the Sudoku puzzle, values are numbers from 1 to 9, which are assigned to each empty cell.

In this example, the backtrack (BT) search will be ordered in a very simple-minded way, going through the cells by row and column starting with the cell in the upper left-hand corner. Since this cell already has a number, this must be its value; we can consider it as assigning the only value in a domain of size 1. Then BT will try cell (1, 2), the second cell in the top row. Here, any number can be assigned; here, we will try them in order beginning with 1. This number goes with the 4 in cell (1, 1), so BT proceeds to cell (1, 3) and then (1, 4).

When the search gets to (1, 4), this will be the first time that a 1 assigned conflicts with another number. (In this case the conflict is with the 1 just assigned to cell (1, 2) — since no two cells in a row can have the same number.) Since this doesn't work, we must try the next number 2. Then, for cell (1, 5), BT tries 1 and 2, neither of which goes with the assignments already made, before settling on 3 for this cell.

Notice that in this procedure BT only checks backwards, in order to ensure that consistency is maintained. In particular it takes no notice of the 1 in cell (1, 9), which will conflict with any 1 assigned to any other cell in this row. Only when the search gets to cell (1, 9), is the conflict detected. Then, since that 1 is the only value that can be assigned to cell (1, 9), search immediately runs out of values to use. So what does it do then?

In cases like this, BT backs up to the variable that preceded this one, and tries a new value. This is where this method of search gets its name. Each time one runs out of values to test, one backs up to the previous "level" of search. And one repeats this as often as necessary. This is what guarantees that search is complete. At the same time, as this example shows, searching in this fashion can be very time-consuming. In this particular case every combination of values between cells (1, 2) and (1, 9) will be tried before search finally backs up to cell (1, 2) (which was the actual cause of the problem) and discards the 1, replacing it with a 2.

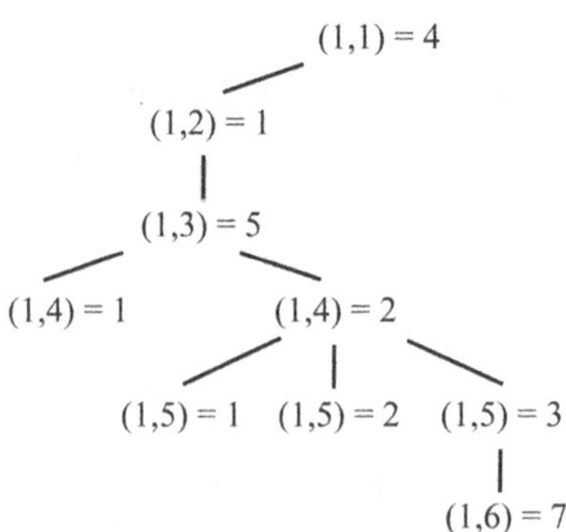

Before proceeding further, I want to point out that a search method of this sort can be thought of as moving from state to state, where each state is a partial assignment. Since we always go forward one step at a time, and back up one step, the search process takes a very simple form, distinguished by a tree-like branching pattern. For this reason, it is called a "search tree". For the Sudoku search just described, the (partial) search tree looks like the inline figure on the previous page.

Each of the assignments indicated is called a "search node". Here, instead of showing the entire set of assignments (which is the full state) at each node, I only show the last one made. (In this case, the full partial assignment can be read off the tree.) When there is more than one branch descending from a node, this means that search has backed up. In such cases we assume by convention that search first went to the leftmost node, then to the one on its right, etc. In this little tree no actual backtracking is depicted (as noted above that will come later in search), although backtracking will not alter the basic structure of the tree. What one sees are entire subtrees descending from a single branch. For example, when (1, 2) is reassigned the value 2, the "(1, 3) = 5" node will appear again under it, then the (1, 4) nodes, etc.

In this particular case, if search is run to completion, the solution is found after exploring 332,421 search nodes (in which search backtracks 93,553 times). Although this seems like a lot (and, in fact, it is), it is much, much less than the nine tredecillion possibilities that make up the entire search space. From that fundamental perspective, backtrack search, even when poorly ordered (as in this case), is tremendously effective.

I said earlier that backtrack search is a complete algorithm. Some readers may be wondering how this can be true if it ignores so many possibilities. The reason is that it manages to cover the entire search space implicitly. Consider, for example the branch ending in "(1, 4) = 1". When search replaced the value 1 with 2, it avoided searching through all the possibilities for the other not-yet assigned variables associated with the assignment of 1 to (1, 2) and 1 to (1, 4). In fact there are 9^{43} of them. Since a good, or valid, solution must satisfy all constraints, and we had already shown that the two assignments just mentioned were in conflict, we also proved that any full set of assignments with "(1, 2) = 1" and "(1, 4) = 1" cannot be a valid solution. In this way, we "pruned" the search tree — to the tune of 9^{43} nodes.

As I said, 332,421 nodes is still a pretty large number, and we can do much better than this. In fact, we have already seen how to make search more efficient — by carrying out arc consistency processing before even starting to search. If we do this in the present case and carry out search in the same (poor) order,[13*] a solution is found (for this problem it is the only one) after exploring 81 nodes. Since there are a total of 81 variables, this means that, following (full) arc consistency, search can be done without backtracking — or even altering any assignments once they are made. In fact, all modern forms of BT use preprocessing of this sort, and in addition similar procedures are mixed in during search. One method in particular performs arc consistency after each assignment has been made. While this isn't necessary for this Sudoku puzzle, which turns out to be a very easy-to-solve CSP, for many problems arc consistency is not really effective until a few assignments have been made (i.e. until the possibilities for one part of the problem have been greatly reduced).

The force of this example will not have escaped the notice of the thoughtful reader. In this case, a logic puzzle that presents a real challenge to a human puzzle-solver becomes trivial when certain systematic search procedures are applied. The key difference is that these methods depend on a representation of the problem that is in a deep sense complete. With such a representation, it becomes possible to manage the myriad possibilities that are involved even in this simple problem with astonishing efficiency. In a real sense, this is the 'secret' behind AI. To a large degree, therefore, successes in AI are due to the solution of certain memory problems — coupled with systematic methods of search.

To round out this discussion, I want to give a brief account of an incomplete, heuristic search method. I will apply it to the same problem, although in this case since we can solve this problem with complete methods in a retraction-free manner, heuristic methods will not do better in this case. On the contrary, especially for someone unfamiliar with these methods, the question is, will they work at all?

The method starts with an initial solution; this may be based on best guesses or it may be completely random. For purposes of demonstration, I will begin here simply by assigning the value 1 to each blank square. This is obviously not a valid solution; in fact, it's not even close. The method proceeds in this way. A variable is chosen that has an assignment that is inconsistent with one or more other assignments. Then a value is

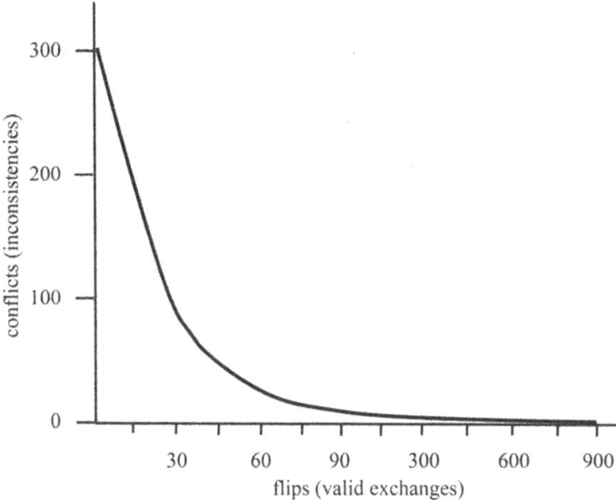

Figure 9.16. Heuristic search with the Sudoku puzzle. Number of inconsistencies remaining in the full assignment after the number of value exchanges ("flips") shown on the x-axis.

chosen that minimizes the number of conflicting assignments. Then search moves on to another variable in conflict, etc. In the variant I'm using here there is another twist: every once in a while (determined by some threshold value) instead of seeking a value with the least number of inconsistencies, a new value is chosen at random, even if this choice increases the number of inconsistencies.

The curve above shows the progress of search. (Note the change in scale after 100 "flips" to accommodate the entire search in a small graph.) Search begins with a full assignment that has 294 inconsistencies. After about 891 flips, i.e. changes of assignment, the number of inconsistencies is reduced to zero and the solution is found. The entire process was completed in 0.05 seconds, which is within range of the time taken by the best version of complete search. Beginning with a more sensible initial assignment would have reduced the time further, but obviously not by much. Anyway, the point of the demonstration was to show that good heuristic methods are generally so powerful that a good initial solution is not required for them to be effective. Incidentally, the curve above is typical for this kind of search in that it shows a rapid initial descent followed by smaller intermittent improvements.

Although this section began with an overview of constrained optimization, I haven't actually talked about optimization as such. In these particular examples a feasible solution was sufficient. However, especially in relation to the heuristic search, we can view the Sudoku puzzle as a kind of optimization in which we wish to minimize the number of inconsistencies. We can then generalize this idea to problems where the minimum number is greater than zero; obviously, the same method can be used in these cases. Going further, we can imagine a situation where there are lots of feasible solutions (i.e. complete assignments that satisfy all the constraints), but these solutions differ in quality, e.g. one solution is less expensive than the rest — so that in this respect it is optimal. The methods I have described can be extended to handle these cases, while other optimization problems can be handled by methods developed within the fields mentioned at the beginning of the section.

The way of thinking described here involves the recognition of constraints. This is a major advance in human thought, which unfortunately has not yet filtered down to the educated populace. This means it has not yet achieved the status of a concept like probability, where most people have some notion of what the idea is about even if their understanding is limited.

The Ubiquity of Constraints

When I said earlier that "constraints are everywhere", I genuinely meant it. And increasingly over the years the realization of this basic truth has been growing in a number of fields of science. In this case, I am referring to fields of empirical science and to developments that have taken place during the last 30 years. So now I will turn away from the "sciences of the artificial" for a moment and consider these other areas.

Perhaps the most significant developments have been in the fields of evolutionary and developmental biology.

Before beginning this discussion, I want to forestall one potential misunderstanding. Some readers may be familiar with the term "bioinformatics", which includes the application of techniques like those described in the last section to problems in molecular biology such as DNA sequencing. That is not the topic of discussion here. In fact, this is just another example of applying techniques like constraint satisfaction to practical problems, and in that sense it is no different than solving scheduling problems or logic puzzles. The subject here is different; it is the use of constraint concepts within the explanatory structure of a particular field of science.

In other words, in this section we are switching from a focus on the "sciences of the artificial" — where we make the things we study — to the natural sciences, i.e. those where we study phenomena found in nature. This brings with it attendant empirical problems. In particular, problems of proper identification and characterization of phenomena loom much larger.

The concern with "constraints" in evolutionary biology is fairly recent; in fact, the term only gained currency in the 1980s, although the ideas are implicit in earlier work, especially in the field of morphology (the study of organic form). The significance of this development is well expressed by the following passage from a paper by a contemporary evolutionary biologist:

> "Recognition of constraints (sensu lato) is one of the most profound and important shifts in the views of evolutionary biologists, comparable to the acceptance of "non-Darwinian" neutral evolution. Continuing resistance attests to the significance of this shift ..."[14]

Initially, the constraints evolutionists had in mind were factors like body plans, which seemed to serve as constraints on later evolution.

Thus, it has been a long-standing question as to why all of the major animal phyla appear to have emerged in the Cambrian era and there have been none since. (An even more general limiting factor of this sort is the DNA code, which with very minor exceptions is universal throughout the biological world.) It appears that once certain lines of organic development are set down, for example those resulting in basic body plans, then it is unlikely that evolutionary processes will be able to act outside the constraints imposed by these features. In other words, they now constitute constraints on further organic evolution.

A classic demonstration of an apparent "developmental constraint" involves the coiling process by which snail shells are produced.[15] Coiling can be considered to occur around a perpendicular axis (the coiling axis), where beginning from a point, the open mouth or whorl moves about the axis while both enlarging in size and possibly shifting downward at the same time. Then varying certain well-defined parameters, such as the rate

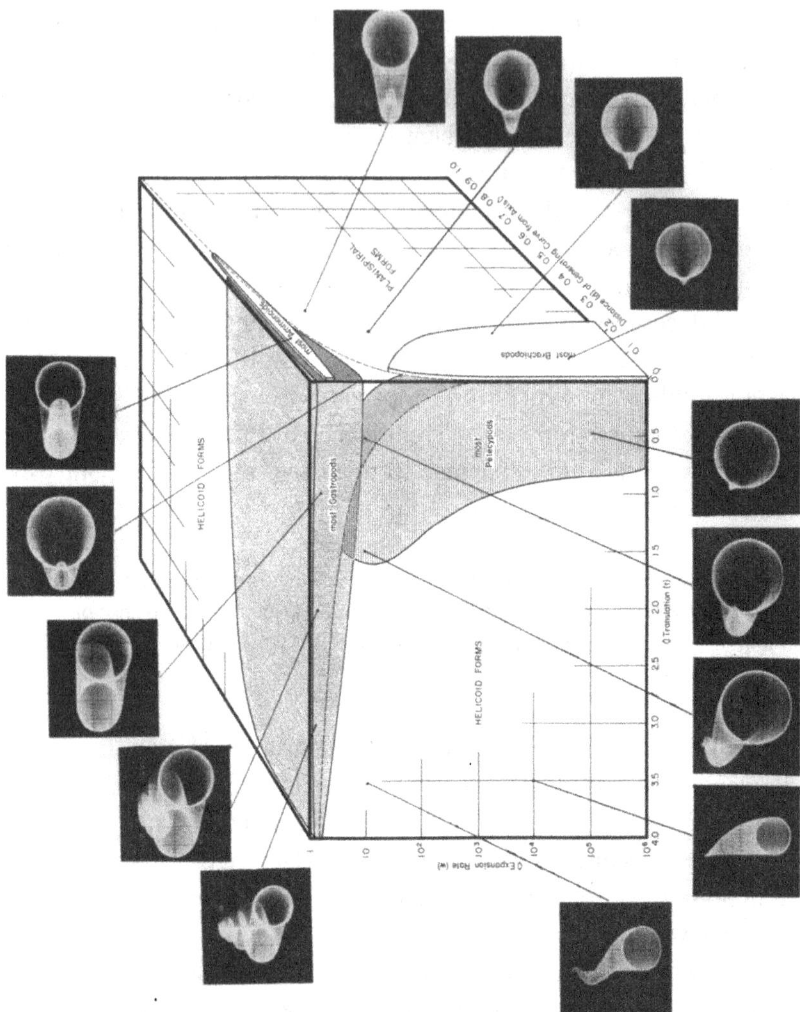

Figure 9.17. The various forms of snail shell structure produced given the basic constraints imposed by the coiling process. See text for further explanation. (Reproduced from Raupp, 1966, Figure 4, courtesy of the SEPM Society for Sedimentary Geology.)

of downward shift and the rate of whorl expansion, produces the different shell shapes. For example, to produce an ordinary snail shell seen in the far upper left of diagram in Figure 9.17,[16] the whorl must both expand and shift downward at a fairly constant rate; if the downward rate is lessened and the whorl expansion rate increased, then the shell-pattern to its right is produced.

There are four parameters in all, three of which are diagramed in the figure above. (The fourth is the shape of the opening; here it is always circular.) Together these create a space of possibilities. But in fact only a small subset of these possibilities are found in the natural world. These possibilities are located in the shaded areas of the cube.

Now, it may be that when other possibilities occur the organisms which are disadvantaged in some way are therefore selected against. Alternatively, there may be constraints on the developmental process that prevent these possibilities from ever occurring, constraints that can be expressed as restrictions on the relations among parameters.

Since the idea of a constraint is so general and because the problem of verifying the existence of a constraint in any given case is not straightforward, it is not surprising that differences and even contradictions and confusions have arisen in this area. Some order can be induced by classifying constraints into various types. The most straightforward division is between physical constraints and developmental and/or phylogenetic constraints, which has been suggested by several authors.

Physical constraints are perhaps the most obvious category of constraints. Since organisms operate in the physical world, their organization and their actions are constrained by various physical laws. For example, there are constraints on the size that an animal can be, given that there is a relation between size and the weight that must be supported and perhaps moved. (As the former increases quadratically, the latter increases cubically.) Another example, given by Maynard Smith *et al.* (1985), is that there is a reciprocal relation between the speed at which a part of the body can be moved and the force it can exert.[17] Another example: for any tube through which fluid flows (such as blood vessels), increasing the diameter of the tube will reduce friction but will require greater force due to the greater volume of liquid.

More interesting are the developmental constraints. Our introductory example of snail shell coiling belongs to this class. Closely associated with these are "phylogenetic constraints". These are constraints that limit the trajectories that evolution can follow. In fact, many if not all developmental constraints also give rise to phylogenetic constraints.

However, there are other ways in which constraints can be classified. They can be also distinguished with respect to the degree that they are unconditional or contingent. Even constraints due to physical laws may also be contingent on earlier 'decisions', i.e. on basic features of the organism that can be taken as givens. An obvious example is the exoskeleton of arthropods vs. the interior skeleton of vertebrates; the former imposes much tighter constraints with respect to size. (So outside of the movies, one will not encounter spiders and wasps that are the size of automobiles.) Thus, while body size per se is not so heavily constrained, once the 'decision' has been made to support the body with an exoskeleton, then it is.

Maynard Smith *et al.* also made a distinction between global and local constraints. An example of the former is the exclusive use of L-isomers of amino acids throughout the living world, although there is no apparent reason why D-isomers could not serve equally well. (This, therefore, may be a global contingent constraint.) A local (contingent) constraint is the example involving skeletons that was given in the last paragraph. As just implied, this division appears to be orthogonal to the one made in the previous paragraph. As a result we can devise four categories: global-unconditional, global-contingent, local-unconditional, and local-contingent. Examples have already been given for three of these categories; it is not clear whether any constraints fall into the local-unconditional group.

In many cases, such constraints tend to be "soft" rather than "hard". This means that a certain amount of deviation is allowed with respect to some ideal point. This seems to be the case in the skeleton example, since both arthropods and vertebrates show a rather large range of body sizes. Thus, having an exoskeleton does not constrain one to a body size of 3 cubic centimeters.

At this point the question must be raised as to whether these ideas are actually related to the notions of constraint satisfaction discussed previously. Or is this just a matter of common terminology, applied to vaguely similar phenomena? In the first place, these evolutionary systems introduce a factor of temporality that was not present before, so that we have constraints emerging over time. But, given this emergence, if we view organismic development as operating under a given set of constraints, then it is possible to construe the resulting organism as a solution to a constraint satisfaction problem.[18*] In short, there does seem to be real connections between these recently formulated ideas in evolutionary biology and notions of optimization under constraints discussed earlier.

*

Notions of constraints have also turned up in several places in psychology and cognitive science. Models in which some notion of constraints plays a critical role, and which are even called constraint satisfaction models, have been proposed within the field of attitude and attitude change and in the field of preferences and decision making. A prominent target for such modeling exercises has been the still problematical phenomenon of cognitive dissonance.

Unfortunately, it is not completely clear that some of the purported effects that the models seem to account for really are cognitive dissonance effects (in addition to their sometimes being difficult to replicate). For this reason and because of some issues I have with the models themselves,[19*] I will pass over work on these topics and instead look at some effects that clearly involve constraints as described in this chapter.

Ideas of constraints have become increasingly prominent in the field of linguistics, especially since the 1980s. They now form part of some phonological models as well as theories of syntax and semantic-syntax relations.

A simple example of a linguistic phenomenon that involves constraints in some fashion is case government. In languages such as German where articles and adjectives have case markers, the case of the word is sometimes determined by the associated preposition. For example, the preposition "mit" (meaning with) requires that the following modifiers be in the dative case, while the preposition "gegen" (meaning, roughly, toward or against) takes the accusative case. So, considering the masculine form of the definite article, which in the nominative case is "der", the following constructions are required:

mit dem
gegen den

where "dem" and "den" are the dative and accusative forms of the article.

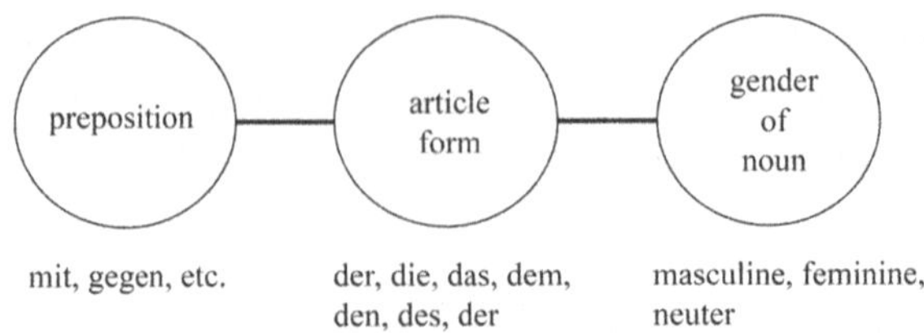

Figure 9.18. Constraint network to represent some basic grammatical relations in German.

At the same time, the gender of the article is governed by the gender of the noun it refers to. So, if the noun is masculine, the "der" form is used, while if the noun is feminine, the article "die" is used. So if the noun is the masculine word "Mann" (man), the constructions

mit dem Mann
gegen den Mann

would be used, while for the feminine word "Dame" (lady), the same article in situ would become:

mit der Dame
gegen die Dame

In these instances the form that the article takes is determined by constraints associated with both the preposition and the noun they are associated with in the sentence. This can be represented by the simple network shown in Figure 9.18. As before, nodes (circles) represent variables, the meaning of which is indicated by the names inside the circles, while some of the possible values that can be assigned to these variables are shown beneath. The two arcs represent constraints.

Similar kinds of constraint networks could be drawn to represent correspondence in number. In English such constraints hold between nouns and associated verbs; thus, we say "He runs" and "They run". In German there are further constraints of this type involving the article form.

The previous examples are examples of prepositional phrases. In either English or German these are also subject to constraints regarding word order as well as placement in a sentence. Thus, in simple declarative sentences in both languages, the subject comes before the verb:

Er sprach mit dem Mann.
He spoke with the man.
Er sprach mit der Dame.
He spoke with the woman.

Sentences such as these are most often analyzed using some form of Phrase Structure Grammar. Thus, the sentence, "He spoke with the man" would be considered to have a noun phrase ("He") followed by a verb phrase ("spoke with the man"); the latter can, in turn, be divided into a verb ("spoke") and a prepositional phrase ("with the man"), and the prepositional phrase is made up of a preposition and a noun phrase ("the man"). These various words and phrases form a nested structure that can be diagramed as a tree, as shown in Figure 9.19.

Within each structure (phrase) there are constraints on order. (So, for example, one cannot say "with man the" or "the with man".) In addition, substitution rules generally restrict references to entire phrases, e.g. nominal substitutions must be with noun phrases and not nouns within phrases. ("He spoke with him" is grammatical, but not "He spoke with the him".)

Restrictions on phrase structures such as these are most often modeled with rewrite rules of the form X → Y, which allow a sentence to be 'unwound' from a single symbol by substituting single symbols to the left

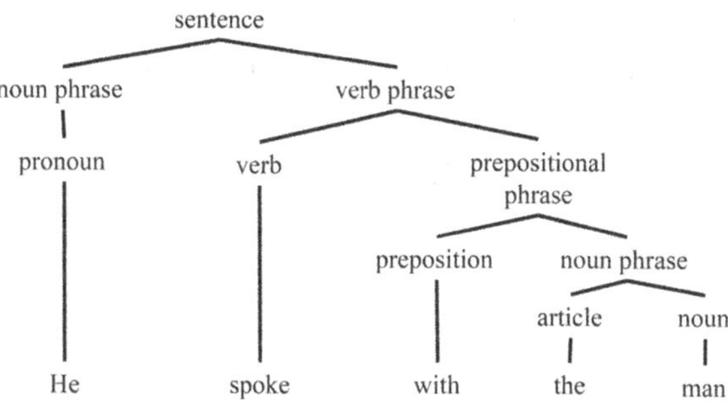

Figure 9.19. Phrase structure representation of simple declarative sentence.

of the arrow by phrase designations and then by individual rules on the right. So for the sentence above the rules might be:

S → NP VP
NP → pronoun
VP → verb PP
PP → preposition NP
NP → article noun
pronoun → he
verb → spoke
preposition → with
article → the
noun → man

Notice that these rules will not produce phrase forms like "with man the" while allowing the string that is grammatical. Hence, this kind of approach if it can be generalized to produce more valid sentences constitutes a theory of grammar. (Grammars in this form are called generative grammars.)

However one construes structural models of this type (and currently grammars that use phrase structures explicitly are only one class of grammatical theories), the fact remains that sentences are composed of recognizable building blocks, or constituents, and these constituents can either be single words or phrases. And in both cases constituents must be arranged in certain orders for the sentence to be considered grammatically correct.[20*] This can be shown by various kinds of allowed substitutions, an example of which was given above.

But the point of significance for this discussion is that the fitting together of constituents is subject to various restrictions, or constraints. Constraints can take many forms, in addition to the kind of precedence rules involved in the typical 'grammatical' constraints. To illustrate, consider the following sentences taken from a well-known text on generative grammar[21]:

(1) The detectives have all read the letters in the garden shed after lunch.
(2) They will wonder whether Poirot will abandon the investigation.

Now, in each case I find the phrasing to be 'not quite right', so I would dispute whether it is a proper English sentence. In sentence (1) "after lunch" doesn't really fit the preceding part of the verb phrase. The problem seems to be with "have"; so the following variation seems okay:

(1') The detectives all read the letters in the garden shed after lunch.

But this is even better (even if it still isn't completely acceptable, due to an ambiguity involving the phrase "in the garden shed"):

(1") After lunch, the detectives all read the letters in the garden shed.

In sentence (2), again, the auxiliary verb seems out of place, so that the following variant seems more acceptable (although still a little odd):

(2') They wonder whether Poirot will abandon the investigation.

Again, to my mind, a better construction is:

(2") They are wondering whether Poirot will abandon the investigation.

In both cases, there are constraints having to do with temporal relations that are violated in the original sentences. Take sentence (1). The verb "have" carries the inference of a state of affairs that has been achieved rather than describing narrative succession. In contrast, "after lunch" specifies the time of occurrence of an event.[22*] So one could say, "The detectives have all read the letters in the garden shed by now."

In the last 20–30 years, considerations such as these have given rise to entire grammatical systems that are built around the notion of constraints, rather than including them in a more or less ad hoc manner. In particular, "construction grammars", and more recently, "property grammars" have been proposed. In the latter systems, restrictions on word or phrase order are realized as precedence constraints; in addition, there are co-occurrence and exclusion constraints between word categories, dependency constraints, uniqueness constraints to prevent ungrammatical duplications, etc.[23] As an alternative to grammars based on rewrite rules, these grammars may be better able to deal with important linguistic phenomena such as idiomatic constructions, sentence fragments, as well as degrees of grammaticality and even sentence quality within a common framework. At any rate, this work certainly shows that constraints play a fundamental role in the construction of proper English sentences.

Another aspect of human cognition where constraints seem to play a pivotal role is that of coherence in thought and argument. The observation is that certain assertions or ideas form a pattern in which the parts adhere and in addition do not conflict with each other. This could be a connected piece of text in which the successive sentences are related. We can call this coherence of discourse. The same idea also applies to explanations in which there are no contradictions and every assertion has some connection with at least one other assertion. On the other hand, disconnected prose (or speech) or explanatory structures that do not have this property can be said to be incoherent on just this account.

To give a simple example of coherence of discourse, consider first this sentence:

Time flies.

And then these:

You can't. They move too fast.[24]

The most straightforward interpretation of the first sentence is as a simple declarative in which "time" is the subject and "flies" is an intransitive verb. But when we consider it together with the other two sentences, there is no obvious interpretation that is coherent. But if we alter the interpretation of the first, so that it becomes an imperative sentence (someone undetermined is ordered to "time flies") then "flies" is now a plural noun, and a relation of co-reference is established between "files" and "they" in the third sentence. Now we can make sense of the second and third sentences in relation to the first: the second says that the imperative cannot be carried out, while the third gives a reason for this.

Now, how does this involve constraints, as that term has been used in this chapter? In the first place, we can model the requirements of anaphora, where the essential condition is co-reference, as an identity relation, that must also satisfy the constraint of equality in number. (In other languages, there might also be constraints on gender and case for the sentences to cohere in this manner.) So if we interpret "flies" as a plural noun, then we can satisfy these constraints. There is also a co-reference between the original imperative and the contradiction that is now satisfied ("You cannot time flies").

Whether or not these sorts of relations can be handled adequately by simple networks of the kind described earlier (and I think that in this case the representation would have to be elaborated beyond one based on discrete domains and extensional relations), it is clear enough that some sort of network of relations stands behind a proper interpretation of groups of sentences such as these, and that these relations must be satisfied in order for the discourse to be coherent.

Explanatory incoherence can arise when an observation is reported that contradicts a theoretical prediction. For example, Count Rumsford's demonstration that the specific heat of brass in the form of slag remained the same although a tremendous amount of heat was released in its production was at variance with the caloric account of heat, which predicted that the specific heat should be less.

Cases such as this have been dealt with by Thagard and his collaborators, who have used constraint satisfaction models explicitly to represent examples of explanatory coherence.[25] For this purpose, they devised a simple kind of constraint network. An example is shown in Figure 9.20.

In this figure, the nodes are propositional elements; these are the variables in the model. Each has a binary domain whose values indicate whether that proposition is true or not. For this purpose, one could use the values {0, 1} or {−1, +1} or even {F, T}. The thin lines in the figure, called "positive constraints", are actually equality constraints, i.e. the propositions

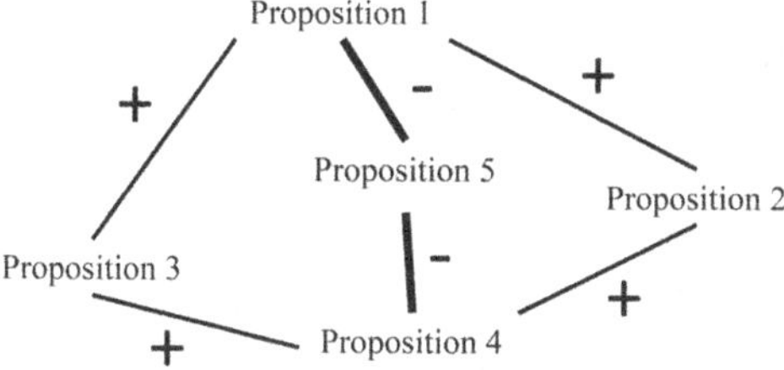

Figure 9.20. Network of propositions, where constraints represent mutual compatibility (thin lines with +) or incompatibility (thick lines with −) with respect to their truth or falsity, based on Thagard's model of conceptual coherence.

associated with such a constraint must be assigned the same value. The meaning is that either both are true or both are false. The thick line is a "negative constraint", in fact an inequality constraint. Its meaning is that if one proposition associated with the constraint (say, 1) is true, then the other (5) must be false, or, conversely, if 1 is false, then 5 must be true.

In this model, maximal coherence is achieved by maximizing the number of satisfied constraints. So this is a CSP model in all its details, where the constraints are "soft" in the sense that they may or may not be satisfied in an optimal solution.[26]

To illustrate these ideas, I take a few propositions from a published example.[27*] This has to do with the chemical explanation of combustion. Two competing explanations are considered: Lavoisier's account based on oxygen, and the older phlogiston hypothesis. Here are two specific hypotheses based on each account (OH-x for oxygen hypotheses, PH-x for phlogiston hypotheses) plus two kinds of evidence (E-x).

- OH-1: Pure air contains oxygen.
- OH-3: In combustion, oxygen from air combines with the burning body.
- PH-1: Combustible bodies contain phlogiston.
- PH-3: In combustion, phlogiston is given off.
- E-1: In combustion, heat and light are given off.
- E-3: Combustion only occurs in the presence of air.

These hypotheses and statements of evidence can be organized into the network shown in Figure 9.21.

In this network, solid lines are the positive constraints while the dashed lines are the negative ones. In addition, it is supposed that evidential nodes are set to +1. To be consistent, the hypothesis nodes linked to them must also be set to 1. But then the negative constraints cannot be satisfied. In this case there is no solution that will satisfy all the constraints, but a maximal solution will set the OH nodes to 1 and the PH to 0. (In fact, the only constraints not satisfied in this case will be those between E-1 and PH-1 and –3.)

As far as I am aware, this work has never gotten beyond the stage of simple demonstrations of this sort. Moreover, there is a certain degree of

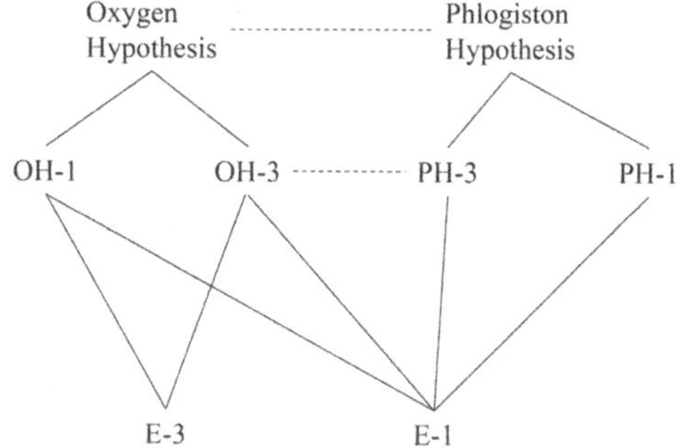

Figure 9.21. Propositional network associated with competing explanations for chemical reactions involving oxygen. (Based on discussion in Thagard, 1989.)

Figure 9.22. A Julesz random dot stereogram. When viewed stereoscopically, the two highlighted portions of the figures fuse to form a rectangle that seems closer to the viewer than the rest of the stereogram, which forms a background.

gimcrackery in the claim that scientific arguments can be adequately described by these rather simple-minded Boolean networks, together with algorithms that find the maximal number of simultaneously satisfied constraints. Nonetheless, there is clearly something to these ideas, and, what is most important for our purposes, they highlight the fact that constraints and constraint satisfaction may play a critical role in argumentation and discourse, as reflected in the 'coherence problem'.

As far as I know, the next example has not been associated with constraint concepts in the literature, or at least not with this terminology. But I would contend that it, in fact, involves a form of constraint satisfaction.

Among its many other functions, the human visual system allows us to see the world in three dimensions. To do this, it must extract the necessary information from the two-dimensional pattern of excitation on the retina. One powerful cue is due to the fact that an image of an object in the real world is transmitted to both eyes so that it falls on both retinas. But depending on how far the object is from the point of focus, these images will fall on slightly disparate parts of the two retinas. By using random-dot stereograms in which there are no discernable figures that can be matched in the brain, Juelez was able to show that retinal disparity alone can produce the perception of depth. A simple demonstration is shown above. If the reader views it from close range so that he can fuse the two images (in this case three squares will be seen), then in a little while he should see a small square floating above the larger square, which is now in the background.[28]

The basic explanation for this effect is that disparity detectors in a given part of the visual field give rise to a perception of depth at a certain distance. If these detectors excite other detectors while inhibiting detectors associated with different depths, then they can arrive at a coherent perception of depth in the visual field, much like the nodes and links in the coherence networks just discussed. This, therefore, is a kind of constraint satisfaction process. This also implies that some parts of our nervous systems are 'hard-wired' to carry out computations that solve constraint satisfaction problems.

My final example is more mundane. This pertains to the constraints that are employed throughout everyday life and are imposed by convention. Examples include the use of waste baskets for refuse (most of us don't throw refuse on the floors of our homes), the use of utensils to eat, room arrangements in houses, and the use of paper of a particular size for writing. All of these confer benefit in terms of efficiency, sanitation, etc. (contrary to the assertions of adolescent dissidents of various ages).[29*]

So, as I said before …

Constraints, Search, and Human Intelligence

But how is all this related to intelligence as we ordinarily think of it? As I have just demonstrated, much of what is called intelligence, including that embodied in AI systems, is organized to handle constraints, or more accurately, to find solutions to problems where constraint handling is necessary.

In fact, the examples given in the previous section show that portions of human intelligence must be organized so that constraints can be dealt with. At the perceptual level, there seem to be special-purpose algorithms that deal with specific classes of constraints surpassingly well. There are also systems at the 'cognitive level' that appear to be more flexible, though less efficient, and which are required for coherent thought.

On the other hand, human beings seem to be at a distinct disadvantage when it comes to problems like scheduling and complex configurations. In considering this fact, it is important to note that such problems seem only to have arisen with the rise of mass society and industrialization. This was when companies had to devise schedules of operation so that a medley of orders could be handled, or maintain inventories with thousands of items, etc.

Historically, such tasks have been done by designated or de facto 'experts', people who were capable of handling the exigencies involved in putting together reasonable, efficient schedules of tasks to be done. In performing such jobs, these people appear to rely on heuristics as well as generate-and-test strategies, and perhaps primitive forms of heuristic search.

As a result, human beings typically aren't very good at such tasks, although some can do a remarkable job. In these cases, therefore, automated combinatorial search constitutes a marked advance over unaided HI. All such methods and systems are examples of AAI or HAI. Note that all the advances in this field were due to human beings, and this continues to be the case up through the present. In other words, we made the tools that enabled us to solve CSPs in novel situations. So here again, in each instance, HI and AI must be considered as two parts of the same system.

In addition, some of the problems posed by large-scale industrial and social developments seem have been solved implicitly, through trial and error across groups of people, resulting in various forms of what I have called "group intelligence". This can be seen, for example, in the historical development of supply chains.

In short, an awful lot of intelligence involves handling constraints.[30*]

Endnotes

1. See J. E. Doran & D. Michie, "Experiments with the graph traverser program", *Proceedings of the Royal Society*, 1966, 294A: 235–259. Work on the analysis of this puzzle and the development of powerful search algorithms is an interesting story in itself. In this case it led to a series of important algorithms beginning with the breadth-first A* algorithm (P. E. Hart, N. J. Nilsson & B. Raphael, "A formal basis for the heuristic determination of minimum cost paths", *IEEE Transactions of Systems Science and Cybernetics*, 1968, SSC-4: 100–107). An important summary work is: J. Pearl, *Heuristics: Intelligent Search Strategies for Computer Problem Solving*, Addison-Wesley, 1984.
2. A related concern of the Blocks World project was to enable a robot to manipulate objects in the layout, but this is tangential to the present discussion.
3. An introductory account of the elementary processes of robot vision, including the early blocks world systems, can be found in V. Daniel Hunt, *Smart Robots*. New York: Chapman and Hall, 1985.
4. See M. B. Clowes, "On seeing things", *Artificial Intelligence*, 1971, 2: 79–116; D. A. Huffman, "Impossible objects as nonsense sentences", In: B. Meltzer & D. Michie, editors, *Machine Intelligence 6*, Edinburgh: Edinburgh University, 1971, pp. 295–323.
5. The procedure described is due to D. Waltz, "Understanding line drawings of scenes with shadows", In: P. H. Winston, editor, *The Psychology of Computer Vision*, New York: McGraw-Hill, 1975, pp. 19–91.
6. The basic reference here is A. Mackworth, "Consistency in networks of relations", *Artificial Intelligence*, 1977, 8: 99–118.
7. Even with this brief discussion, it will not surprise the reader that the literature on this subject is quite technical; most if not all of it is still only found in primary sources. A relatively accessible paper is M. A. Trick, "A schedule-then-break approach to sports scheduling", In: E. Burke & W. Erben, editors, *Practice and Theory of Automated Timetabling III* (Lect. Notes in Computer Science No. 2079), Berlin: Springer, 2001, pp. 242–252. A more recent review is R. V. Rasmussen & M. A. Trick, "Round robin scheduling — A survey", *European Journal of Operational Research*, 2008, 188: 617–636.
8. M. Trick, "Scheduling major league baseball", Michael Trick's Operations Research Blog, November 6, 2013, http://mat.tepper.cmu.edu/blog/?p=1832.
9. Here I include some standard abbreviations, such as OR for operations research and CSP for constraint satisfaction problem.
10. The idea of satisfiability actually originated outside the field of AI, in connection with symbolic logic. But since it is so closely related to the CSP formulation (in fact there are equivalences between the two) and because these equivalences are often taken advantage of (and because AI is so deeply tied up with logic), I have put the two together here under one heading.

11. In fact, an alternative constraint-satisfaction based approach to this sort of global optimization problem has been devised during the last few decades, involving bounds on the values that the equations can take (basically boxing in portions of the space where the optimum must be found with successively smaller boxes until a minimal criterion for the size of the box is reached).
12. Two examples are given here to impart some idea of the kinds of problems addressed in operations research and global optimization.

    Operations research (OR) is now a vast area of endeavor, and it has spawned a wide variety of models. However, they are all based on a generic scheme where a goal (called an objective) is expressed by means of an equation, coupled with a series of constraints, also expressed as equations or relational expressions. So let's consider a simple case involving a form of mathematical programming called linear programming — where the objective and the constraints are all expressed as linear relations, i.e. with the form $y = ax_1 + bx_2 .. +kx_k$. (This example is taken from F. S. Hillier & G. J. Lieberman, *Introduction to Operations Research* (Fifth Edition), New York: McGraw-Hill, 1990, by permission.)

    Suppose there is a company that has three plants, which manufacture either or both of two products, glass frames and glass doors. Glass frames yield a profit of \$3 per unit; glass doors yield \$5. Each product has a certain required capacity, and each plant has an overall capacity. These features are summarized in the table below:

plant	product requirements 1	2	Plant capacity
1	1	0	4
2	0	2	12
3	3	2	18
unit profit	\$3	\$5	

Now, we can turn this into a linear programming model by considering two variables, the units of glass frames to be manufactured and the units of glass doors, which we will denote as x_1 and x_2. First we express the total profit with the equation:

$$Z = 3x_1 + 5x_2$$

In this case, the objective is to make Z as large as possible. However, we can only do this within the constraints imposed by the capacity requirements. These we can represent as follows:

$$\begin{aligned} x_1 &\leq 4 \\ 2x_2 &\leq 12 \\ 3x_1 + 2x_2 &\leq 18 \end{aligned}$$

In this case profit is maximized when $x_1 = 2$ and $x_2 = 6$, which gives a total profit of 36. Note that when these are substituted for the variables in the constraint relations, all constraints are satisfied. Notice that at plant 1 x_1 could be as much as 4; but in this case because of the constraints at plant 3, x_2 could be no more than 3; so in this case the total profit would only be $3 \times 4 + 5 \times 3 = 27$. So, although $x_1 = 4$, $x_2 = 3$ is a feasible solution (it satisfies all the constraints), it is not the optimal one. (The main method for finding optimal solutions for such systems of equations is the famous simplex algorithm, which we don't need to go into here. A simple problem like this can also be solved graphically, as shown in the text cited.)

A number of engineering problems ranging from transistor modeling to chemical plant production can be expressed as complex equations. A example is the equation,

$$\sum^{5} i\cos(i+1)x+i)$$

which when graphed over part of its range looks like this:

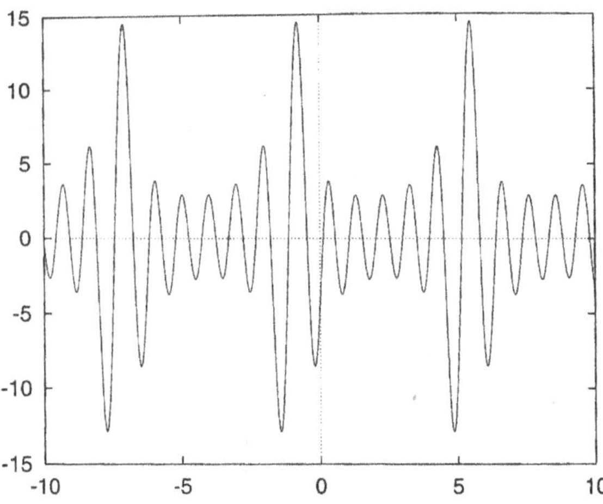

A global optimization problem associated with this equation would be to find the global minimum. Notice that in this case there are many places where the curve dips to a local minimum before rising again, so finding the global minimum (the deepest dip) is not a trivial problem. (The example is taken from P. Van Hentenryck, L. Michel & Y. Deville, *Numerica*, Cambridge, MA & London: MIT, 1997, pp. 9–10. The figure is reprinted from a portion of Figure 1.3, by permission.)

13. A much more reasonable way to order backtrack search is to assign the variables with only one possible value first, so they are all at the top of the search tree. Then each assignment to a blank square checks that assignment against all squares with an obligatory assignment that might be in conflict. Doing this reduces the number of

search nodes to 942 (with 74 backtracks), while the time (in my implementation) is reduced from 2.07 seconds to 0.01 seconds.

14. D. J. Futuyma, "Evolutionary constraint and ecological consequences", *Evolution*, 2010, 64: 1865–1884, p. 1865.
15. See D. M. Raup, "Geometric analysis of shell coiling: General problems", *Journal of Paleontology*, 1966, 40: 1178–1190.
16. *Ibid*., Figure 4.
17. J. Maynard Smith *et al.*, "Developmental constraints and evolution", *Quarterly Review of Biology*, 1985, 60: 265–287.
18. In some cases the basic CSP model may not be sufficient. However, there are some interesting extensions available. One, called the conditional CSP, incorporates conditionality into the basic model itself, so that certain constraints or even variables do not appear unless other variables take on certain values. (See M. Sabin, E. C. Freuder & R. J. Wallace, "Greater efficiency for conditional constraint satisfaction" In: F. Rossi, editor, *Principles and Practice of Constraint Programming — CP 2004*, Lect. Notes in Computer Science No. 2833, Berlin: Springer, 2004, pp. 649–663 and references therein.) There are also hierarchical models in which variables at one level become entire subgraphs at another. (See, for example, D. Sabin & E. C. Freuder, "Configuration as composite constraint satisfaction", In: *Proceedings of the AAAI 1996 AI and Manufacturing Planning Workshop*, Menlo Park, CA: AAAI, 1996, pp. 153–161.)
19. I see several problems with this area of research, which is why I have chosen not to review it in the main text. Regarding the models themselves, these are billed as neural network models, which gives them a surface plausibility by virtue of the fact that there are networks composed of real neurons that underlie cognition and behavior. However, in these models, the "neural networks" are built with 'magic units', which have many of the same properties as the system whose behavior they are supposed to account for. It's not clear to me that this is the kind of model that is wanted as an explanation at the psychological level. But perhaps an even more important problem is the status of cognitive dissonance itself. In the first place, I am not convinced that cognitive dissonance as described by Festinger is a real process, i.e. that it operates in the manner postulated by his theory. For example, there is an old but significant literature that shows that people sometimes seek out information that is at odds with their opinions, and this flatly contradicts the assumptions of Festinger's theory, which supposes that people always act to reduce dissonance. Perhaps I don't fully understand all the nuances of this field, but it isn't clear to me why one would want to model effects that may have very different causes, and in some cases may even be mythological.
20. In this context a telling observation — so it seems to me — is that when faced with an ungrammatical sentence, often one can understand its meaning and recognize that it is ungrammatical at the same time. This suggests to me at least that there is something like a generative system that supports grammaticality, above and beyond 'constructions' such as idioms, constraints on pairing verbs or nouns with adjectives,

different shades of meaning of a word depending on the phrase or sentence it appears in, etc. (Of course, Chomsky's old "Colorless green ideas sleep furiously" example, which is a perfectly good English sentence albeit meaningless, is perhaps an even more telling demonstration of the separation of syntax and semantics.)

21. L. Haegeman, *Introduction to Government & Binding Theory,* 2nd edition. Oxford: Blackwell, 1994
22. These distinctions are discussed in R. Huddleston, *English Grammar: An Outline*. Cambridge: Cambridge University, 1988, pp. 76–77. In this passage, Huddleston contrasts, "I arrived here last week" with "I have arrived here last week", arguing that the latter is unacceptable for reasons very similar to the objections to sentence (1) given in the text.
23. For an account of construction grammars, see M. Hilpert. *Construction Grammar and its Application to English*. Edinburgh University, 2014. For a discussion of property grammars, see P. Blache, "Property grammars: A fully constraint-based theory. In: H. Christiansen, P. R. Skadhauge & J. Villadsen, eds. *Constraint Solving and Language Processing*. Springer, 2004, pp. 1–16, as well as the recent volume edited by P. Blache, H. Christiansen, V. Dahl, D. Duchier & J. Villadsen, *Constraints and Language*. Cambridge Scholars, 2014.
24. This example is taken from M. A. K. Halliday & R. Hasan. *Cohesion in English*. Longman, 1976, p. 4.
25. See, for example, P. Thagard & K. Verbeurgt, "Coherence as Constraint Satisfaction" *Cognitive Science*, 1998, 22: 1–24, and P. Thagard, *Coherence in Thought and Action*, Cambridge, MA & London: MIT, 2000.
26. P. Thagard, "Explanatory coherence", *Behavioral and Brain Sciences*, 1989, 12: 435–502.
27. *Ibid*. It should be noted that in the paper from which this example was taken, the notion of constraint satisfaction was not yet applied in this context. Instead, Thagard's discussion is in terms of a "connectionist" model (a kind of neural network model). However, the translation to constraint networks can be done in a straightforward fashion, as the example shows.
28. B. Julesz, *Foundations of Cyclopean Perception*, Cambridge, MA: MIT, 1971.
29. Still another area in which the notion of constraints arises is called "constraints on learning". The term refers to various ways in which the efficiency of learning is affected by features of the organism or its environment. Organismic features include species-typical tendencies, for example, making it difficult for a rat to learn to press a bar to avoid a noxious stimulus, since its species-typical proclivity is to flee. Environmental features include relative spatial locations; for example a cue stimulus may be harder to associate with some action if it is not spatially adjacent to the direction of action. Such examples are not really constraint satisfaction problems, since they have to do with discovering relations rather than satisfying them. But from a broader perspective they too exemplify the presence of constraints in a real-world

situation. For general reviews, see M. E. P. Seligman (1970). "On the generality of the laws of learning". *Psychological Review*, 77: 406–418.; S. J. Shettleworth (1972). "Constraints on learning". In: D. S. Lehrman, R. A. Hinde & E. Shaw, eds. *Advances in the Study of Behavior. Vol. 4*. New York: Academic Press, pp. 1–68. For some specific examples, see R. J. Bolles (1970). "Species-specific defense reactions and avoidance learning". *Psychological Review*, 77: 32–48, and R. L. Gallon (1974). "Spatial location of a visual signal and shuttle box avoidance by goldfish (Carassius auratus)". *Journal of Comparative and Physiological Psychology*, 86(2): 316–321.

30. In this chapter I have focused on my own field of expertise, which is constraint satisfaction. However, chapters with an equivalent thrust could be written about reasoning under uncertainty (especially the work on Bayes nets) and machine learning. Interestingly, these fields, like constraint satisfaction, are both heavily algorithmic, so that again one finds that the great advances in these areas are due to the discovery of algorithms for handling problems that are combinatorial in nature. So in that sense the present chapter can 'stand in' for all of these topics, in that the conclusions drawn here can be drawn from them as well.

Part IV

Human Intelligence and Its Discontents

10

AI: Critics and Cheerleaders

Critics of AI and the AI Program. I. Attempts at Refutation

Given the over-exuberant claims of some early AI researchers, it was inevitable that the AI program would inspire a host of critics to 'rise to the challenge' and examine and pass judgment upon it. Unsurprisingly, many, perhaps most, of these judgments were dismissive.

In general two different tacks have been taken. Either the author tries to fashion a decisive argument to the effect that AI can never match certain fundamental features of human intelligence, or the author adduces evidence from psychology or the neurosciences that he thinks reflect special properties that are incompatible with machine intelligence. In this chapter, I will consider each approach and discuss the leading proponents of each strategy.

*

Perhaps the two best-known attempts to fashion a 'killer' argument are those by the philosopher John Searle and the physicist Roger Penrose.

Searle has made two major arguments against what he calls "strong AI" as opposed to "weak AI". Since this distinction is important to Searle, if not to us, it is worth recounting at the outset:

> "According to weak AI, the principal value of the computer in the study of the mind is that it gives us a very powerful tool. For example, it enables us to formulate and

test hypotheses in a more rigorous and precise fashion than before. But according to strong AI the computer is not merely a tool in the study of the mind; rather the appropriately programmed computer really is a mind in the sense that computers given the right programs can be literally said to understand and have other cognitive states. And, according to strong AI, because the programmed computer has cognitive states, the programs are not mere tools that enable us to test psychological explanations; rather, the programs are themselves the explanations."[1]

Note that the terms "cognitive states" and "understand" are used to demarcate intelligence, terms that designate unobservables or can only be vaguely defined.

To refute the claims of strong AI, Searle proposed a thought experiment, now known as the Chinese Room argument. The inspiration for the argument came from a particular AI project carried out by Roger Schank and his colleagues, the goal of which was to write programs that could understand written English, beginning with sentences, but later including simple narratives and even news reports.

To adequately understand the argument, one must know something about how the Yale programs worked, as well as the basic ideas behind them.[2] It begins with the idea — or intelligent observation — that understanding involves making inferences. For example, if we read (or hear) the sentence,

John gave the book to Mary,

we can infer that the book is now in Mary's possession. We are also likely to make other inferences: that John and Mary probably know each other, that either Mary wanted to read the book or that John thought she might be interested in reading it, and so forth. Of course, if the sentence is spoken in some immediate context, in which the hearer knows the parties involved (and the speaker in turn knows this, so that a brief message of this sort is sufficient), then inferences like these will be made with greater certainty. I think it is fair to say that all these notions that are aroused are part of our understanding of the sentence.

In keeping with this line of reasoning, one kind of evidence for comprehension is the ability to answer questions regarding a sentence or a sequence of sentences that forms a narrative. In particular, a system that understands such material should be able to give answers to questions that require a degree of background knowledge about the general situation referred to by the narrative.

Here is an example, produced by a program called SAM (for Script Applier Mechanism).[3] The input text was:

> "John went to a restaurant. He ordered a hot dog. The waiter said they didn't have any. He asked for a hamburger. When the hamburger came, it was burnt. He left the restaurant."

Given this input, SAM answered the following questions:

Q: Did John order a hot dog?
A: Yes.
Q: Did John eat the hot dog?
A: No, the waiter told John the management was unable to give it to him.
Q: What did the waiter serve John?
A: The waiter served John a hamburger.
Q: Why didn't John eat the hamburger?
A: Because the hamburger was overdone.
Q: Did John pay the check?
A: No, John was angry because the hamburger was overdone and so he left the restaurant.

So how does a program work that understands sentences and narratives in these terms?

SAM and other programs in this series were based on a theory about the meaning of sentences called conceptual dependency (CD). The basic idea is that meaning involves certain basic concepts, and that these have necessary associations via dependency relations. When someone encounters a statement or a connected sequence of statements such as that above, certain basic concepts are evoked, which lead to other concepts being evoked via the dependencies.

A key idea was that there were a small number of conceptual "primitives" that dependency networks could be built around. It was possible to conceive of a system of primitive concepts in this way because Schank and his coworkers considered actions (which they called ACTs) as the basic concepts, and this was related to the idea that a sentence is basically the expression of an act. Conceptual primitives included transfer of a possession (called ATRANS), change in location (PTRANS), communication (MTRANS), as well as movement per se (MOVE), attending (ATTEND), and others, totaling a little over ten.

In addition to ACTs, there were concepts related to objects, called Picture Producers (PP), and two classes of modifiers, one related to ACTs (AA, for action aiders) and one related to Picture Producers (PA).

Consider again the sentence,

John gave the book to Mary.

When this is interpreted by the CD system, the verb "give" is translated into the ACT primitive ATRANS, which means a transfer of possession. The dependency network can be represented diagrammatically by a graph with different types of edges, which are also annotated in different ways. In this case it looks like this:

$$\text{John} \overset{p}{\rightleftarrows} \text{ATRANS} \overset{o}{\longleftarrow} \text{book} \overset{R}{\longleftarrow} \begin{cases} \xrightarrow{\text{to}} \text{Mary} \\ \xrightarrow[\text{from}]{} \text{John} \end{cases}$$

The annotations are as follows: "p" indicates that the ACT takes place in the past, "o" indicates that this is an object-dependency, "R" indicates a recipient-dependency on "book". The double arrows indicate the mutual dependencies between ACT and ACTOR; in other cases, the arrowhead points toward the governing concept in a particular dependency.

Here, let me introduce another important idea, related to that of inference in deriving meaning. This is that one can also use these networks to predict parts of a sentence not yet encountered as well as subsequent actions in connected discourse. For example, ATRANS will engender certain predictions such as a donor and a recipient, while MBUILD would engender different predictions.

By itself, the CD system was insufficient to interpret connected prose in the form of short stories. Therefore, programs like SAM were equipped with further features, which were built on top of the CD framework. In addition, the emphasis shifted somewhat from ACTs to EVENTs, so that the latter became the central concept; clearly, it is related to the sentence in much the same way that the ACT is related (with appropriate caveats) to the verb. Along with this, the CD graph above was treated as an element in a larger structure. At the same time, it took on more frame-like characteristics, as can be seen in the following description[4]:

Every EVENT has:
  an ACTOR
  an ACTION performed by that actor
  an OBJECT that the action is performed upon
  a DIRECTION in which that action is oriented

Taking our previous example,

John gave the book to Mary,

the program puts John in the ACTOR slot, Mary in the OBJECT slot, while DIRECTION is from John to Mary. As before, the ACTION is ATRANS.

However, connecting CDs together still doesn't solve the problem of creating a coherent representation of most narratives. The problem, as Schank and Rieger put it, is that "frequently texts seemed to make long "leaps of faith". That is, you often could not determine the causal connectedness because you needed a great deal of detailed knowledge about a situation in order to determine the causal relationships involved."

These authors give the following example, which seems perfectly comprehensible to us[5]:

> "John was hungry. He went into Goldstein's and ordered a pastrami sandwich. It was served to him quickly. He left the waitress a large tip."

The authors go on to say: "People are capable of responding rather easily, and with a fair amount of certainty, to the following questions:

What is Goldstein's?
What did John eat?
Who made the sandwich?
Who took John's order?
Who served the sandwich?
Why did John leave a large tip?

This leads naturally to the idea, which harks back to earlier notions of schemas and frames, that people have basic situations and scenarios stored in long-term memory, which they use to interpret text. In program form, such schemas were called "scripts". Scripts could be invoked when keywords (such as "hungry", "sandwich", "waitress") were detected, after which the program looked for other elements of the script, so that the elements of the story could be fitted into a coherent pattern.

In addition, a notion of goals and planning for those goals was introduced. This was meant to enable a program to understand narratives like this one[6]:

> "John needed money for a down payment on a house. He called his sister."

In this case, some notion of John's goals and strategies for achieving those goals seems necessary if a program is to 'make sense' of a story like this.

There have been a number of other important developments in this line of research that I will mention briefly. First, it was found that the interpretation of many narratives involved representing multiple goals as well as recurrent goals; it was also necessary to recognize conflicting goals held by different actors in order to explain stories such as the following.[7]

> "John wanted to win the stockcar race. Bill also wanted to win. Before the race John cut Bill's ignition wire."

It was also necessary to assess the significance of events for different actors (loosely called affect or emotion by authors like Dyer), which determines whether a possible goal is likely to be relevant (e.g. consider a wealthy banker losing a dollar bill as opposed to an indigent). Other work has addressed the general problem of how long-term memory should be organized in order to support ongoing interpretation of streams of events.[8]

Needless to say, the Stanford-Yale programs for story understanding and related topics are subject to the same reservations and caveats that were considered in Chapters 2-5. In fact when one examines the actual code, some of which is available, one finds all sorts of peculiar features, some of which look distinctly like kludges. Thus, the same issues arise concerning AI systems as reflecting human intelligence, and once again the conclusion is that they are more properly seen as extensions of human intelligence than as something independent of it.

And, of course, there are also legitimate questions concerning the nature of "understanding" in these systems, questions that revolve around whether the outputs are ultimately just canned responses, despite the fact that they are based on elaborate inferences and data structures.

Another question raised by this work is whether conceptual structures are really this ACT/EVENT oriented. A related problem is that it is unclear how nominals (nouns) are handled as such. Such concepts appear frequently in discussions of systems like SAM, but an overall conceptual scheme is not described.

And, as occurs so often in early AI systems, there are cases where complex concepts appear to be finessed by simple labeling. An example is found in the chapter by Cullingford in the collection edited by Schank and Riesbeck. In this case, an incident in which a person died in a car accident is modeled with a "$VEHICLE-ACCIDENT" script, that supposedly represents the fact that "a negative change in the physical state of a bodypart (belonging, by inference, to Mary Jones) caused a terminal change in her health".[9*] I for one am not convinced that the #bodypart, #person, and #physical-object slots of $VEHICLE-ACCIDENT are sufficient to convey a proper understanding of the relations involved in this case.

More generally, the concept-label strategy seems in the end to be terribly inadequate. For one thing, there is no implication in this that concepts can be mined for deeper meaning. And finally, since a multitude of words are mapped into a relatively small number of 'meanings', Schank et al. never deal with the question of why there should be so many terms (i.e. words) with the same meaning. Given their scheme of things, it is natural to ask why something so rich and prolix as ordinary language was fashioned on the anvil of natural selection.

However, the pertinent question for us is whether these systems can be said to embody some form of understanding. And in this case, I think the answer is yes. In short, given what seems like a reasonable conception of understanding, since the Yale programs can make such inferences based on their background knowledge, they can be said to embody elements of understanding. (I would certainly agree that the scope of their understanding is limited, but that's another issue.[10*,11*])

But Searle will have none of this.[12*] So let us turn now to his arguments, beginning with the Chinese room. (Here, I will recount it in what I take to be its original form, which spoke directly to the work of Schank *et al.*[13])

Imagine yourself in a room. Your task is to carry out certain instructions involving Chinese characters; it is assumed that you know essentially nothing about Chinese; that is, you cannot recognize specific Chinese characters or even tell whether a similar pattern of marks is a genuine Chinese character or not. However, you have been given "a set of rules" (in English) that allows you to "correlate" a batch of Chinese symbols with another batch on the basis of their physical features. Other rules allow you to correlate a third batch with the other two, "and these rules instruct" you "how to give back certain Chinese symbols with certain sorts of shapes in response to certain series of shapes given" "in the third batch". In fact, the first batch is called (by those who understand Chinese) a script, the second is a story, and the third is a list of questions. We also "suppose" that you become so skilled at following the rules that the responses (answers) you give back "are absolutely indistinguishable from those of native Chinese speakers". From this Searle concludes that one can meet the requirements set up by Schank and others for demonstrating story understanding without having to understand the language at all — nor any stories written in that language.

To begin with, I note that in the original 1980 article the argument is introduced with this remark: "One way to test any theory of the mind is to ask oneself what it would be like if my mind actually worked on the principles that the theory says all minds work on." Now, if this were true, and one could really test theories of anything in this fashion, then this would run counter to all that we know about the scientific method and how empirical investigation must be carried out. For serious scientific testing (which is all that will be considered here), asking oneself "what it would be like" simply doesn't pass muster. Moreover, since we are dealing with processing that must be largely unconscious (we are not conscious of how we access word meanings or how we make the kinds of inferences that are required to answer questions about the situation referred to by a short narrative, although the processes can be elucidated by measuring reaction times in carefully arranged situations), it isn't possible to determine how one's "mind works" in this case by examining 'it' from 'the inside' in the way that Searle is assuming.[14]

So it seems pretty clear that Searle has gotten off on the wrong foot even before he presents his actual arguments. But more interestingly, he has revealed a fundamental flaw in his mode of thinking right at the beginning of the discourse.

Now let's consider the argument itself. In the first place, the Chinese Room argument assumes that one can have a perfect list of linguistic equivalents, as well as rules specified at the level of symbol matches for every question asked. But is this even possible? Note how this was slipped into the argument as a given. One has to ask how anyone could be expected to refute an argument when it is based on such dubious assumptions. This is a big problem with non-empirical arguments like this one; too often they are intellectual sleights-of-hand. (In this connection, notice that the entire argument is couched in terms of achievements (we do this, we do that), which avoids having to delineate the mechanisms needed to effect them.)

So I would say to Searle: "Build your Chinese room! Show us that your argument is more than mere words. Because as of now you haven't demonstrated that anyone can actually do what you describe."

But to my mind the chief problem follows from the "flaw" that I referred to earlier. In the Chinese room, a human being is functioning as a computing element. In this role, one would not be expected to "understand"; understanding is a system concept. Note that here I'm not attempting to resolve or even shed any great light on the problem of understanding. I'm just arguing that the Chinese room demonstration doesn't refute the possibility of understanding-by-computer.

Searle has more general arguments related to cognition in humans and machines that turn on the idea of consciousness. This seems to have become his all-purpose AI-slayer, as I gather from a recent review of the books by Bostrom and others on AI and its potentials.[15]

The basic argument is that genuine understanding as well as intelligence depends on "consciousness", which is an emergent property of biological neural networks. A proper account of the world-at-large will therefore include both subjective and objective events. In this framework "thoughts and feelings" and other subjective events are put in the same basket as "understanding".[16] One important implication of his position is that Searle is committed to giving subjective mental "states" causal status.

A basic point that Searle elides over is that it may be possible to describe the network of causes underlying phenomena like understanding (not to mention thinking and feeling) in physical terms without discarding the idea that there are (in some sense) mental 'states'. (Here, the term "state" is quite problematic, since it can often be given a definite physical or at least operational meaning, as is done in many parts of biology and neurobiology. Consider, for example, sleep versus wakefulness. Or hunger versus satiety. Or a learned response performed versus extinguished.) This means that a mental "state" can at one time refer to some physical process and at another to a correlated subjective experience.[17*]

In light of the problematic character, and evident multi-facetedness of understanding, one of the things I find odd is the certainty with which Searle propounds this argument. Why is Searle so sure of himself, especially when his entire argument depends on poorly specified terms such as "mind" and "consciousness"? Thinking about this, it's hard to dispel the impression that his stance on this issue is in some ways an act, a kind of bluff.

In fact, he seems to be playing a verbal game: by stipulating that genuine intelligence involves consciousness and stipulating that consciousness is a biological function which machines can't have, then machines can't be intelligent — but this is pure sophistry. And I suspect that someone about to lose his job because an AI system can perform the same activities will not find any consolation in Searle's assurance that because they're not "conscious", AI systems are not really intelligent.

Perhaps the major shortcoming in all this is that Searle assumes that issues such as the nature of thinking and understanding by artifacts can be resolved by clever arguments. In this respect, he seems not to have fully grasped the implications of the scientific revolution. (But then how many of us have?)

But two can play this game. In this spirit, here is an argument in the manner of Searle. Searle assumes that capacities like understanding require something called consciousness, which he assumes is an emergent capacity of biological neural networks. Schank *et al.* have demonstrated that computer systems can behave in a way that is commensurate with understanding. There is no need to assume that while the program is running the computer is conscious. (In fact, the activities of the computer program mirror what are obviously unconscious activities in human cognition.) I think we can conclude from this that consciousness, however one construes it, is not required for understanding.

The key word here is "capacity". Searle needs to show why Schank et al's demonstrations do not demonstrate such a capacity, even if it is in a very limited form. And, of course, to say that consciousness is required is to say nothing whatsoever regarding the functions that are required for a system to demonstrate this or any other cognitive capacity.[18*]

At this point, let's reconsider the reaction time experiment discussed in a footnote to Chapter 1. Is there anything in a Searlean account that could explain why it takes 80 milliseconds longer to decide that "a" and "A" are the same letter than to decide that "A" and "A" are the same? Note that under both conditions we can assume that the subject is conscious of the two letters; so obviously, invoking this as an explanation doesn't get us very far. (In fact, the whole reaction time literature seems to me to be a kind of tsunami that has more or less obliterated arguments such as these, if one had only noticed.)

Searle also seems to assume that human understanding is basically unproblematic, that understanding does not have its vicissitudes. But as any pedagogue should know, human beings show all sorts of deficiencies in this department. Moreover, they are blighted by what could be called the "illusion of understanding". That's why we have to give tests!

A nice demonstration of the problematic character of 'understanding' is found in an old paper by E. L. Thorndike.[19] Thorndike was trying to show the close relation between reasoning and mental habits. (In fact he thought that reasoning consisted solely of "the organization and cooperation of habits" of varying degrees of coarseness and refinement.) To do this, he used common high school algebra tasks, presenting them to subjects either in their usual form or with the terms altered, so that the appearance of an expression or equation was less familiar. Examples included:

Ordinary	Changed
What is the square of $x + y$?	What is the square of $b_1 + b_2$?
Multiply x^a by x^b	Multiply 4^a by 4^b

These and other problems were given to graduate students, who could be expected to "understand" the mathematical rules involved and how to apply them. (Remember, this was in the 1920s.)

In most cases, however, Thorndike found that the time to solve the problem and the error rate both increased when the format of the problem was altered, sometimes dramatically. So, in the first case above, the problem in its ordinary form was done incorrectly by 6% of the subjects while with the changed form the error rate was 28%. For the other case, the error rate went from 55 to 71%.

The relevance of this experiment to the present argument is that it shows quite clearly that one cannot discuss or describe human "understanding" without some analysis of the mechanisms that underlie performance. And when this done, through empirical investigation of course, one finds that understanding cannot be simply taken as a given, a property of the "mind".

Suppose I told you that I understood String Theory (which I don't, in fact). How would you go about determining whether this was true? I think we can safely assume that if you actually know something about the theory, you will question me about it. You might ask me to give an account of some relevant phenomenon that the theory bears on. If you were to give me a formal test, you would ask me to solve problems whose solution depends on a knowledge of the subject. You might also ask me 'trick' questions to see whether I could detect errors in reasoning in this field of discourse, and more importantly whether I could explain to you why they were errors. Now, doesn't all this have to do with making inferences? And isn't this therefore the sine qua non of genuine understanding?[20*]

Finally, isn't Searle telling us, in effect, that mechanical fish don't really swim and planes don't really fly? And in the end that may be all one needs to say about his arguments.[21*]

Also, note that, in sharp contrast to Searle's arguments, the research program of Schank and his coworkers raises all sorts of interesting specific questions about how we understand text and thereby sheds considerable light on the phenomenon of understanding. To my mind, that's what genuine intellectual contributions are supposed to do.

*

In his books, *The Emperor's New Mind* (1989) and *Shadows of the Mind* (1994),[22] Penrose takes a different approach to the question of artificial intelligence that is in some ways more interesting, although, again, ultimately questionable. Its special interest lies in the fact that he brings the fundamental work on computability by Turing and others to bear on the discussion. In fact, that work hovers over any discussion of the nature and limits of artificial intelligence. (To distinguish specific references to one or the other volume, I will use the acronyms ENM AND SM.)

At the same time, Penrose, like Searle, conflates the question of the possibility of genuine artificial intelligence with the question of whether the performance of a computer can be equated with having a "mind", which he in turn equates with being "conscious". The present work skirts such issues on the assumption that intelligence can be discussed without having to delve into the vexed issues surrounding the idea of consciousness and its relation to the physical world as we now know it.[23*,24*]

Nonetheless, we can tease out the parts of his argument (in Chapters 2–4 of ENM) that bear on the question of whether human beings possess cognitive capacities that cannot be realized in computer systems. Here, Penrose argues that this question can be linked to the question of whether there are solutions that human beings can derive that are not computable.[25*] In essence, Penrose is using mathematics, and particularly some of the deep questions regarding completeness and consistency of mathematical systems, in order to come to grips with questions about the 'ultimate' adequacy of AI in a way that is sound and convincing.

The following paragraph, from the end of the third chapter, gives the flavor of his argument:

"In Chapter 1, I discussed at some length the point of view of strong AI, according to which mental phenomena are supposed to find their existence within the mathematical idea of an algorithm. In Chapter 2, I stressed the point that the concept of an algorithm is indeed a profound and 'God-given' notion. In this chapter I have been arguing that such 'God-given' mathematical ideas should have some kind of timeless existence, independent of our earthly selves. Does not this viewpoint lend some credence to the strong-AI point of view, by providing the possibility of an etherial type of existence for mental phenomena? Just conceivably so — and I shall even be speculating, later, in favour of a view not altogether dissimilar from this; but if mental phenomena can indeed find a home of this general kind, I do not believe it can be with the concept of an algorithm. What would be needed would be something very much more subtle. The fact that algorithmic things constitute a very narrow and limited part of mathematics will be an important part of the discussions to follow."[26]

The basic argument, developed at length in the aforementioned chapters, is that, against the incompleteness of certain formal systems as demonstrated by Gödel and Turing, there is the fact that we as observers of the proof process can discern that the proposition that is shown to be incapable of being proven within the system is nonetheless true. So that our capacity for understanding does not appear to be limited in the same way as computable functions have been shown to be.[27]

Gödel's incompleteness theorems arose in connection with an effort inspired by the German mathematician David Hilbert to place all of mathematics on a sound foundation. To this end, procedures were sought for ensuring that for every mathematical system it could be shown that, (i) the axioms of the system were consistent with one another, so that one could never derive a theorem T as well as its contradiction ~T, (ii) any true statement in the system could be derived from a set of axioms; this is the property known as "completeness". With the work of Frege, Russell and Whitehead showing that much of mathematics could be expressed as formulas in the propositional and predicate calculi, Hilbert's program became bound up with their logistics program. What Gödel showed was that it was possible to state a theorem, or formula, within a suitably complicated area of mathematics, specifically one that includes arithmetic, which cannot be determined to be true or false within the system itself (i.e. by using the proper rules of inference and the axioms of the system). He was also able to deduce (by reasoning outside the formal system itself) that the formula was true; hence there was at least one statement within the system that was not derivable (and therefore not decidable), and hence the system was incomplete.

The original formula devised by Gödel had the property that it was self-referential; basically, it stated that it was not decidable. (This property was also the key to generating such statements for any extension of the system in which earlier statements of this type could be proven.) Since then it has been possible to demonstrate undecidability for more ordinary statements within mathematical systems.

Given these basic incompleteness theorems, Penrose argues that since a human being who understands Gödel's argument can discern that the given formula is true even though it cannot be proven so within the formal system in which it is stated, and this can be done for any system of sufficient complexity, then the human mind has properties that cannot be duplicated by a mechanical system. Since the formal system in question can also be realized by a Turing machine, Penrose's argument also implies that human mentation cannot be reduced to Turing machine capabilities. Hence strong AI is impossible.

One counter-argument can, I think, be readily dismissed. This is that it is possible to build a formal system that subsumes the system in question, in which the said formula can be proven. But, as noted above, it is always possible to devise self-referential formulas within this new system that cannot be proven within it. And this process can be repeated indefinitely. But as Penrose noted, a person can comprehend this infinite sequence of reformulation and counter-formulation, whereas none of these formal systems is capable of computing this as an outcome.[28]

As far as I can tell, what the argument does show is that a given human 'mind' cannot be duplicated by any particular algorithm. But to quote from the well-known exposition of Gödel's proof by Nagel and Newman, it does not mean:

> "that there are arithmetical truths which are forever incapable of becoming known, or that a "mystic" intuition (radically different in kind and authority from what is generally operative in intellectual advances) must replace cogent proof. It does not mean, as a recent writer claims, that there are "ineluctable limits to human reason". It does mean that the resources of the human intellect have not been, and cannot be, fully formalized, and that new principles of demonstration forever await invention and discovery."[29]

In addition, the Gödelian argument does not preclude the possibility that anything produced by 'mindwork' can also be produced by a suitably constructed program. And that is exactly what we have seen during the past half century. (In this connection, it is interesting that Gödel's proof has been verified with an automated proof checker.[30])

A key problem with such arguments is that the brain is not a fixed system, nor is it ever well defined, whereas proofs of incompleteness all rely upon carefully defined formal systems with a fixed set of axioms. One therefore has to ask whether the rigorous notions of correctness and consistency that are vital to Gödelian arguments even apply to human brains. Based on all the empirical evidence, including the problems adduced during the extensive discussion over Penrose's books, the answer would have to be, "No".

To take one example of the latter: in a discussion of the Gödelian thesis, Feferman lists several errors made by Penrose in his discussion of the incompleteness theorems in SM.[31*] Now, what does this imply about human cognition, and especially about "insight"? For one thing, the latter certainly doesn't appear to be a process with supermundane qualities, like an arrow that always finds its target; indeed, it seems to be excessively error-prone. It also appears that human brains have consistency problems of their own.

The following case is also instructive. The famous 4-color theorem was thought to have been proved during a period of about a decade in the late 19th century. But then someone demonstrated — with a concrete counter-example — that the proof was incorrect. Where was the "insight" that should have shown this in the first place? Why did it fail to function?

In line with this is the fact that mathematical rigor has always depended on prosthetic devices beginning with developments in mathematical notation. Without these accoutrements, it is doubtful that modern mathematics would have come into being at all. Automated theorem proving is just another development within this stream of intellectual development.

This brings us back to the view of intelligence presented in the present work, in which intelligence is always based on a network of agents, some human or biological and now some artificial. It seems to me that this simply adds to the case against Penrose. In fact, if one cannot draw a clear line between human and artificial intelligence, then arguments like those of Penrose lose their force and even their coherence. Although, while it adds another level of interacting parts to the interacting parts within an individual agent, it doesn't seem to add any new difficulties to those already noted (e.g. by Minsky and Sloman) for a single agent of the complexity of a human being.

At the same time, the conception of intelligence presented here does not conflict with Penrose's (or Turing's) characterization of AI in any way that single AI agents do not. This is because at any point in time an intelligence network can be realized by an equivalent Turing machine if it can be represented as a collection of computing elements. In this case, it can be encompassed by the general notion of computability as worked out by Turing and others. When the network has an evolutionary character so that new nodes can be added (and nodes themselves can acquire new properties), then it can acquire computational capacities (i.e. programs) that it didn't have earlier; but these can again be realized by another Turing machine (although the evolutionary trajectory itself may be a problem for this perspective, especially when the evolving network involves so many actual and potential interactions).

When we consider general questions of intelligence in relation to the idea of computability, there are also issues of definition and precision, specifically, the problem of ill-defined inputs. The basic theory of computability assumes well-defined inputs, but in the case of human beings acting in the real world, this condition often cannot be met. So where does that leave us?[32*]

However, judging from the success of neural networks in recognizing real-world inputs ranging from written text to scene recognition, not to mention the success of biological neural networks in handling sensory input, it is possible that there are descriptors powerful enough to discriminate an indefinite number of real-world inputs despite the lack of clear definition in the latter. In addition, algorithms that can seek out solutions of maximum coherence when faced with data from various sources (as discussed in the previous chapter), may allow a system to 'make sense' of the situation overall. And this can be done even when the data obtained is ill-defined or even partly contradictory. In this case, we are, potentially at least, back in the realm of computable functions, where Turing's arguments (and the general AI thesis) apply. However, at this point in time it seems impossible to make an airtight case.[33*]

Critics of AI and the AI Program. II. Claims from Counter Evidence

Now, I want to consider the second general approach that the critics of AI have taken. Rather than coming up with 'killer' arguments, these authors argue that empirical evidence exists that suggests that either there is an unbridgeable gulf between human beings and machines or that good-old-fashioned AI at least will not prove adequate for the task of creating a system with general intelligence. I will begin with the earliest example of this line of thinking, the work of the philosopher Hubert Dreyfus.

Back in the 1970s, Dreyfus published a book with the provocative title, *What Computers Can't Do*. (A 1992 reissue was titled, *What Computers Still Can't Do*.)[34] In this work, he tried to explain why the AI programs of the time had fallen short in their performance of difficult cognitive tasks that at least some human beings were capable of. But he went further and claimed that there were fundamental limitations to the basic ideas of AI that would prevent programs built according to these principles from ever accomplishing what unaided human intelligence could do. I should say that, despite the severity of the criticisms that will follow, I consider Dreyfus' book a careful treatment of the major positions of people in AI and cognitive science, which he develops in sufficient detail to make this a work of genuine significance.

An example of the way in which Dreyfus approaches a particular AI problem is his discussion of chess playing programs and their limitations. Dreyfus was writing in the 1970s, so at that time his arguments appeared to be weightier than they do now. In those days these programs were still very weak players in comparison with experts.

Very tellingly, the section about chess is titled "Fringe consciousness vs. heuristically guided search", as if the two were mutually exclusive (and as if "fringe consciousness" could be compared and contrasted with a physical process such as search). Basically, the idea is that human beings can perceive relationships among pieces on the board so as to "zero in" on weaknesses in the opponent's position, and this seems to involve elements both inside and outside the current focus of attention. Moreover, we know that such skills depend on experience gained from playing a large number of games. Summarizing his argument, Dreyfus says:

> "Applying these ideas to our original protocol, we can conclude that our subject's familiarity with the overall chess pattern and with the past moves of this particular game enabled him to recognize the *lines of force, the loci of strength and weakness*, as well as specific positions."[35] (emphasis added)

On the basis of these sorts of vague, hand-waving assertions (cf. the italicized part of the passage), Dreyfus makes a further and to my mind unwarranted inference:

> "There is no evidence, behavioral or introspective, that counting out is the only kind of "information processing" involved in playing chess, that "the essential nature of the task [is] search in a space of exponentially growing possibilities."[36]

Now, while one can agree with the first assertion about "counting out" (i.e. "brute force enumeration" of possible moves), this does not entail the second. In fact, given that chess has a game tree structure, choosing a move in chess necessarily involves "search in a space of exponentially growing possibilities", whether this is done explicitly or by some process that occurs outside of awareness. This should be obvious, but let me point out in addition that if it weren't true, then Deep Blue would never have beaten Kasparov.

However, Dreyfus is certainly correct in saying that the means by which human beings search the space is very different from the way that most chess playing programs do it. And he is correct to emphasize the importance of experience. In fact, this was a critical part of the success of the world champion backgammon program — and one could even describe some of Deep Blues's programming, which involved storing moves of former grand masters, as providing it with canned experience (showing that AI subsequently developed in ways that Dreyfus could not envisage at the time). But at the same time, he has not shown that the processes involving "fringe consciousness" are not sophisticated kinds of heuristic — as opposed to fixed algorithmic — methods for cutting down the search space. (In fact, what else could they be?) Or that some kind of complex feature detection is not at the heart of 'zeroing in' on an effective strategy — which could, therefore, be expressed in the form of rules, even if the human player cannot express these rules himself.

Dreyfus seizes upon the fact that human players can quickly size up a game board, thus showing 'insight' into the best line of attack. What he leaves entirely up in the air is how such insights come about. Consider Deep Blue again, and in particular the moment when it outsmarted Kasparov — was this not insight? And what is "insight" if not the selection of a solution from within a collection of possibilities?[37*]

Other discussions, which consider limitations of machine translation programs, pattern recognition programs, simulations of human cognition, and problem solving programs, have a similar thrust. In all cases, poorly understood processes are discussed impressionistically (moreover, this is carried out as if it were a virtue), and the conclusion is drawn that the then-current approaches could never succeed in matching human abilities. Here is a revealing quote from a discussion of pattern recognition:

> "Simulating recognition of even simple patterns may thus require recourse to each of the fundamental forms of human "information processing" discussed this far. And even if in these simple cases artificial intelligence workers have been able to make some headway with mechanical techniques, patterns as complex as artistic styles and the human face reveal a loose sort of resemblance which seems to require a special combination of insight, fringe consciousness, and ambiguity tolerance beyond the reach of digital machines. It is no wonder, then, that work in pattern recognition has had a late start and an early stagnation."[38]

As an example of hand waving and unwarranted complacency, this passage is pretty hard to beat. More than anything, it impresses me with how easy it is to string together vague notions in this way, while imagining that one is saying something of substance. And, of course, the inadequacy of this way of thinking has become almost painfully apparent now that there are pattern recognition systems that can recognize faces and AI programs that can simulate artistic styles.[39]

One thing that Dreyfus seemed not to have appreciated is that in studying any difficult problem one has to start somewhere. And one can almost anticipate that early attempts at solutions to a problem of depth and complexity will come up short. But it is only by doing this that one can be guided to more powerful solutions. In fact, there is a search process here that Dreyfus seems entirely insensitive to, although in all fairness, this was also true to perhaps a large extent among the AI researchers whom he criticized. (On the other hand, I think that many of the people who have worked on these problems have had a sense of this, if only in fringe consciousness, in odd contrast to Dreyfus. Moreover, they knew that there was a sound logic underpining some of their investigations, as with game playing, and to a more limited degree machine translation.)

In Part II of his book, Dreyfus examines what he discerns are four kinds of assumptions behind AI: biological, psychological, epistemological, and ontological.

In his discussion of brainwork, Dreyfus assumes that the central nervous system is some sort of analog, as opposed to digital, device. The way he goes about his argument is telling:

> "The brain, operating with volleys of pulses, would be a digital computer only if each pulse were correlated with some symbol in an information-processing sequence; if, however, the rate at which pulses are transmitted turns out to be the minimum unit in an account of the relevant activity of the nervous system — as von Neumann seems to hold — then the brain would be operating as an analogue device.
>
> "Once this conceptual confusion has been cleared up, von Neumann can be understood as suggesting that the brain functions exclusively like an analogue computer, and subsequent work has tended to confirm this hypothesis."[40]

EOA[41*]

However, the idea that pulse rate is a "minimum unit" is at best premature. (These were only speculations on the part of von Neumann. And a latter quote from T. H. Bullock is equally speculative.) And it does not preclude the existence of an information handling system with digital properties, especially since nerve cells are separate elements in a network and thus can be stimulated (i.e. turned on or off) independently. In addition, one is more likely to find digitalization of some sort in systems that subserve knowledge functions as opposed to functions that have a more continuous character, like the control of movement.

Moreover, his general skepticism concerning digital processes in biological systems is not well taken. We now know that at the subcellular level digital processes have evolved that regulate genetic transcription (the enhancer-promoter system); moreover the construction of macromolecules is itself highly digital in character. Now, mightn't there be developments of the same kind at the neuronal level? For example, speech recognition is based on distinctive features and thus seems to have a digital character. And language in general seems to be the product of discretization.

In addition, as Helmholtz and others realized, the human brain carries out inferences when it perceives as well as when it thinks. A nice example of this is size constancy in the visual system, which depends on the size of the retinal image together with assessment of distance. Helmholtz called the processes underlying such phenomena "unconscious inference". As such it is similar and possibly equivalent in a functional sense to symbol handling as discussed by Newell and Simon.[42*]

Even in the case of simpler animals, we often find that their behavior is guided by distinct cues (via releasing mechanisms, to borrow the term used by classical ethologists[43]). This demonstrates that even elementary forms of behavior can involve discretization and information transfer.[44*]

In the chapter on psychological assumptions, Dreyfus continues his examination of the propriety of equating human intelligence with computer programs designed to exhibit intelligent activity. He is concerned in particular with the "assumption that the mind can be viewed as a device operating on bits of information according to formal rules".[45] Some of this discussion does not concern us directly since it reflects the then contemporary melding of AI and the computer simulation of human cognition, especially by Newell and Simon. However, there are some general arguments that are pertinent.

At the very beginning of the chapter Dreyfus tries to bring into question the entire information processing framework that is taken for granted by both cognitive psychologists and researchers in AI. To do this, he seizes on the distinction between the basic definition of information processing as message detection and the problem of interpreting the meaning of a message. However, while the former does not necessarily help us with the latter (and this is why interest in information theory in psychology waned after a brief period of intense interest in the 1950s), the two are not mutually exclusive, as Dreyfus seems to think. In fact, interpretation and meaning presuppose information processing;

so, pace Dreyfus, they must be analyzed within a general information processing framework. Therefore, AI pioneers like Newell and Simon cannot be faulted on this basis. (And needless to say, they were perfectly aware that interpretation and meaning were at the heart of the AI project rather than simple information transmission.)

In this chapter, Dreyfus brings his background in phenomenology to bear on certain psychological issues in a way that to my mind is unconvincing and even deceptive. An egregious example is his discussion of a passage in Fodor's book *Psychological Explanation* that deals with the abstraction of patterns or perceptual constancies from varying stimulus inputs, specifically the perception of a similar melody despite this sort of variation. This is in fact a deep scientific problem, which is still a lively area of inquiry after decades of research.

> "... indeed on the level of physical energy it is no doubt true that inputs of energy of various frequencies are correlated with the same perceptual experience. The energy transformations involved will presumably someday be discovered by neurophysiologists. But such *physical* sequences of tones cannot be "heard" — we do not hear frequencies; we hear sounds — and thus *a fortiori* these frequencies cannot be "heard as similar." If, on the other hand, we try to understand the input as sequences of *phenomenal* tones, which it would make sense to "hear as similar," then we are on the level of perception, and unfortunately for Fodor the problem of how we hear these sequences of tones as similar vanishes; for in order to pose the problem in the first place we have already assumed that the phenomenal tone sequences are heard as similar."[46] (italics in original)

Here, with what might appear to some as a deft argument, Dreyfus manages to sweep a real problem under the rug. But he can only do this by shifting back and forth between the languages of physical description and phenomenology, claiming that at the level of phenomenology no explanation is needed because the phenomenon of hearing a melody is simply a given.[47*,48*]

On the other hand, if we take a behavioristic stance and consider a person's ability to decide on similarity, then we have the real problem located at the psychological level, i.e. at the level of the perceiving/behaving organism. And in addition to trying to explain this ability, we can imagine how one might go about designing machines to carry out the same task. Incidentally, one can see in these flippant arguments why scientists and engineers often find it difficult to take philosophers seriously.[49*]

In the rest of this discussion Dreyfus continues to assume that Fodor is treating the brain as essentially isomorphic to a digital computer, so that the latter's discussions of "stimulus information" and "data processing" are somehow meaningless. But of course there is no need to assume such isomorphism to apply general ideas of information processing to psychological capacities. (Again, one can cite the reaction time literature as supporting such arguments and the general behavioristic point of view.)

In the chapter on epistemology, having supposedly refuted claims that human intelligence can be explained in terms of "heuristic rules" that could be realized by computer operations, Dreyfus turns to the question of whether it is even possible to formalize human capacities "in terms of such rules".[50]

To get a sense of the largeness of Dreyfus' claims in this chapter, we can begin with his first example: a man riding a bicycle. He first re-asserts that while a rule such as "wind along a series of curves, the curvature of which is inversely proportional to the square of the velocity"[51] may express the man's competence, it is not an explanation of performance. But he goes further and claims "that unlike the technological application of the laws of physics to produce physical phenomena, a timeless, contextless theory of competence cannot be used to reproduce the moment-to-moment involved behavior required for human performance; that indeed there cannot be a theory of human performance".[52]

It seems to me that one of the conclusions one must draw from this argument is that robots will never be able to ride bicycles. Now, as far as I know this feat has not yet been accomplished. But the success in building robots that can walk over various terrains (which should be subject to the same arguments as those made for cycling) should give one pause.

But the main topic of the chapter is whether — in contrast to modeling physical systems — it is possible to model the competence of thinking human beings so as to produce artificial intelligence that is equivalent in capacity. Here, he makes use of linguistics, and in particular questions of context and interpretation ("linguistic use"[53]) to argue that humans can somehow transcend all rules:

> "Programmed behavior is either arbitrary or strictly rulelike. Therefore, in confronting a new usage a machine must either treat it as a clear case falling under the rules, or take a blind stab. A native speaker feels he has a third alternative. He can recognize the usage as odd, not falling under the rules, and yet he can make sense of it — give it a meaning in the context of human life in an apparently nonrulelike and yet nonarbitrary way."[54]
>
> "To assume … that the rules covering all cases must be explicitly built in or learned — since this is the only way a digital computer could simulate the human ability to cope with odd uses — runs counter to logic and experience."[55]
>
> "Logically, it is hard to see how one could formulate the rules for how one could intelligibly break the rules; for, no matter what metarules are formulated, it seems intuitively obvious that the native speaker could break them too and count on the context to get his meaning across to another speaker."[56]

Ironically enough, when these words were written Roger Schank was embarking on a project (described above) that would result in programs that could to some degree perform in the manner Dreyfus believes could not be performed by rule-based computer programs.[57*]

The chapter on ontology continues the idea that because AI systems "must in principle be understandable in terms of a set of determinate independent elements",[58] they will never be able to duplicate the capacities of human beings. Here, Dreyfus disputes the assumption that our phenomenological world is based entirely on elements that are at least potentially explicit as facts. Although, he admits that this basic rationalistic maneuver has been successful in describing the physical world, he does not think it can successfully handle human situations such as being "at home", which depends on a welter of conventions regarding what it is to have a home and to be there (e.g. if one is in the backyard, one is still at home). Nor does he think that situations in general can be reduced to sets of features or facts; instead, they "might be of a radically different order and fulfill a totally different function than any concatenation of facts".[59] Moreover, it is the situation that "determines the significance of the facts involved", and "it is our sense of the situation which enables us to select from the potential infinity of facts the immediately relevant ones, and once these relevant facts are found, enables us to estimate their significance".[60] Instead of speaking immediately to these specific points, I will discuss them in connection with the final arguments of the book, found in Part III, since the latter are a continuation of them.[61*]

In these arguments, Dreyfus, like Searle, makes use of the general notion of 'embodied' cognition. And here, I think he is saying something of significance (which, incidentally, I did not get out of Searle's arguments). Unfortunately, the valid part of this discussion occurs side by side with more questionable arguments that continue the lines of thinking already discussed.

The significant part of his argument is a criticism of the symbol manipulation ideas put forward most forcefully by Alan Newell and Herb Simon; that is, that intelligence is based upon symbolic representations of relevant aspects of the world, which can then be operated on to produce solutions in line with certain criteria (i.e. goals) that are also represented symbolically.

Now, in fact, because biological organisms are so well interfaced with the world around them, in many cases it is not necessary for them to have anything like a complete symbolic representation of their outside environment. Instead, their understanding is based in part on the interactions that they have with the world around them.

A number of significant 20th century thinkers arrived at a similar viewpoint. These include Heidegger and Wittgenstein, whom Dreyfus draws upon directly, as well as the biologist Maturana.

At the same time, it must be emphasized that this is an analysis of certain aspects of human cognition. As such, it doesn't mean that capacities which are based on such processes cannot be realized by other means, including more explicit symbolic representations. Or that generative systems could not be built to produce coherent knowledge to fit a given situation.

However, in Dreyfus' telling, this "bodily side of intelligent behavior"[62] is made to appear as something beyond analysis, so that it cannot be realized in a computer program. At this point in his discussion, Dreyfus draws upon Gestalt accounts of perception, in which the whole is more than a 'sum' of its components and there is a background as well as a foreground to any perception, both of which are significant components. In addition, he draws heavily on the tradition of phenomenological thought (especially Husserl, Heidegger, and Merleau-Ponty). In his words:

> "There is a kind of answer to this question [of how humans recognize situations and act intelligently in relation to them] which is not committed beforehand to finding the precise rulelike relations between precisely defined objects. It takes the form of a phenomenological description of the behavior involved. It, too, can give us understanding if it is able to find the general characteristics of such behavior: what, if any one thing, is involved in seeing a table or a house, or, more generally, in perception, problem solving, using a language, and so forth. Such an account can even be called an explanation if it goes further and tries to find the fundamental features of human activity which serve as the necessary and sufficient conditions for all forms of human behavior."[63]

The major problem with all of this is that phenomenology — or reasoning from introspection — is not capable of telling us how perceptions are actually derived from the stimulation that impinges on the organism, or how solutions to problems are obtained when a person is faced with a task, since conscious perception is essentially output of a certain kind, and therefore 'after the fact'. It is certainly possible that there are features that signal a particular context, and allow what Dreyfus calls "a certain sort of indeterminate, global anticipation"[64] of a particular situation without one being aware that this is happening. And it is equally possible that transformations occur outside of our awareness that are critical for arriving at solutions. But this doesn't mean they can't be analyzed. In other words, Dreyfus is taking the fact that a conscious human being cannot analyze all aspects of his perception and making the unwarranted inference that these aspects cannot be analyzed at all. (Since this difficulty seems basic to this way of approaching problems of human cognition, it merits a name; call it the "phenomenological fallacy".)[65*,66*]

Later in the book Dreyfus derides Neisser and Minsky for their (to him) naïve ideas about models of the external world that are built up from sensory inputs (combined with background knowledge).

> "The whole I/O model makes no sense here. There is no reason to suppose that the human world can be analyzed into independent elements, and even if it could, one would not know whether to consider these elements the input or the output of the human mind."

> "If this idea is hard to accept, it is because this phenomenological account stands in opposition to our Cartesian tradition which thinks of the physical world as impinging on our mind which then organizes it according to its previous experience and innate ideas or rules."[67]

He even goes so far as to say:

> "The claim that we are nonetheless carrying on such operations unconsciously is either an empirical claim, *for which there is no evidence* or an a priori claim based on the very assumption we are here calling into question."[68] (emphasis added)

In fact there is a wealth of evidence that bears on this question. For example, neurophysiological analysis of individual cells in sensory pathways and the cerebral cortex shows that some sort of feature detection occurs prior to more sophisticated forms of neuro-computation (such as spatial Fourier analysis). Moreover, this work shows that there are regions specialized for different aspects of perception, such as registering color as opposed to form in visual perception. This means that the original input is being 'broken down' for analysis.

There are several lines of investigation that bear on such questions in relation to human cognition. As already noted, reaction time studies reveal both coding processes and even levels of processing that bear a close resemblance to the speculations of Minsky and others that Dreyfus derides. In addition, beginning with Bartlett, there is ample evidence for the schemapiric nature of perception and understanding. Also, in the area of clinical neurology we have evidence for information transfer in the form of "disconnection syndromes" that arise when parts of the cerebral cortex are separated from each other. An example is the failure to recognize written or printed language when the visual cortex has been separated from the areas involved in language comprehension. How one could explain a syndrome like this other than in terms of processing and transfer of information is certainly not clear to me.

Another assumption that Dreyfus makes is that all of the requisite knowledge would have to be coded 'up front'. Here, he failed to anticipate the enormous advances that would be made in machine learning (which was barely a presence when he wrote his original work in the 1970s). An important implication of these advances is that they allow forms of machine intelligence that do not have to be programmed up front.

A less fundamental error that I see in Dreyfus' discussion is that he applies arguments concerning the general capacity to behave intelligently in an indefinite number of situations to specific problems such as chess playing or machine translation. Chess playing in particular requires highly specialized skills that pertain only to that domain. Hence, even if his basic arguments have some validity (and I suspect that they do), one cannot deduce from them that chess playing programs cannot be devised that will allow play at the master or grandmaster level. And, of course, as already discussed at length in earlier chapters, it has proven possible to do this, so that this part of Dreyfus' argument has been decisively refuted. On the other hand, the success of programs like Deep Blue by no means undermines the arguments about general intelligence.

Bound up in the discussion of context and situationality is the problem of relevance: what features of a situation are relevant to one's current concerns? To take one of his examples, when playing chess, the weight and size of the pieces is irrelevant; but if one is manufacturing a chess set then they are very relevant.

One of Dreyfus' points is that one often cannot tell what will be relevant in advance. Thus, in betting on a horse, in addition to its age and track record, it might be relevant if the jockey's mother had died the day before. And a human being if apprised of such information might very well take it into account. But how would a computer program know to do so?

One thing overlooked by Dreyfus in examples like these is that he isn't giving us a blow-by-blow account of an ongoing situation in-the-world. Instead, this is a made-up (i.e. disembodied) example. In this case the question is, how did he come up with it? And in considering the question it is hard to see how one could come up with a pertinent example like this if one did not use certain rules. Thus, to come up with the idea that a jockey's mother might be relevant, one draws on knowledge of the class to which the jockey belongs: human beings. Then one can note that members of this class all have mothers and fathers, that there are certain close relations in such cases so that one would likely be affected if something untoward happened to such people, etc. My point is that the very fact that one can come up with examples like this outside of an actual situation (or a genuine embodiment of the terms and relations in question) suggests that in fact cogitations of this sort do involve abstract rules. (It also suggests to me that the whole business about "embodiment" and being-in-the-world is overblown; to some degree it may be more a matter of rhetorical maneuvering rather than actually 'seeing' into the real world.)

Within mainstream AI, there have also been attempts to build systems in which background knowledge can be applied to specific tasks. And, of course, this means representing background knowledge explicitly within the constructed program. Examples include Minsky's idea of frames (which are knowledge structures activated by features, which then impose a certain significance on other features as well as indicating which other features are relevant) and the work of Schank and his collaborators described earlier in this chapter.[69*]

An important aspect of human intelligence completely overlooked by Dreyfus is that present-day intellectual endeavor involves a medley of specialized tools, without which human beings could not carry out many intellectual tasks. This began with the invention of writing, and then numerical symbols, and continued with mathematical and logical notation (as well as the devices necessary to carry out quantitative physical science). All of these serve to make human thinking more precise — essentially by discretizing it. From this we can conclude that the unaided human intelligence lauded by Dreyfus isn't a powerful problem solving system in and of itself, or at least that it has some very definite limitations. (How else can one account for all these inventions and the advances that ensued?)[70*]

A related group of 'counter-examples' are the algorithms that people must learn in order to do basic arithmetic. Surely one can see that these are founded on atomic operations (e.g. rules for summing single-digit numbers), which must be performed in the proper sequence in order to carry out operations like adding or multiplying correctly. And this certainly suggests similarities between brains and digital computers. (Or does Dreyfus think that the brain is not engaged in "information processing" while doing these tasks, while the computer is?)

After considering critiques like those of Dreyfus (and Searle) that were first proposed when the field was in its early stages, one can better appreciate the essential service that a program like Deep Blue has provided. Whatever else it accomplished, it has taken the wind out of their sails (whether or not they deign to notice). And I suspect that nothing less than beating the world champion would have done this. Whatever the similarities or differences between the processes embodied in AI programs and those that underlie human cognition, one can no longer look disdainfully at the former under the assumption that they simply cannot come up to the level of the best representatives of humanity. That question at least has been answered decisively.[71*,72*]

On a more positive note, it seems to me that some of Dreyfus' more compelling arguments may be construed as arguments for the necessity of some sort of robotic intelligence rather than an intelligence that does not have to concern itself with negotiating with the outside world on a continual basis. This may well be the case if one wants to build a system with general-purpose intellectual capacities. But as far as I can see, this is not a critical issue for the present thesis.[73*,74*]

*

Interestingly, this kind of thinking has inspired a line of research within the field of AI itself, initiated in the 1980s by Brooks and others in connection with autonomous intelligent robots. A major theme of this work is that general intelligence does not require explicit (symbolic) representations, and that since it is manifested in the agent's interactions with the world, these interactions serve as de facto representations.[75] Or, as Brooks likes to put it, "the world is its own best model". (Although it's not clear, it is conceivable that Dreyfus' arguments had some influence on these ideas.[76*])

Brooks also proposed an architecture for supporting general intelligence that he called the "subsumption architecture". The basic idea is to have a loose hierarchy of subsystems in which each system has its own input and output and therefore its own goals. So a lowest level system might simply be concerned with moving forward in a physical environment and avoiding obstacles in the process. The next subsystem above might be concerned with exploration or patrolling within some environment, while relying on the first system to carry out the details of moment-to-moment navigation. A subsystem above that might be concerned with maintaining the energy needed for locomotion (a kind of "hunger/feeding" system). Thus whenever the robot's batteries run low, it takes over to guide the system to a place where the batteries can be recharged. And so forth.

From the general vantage point assumed in the present work, while Brooks' proposals are of some significance, they certainly do not preclude speaking about intelligence based on other architectures and AI programs. After all, why should something as general as intelligence be restricted to one's own favorite architecture? One could no more restrict the idea of life to a particular class of organisms.

To my mind, Brooks makes a serious error when he confounds intelligence with autonomous action. Now, it is true that a working robot such as Herbert or Toto (two of the Brooks brood) solves certain problems of locomotion in an environment, and this is therefore an expression of intelligence. But the source of this intelligence is the designer. There is really nothing going on here that cannot be found in any servo-mechanism or even in the actions of a thermostat.

Regarding the issue of whether intelligence requires explicit or symbolic representation, I strongly suspect that this depends on the flexibility and sophistication of the system that one wants to build. Even at the level of the senses it has been realized ever since Helmholtz that sensory systems carry out various forms of inference, albeit unconsciously. The motor system in turn is intimately connected with the sensory systems, so that in some ways it resembles them.[77] The result is a highly flexible system that can respond to a variety inputs in complex ways in a wide range of environments. In contrast, a simple feedback system carries out one kind of 'hard-wired' inference: if mismatch between input and setpoint, then perform action.

Moreover, simpler systems, such as the lower levels of a subsumption hierarchy, are highly restricted in their inputs. This reflects a decision made by the designer — so that again, their performance requires intelligence. And this is coming from elsewhere in a network.

On the other hand, I agree with Brooks that the symbol-centric depiction of intelligence as presented by Newell and Simon and discussed in Chapter 8 is not the ultimate general framework that it was purported to be. For one thing, if one examines either animals or robots, one finds that analog and (in the case of nervous systems) ensemble systems are of critical importance in producing what I would call intelligent behavior.

Oddly enough, however, there are points of contact between Brooks' (and Dreyfus') ideas and some of Newell's ruminations in his knowledge level paper. In the latter work, Newell describes what he calls "knowledge" in very functional terms: "Knowledge is to be characterized entirely functionally, in terms of what it does, not structurally, in terms of physical objects with particular properties and relations".[78] However, Newell assumes the necessity of the employment of a symbol system for fulfilling the functions necessary for intelligent action.[79*]

Here, the reader should also recall that in Chapter 8, it was noted that concepts such as working memory (which Newell argues are fundamental to the operation of a symbol system) are clearly found in animals at a sufficient level of complexity, e.g. in birds and mammals. And it is hard to see how these processes could operate except by using symbols or descriptors of some sort, since what is being represented are alternative actions or outcomes, which the animal must choose between.

The resolution of these issues may be that certain kinds of intelligence do not require symbol systems in the sense of Newell. But for certain basic kinds of tasks, such as those involving flexible choice, symbol systems may be necessary. And, of course, symbol systems are required for communication.[80*]

*

Another critic of AI in its 'standard' or classical form, i.e. based on functionalist assumptions and manipulation of symbols, is Jeffrey Hawkins.[81] Early in his book, Hawkins makes the claim that real intelligence involves thinking and understanding, so that intelligent output alone (the sine qua non of AI) is a sort of red herring. However, I would question whether thinking per se can ever be taken as an indicator of intelligence. In this connection, Faulkner's depiction of Benji (in *The Sound and the Fury*) comes to mind. Although not genuine empirical evidence, if the depiction is accurate in its essentials, it shows that thinking of a sort (and memory-based thinking at that! Cf. below) can go on where there is only a limited degree of intelligence. In fact, I suspect that the depiction is accurate in that it reflects the (likely) fact that many cognitive/computational processes in the brain of an idiot are running off in a normal fashion. But because other processes are not, the person's overall intelligence is severely limited. In other words, one really does require a demonstration of effective action before one can assert that a system exhibits intelligence.

At any rate, this particular claim is independent of the main thesis of the book, which is that genuine intelligence cannot be achieved unless the underlying system has an architecture similar to the human brain, specifically the neocortex. Most of his book is devoted to an elaboration of this idea, including an extended discussion of how he thinks the cortex works.

Speaking of the efforts of AI researchers to build artificial systems that can support specific functions such as vision or language, Hawkins says:

> "When they try to understand vision or make a computer that can "see," they devise vocabulary and techniques specific to vision. They talk about edges, textures, and three-dimensional representations. If they want to understand spoken language, they build algorithms based on rules of grammar, syntax, and semantics. But if Mountcastle is correct [about the neocortex carrying out one basic algorithm], these approaches are not how the brain solves these problems, and are therefore likely to fail."[82]

Here, Hawkins is using neuroanatomical and neurophysiological data to make much the same case that Dreyfus did. Again, there is the fallacious assumption that certain functions can only be done in one way or with one kind of architecture.[83*] Since I question Hawkins' basic notions of intelligence, which he himself qualifies by stipulating functional equivalences between the systems he wants to build and the human brain itself, the important issue is whether there are cognitive functions that a neocortex-like architecture supports that cannot be supported by symbolic AI programs of the kind that have been built to date.

According to Hawkins, what passes muster as intelligence for him is based first and foremost on prediction, which in order to be adaptive must be memory-based, i.e. not 'hard-wired'. This is because the processes that underlie these functions must operate on a moment-to-moment basis in an almost unlimited number of situations. This is illustrated by a mundane but instructive example: the ability to recognize that the front door to one's house, which one passes through nearly every day, has been altered in some subtle way:

> "Suppose while you are out, I sneak over to your home and change something about your door. It could be almost anything. I could move the knob over by an inch,

> change a round knob into a thumb latch, or turn it from brass to chrome. I could change the door's weight … I could make the hinges squeaky and stiff … I can imagine a thousand changes that could be made to your door … When you come home that day and attempt to open the door, you will quickly detect that something is wrong. … As your hand reaches for the moved knob, you will realize that it is not in the correct location. … Or if the door's weight has been changed, you will push with the wrong amount of force and be surprised. The point is that you will notice any of a thousand changes in a very short period of time.
>
> "How do you do that? … The AI or computer engineer's approach to the problem would be to create a list of all the door's properties and put them in a database … When you [?] approach the door, the computer would query the entire database, looking at width, color, size, knob position, weight, sound, and so on. While this may sound superficially similar to how I described my brain checking each of its myriad predictions … [the] AI strategy is implausible. First, it is impossible to specify in advance every attribute a door can have. The list is potentially endless. Second, we would need to have similar lists for every object we encounter every second of our lives. Third, nothing we know about brains and neurons suggests that this is how they work. And finally, neurons are just too slow to implement computer-style databases. …
>
> "There is only one way to interpret your reactions to the altered door: your brain makes low-level sensory predictions about what it expects to see, hear, and feel at every given moment, and it does so in parallel."[84]

First, let me comment on the cortex versus AI side of this argument. While it is unlikely that one could sit down at one's desk and write an exhaustive list of attributes, this simply shows that a one-shot approach to the knowledge problem in this case will probably be inadequate. It certainly doesn't rule out the possibility that a human-engineered solution can be found, even within the current AI paradigms.

On the other hand, Hawkins is certainly correct in claiming that such predictions are a ubiquitous part of human perception and cognition, and he may be right to claim that the ability to make predictions of this sort in every sort of situation one encounters is fundamental to general-purpose intelligence.

So how does Hawkins think the cortex manages this feat? Building on ideas in the neurosciences that are still more or less current, he describes a model of cortical action that in broad outline is quite compelling. Here, I will only sketch out his conception of cortical information processing, since a more detailed account would take us into areas outside the focus of the present work.

Hawkins starts with an observation by Mountcastle that despite the existence of different senses (sight, hearing, smell, etc.) and cortical involvement in both sensory processing and motor control as well as higher level processes such as language, every part of the cortex seems to have a similar organization. In all parts of the neocortex the same layered structure can be discerned, with the same types of nerve cells in each layer. Moreover the pattern of connectivity is everywhere the same. This suggests that all areas of the cortex are handling the information they receive in the same fashion. In other words, there seems to be a common form of representation, or common language that is sufficient to express both perceptions and motor commands, and information in this form can be processed by a single 'master algorithm' or algorithmic schema.

Referring again to the issue of AI versus brain-based intelligence, it seems to me that this is consistent with what Newell and Simon and other AI researchers have been saying all along. Namely, that, if one can fulfill certain basic requirements such as those embodied in the symbol systems idea, then information about any aspect of the world can be processed by a single system.

A basic principle of cortical neurobiology is that the neocortex is composed of areas related to the different major senses (vision, audition, and touch), and within each of these areas there is a set of regions arranged in a hierarchy, where regions higher in the hierarchy detect more abstract patterns than the lower regions. For example, the lowest region in the part of the cortex concerned with vision might only detect edges, while a region much higher in the hierarchy might contain cells that detect a complex of features associated with a human face. Even higher in the hierarchy are the 'suprasensory' regions that might be responsible for concepts such as human versus animal or going to the supermarket.

At a finer grain, Hawkins makes use of the well-known (but more problematic) idea that there is a functional unit of the cortex that takes the form of a column of nerve cells, all of which are activated by the same stimulus, such as pressure on a certain patch of skin or an edge oriented at a particular angle in a specific location in one's field of vision. Hawkins makes the bold claim that such columns are the units of prediction. He then cites various facts about the anatomical connections of the neocortex to buttress the idea that there are both feed-forward and feedback relations between columns, especially those lower and higher in the sensory hierarchies, which can support sequential predictions across varying degrees of abstraction.[85*]

One compelling aspect of this account is that the neurological findings do support the idea that cortical nerve cells always operate within an enormous context in that they are continually influenced by the activity of cells in nearby columns and in many other regions. In fact, according to Hawkins, almost 90% of the synaptic connections impinging on a single cortical cell come from outside the column where it resides. Coupled with as yet unknown memory mechanisms, an architecture of this sort seems potentially able to support the capacity to make predictions in an almost infinite number of situations.

However, I think it is still too early to fully embrace the notion that this is all that the cortex is doing, or that prediction is the ultimate basis of general-purpose intelligence. First, one should note that the cerebral cortex seems to handle other functions than prediction. Earlier I gave a short account of depth perception based on retinal disparity; it's not clear to me how comfortably such functions fit under the rubric of prediction. Nor, to take an example that Hawkins discusses at one point, does it explain how we can have a mathematical conception of a circle despite our never having seen a perfect circle.

How well can a memory-prediction model handle the task of reading a book for the first time and comprehending it (especially if the latter requires some extended thought)? Does prediction subsume comprehension or vice versa? And generalizing this line of thought, how is prediction different from a capacity for making inferences? As opposed to being a specialized instance of this more general capacity.[86*]

Nevertheless, Hawkins has thought deeply about how cognition and representation can occur when these are embedded in a continual flow of events. And in doing this, he has given us a kind of cybernetic conception of cognition that must be taken seriously by any AI researcher.

Moreover, his argument suggests that effective real-world knowledge should be built around generalized descriptors, such as contrast or edge detectors in the visual system, plus the capacity to use these to make predictions. He has also made a compelling case that some form of hierarchical representation must underlie any form of general-purpose intelligence.

And finally, the claim that cortex-based intelligence is memory-based rather than logic- or inference-based (including systems that employ search to a large degree) is an important one.

To highlight these differences, Hawkins' treatment of time can be compared with that of standard AI. Early in his book Hawkins makes the claim that any general-purpose intelligence must handle time. At this point it isn't clear that what he has in mind is a system that can work at a high level of complexity in real time (via the processes described above). In contrast, in AI in the late 1980s and early 90s there was considerable interest in representing temporal relations by various logical and algebraic systems. Such logical systems handled relations such as <before> or <during> and provided a basis for automated reasoning about them. But (obviously) this does not even speak to the problem of developing and maintaining representations based on temporal sequences that occur in real time, which is the focus of Hawkins' discussion.[87*]

So even if he hasn't made his case in its most general terms (which is how he posed it in the first place), Hawkins has made the case that certain functions must be subserved by any general-purpose system, which clearly are not well handled by current AI systems. And he has shown that the neocortex has certain features that might support these functions.

Before ending this subsection I want to make one further point. In a recent talk on the progress and future of AI titled "On Boolean wings", Ken Ford made the significant point that in the past technology has only made the most significant gains after it had discarded specific and irrelevant features in favor of understanding general principles. A telling example is the history of aviation. In the early days, inventors tried all sorts of devices based on known models of flight, namely birds. So that contraptions were built with feathers and flapping wings, and so forth. The giant step was taken when the Wright brothers worked out some of the basic principles of aerodynamics and then built their flying machine in accordance with those principles. And of course, their original vehicle and all of its descendents have no immediate similarity to the apparatus that birds use to fly. Certainly, this is in part due to the fact that birds have other requirements than flying, such as sleeping or nesting, and these impact on their means of flight — while being irrelevant to the aims of human inventors.

The moral of this story is obvious: if we are to have general intelligence, we had better understand the basic principles involved. Otherwise, we are likely to be mimicking features of biological systems that are not really relevant to the quest. But, on the other hand, we certainly should not ignore existing systems, especially when they have capacities that go beyond any artificial systems that have been built. Moreover, intelligence as such may be of a different order than flying. In this case, perhaps, it makes more sense to be guided by an existing natural system. At present, I think, these issues are entirely open.

*

An interesting feature of this body of work is the degree to which it stands to one side of the actual developing field, much as journalistic accounts of a scientific subject with rare exception are never absorbed into the field itself. It is also telling how the abstract rationalistic arguments discussed in this section seem to slide by concrete empirical investigations — like the proverbial two ships in the night.

In many cases, also, the critics do not seem at all interested in what these systems can actually do. Instead of examining actual programs, they tend to sound off about the general question of artificial intelligence. And once this adversarial stance is assumed, it is never forsaken. But isn't this telling?

It is especially ironic that Dreyfus never seems to have realized that it was the engineers and computer scientists who were "in the world". Indeed, the papers they wrote were only a part of the endeavor they were engaged in — while for Dreyfus the words he wrote were everything. And since intelligence-in-the-world is the focus of the present work, it should be obvious which side the present writer comes down on.

Most of these discussions are also ad hoc, i.e. a response to concrete achievements. That this is a more important point than may be evident at first is something I will try to show in Chapter 11.

One particular refrain is that these systems don't "understand". This notion of understanding is constantly brought into the argument by the critics of AI — but without ever grappling with what the word actually means. As a result, there is always something evasive about such arguments. Moreover, in these statements I never see any acknowledgement that Schank and others have tackled this very problem with some success. In fact such work is never mentioned at all (except by Searle who was attacking this work directly.)

Naturally, among these criticisms are some very interesting arguments concerning the nature of human intelligence. The question is whether any of their points actually contradicts the AI project — as nearly all of them seem to think.

With their constant harping on the supposed deficiencies of this or that syatem, the critics almost appear to be willfully misconstruing the basic aims of AI. Is this why they raise the issue of "understanding" almost like a red flag — without delving further into what this criticism actually means? Are we seeing another one of the endless vagaries of human discourse and argumentation that characterize our species?

In considering these issues, it is also worth examining human intelligence with a more critical eye. Because it is a fact of life that too often one encounters failures of intelligence in the real world. One example (which is almost a pet peeve) is the inability to recycle items properly. People, who I assume are well-intentioned, seem utterly unable to make the simple classifications required, and as a result all sorts of refuse ends up in the recycle bins.

Quite another problem is the confabulatory aspect of human intelligence. Especially in our age, we are not only deluged with 'information' as the critics say, but we seem fated to spend much of our lives in an endless swamp of bad arguments. Not just questionable arguments, but silly arguments, sophistry, and so forth.

Viewing these and other examples, one is tempted to ask, "Just what human intelligence are we talking about?"

One more remark before leaving this topic. It is worth asking whether anything of fundamental value has come out of this kind of discussion, as well as the to-do over the Turing Test. What have we learned from all of it? And have any of the numerous critiques of AI actually influenced the field, or the more general discipline of cognitive science, or led to any substantive results, in the way that Hayes' critique of the anti-logic position or Clancey's analysis of expert systems led to actual changes in later developments? In short, is there anything that has truly been added to our collective intelligence? And if not, why not?

As far as I know, in only one instance has a critic of AI made a substantive prediction about what an AI system can or cannot do in a particular situation. This was Dreyfus' prediction that a chess program would never be able to play chess at the level of a ten-year old. If nothing else, this shows how little these people know about working cognition, and what it takes to solve a particular problem.

What is astonishing about these efforts is not that they're wrong or even very wrong but the incredible presumption of knowing that attends such exercises. Critics tend to belittle what in fact are impressive and even formidable achievements — that could not have been predicted beforehand. This is so obviously some kind of psychological 'game' in play that one wonders how people of intelligence can carry it off without apparent doubt or self-conflict.[88*]

The fact that they have been wrong on every substantive question never fazes them. And that should tell us something.

It is hard to shake off the idea that most of these people (Brooks and Hawkins are exceptions) are attempting to retreat back into old complacencies, raising barricades to protect certain cherished beliefs. In fact, it's still not clear that the so-called powers of the human intellect involve anything more than the capacity to delude oneself and others in various and sundry ways. In accordance with this, the somewhat depressing effect that robotic intelligence engenders may be due to the lack of an accompanying aura (meant for human consumption) that attends parallel flights of fancy by human beings.

In the end, what these arguments and controversies may have demonstrated is that "mind" is the last citadel of sophistry. In that case, since we now have the fort surrounded, all that remains is to give the war whoop and plunge in.[89*]

AI and the Prospect of Superintelligence

It should come as no surprise that advances in AI have brought forth advocates and promoters in their wake. It is interesting to observe that assessments of this sort are usually futuristic in character: we are either rushing headlong toward a better world or to some ultimate demise. As with the body of work that criticizes AI research, it looks as if the emergence of AI on the world stage has set off a reaction that then follows its own logic.

The best-known exponent of superintelligence is Ray Kurzweil. Like Hawkins, he has important engineering achievements under his belt, but for some years (his first book on the topic was published in 1990) he has been engaged in extrapolating trends and weaving together imaginary scenarios for the future. There is something of the intellectual impresario (or carnival barker) in Kurzweil; this is reflected in the title of his major work, *The Age of Spiritual Machines*, with its gratuitous use of the word "spiritual", as if with increased computing power this was an add-on to be had for free.[90, 91*,92*,93*]

Kurzweil's thesis rests heavily on the idea that in our world events in the large do not change linearly; instead they develop in an accelerating or decelerating fashion. This gives an exponential character to trends over time. So that progress, instead of proceeding at a steady pace, which would give a curve like this,

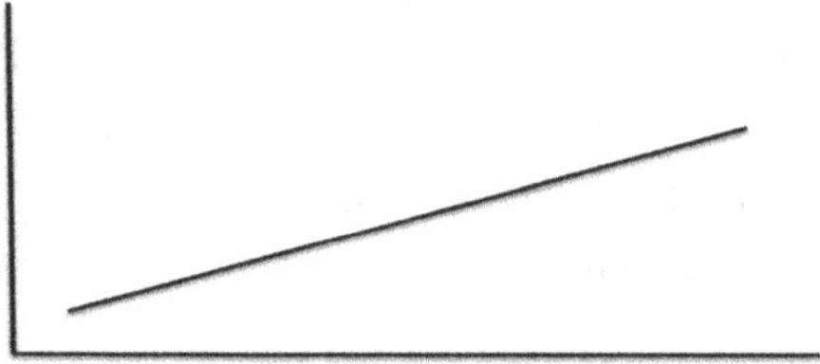

develops in an ever more rapid fashion, which gives a curve like this (in both cases, time is represented on the horizontal axis):

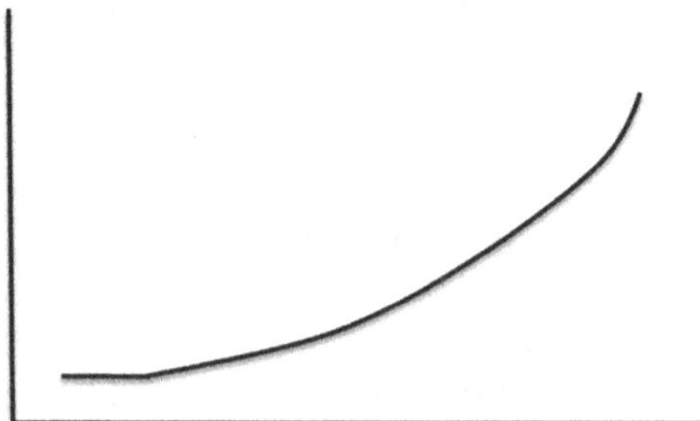

By the same token, these curves can be flipped over (rotated around a horizontal axis intersecting their highest point) to depict regressive developments as decreasing linear or exponential trends, respectively.

For example, beginning with the first few trillioniths of a second following the Big Bang,[94*] changes in the organization of matter in the universe have been taking place at a rate that is slowing down exponentially. On the other hand, the evolution of complexity in biological systems and the evolution of human technology both show accelerating trends. The former exemplifies what Kurzweil calls the "Law of Increasing Chaos", while the latter exemplifies the "Law of Accelerating Returns". The latter, in particular, is used extensively in the book to give an appearance of certainty to his musings about future gains in intelligence.

But all this, of course, is make-believe, since these "laws" are not genuine scientific laws, although to be sure, complex systems do sometimes show positive feedback effects of the sort described. But instead of trying to explain why such effects occur (which would take real intellectual effort), Kurzweil simply takes them for granted and elevates such observations to universal principles. (Such is the way of the intellectual impresario.)[95*]

Before launching into his futuristic account, Kurzweil gives a brief overview of AI's most successful techniques. Here, he discusses what he calls the "recursive formula", as well as neural networks and evolutionary algorithms. And this is really all he has to say about the basis of intelligence.[96*]

As usual, the treatment is superficial and in some ways misleading. For example, neural nets do not simulate neurons (p. 76); their units are simply weights that can be combined with other weights via the network connections. And evolutionary algorithms do not involve "repeated struggle among competing designs" (p. 101); instead, they involve multiple candidate solutions that are evaluated and selected according to a common criterion (called an "objective" or objective function). In fact, as noted in Chapter 9, evolutionary algorithms form one class of heuristic search methods.[97*] Finally, the idea of a recursive formula refers to the structure of problems that can be solved with the complete methods that were described in the last chapter as well as heuristic methods, which include evolutionary algorithms.

The chapter that follows (Chapter 6: Building new brains ...) is the one that I found most diverting, perhaps because here Kurzweil is in his natural element, and his concern here is with descriptions as opposed to speculations. In this chapter he regales the reader with spirited discussions of DNA and quantum computers, exhaustive brain scanning which might someday enable one to duplicate a person's brain and perhaps the person himself, and other tidbits of current scientific research. I'm not sure what I actually learned from all of this (I guess I know a little bit more about quantum computing than I did), but it does manage to be a kind of high entertainment. In some ways, reading an account like this resembles a perambulation through a modern department store, with its aisles and aisles of goods laid out for perusal. There is the same sense of abundance without any real significance.

Then, after a chapter where he muses about the ways in which the human body might also be refurbished or replaced (as housing for the now-enhanced mind), we are launched from the present (1999), where many aspects of life (including the arts[98*]) have been subject to infiltration by artificial intelligence and other forms of information technology, into the near future, with brief stops in 2009, 2019, 2029, and 2099. So, in 2019 computing elements "are embedded everywhere". "People routinely use three-dimensional displays built into their glasses". "People communicate with computers the same way they would communicate with a human assistant", whose personality the user can model. Another pet idea is included: "significant progress has been made in the brain-scanning reverse engineering of the human brain." And in this brave new world,

> "People are beginning to have relationships with automated personalities as companions, teachers, caretakers, and lovers. Automated personalities are superior to humans in some ways, such as having very reliable memories and, if desired, predictable (and programmable) personalities. They are not yet regarded as equal to humans in the subtlety of their personalities, although there is disagreement on this point."[99]

One can almost believe an automated assistant wrote this text.

Idle fantasies aside, Kurzweil's futuristic projections are based almost entirely on the speed of computation and number of computing elements (another intellectual sleight of hand). This allows him to calculate and graph trajectories of expected advances in intelligence and to compare machine and human 'intelligence' with one metric. (Intriguingly, all the computations in this imagined world still involve neural nets and evolutionary algorithms; in this case, it seems, his imagination falters.) Here is an example of this sort of thinking:

> "The memory capacity of the human brain is about 100 trillion synapse strengths (neurotransmitter concentrations at interneuronal connections), which we can estimate at about a million billion bits. In 1998, a billion bits of RAM (128 megabytes) cost about $200. The capacity of memory circuits has been doubling every eighteen months. Thus by the year 2023, a million billion bits will cost about $1,000. However, this silicon equivalent will run more than a billion times faster than the human brain. There are techniques for trading off memory for speed, so we can effectively match human memory for $1,000 sooner than 2023."[100]

Oddly enough, when reading over this passage I was reminded of some of the haiku-like poems produced by Kurzweil's software poet, examples of which are given on pp. 163–6.[101*]

Because it really doesn't rest on firm foundations, it is hard to draw any significant conclusions from this book. And given the crude notions of intelligence and its basis, it is also difficult to give any cogent assessment of its arguments with respect to the character of intelligence and its future evolution.[102*,103*]

*

Although it appeared a decade before the Kurzweil book, Moravec's *Mind Children: The Future of Robot and Human Intelligence*[104] gives a somewhat clearer picture of what artificial intelligence is, as well as explaining some of the deep problems involved in creating effective AI, in this case in the form of robots that can carry out various tasks in real-world environments. At least this is true at the beginning, as in the first chapter, which contains an interesting account of then-contemporary robotics and some of the major problems that were in the process of being solved such as locomotion across an irregular terrain, moving in an area with other objects that one needs to avoid colliding with, recognizing objects, lifting and manipulating objects. And in subsequent chapters there are interesting discussions of the evolution of computer power and of the human-computer interface, as well as the emergence of software parasites (Trojan horses, viruses, etc).

Unfortunately, the bulk of the book is taken up with fantasies about the future, including numerous vignettes — scenes that might possibly occur when robots and artificial intelligence are really, really advanced. Some scenarios resemble the advances that have been made in virtual reality, which still hasn't really taken off. Other ideas, like the intelligent bush with telescoped branches that end in a trillion 'fingers' that can sense surfaces at the sub-microscopic level are intriguing and suggestive, but these are still just word-play, or vapor-ware. So while ruminations of this sort might be viewed as a kind of high entertainment, they do not qualify as serious discussion of questions related to human and machine intelligence.

Eventually the author becomes so carried away by these ideas that he begins to commiserate with the poor, limited human beings who must now take a back seat to their robot creations:

> "The thought of being grandly upstaged … by our artificial progeny is disappointing. Long life loses much of its point if we are fated to spend it staring stupidly at our ultra-intelligent machines as they try to describe their ever more spectacular discoveries in baby-talk that we can understand."[105]

But hope is at hand. If we can build "ultra-intelligent" systems, then why not re-engineer ourselves, so we too can be super-intelligent? This idea leads to another vignette, where 'you', a person of the future, are having yourself copied and stored so your intelligence can be amplified (and your old body discarded) to create a new and better you. (Nose jobs are nothing compared to Moravec's ideas about self-transformation.)

> "Layer after layer the brain is simulated, then excavated. Eventually your skull is empty, and the surgeon's hand rests deep in your brainstem. Though you have not lost consciousness, or even you train of thought, your mind has been removed from your brain and transferred to a machine. In a final, disorienting step the surgeon lifts out his hand. Your suddenly abandoned body goes into spasms and dies. For a moment you experience only quiet and dark. Then, once again, you can open your eyes. Your perspective has shifted. The computer simulation has been disconnected from the cable leading to the surgeon's hand and reconnected to a shiny new body of the style, color, and material of your choice. Your metamorphosis is complete."[106]

In these passages Moravec reaches the same plane of precocious inanity that Kurzweil was to ascend to ten years later. Like the latter author, his discussion is pervaded by an air of knowingness, a presumption of certainties which in fact are not apparent and may not even be possible to determine.

Like Kurzweil, Moravec is entranced by calculations of computing capacity, and these are the basis for his predictions regarding the advent of superintelligence:

> "If the retina's processing can be matched by 1 billion computer calculations per second, what can we say about the entire brain? ... By multiplying the computational equivalent of the retina by a compromise value of 10,000 for the ratio of brain complexity to retina complexity, I rashly conclude that the whole brain's job might be done by a computer performing 10 trillion (1013) calculations per second. ...
>
> "... it would be foolish to expect consensus opinion about a comparison of radically different systems executing dimly understood functions. Nevertheless, my estimates can be useful even if they are only remotely correct. Later we will see that a thousandfold error in the ratio of neurons to computations shifts the predicted arrival time of fully intelligent machines a mere 20 years."[107]

As a result of these ruminations, Moravec predicted that the fastest computers would reached 'human capacity' by around 2010, and personal computers would achieve this by 2030. How did he fare? Well, we're now ten years past the first milestone, and I am still frustrated by the limitations of automated voice systems, and I still carry out most household chores myself. So although Moravec has given himself some leeway, and more impressive achievements are bound to appear over the next ten years, it doesn't look like such calculations give any sound basis for making predictions. More importantly, they provide no insight into any important issues regarding machine intelligence and its future growth.

In this work there is also the same confusion between "consciousness" and effective intelligence that appears in Penrose, the latter referring in this case to requirements for properly representing the world:[108*]

> "A verbal interface keyed to these programs would meaningfully answer questions like, "Where are you?" ("I'm in an area of about twenty square meters, bounded on three sides, and there are three small objects in front of me") and "Why did you do that?" ("I turned right because I didn't think I could fit through the opening on the left.") In our lab, the programs we have developed usually present such information about the robot's world model in the form of pictures on a computer screen — a

direct window into the robot's mind. In these internal models of the world I see the beginnings of awareness in the minds of our machines — an awareness I believe will evolve into consciousness comparable with that of humans."[109]

This seems to me an almost whimsical take on the problem of mind in relation to the physical world, which the author did not even take the time to think through. (Kurzweil, incidentally, has a much more adequate discussion of these issues; he is also more circumspect about whether the consciousness problem will simply take care of itself, although he basically ignores the issue thereafter.)

On the whole, then, this work is little more than a self-indulgent exercise. In the end it feels even less substantial than Kurzweil's multitudinous effusions.

*

A recent work on the same topic has received a great deal of attention and apparently achieved considerable sales, perhaps on the strength of its title. This is Nick Bostrom's *Superintelligence*.[110] More than the two previous works, which were carefree romps through imagined landscapes, this attempts to be a sober, systematic assessment of the issue and possible future outcomes. Unfortunately, it does not escape the limitations of this sort of writing, so that in the end one is left with the same sense of intellectual vacuity. Nor does it overcome the seemingly irresistible tendency to attempt to impress the reader with dramatic invention in its discussions of what lies ahead.[111*]

In fact, a melodramatic note is sounded on the first page of the volume. Here, Bostrom gives us the fable of the Sparrows and the Owl in order to pose the question: are we incorporating entities into our human world in the name of progress, etc. that will eventually overturn that world altogether? Following this, on the first page of the Preface, we find these remarkable comments:

"If some day we build machine brains that surpass human brains in general intelligence, then this new intelligence could become very powerful. And, as the fate of the gorillas now depends more on us humans than on the gorillas themselves, so the fate of our species would depend on the actions of the machine superintelligence.

> "We do have one advantage: we get to build the stuff. In principle, we could build a kind of superintelligence that would protect human values. We would certainly have strong reason to do so. In practice, the control problem — the problem of how to control what the superintelligence would do — looks quite difficult. It also looks like we will only get one chance. Once unfriendly superintelligence exists, it would prevent us from replacing it or changing its preferences. Our fate would be sealed"[112]

Now, let's unpack this passage. Notice first of all how casually the thought, "we could build a kind of superintelligence that would protect human values" is trotted out by the author, as if this was a reasonable programming project (which in turn assumes that it makes sense to even talk about such aims in these terms). And notice how the idea that, "Once unfriendly superintelligence exists, it would prevent us from replacing it" is proffered as if it was a straightforward observation about likely events. In fact, such thoughts are better suited to brainstorming sessions for movie scripts than a serious discussion of automated systems and society. And as always with such thinking, AI is regarded as something alien and apart, its autonomy and omniscience imparted as a kind of divine afflatus by otherwise limited and short-sighted human investigators.

And I'm afraid that this is pretty much how it goes throughout the book.

It is evident from even a cursory reading of this book that Bostrom labors under the handicap of not knowing the field in depth. (This comes out quite clearly from time to time, as in his reference to Deep Blue as a "simple program".) This is not always a fatal shortcoming — witness the many excellent journalistic accounts of 'science in action'. But it does hamper anyone trying to work through basic issues regarding human versus artificial intelligence and their implications for the future.

A nice example of the level of discussion is an idea that the author introduces early on called "AI-completeness".[113*] A task is considered to be AI-complete if being able to perform it requires general human-level intelligence. Of course, since the latter is cannot be clearly defined, the idea is essentially vacuous. What is interesting about this is that it is obviously derived from a fundamental idea in a branch of mathematics called complexity theory. The original idea involves a class of problems of similar difficulty, and problems in that class that are at least as hard to solve as any of their class-mates. If X is the name of the class, then the latter problems are called "X-complete". The difference between this and AI-completeness is that all the concepts in the former case are rigorously defined; they also emerged in a natural way as the analysis of algorithm performance was developed into a science. The latter idea is essentially an attempt (done consciously or unconsciously) to adopt a term used by genuine computer scientist-mathematicians, thereby giving the discussion a certain scientific patina without underpinning the new term with the logic or empirical grounding that would give it real substance.[114*]

The main text begins with a short account of the growth of world GDP over time, together with graphs that demonstrate the sudden rapid growth over the past two or three hundred years, after millennia of stasis. This is then likened to the exponential growth of intelligence that can be expected now that we are able to 'create' it artificially. But it's not at all clear that the two are really comparable. To be sure, there has (already) been an exponential growth of knowledge, especially during the past century. And in some very definite ways, this has added to the world's intelligence, as defined in the present work. Moreover, if we recognize that application programs like those that handle banking transactions and airline reservations, as well as all the manifold capacities now present on the Internet, are also manifestations of intelligence, then we see that there is a sense in which the 'amount' of intelligence in the world has already risen exponentially.

But if I am correct in ascribing intelligence to networks of agents rather than to agents with near-deific capacities, then the future of intelligence becomes more problematic, and an overall rise in intelligence is not assured. (In fact, one can foresee possible declines in intelligence if some of the phenomena described in the next chapter take place on a larger scale.)

The same chapter continues with a brief history of AI, including descriptions of some major discoveries such as Bayes nets, machine learning techniques, and programs that produce effective schedules of operations. Bostrom singles out two important challenges: learning and handling uncertainty. I think no one would disagree that these are two fundamental problems for AI. This is followed by a discussion of some genuinely impressive achievements, in particular, the successes at game playing. Finally, there is a rundown of current opinion in the field as to when we can expect "human level machine intelligence" to arrive, and then how long it will be after before we have "super-human machine intelligence".

Again, from the perspective of the present work, all this is off the mark (and more than a little off the wall). In fact, with the first program that could take advantage of the computer's capacity to work its way through logical conditions of any complexity, we had created a kind of intelligence far beyond any unaided human abilities along the same lines; in other words, at that moment super-human intelligence had arrived. And this will continue to be true for any area in which the combinatorics (i.e. the number of possibilities to be considered) overwhelms human capacities. All that is required is a proper representation of the problem; after that the search capacities of computer-based programs can deal with the situation more effectively than any human being working without such aids.

In the next chapter (titled "Paths to superintelligence"), Bostrom first disarms the reader with a we'll-know-it-when-we-see-it definition of superintelligence:

> "any intellect that greatly exceeds the cognitive performance of humans in virtually all domains of interest"[115]

Interestingly, in a footnote other similar definitions are referenced going back over half a century, which shows that Bostrom is not the first to have satisfied himself with this sort of hand waving. Then he makes the following argument:

> "We know that blind evolutionary processes can produce human-level general intelligence, since they have already done so at least once. Evolutionary processes with foresight — that is, genetic programs designed and guided by an intelligent human programmer — should be able to achieve a similar outcome with far greater efficiency."[116]

One thing that strikes me on reading a passage like this is how easy it is to write this sort of stuff. But of course that's the problem: when talking about realms where definite observations cannot be made, as for example the future, there are fewer checks that would forestall dubious assertions or force one to confront vagueness of conception. And, tellingly, Bostrom seems to feel quite at home in these realms.

Here and elsewhere evolutionary algorithms are discussed as if their performance was somehow analogous to biological organisms evolving over time. On the basis of this analogy the author indulges in the same kind of numerical speculations that Kurzweil and Moravec are so fond of. In this case, biological evolution is quantified by estimating the number of steps required; this is followed by a calculation of how long it would take an evolutionary algorithm to complete the same number of steps. From this, Bostrom concludes that it is feasible to produce human-level intelligence in this fashion.

In all of this, there is an evident hankering after the kind of certainty that comes with having concrete evidence and an attempt to achieve this by means of numerical calculations. This seems to be an enduring temptation among futurists; one can't help thinking of the moth drawn toward the flame.

Bostrom then considers other possible routes to superintelligence, including ones based on whole brain emulation. Here, the reader meets with the same sorts of fantastic speculation found in the other books, although there the effect was leavened by setting it off as somewhat light-hearted speculation. Although musings along these lines seem to be another favorite occupation among futurists, I haven't as yet seen anything that would actually support these speculations. At one point, he more or less gives the game away with this statement:

> "In the unrealistic limiting case, we could imagine emulating a brain at the level of its elementary particles using the quantum mechanical Schrödinger equation."[117]

Not only is this "unrealistic", it is gobbledygook — what on earth does it mean to use the "quantum mechanical Schrödinger equation" in this fashion? At this point the author is just stringing together words picked up in his reading. In Sokal and Rolf's words, it is "fashionable nonsense".

More interesting than the arguments themselves, which are no more than piffle, is the false note that runs through the entire discussion. On the one hand, Bostrom has assured us that he is worried about our future prospects — and that we should be too. But then he lays out all these grotesque scenarios with obvious enthusiasm. And they are presented as if they were givens, as developments that will just happen and that we must be prepared for, not as human choices. Such abdication of responsibility bespeaks a kind of paralysis, a gelding of the moral will. At the same time, there is an overweening hubris, as if the author were revealing deep truths to his readers like the angel in Tintoretto's painting bearing the light. Of course, all this may just be another demonstration of what can happen when one doesn't have to do real work for a living.

With this 'foundation' in place, Bostrom then considers the features of the world that is about to spring forth and engulf us. First, there is a short chapter on the possible forms that superintelligence might take, which is really another empty exercise: superintelligence may just occur at a faster rate than human intelligence, or it may be "vastly qualitatively smarter" (p. 56). (As Gore Vidal would say, "Yes.")

Intriguingly, in this chapter one of the alternatives considered is "collective intelligence", and in his description Bostrom lays out something very similar to the central conception of the present work. However, he envisages this as another alternative form of intelligence, not as the fundamental form that all intelligence must take. And it is shoehorned into his basic perspective:

> "To obtain collective superintelligence from any present-day collective intelligence would require a very great degree of enhancement. The resulting system would need to be capable of vastly outperforming any current collective intelligence or other cognitive system across many very general domains."[118]

And so on and so forth. Later in the same section, because he has no clear idea of what he means by intelligence, his conception of collective intelligence devolves into something like Le Bon's crowd, subject to rumors and false information and other sorts of unintelligent actions.

After this there are more chapters of futuristic fantasies. One considers possible timelines for the growth of superintelligence once it exceeds the human 'threshold' (slow, moderate, fast), and plays with a notion of "recalcitrance", which is simply the difficulty encountered in proceeding. Here, the reader is treated to passages such as the following:

> "In some situations, recalcitrance could be extremely low. For example, if human-level AI is delayed because one key insight long eludes programmers, then when the final breakthrough occurs, the AI might leapfrog from below to radically above human level without even touching the intermediary rungs."[119]
>
> "The upshot of these several considerations is that it is difficult to predict how hard it will be to make algorithmic improvements in the first AI that reaches a roughly human level of general intelligence."[120]

(Cue in Vidal again.)

The chapter after this considers scenarios where various superintelligences emerge in different places. The following question is posed:

> "Will one machine intelligence project get so far ahead of the competition that it gets a decisive strategic advantage — that is, a level of technological and other advantages sufficient to enable it to achieve complete world domination?"[121]

To fill out the discussion there are references to technology races in the past including the Cold War arms races.

The next two chapters (6 and 7) contain musings about the forms that superintelligence might take and the goals that an autonomous system of this sort might have. In the latter chapter two ersatz principles are introduced, one that posits the independence of intelligence and motivation and one that assumes a kind of convergence of goals. In addition to appearing to contradict each other, the former is at least partly undermined by the discussion in the text. At any rate, since both are merely presumed, they add little of substance, while continuing the air of carrying out serious analysis. The next chapter is a culmination of sorts where various scenarios involving malevolent intentions are considered. As such, it is a strange mixture of intellectual pretense and lurid imaginings. For example, at the beginning this chapter the author says:

> "Proceeding from the idea of first-mover advantage, the orthogonality thesis, and the instrumental convergence thesis, we can now begin to see the outlines of an

> argument for fearing that a plausible *default* outcome of the creation of machine superintelligence is existential catastrophe."[122] (emphasis added)

Since the entire argument is insubstantial, it is easy to come up with scenarios that don't actually make sense:

> "the instrumental convergence thesis entails that we cannot blithely assume that a superintelligence with the final goal of calculating the decimals of pi (or making paperclips, or counting grains of sand) would limit its activities in such a way as not to infringe on human interests. An agent with such a final goal would have convergent instrumental reason, in many situations, to acquire an unlimited amount of physical resources and, if possible, to eliminate potential threats to its goal system. Human beings might constitute potential threats; they certainly constitute potential resources."[123]

This thought is continued in the next paragraph:

> "If we now reflect that human beings consist of useful resources (such as conveniently located atoms [??]) and that we depend for our survival and flourishing on many more local resources, we can see that the outcome could easily be one in which humanity quickly becomes extinct."[124]

And this is pretty much how the chapter goes — from one scary scenario to another. Of course, in keeping with the spirit of the work all this is given an impressive-sounding name: "malignant failure modes".

In some ways this sort of writing resembles the discourse of people who are heavily engaged in role-playing games. Typically, the latter accumulate all sorts of ersatz knowledge about these games without also having to master a body of argument that would make that knowledge of real substance. As a result, their discourse carries a veneer of objectivity without respecting the kinds of constraints that make genuine objective knowledge useful and effective. This is why it never leads to anything beyond itself and is eventually put aside and forgotten.

After expounding on an imaginary crisis, the author develops, in equally excruciating detail, various plans for meeting it. First, a taxonomy of strategies is laid out, including such ideas as restricting its access to resources ("boxing"), making sure the system does not develop malicious goals ("incentive methods") and limiting its capacities ("stunting"). Note that each of these is an obvious idea that that would occur to anyone; moreover, it is also unalterably vague. But this allows the author to give the impression in subsequent chapters of applying his strategies in various situations. The latter include question-answering systems and various kinds of software tools.

And on and on it goes: through visions of "multipolar" scenarios, where various kinds of economies evolve, to lengthy discussions of how values might be incorporated into superintelligent agents (which includes a somewhat useful review of notions of goals, utility and similar ideas without, however, considering this material at all critically), and finally some prescriptions regarding how humanity might proceed in the face of the "existential risk". The latter is replete with the same cotton candy reflections encountered earlier in this work, as in this passage:

> "We have seen in earlier chapters that the introduction of machine superintelligence would create a substantial existential risk. But it would reduce many other existential risks. Risks from nature — such as asteroid impacts, supervolcanoes, and natural pandemics — would be virtually eliminated, since superintelligence could deploy countermeasures against most such hazards, or at least demote them to the non-existential category (for instance, via space colonization)."[125]

Perhaps unsurprisingly, the idea of brain emulation pops up again in these discussions, viewed as a kind of application software package that might be available, although the notion is entirely whimsical and has little bearing on issues of artificial intelligence. But this in keeping with the general character of the work.

I have to admit that at the end of the day I prefer Kurzweil's giddy flights of fancy to Bostrom's ponderous ruminations, although both are equally vaporous. From the present perspective, the most interesting aspect of these works is that they illustrate vagaries and shortcomings of human thought, a topic that will be explored further in the next two chapters.[126*]

*

As with the critics, it is important to note that these discussants occupy a place off to the side of the actual field. AI researchers that I've talked to, while vaguely aware of such goings-on, have not actually bothered to delve into this material. On the other side, it isn't clear to me how much interest people like Kurzweil and Bostrom have in the actual subject of cognition and knowledge, as opposed to grandiose ideas like superhuman AI.

Perhaps the most striking thing about "superintelligence" is its phantasmagoric quality — which I have tried to counter in this book by giving an account of AI as it is actually implemented, and as a living science with specific attributes and a particular history. It is also interesting that there is very little discussion in books such as Kurzweil's or Bostrom's of any of the deep issues facing AI researchers, which have been discussed (however fleetingly and superficially) in these chapters.

Once one has grasped the fact that human intelligence (HI) and artificial intelligence (AI) can only exist within a network of agents, then one sees that most of the discussion about superintelligence is essentially off-base. To put the matter simply, it should be obvious that superintelligence is not something that's going to come in a box.

By now the reader should not be surprised if I say that superintelligence is already with us; in fact, it's been here for some time. One form in which it manifests itself is called subatomic physics; another is called genomics, another solid-state engineering, and so forth. In each of these disciplines intelligence is exhibited that would have been unimaginable even 50 or 100 years ago. And even earlier, advances in what is now know as the calculus gave us a form of superintelligent capacities far in advance of those of earlier generations of mathematicians or users of mathematics.

In a somewhat similar vein, the automobile and the airplane are examples of super-locomotion. But as far as I know, no one is having kittens over this. (Once could also cite spell-checking systems in this vein.) All of this suggests that there are quirky psychological influences lurking in the background and driving this particular line of discussion.

The idea that intelligence of any kind occurs within an agent-in-a-network framework in turn suggests that AI is better thought of as Artificially-Aided Intelligence (AAI). And this leads naturally to the next topic that will be considered in this work.

Coda

Interestingly enough, neither the critics nor the 'cheerleaders' consider issues that are at the heart of the present work. Nowhere in all of this have

I encountered anything that resembles the present conception of intelligence.[127*]

In short, something extraordinary is going on under the label of "artificial intelligence", and no one on either side of the aisle seems quite able to come to terms with it.

After combing over the arguments recounted in this chapter, it occurred to me that the world may be ready for a work to complement George Bernard Shaw's *The Adventures of the Black Girl in Her Search for God.*[128] It could be called *The Adventures of the Black Girl in Her Search for Superintelligence.* Certainly, there are a sufficient number of gurus on call to fill a small volume, just as there were when Shaw wrote his sparkling satire.

Endnotes

1. J. R. Searle, "Minds, brains, and programs" *Behavioral and Brain Sciences*, 1980, 3: 417–457 (with comments); quotation on p. 417.
2. I will note in passing that this is in fact a worthwhile side-trip, since the Yale project was one of the most interesting and productive of the early AI projects (and wasn't referenced earlier in this volume). For further reading I would recommend R. C. Schank & C. K. Riesbeck, *Inside Computer Understanding*, Hillsdale, NJ: Lawrence E. Earlbaum, 1981 and J. L. Kolodner, *Retrieval and Organizational Strategies in Conceptual Memory*, Hillsdale, NJ: Lawrence E. Earlbaum, 1984.
3. R. Cullingford, "SAM", Chapter 5 in Schank & Riesbeck, *op. cit.*
4. Schank & Riesbeck, *op. cit.,* p. 11.
5. *Ibid.*, pp. 29–30
6. *Ibid.*, pp. 33–34.
7. These problems were addressed by the PAM program, which is described by R. Wilensky in Chapter 7 of Schank & Riesbeck. This example appears on p. 140.
8. The organization of memory is discussed in R. Schank, *Dynamic Memory*, Cambridge, 1982. Other important developments are described in M. Dyer, *In-Depth Understanding*, Cambridge, MA & London: MIT, 1983 and J. Kolodner, *Retrieval and Organizational Strategies in Conceptual Memory: A Computer Model*, Hillsdale, NJ: L. E. Earlbaum, 1984.
9. R. Cullingford, *op. cit.,* p. 111. In this case it is intriguing to note that the author seems to have some difficulty himself in verbally formulating the causal relations.
10. In fact, one of the most impressive achievements of this work is the light that has been shed on the meaning of understanding itself. In hindsight, it is not surprising that "understanding" should turn out to be an inherently vague term that in actuality

refers to many different kinds of inference and information handling. But without the work of Schank *et al.* this would not have been so obvious or so well demonstrated.

11. One of the annoying features of much of the early AI work is that these people seemed to take no cognizance of work that was done before them. For example, in connection with basic primitives for thinking, the work of Kant immediately comes to mind. And the strange thing is that on going over Kant's efforts to establish the foundations of human knowledge, there is very little that fits into the Yale scheme. Where, for example, are the basic categories of quantity, quality, modality and relation or the categories that fall under them? (One does find discussions of causality, a conception that Kant thought was fundamental and a priori, and the need for the system to handle causal relations. But I don't see many other similarities.)

    Yet, even while saying this, I have to admit that there are aspects of the work of Schank et al. that seem to have a bearing on important philosophical problems. (Certainly, their work was philosophically primitive; but is this a devastating criticism?) So maybe they were right to ignore the older armchair discussions while trying to get their programs to work and do interesting things while operating on well-defined inputs.
12. In fairness, and in order to make clear what the issues are here, I should add that I think that Searle would agree that, considered as experimental tests of certain ideas about cognition, these programs are very instructive. His shtick is that they do not embody 'real' understanding, in contrast to human intelligence. My position is that they do embody understanding of a sort and thus approximate the understanding that human beings are capable of. But at the same time, their achievements cannot be separated from the intelligence network within which they were created.
13. J. R. Searle, op. cit.
14. See for example, R. E. Nisbett & T. D. Wilson, "Telling more than we can know: Verbal reports on mental processes", *Psychological Review*, 1977, 84: 231–259.
15. J. R. Searle, "What your computer can't know", *New York Review of Books*, Oct 9–22, 2014, pp. 52–55
16. J. R. Searle, *The Rediscovery of the Mind*, Cambridge, MA & London: MIT, 1994 (orig. 1992), p. 8.
17. One thing I have noticed here and elsewhere in Searle's work, is that he sometimes makes important use of terms, like "state" or even larger expressions (like sentence number 4 of his is-to-ought argument[17a]), that can have more than one interpretation. This seems to allow him to move between categories while denying that there is any problem in doing so. Here, it may enable him to finesses issues having to do with mind-brain relations, where more circumspect souls encounter serious difficulties.

17a. J. R. Searle, *Speech Acts*, Cambridge: Cambridge University, 1969, p. 177.

18. I will note parenthetically, since I don't wish to go into these issues in this work, that in coming up with another verbal formula that allows him to exorcise the

AI 'demon', Searle has chosen "consciousness" as his trump card. But in fact it's the joker in the deck.

19. E. L. Thorndike, "The effect of changed data upon reasoning", *Journal of Experimental Psychology*, 1922, 5: 33–38.
20. Regarding the Chinese room and suchlike arguments, I'm reminded of the rubber duck that used to swoop down from time to time on the old Groucho Marx "You Bet Your Life" show, whenever someone uttered the 'magic word' of the night. It would drop down out of the blue, cause a brief disturbance, and quickly disappear again without having any connection to what was actually happening onstage.
21. In fact, Searle cuts an impressive figure in contemporary philosophy (I for one agree with those who think that his books on speech acts and the "construction of social reality" are classics), and more often than not he strikes me as eminently sane and sober in his thinking. So why did he end up inside the Chinese room? My own pet theory is that Searle has an inner sophist that he doesn't always manage to keep in leash. (This sort of thing seems to be an occupational hazard for philosophers.) This sophist, like most members of the breed, is overly fond of verbal arguments. So amidst the many impressive analyses, sometimes we get the occasional oddity, such as instructions on how to turn "is" into "ought" and excursions into the Chinese room. The result is that we are faced with a perplexing combination of straightforward common sense and utter obtuseness. If I am correct in my assessment, then this is such an interesting case of sophistry that I'm inclined to invoke a well-known notion and say that if John Searle didn't exist it would be necessary (or at least very useful) to invent him.

    Moreover, when it comes to questions of artificial intelligence, he really seems to lose it and immerse himself in what to me are sophistical arguments. In particular, I don't think that questions about intelligence should be conflated with the problem of consciousness; yet his entire argument against AI turns on this. This may also be because, like other contemporary secular philosophers he wants to treat consciousness as another physical-biological phenomenon, but one that somehow escapes the nets of engineers. In fact, there's a having-your-cake-and-eating-it character to this entire line of thought.
22. R. Penrose, *The Emperor's New Mind*, Oxford: Oxford University, 1989. R. Penrose, *Shadows of the Mind*, New York & Oxford: Oxford University, 1994.
23. Throughout Penrose's book there seems to be a confusion between psychological processes and experience. For example, on p. 17, we find the statement, "One of the claims of AI is that it provides a route towards some sort of understanding of mental qualities, such as happiness, pain, hunger." He then goes on to discuss a simple feedback system in an early robot ("Grey Walter's tortoise") that causes it to return to a charger whenever its battery runs down, to illustrate the 'AI' account (which is, in fact, a behavioristic account) of hunger. In fact, Walter's demonstration meshes with a large body of physiological and behavioral studies that lead to similar conclusions regarding the mechanisms of hunger. For example, some of the signals for

'hunger' (i.e. food seeking and eating) and satiation have been elucidated, and the evidence for feedback control (physiological and behavioral homeostasis) is very strong. None of this work involves asking whether the organism "actually feels" hunger; likewise for pain and other motivational phenomena. (I might add that I found it passing strange to encounter a section title, "An AI approach to 'pleasure' and 'pain'", since these are not topics normally associated with AI, as any textbook on the subject would indicate.)

In the same vein, in a subsequent discussion of whether a computer system can be said to understand, this issue is (to my mind) conflated with the question of whether a system that behaves as though it understood (e.g. by answering questions posed to it appropriately) has the same "'mental state'" as a human being who performs equivalently. To me it is obvious that everything depends on what one means by "mental state": if we mean a state of the system capable of producing the output, then the system can be said to exhibit some form of understanding, but if we mean some capacity for experience, then the question seems unanswerable, although I for one would be skeptical concerning the machine's capacities in this regard. But, again, for the purposes of the present work, the latter question is irrelevant.

Penrose does not consider the possibility that discussions of conscious awareness are simply incommensurate with discussions of what a system is capable of doing. In particular, the 'threat' posed by artificial intelligence does not depend in the slightest on whether these systems are conscious.

When an entire argument turns on an idea that cannot be adequately defined, warning signals should flash.

(Here I might add that use of a phrase like "the unconscious mind" is an acknowledgement that 'consciousness' is not required for mental activities.)

24. Although it has no direct bearing on the present work, perhaps I should say something about my views on the perplexing question of consciousness, in part because it really seems to me that most discussions of consciousness are either vacuous or incoherent. At present while I have no strong views on the matter (not having studied the question or the literature on the subject in any depth), my intuitive view is what I would call genuine dualism. By this I mean the same dualism that applies to, say, a linear program (as a system of linear equations with an objective to be maximized or minimized), or to various other mathematical systems; i.e. there are alternative descriptions ("duals") of the system that are formally equivalent. I call it "genuine" because I do not think that the 'ghost-in-the-machine' form of dualism is a genuine dualism; instead, I would call it a duple-ism. So what are the duals in this case? I would say that there seems to be a dualism between the individual and, in some sense of the word, the universe. In other words, it is a form of micocosom-macrocosom dualism.

Mind you, this is in no way an explanation of this consciousness business, since I have no idea of what it really means or how it could be true. I would not even go so far as to call it a hypothesis. It is simply a tentative, intuitive view of the matter, or, if you like, a suspicion. Incidentally, I find a similar adumbration in an apothegm of Meister Eckhart: "God sees the world through my eyes". (In other cases, where he seems to actually equate the I with God, I would be inclined to agree that he should have been burned at the stake for heresy — but in this particular instance I see an intuition similar to mine expressed within the Christian framework.) And of course there is the Hindu Atman-Brahmin dualism, which also seems very similar to my intuitions.

Putting this another way, by the term "consciousness" I am referring to the thatness of the world and the fact that this depends in some unknown way on my physical existence (and state). So there is some sense in which I bring the world into being.

Along these lines, one thing that people can do that seems to be outside the realm of computability is that they can contemplate existence. For example, I can take up a pebble or a leaf and simply regard it as such. (And isn't this also what is involved in most purely intellectual endeavors?) I have no idea how this could be achieved by a computer program (by repeating the algorithms again and again? by making them go faster and faster?). Or even what it means in terms of computability. But since the present work is concerned with what AI systems can do, we can put this issue aside. (Note also that the 'threat' of AI does not depend in the slightest on whether consciousness enters into the activities of these systems. Moreover, I draw no conclusions concerning the possibility of building a machine that can support consciousness, i.e. one that is conscious.)

25. Penrose's arguments about "non-algorithmic" thinking are relevant to constraint satisfaction.
26. ENM *op. cit.,* pp. 127–128.
27. A much fuller account of these matters can be found in the ENM book, as well as E. Nagel & J. R. Newman, *Gödel's Proof,* New York: New York University, 1958. For Turing's work, the best short introduction I've found is the Wikipedia article on Turing Machines.
28. ENM *op. cit.,* p. 143.
29. Nagel & Newman *op. cit.,* p. 101.
30. A. Quaife, "Automated proofs of Löb's theorem and Gödel's two incompleteness theorems", *Journal of Automated Reasoning*, 1988, 4: 219–231.
31. These errors are quite technical, e.g. use of a specialized form of consistency (ω-consistency) in places where one would have expected the usual definition of soundness, which makes some of the subsequent arguments ambiguous. The point is that they tend to undermine a thesis that endows human beings with special intellectual gifts beyond the powers of mere machines. After all, what do Penrose's own insights actually amount to if he manages to introduce confusion into the arguments he is making?
32. A related idea, having to do with the development of novel concepts in ill-defined situations, has been termed "ontological uncertainty". See D. A. Lane, "Ontological uncertainty and innovation", *Journal of Evolutionary Economics*, 2005, 15: 3–50.

33. In the last chapters of his book, Penrose argues that the human brain may have objectively identifiable capacities that are outside the scope of physical, deterministic computing systems. His argument (which of course is tentative) rests on the existence of phenomena at the quantum 'level', such as quantum superposition, that cannot be handled by the methods of classical physics. Since this material is outside my range of competence, I can't comment on it directly or at length. However, the more I think about it, the more skeptical I am. This is because even the simplest neural processes involve perhaps billions of molecules. Consider synaptic transmission: in this case each synaptic vesicle contains hundreds or thousands of transmitter molecules, and while its merging with the membrane to discharge its contents into the synaptic cleft involves atomic processes, these occur in such great number that it is hard to see how quantum effects could play any kind of significant role. The same arguments could be made for action potentials, post synaptic potentials and so forth.

    In any case, this seems to me to be a much weaker and therefore at present a less interesting argument than the one based on the limits of computability. Fortunately for us, whatever the ultimate answer is, it does not really affect the thesis of the present work. Instead, it could possibly set limits on the capacities that can be imparted to nodes of a particular character within an intelligence network.
34. H. L. Dreyfus, *What Computers Can't Do* (revised), New York: Harper & Row, 1979. (The first edition was published in 1972.)
35. *Ibid.*, p. 105.
36. *Ibid.*, p. 106.
37. A few pages later in a discussion of the ability to discriminate the "essential" from the "inessential", Dreyfus discusses the notion of insight further:

    "For example, Gestalt psychologist Max Wertheimer points out in his classic work, Productive Thinking, that the trial-and-error account of problem solving excludes the most important aspect of problem-solving behavior, namely a grasp of the essential structure of the problem, which he calls "insight". In this operation, one breaks away from the surface structure and sees the basic problem — what Wertheimer calls the "deeper structure" — which enables one to organize the steps necessary for a solution." (p. 114)

    Later Dreyfus says:

    "This lack of progress [in building powerful problem solvers] is surprising only to those, like Feigenbaum, who do not recognize the ability to distinguish the essential from the inessential as a human form of "information processing," necessary for learning and problem solving, yet not amenable to the mechanical search techniques which may operate once this distinction has been made. It is precisely this function of intelligence which resists further progress in the problem-solving field." (p. 119)

Now, I don't disagree with the argument that human beings are superb at perceiving significant clusters of relations ("structure") in a problem or a game like chess, in ways that are still poorly understood. However, Dreyfus appears not to realize, (1) that recognition of a phenomenon does not mean one understands it, and it should be clear to the modern reader that his discussion of these matters is 'hopelessly' vague in its delineations of such abilities (and it is telling that he seems completely oblivious to this), (2) that there may be more than one way to 'skin the cat', especially if one understands the basic formal features of problem solving. This, in fact, is what has happened, so that in many fields now there have been notable successes, which should not have happened if Dreyfus' arguments were as compelling as he thought — because all this has transpired from building upon the insights of the AI pioneers, insights that his book disparages.

38. Dreyfus, *op. cit.,* p. 120.
39. For a recent summary of the state-of-the-art in face recognition, see M. Hassaballah & S. Aly, "Face recognition: challenges, achievements and future directions", *IET Computer Vision*, 2015, 9: 614–626. And for various other recognition tasks, modern machine learning systems such as those involving so-called "deep learning" are approaching human levels of competence Y. LeCun, Y. Bengio & G. Hinton, "Deep learning", *Nature*, 2015, 521: 436–444). For AI approaches to artistic styles see M. Jones, "Robotic arts: current practices, potentials, and implications", *Multimodal Technologies and Interaction*, 2017, 1, doi:10.3390/mti1020005 and J. L. Kirsch & R. A. Kirsch, "The anatomy of painting styles: description with computer rules", *Leonardo*, 1988, 21: 437–444.
40. Dreyfus, *op. cit.,* p. 161.
41. EOA = End of Argument (the sophist's version of QED).
42. H. Helmholtz, *Physiological Optics, Vol. 3*, Optical Society of America, 1924. Although Dreyfus would probably describe it as underdetermined and wholistic, visual perception is normally overdetermined (i.e. there is a high degree of redundancy in the normal retinal image). This is why it typically occurs almost instantly. Interestingly, in some of Julesz's advanced demonstrations of stereopsis, a coherent perception takes several minutes to appear — and one is aware of the process of formation. In these cases, the visual system is being forced to 'think' to a degree that it does not ordinarily have to, and what is going on is clearly a search process of some sort. See B. Julesz, *Foundations of Cyclopean Perception*, MIT, 1971.
43. A discussion of these matters can be found in any textbook of ethology such as R. A. Hinde, *Animal Behavior,* 2nd edition, New York & other: McGraw-Hill, 1970.
44. The following sentence, that appears at the end of the chapter, is also telling: "In fact, the difference between the "strongly interactive" nature of brain organization and the noninteractive character of machine organization suggests that insofar as arguments from biology are relevant, the evidence is against the possibility of using digital computers to produce intelligence." (162; italics added). Here, the vagueness of the terms "interactive" and "noninteractive" should be noted; in what sense is a

system of integrated circuits (or for that matter, a program with multiple subroutines or even multiple classes) "noninteractive"?

45. Dreyfus, *op. cit.,* p. 156.
46. *Ibid.*, p. 183–184.
47. In discussing the same passage from Fodor, Dreyfus also takes issue with terms "type" and "token" to refer to the perceptual equivalence of two stimulus inputs. He says,

    "The perceived phenomenal sound sequence (the melody) cannot be an abstraction (a type) of which the physical energy inputs are instantiations (tokens). The percept and the physical energy are equally concrete and are totally different sorts of phenomena. No amount of complication can bridge the gap between shifting energy inputs and the perception of an enduring sound. One is not the instantiation of the other." (p. 184)

    I think this shows pretty clearly that while assuming the mantle of phenomenologist, Dreyfus is in a fact essentially a sophist (i.e. a labeler, not a looker — but a labeler who has adopted a looker label!). Here, he has basically talked himself around the important problem of perceptual constancies, which is obviously one of deriving a constant perception (in this case a particular melody) from a set of inputs that vary in specific ways (which ultimately can be described in terms of regularities of some sort, i.e. rules — otherwise, there would be no basis for the perceptual constancy). Of course, as a sophist/labeler he doesn't see that this is what he has done.
48. On pp. 243–247 of his book, Dreyfus takes Neisser to task for not understanding that concepts such as plans or syntactic rules cannot be used as substitutes for Gestalt wholism, and therefore cannot explain the phenomena that come under this heading. Again, this is vintage Dreyfus: take some ill-defined notion like the Gestalt notion of wholes and use it to criticize anyone who would try to define it more precisely (while at the same time claiming that some armchair introspective account is more adequate!) What he does not see is that such arguments are in the end self-defeating, since they rule out any real explanation of the phenomena.
49. Here is another example of the essential fatuousness of Dreyfus' arguments. In a chapter called, "The situation: orderly behavior without recourse to rules", after noting (again) the sheer number of facts that a system with an intelligence comparable to humans would have to deal with, and the deep problem of recognizing and attending to relevant the relevant elements in any particular situation, Dreyfus says this:

    "It [the ability "to zero in on the relevant facts"] has to do with the way man is at home in his world, has it comfortably wrapped around him, so to speak. Human beings are somehow already situated in such a way that what they need in order to cope with things is distributed around them where they need it, not packed away like a trunk full of objects, or even carefully indexed in a filing cabinet." (p. 260)

Voilà! Questions answered. Problems solved.

50. Dreyfus, *op. cit.*, p. 189.
51. *Ibid.*, p. 190.
52. *Ibid.*, p. 190–191.
53. *Ibid.*, p. 200.
54. *Ibid.*, p. 199.
55. *Ibid.*, p. 200.
56. *Loc. cit.*
57. This is another example of how clever arguments like those of Dreyfus manage to obfuscate important issues, especially when one is arguing an extreme position, in this case the impossibility of something ever being realized.
58. Dreyfus, *op. cit.,* p. 208.
59. *Ibid.*, p. 218.
60. *Loc. cit.*
61. Here, it should be pointed out that Dreyfus sidles around the issue of how a situation itself is identified. It is difficult to see how this can happen except through the (possibly implicit or unconscious) identification of features. So his assertion that situations "might be of a radically different order" begins to sound like either evasion or wishful thinking. Especially at the end of this chapter (pp. 221–4), he begins to wax rhetorical (e.g. "There seems to be no way to get into a situation and no way to recognize one from the outside."(p. 223) and "It seems we simply take for granted this ultimate situation of being people." (p. 221)). This seems to me to be an implicit admission that there is something fundamentally lacking in his argument.
62. Dreyfus, *op. cit.,* p. 236.
63. *Ibid.*, p. 232–233.
64. *Ibid.*, p. 237.
65. In fact, it is here that the essential weakness of Dreyfus' arguments against AI is most apparent. This becomes clear if one examines the strategy of his arguments closely in this case. Dreyfus begins by making the astonishing statement that tasks like pattern recognition and chess playing "cannot be formalized". He then claims that "the nonformalizable form of "information processing" … is possible only for embodied beings". He goes on to say that, "with the aid of concepts borrowed from phenomenology", he will "try to show how pattern recognition requires a certain sort of indeterminate, global anticipation" (!) ... "characteristic of our body as a "machine" of nerves and muscles … and also of our body as experienced by us, as our power to move and manipulate objects in the world", which "cannot be reproduced by a heuristically programmed digital computer — even one … which

can operate manipulators" [i.e. a robot]. And "therefore, by virtue of being embodied, we can perform tasks beyond the capacities of any heuristically programmed robot". (p. 237)

And this is the gist of his argument that machines will never recognize patterns as well as human beings can or play chess as well as the best human players. In fact, this is a rather shallow piece of sophistry, as well as an attempt to settle an empirical question by performing a logical pirouette starting from vague or erroneous assumptions. For one thing, the basic structure of chess can be formalized and already had been when Dreyfus was writing. And "pattern recognition" can be broken down into many specific problems that can be formalized. On the other hand phrases like "indeterminate, global anticipation" (or "fringe consciousness", which refers to the same thing) do nothing to clarify the problem of what information is being used and how it is detected. (Although Dreyfus objects to use of the term "information" in its formal sense in this connection, surely one can accept that there must be features of the situation that in turn must be recognized in order to perform a task properly — through "fringe consciousness" or whatever. In other words, "fringe consciousness" has to involve something more concrete than a Cheshire cat smile.)

One simple problem raised by this argument is: why are "bodies" required to produce things like "indeterminate, global anticipation"? That is, what exactly are the characteristics involved in such functions, and why are "bodies" required to perform these functions?

(Isn't it odd that when you look closely at arguments concerning embodiedness, you rarely find anything of substance? Incidentally, I'm amazed that the people who wrote the Wikipedia article on Dreyfus thought that he had been largely vindicated in his criticism of AI. One wonders if they ever looked at the actual arguments.)

66. Dreyfus also overlooks the fact that a computer does operate with focal awareness plus background information. The former is manifested in the current Central Processing Unit (CPU) operations, while the latter is the information stored in memory. In fact, modern computer systems even have what Husserl, according to Dreyfus, called the "inner horizon" between focal and background consciousness, in the form of cache memory. It should also be noted that these ideas are handled in cognitive psychology in a more objective manner than phenomenologists' introspective accounts in the form of working memory versus long-term memory.
67. Dreyfus, *op. cit.,* p. 266.
68. *Ibid.*, p. 265.
69. What Dreyfus did not (and evidently does not) grasp is that AI is part of an emerging computational paradigm. As such it lays claim to all those processes associated with the human brain that can be called intelligent. Now, the means by which the brain carries out its computations may be very different from the operations of a digital computer. But the claim is that it is carrying out computations nonetheless. In his discussions of Gestalt phenomena, Dreyfus seems to think otherwise.

Evidently, he hasn't grasped the fact that a soap bubble doesn't compute anything insofar as it follows the physical constraints that make it a soap bubble. It is only when such action serves to transmit information (reflected in a coherent perception or a new idea) that it can be said to compute.

70. Why do these philosophers never dwell on the vagaries of human cognition, the lapses in human intelligence? Reading Dreyfus, one has the impression that human beings never make mistakes, that they never overlook relevant information, and that they never respond inappropriately. This is a topic that will be treated at length in the penultimate section of this book.
71. It's interesting how often the idea of "embodiment" pops up as an explanatory device in critical discussions of AI. Not to mention how it tends to be presented without any caveats. I for one find it disconcerting to hear all this fluting about "embodiedness" while never encountering any specific ideas as to how this confers abilities such as responsiveness to context (or why it might allow one to zero in on promising lines of attack in a chess game). To be blunt, I'm afraid that all this has something of the character of an intellectual hustle.
72. Again, let me emphasize that the above counterarguments do not undermine what I think is the substantial claim behind notions of "embodiedness" or being-in-the-world. This is that knowledge in predicated form emerges from interactions with the world that go on at a nonverbal level (which could even be characterized as "stimulus-response", although this terminology ignores the feedback character of behavior at this level). This is what I think Wittgenstein was trying to get at via his language games — as well as showing that language and conceptualization are themselves part of such interactions.

    Part of the problem here may be due (as usual) to terminology. "Body" and "embodiedness" take us in directions away from the basic insight just mentioned that pertain to forms of interaction including basic perception. Perhaps if the term "embeddedness" had been used instead of "embodiedness", this would have forestalled some of the confusion.
73. Incidentally, one has to wonder how with all this contextualization, this formation of the perceptual field in accord with one's needs and concerns, there can be a capacity to analyze. How could the mind extricate itself from this morass in order to carry out any sort of objective investigation? Along with this, Dreyfus never notices that his arguments in and of themselves cannot account for his ability to make such arguments — which are basically of a general, abstract character.
74. One parting shot before leaving this account of Dreyfus' arguments. There is a curious dramaturgical (or attitudinal) side to this book which becomes increasingly apparent as one reads it through. Because he thinks that he has decisively refuted the basic assumptions of the AI program (as well as the emerging field of cognitive science, at least in the form it was taking), Dreyfus uses turns of phrase that reflect his belief that the whole AI project is hopeless. People like Marvin Minsky, John McCarthy and Ulrich Neisser are depicted as floundering about in confusion,

unable to prevent the looming demise of their endeavor. So that after all the striking advances over the last forty years, the impression is one of overarching silliness. By now the dubious character of the arguments — and the blindness of the author to their failings — are excruciatingly obvious.

75. R. A. Brooks, "Intelligence without representation", *Artificial Intelligence*, 1991, 47: 139–159, and "Elephants don't play chess", *IEEE Robotics and Autonomous Systems*, 1990, 6: 3–15.
76. Curiously, Brooks seems to have avoided citing Dreyfus, although at one point in his Intelligence paper, he dismisses the resemblance between his ideas and some ideas from "German philosophy".
77. A nice discussion of this can be found in the book by Hawkins, which is discussed next.
78. A. Newell, "The knowledge level", *Artificial Intelligence*, 1982, 18: 87–127, p. 105.
79. These ideas are also related to the declarative/procedural controversy discussed in Chapter 8.
80. This may be why animal communication systems are for the most part restricted to "call systems", where a small number of distinguishable signals are used to communicate information about sex, danger, etc.
81. J. Hawkins, *On Intelligence*, New York: St. Martin's Griffin, 2004.
82. *Ibid.*, pp. 51–52.
83. Even within the biological world one can find potential counter-examples. An important case is that of bird brains, which seem to have a somewhat different organization than the mammalian neocortex. In particular the laminar architecture so characteristic of the latter is not found in the areas that subserve similar higher cognitive functions. Nonetheless, birds exhibit some of the same signs of intelligence as do mammals. See e.g. T. Matsushima, E.-I. Izawa, N. Aoki & S. Yanagihara, "The mind through chick eyes: Memory, cognition and anticipation", *Zoological Science*, 20: 395–408, 2003; L. Medina, "Do birds and reptiles possess homologues of mammalian visual, somatosensory, and motor cortices?" In: J. H. Kaas, ed., *Evolution of Nervous Systems, Volume 2*, Chapter 2.0.7. Cambridge, MA: Academic (Elsevier), 2007, pp. 163–194.
84. Hawkins, *op. cit.,* pp. 87–88.
85. The reader should be aware that Hawkins is to some degree cherry picking from what is a complex and problematical area. In particular, his account of the connections between the cortex and a subcortical structure called the thalamus, which is closely integrated with cortical activity, is sketchy and misleading. But perhaps the most problematic aspect of his discussion is his emphasis on the cortical columns. In fact, it is still not known whether the various kinds of columnar organization found in the neocortex, which vary from species to species and even between individuals of a species without apparent variation in capacities, represent true functional units or something left over from embryonic development (much like the retina being oriented in the wrong direction so that the receptor layer faces away

from the incoming light — because of a quirk of evolutionary development and not because of some functional requirement). In this connection, see J. C. Horton & D. L. Adams, "The cortical column: a structure without a function", *Philosophical Transactions of the Royal Society*, Series B, 2005, 360: 837–862.

86. The thought may have occurred to the reader that if there is a common algorithmic process being carried out in the cortex, then an alternative candidate is some form of constraint satisfaction, as described in the previous chapter.
87. Although Hawkins doesn't emphasize it, there is an aspect to cortical processing which may indeed distinguish it in a fundamental way from classical AI and symbol system ideas. This is the statistical character of cortical activity. Thus, each pyramidal neuron receives inputs through thousands of synapses, so that any output is a function of some kind of weighted average; moreover, the output itself may be graded in that the frequency of firing of axons can vary. It's not at all clear what notions like symbol systems and the like mean in a system like this. (Of course, this bears on the symbolist-connectionist controversy as well.)
88. However, in all fairness it must be added that in several cases critics were reacting to the same kinds of presumptions (and to downright hubris) on the part of AI researchers. In particular, in the early days of AI there was an extraordinary optimism about how quickly machines with human-level intelligence could be built. This is a recurring problem in this field: that participants — on both sides of the fence — seem always to assume that they know more than they actually do.
89. I should add that despite the sometimes severe criticisms made in this section, it is the case that each of these books contains thoughtful discussions as well as interesting insights on intelligence, cognition, and computation. I would also say that all in all the critics come off better than the cheerleaders, to whom I turn to next.
90. R. Kurzweil, *The Age of Spiritual Machines*, London: Penguin, 2000.
91. An even more egregious example of this sort of thing is found on p. 16, where the author plays with the word "transcendence", moving from the triviality that a functioning machine 'transcends' its components, in that it has properties that they do not have by themselves, to the equally trivial point that the effect of a work of art 'transcends' the materials from which it is made. But in this the suggestion has been planted that artistic effects are somehow commensurate with the actions of machines, which sets the stage for the misuse of the word "spiritual".
92. In contrast to the works reviewed so far, each of which bears a stamp of individuality, *The Age of Spiritual Machines* reads like a 'packaged product'. So in Chapter 1 we are treated to a potted history of the universe in two pages and an equally breathless account of evolution, all to buttress some hand-waving analogies with the evolution of technology that is brought in after that. We are treated to passages like the following:

   "A corollary to the second law of thermodynamics is that in a closed system (interacting entities and forces not subject to outside influence; for example, the Universe), disorder (called 'entropy') increases. Thus, left to its own devices, a system such as the world we live in becomes increasingly chaotic. Many people find this describes their lives rather well. But in the nineteenth century, the laws of thermodynamics were considered a disturbing discovery." (p. 12)

Or to close to meaningless hand-waving, as in this passage about the transition to DNA-based systems:

"For the earliest organisms, the record was written (embodied) in their bodies, coded directly into the chemistry of their primitive cellular structures [and just how was that managed?]. With the invention of DNA-based genetics, evolution had designed a digital computer to record its handiwork." (p. 13)

And this passage about technological evolution, in which we also encounter an out-and-out intellectual sleight of hand:

"Just as the genetic code of the early life-forms was simply the chemical composition of the organisms themselves, the written record of early tools consisted of the tools themselves. Later on, the "genes" of technological evolution evolved into records using written language ..." (p. 14)

(Note that if one takes the comparison in the first sentence seriously, then toolmakers were an irrelevance. Now, I'm sure the author would immediately disown this implication (this is clear from a passage on p. 16), but then why did he write it this way?) Language like this, its vagueness combined with a pervasive aura of knowingness, strikes me at least as a higher form of sophistry; reading it, I have to wonder if the person writing it is "for real". After encountering stuff like this, it is impossible not to continue the work with a sense of foreboding.

93. While reading, one also comes across occasional unaccountable errors. On p. 56, the reader is told that "Giant squids are wondrous sociable creatures" and "A few fortunate human scientists have developed relationships with these clever cephalopods." Now, in fact, squid are solitary carnivores with little social behavior besides mating and (probably) aggression between males. (We don't have information about the latter because so little is known about these animals; this is because they spend most of their time in deep recesses in the ocean floor. So, in lieu of actual information, I am extrapolating from other solitary carnivores.) So Kurzweil's statements about squid are not just wrong; they are nonsense. They read like someone passing the day in idle gossip rather than someone developing an argument that is meant to be considered seriously.

A more egregious error appears in a footnote on pp. 328–9, where there is a discussion of Russell's paradox, which was based on the notion of a mathematical set of all sets that do not contain themselves as a member of that set. The problem is that whether one assumes that the set is included in itself or not, the result is a contradiction. According to Kurzweil, Russell overcame the paradox in the following way by coming up with a "logical computer":

"Russell turns on his theoretical computer … and the logical operations are "executed" in turn. So at one point the answer is Yes, but the program keeps running, and a few quantums of time later the answer becomes No. The program runs in an infinite loop, constantly alternating between Yes and No." "But the answer is never Yes and No at the same time!"

Now, I don't know how Kurzweil came to entertain this idea, but it has nothing to do with any actual solution to Russell's paradox nor (thankfully) to any discussion of it that I have ever encountered. (Did Kurzweil stumble upon a Sokal-type hoax that he took seriously?) Indeed, I cannot for the life of me fathom how anyone could think that this was a solution. It is sheer gobbledygook, leaving one to wonder how seriously anything else in the book should be taken. (Once again, I might add, we are faced with real questions regarding human intelligence.)

94. Actually, according to Kurzweil, changes began even sooner, within the first 10^{-43} seconds.
95. A typical example of how these "laws" are used to support the book's thesis is found on p. 101. After a paragraph about the limitations of brains and DNA as computational resources, Kurzweil says, "But the Law of Accelerating Returns tells us that evolution will not remain stuck at a dead end for very long. And indeed, evolution has found a way around the computational limitations of neural circuitry. Cleverly, it has created organisms that in turn invented a computational technology a million times faster than carbon-based neurons."
96. In this discussion, we encounter yet another error in connection with the Logic Theorist program discussed in Chapter 4. On p. 69, the reader is told that the proofs discovered by the Logic Theorist included "a completely original proof for an important theorem that had never been previously solved." In this case, the basis for the error is obvious: yes, it is true that the Logic Theorist discovered a proof that was more elegant than the one found in the *Principia Mathematica*; no, this was not an unproven theorem, nor did the theorem constitute a significant mathematical discovery; in fact, it was one of the numerous elementary theorems in logic that were proven at the beginning of the work.
97. The key difference between evolutionary algorithms and simpler forms of heuristic search is that in the former case, rather than trying to improve a single candidate solution, populations of potential solutions are maintained, any one of which may be selected at a given time for improvement. This is one way of introducing diversification into the search process, in that many parts of the search space can be explored at the same time.
98. I wonder what Kurzweil would think if someone were to inform him that the era of great literature in the West ended some time ago, and that the field of 'serious' literature has in large measure become a playground for tricksters and poseurs.

99. Kurzweil, *op. cit.,* p. 206.
100. *Ibid.*, p. 103.
101. When one reads a book of this sort, there is a point at which one realizes that a kind of madness informs it. Along with this there is an obscure sense of absence or lack, so that the world that emerges from its pages has a flattened character. I don't think this is a trivial observation, and it is worth developing further, since in this day and age one has to seriously consider the possibility that such madness will eventually prevail.
102. Curiously, there is a passage in Kurzweil's book that in some ways suggests the present conceptions:

    "As we port ourselves, we will also vastly extend ourselves. Remember that $1,000 of computing in 2060 will have the computational capacity of a million human brains. So we might as well multiply memory a million fold, greatly extend recognition and reasoning abilities, and plug ourselves into the pervasive wireless-communication network. While we are at it, we can add all human knowledge — as a readily accessible internal database as well as already processed and learned knowledge using the human type of distributed understanding." (pp. 126, 128)

    Unfortunately, this passage also reflects the fact that by this point in the book a lot of the text has the quality of word salad. Also note the way in which the agent becomes almost indistinguishable from the network itself; I don't think this shows any deep insight, just mushy thinking, almost language on holiday, to use Wittgenstein's phrase. And since this adumbration is just one element in a tide wrack of fantastic conceptions, it is impossible to evaluate its significance overall.
103. I am hardly the first to look askance at some of Kurzweil's more enthusiastic assertions; see the references listed in the Wikipedia article on Kurzweil. One has the impression that this relentless gimcrackery serves a function in some psychological sense.
104. H. Moravec. *Mind Children. The Future of Robot and Human Intelligence*, Cambridge, MA & London: Harvard University, 1988.
105. *Ibid.*, p. 108.
106. *Ibid.*, p. 110.
107. *Ibid.*, pp. 59–60.
108. The fact that Searle and Penrose base their arguments on the impossibility of genuine AI in part on the 'existence' of consciousness while Moravec assumes that consciousness is simply another way of referring to sufficiently complex representations demonstrates again what a slippery concept it is. This seems to confirm the wisdom of my decision to avoid it in my arguments.
109. Moravec, *op. cit.,* p. 39.
110. N. Bostrom, *Superintelligence*. Paths, Dangers, Strategies, Oxford: Oxford University, 2014.

111. Bostrom's book builds on a growing body of work centered on the idea of superintelligence. These people are located at various institutes and hold their own conferences, which as far as I can tell don't make much contact with the field of AI itself. This is an interesting example of the ecology of contemporary intellectual life.
112. Bostrom, *op. cit.,* p. vii.
113. In fact, this term seems to have wide use in the field of superintelligence, as well as being used from time to time by AI researchers themselves.
114. It is also interesting to note that AI-completeness is essentially an empirical notion, while the original idea is a formal mathematical property. So one would not expect to be able to carry it over in the way that it has been. But since it is part of a larger hand-waving exercise, it makes little difference one way or the other whether this aspect of the maneuver is strictly kosher.
115. Bostrom, *op. cit.,* p. 22.
116. *Ibid.*, p. 23.
117. *Ibid.*, p. 33.
118. *Ibid.*, p. 54.
119. *Ibid.*, p. 69.
120. *Ibid.*, p. 70.
121. *Ibid.*, p. 78.
122. *Ibid.*, p. 115.
123. *Ibid.*, p. 116.
124. *Loc. cit.*
125. *Ibid.*, p. 230.
126. In fairness to these authors I should point out that Kurzweil has a discussion of Penrose that makes some useful points. Bostrom has some very brief discussion of learning and uncertainty, although he whizzes by these topics as he does everything else.
127. As pointed out in the main text, there are adumbrations in Bostrom's book, but these are mostly in the form of asides. Also, "collective intelligence" is presented as an alternative, a possible form that superintelligence might take, and not as a defining feature of intelligence.
128. G. B. Shaw, *The Adventures of the Black Girl in Her Search for God*, London: Constable & Robinson, 1934.

11

Cautionary Tales

In this chapter I will discuss some 'negative examples'. These are instances of either failing to create the necessary intelligent network, or even undermining an existing and viable system of human or group intelligence. The discussion is limited to three cases:

- Building maintenance in Africa (HI)
- Nursing in the United Kingdom (HI)
- The American Savings & Loan debacle (HI/GI?)

Together, these examples show how little most of us actually understand about natural intelligence and, much more importantly, how insensitive people are to the presence or absence of intelligence networks if they are not part of those networks themselves. I would call this a major failing of Academia and of high-level decision makers, i.e. a critical shortcoming of the "managerial class".

Moreover, it is also likely that even those who participate in such networks have only a vague understanding of their operation, especially their maintenance through tradition. Among other things, this means that even when people see the network being trashed, they do not have the wherewithal to remonstrate against this, especially to those whose domain of expertise is based on conceptualizations.

In other words, there may be a serious gap in human thinking in regard to intelligence networks that leads repeatedly to problems, and even disasters, without anyone learning from these mistakes.

Building Maintenance in Africa

Turning to the first case, building maintenance in Africa. This seems to be a perennial problem in this part of the world, as indicated by the following quotation from Paul Theroux, in speaking of Kampala, Uganda:

> "The older buildings had not been maintained and looked blighted, haunted relics of an earlier time. It seemed to me that the new buildings would go this way too, fall into disrepair and not crumble but remain, defaced and unusable, while still newer ones were built. This seemed a pattern in the African city, the unnecessary obsolescence of buildings. Nothing was fixed or kept in good repair, the concept of stewardship of maintenance hardly existed."[1]

The present author had a similar encounter with this phenomenon on the other side of the continent, at a university in Nigeria. At the time of that visit, I noticed that many of the buildings seemed in need of repair, or at least needed repainting. My contact at the university showed me a lecture hall where half the chairs were broken and unsuitable for sitting in. Some of the windows were also broken. "But they just installed a flat panel screen," he said, pointing it out on a wall beside the stage at the front. And later, in reference to the general state of disrepair, he said that at the same time new buildings were being built.

Of course, the faculty at that university were perfectly aware of the problem; in fact, it was a major grievance held against the administration. Happily, I know from a later visit a few years later that at least some of these problems have since been fixed, but this required industrial action on the part of university staff members.

Here, I will hazard an explanation of why this situation exists. When the Europeans ruled parts of Africa, they must have brought in the necessary expertise to build buildings in the European style. But when they left and African states gained their independence, the people with the expertise undoubtedly left with them. As a result, the intelligence networks that were required to maintain the buildings no longer existed in the newly independent countries.

Moreover, and the observations recounted above attest to this, little or no attention seems to have been paid to the hiatus that was opening up.

If there had been, then programs could have been instituted to train native Africans, so that indigenous networks could be created that would carry the work of maintenance forward. I suspect this was because the politicians and high-level administrators who carried out the transfer of sovereignty were not aware of — nor could they foresee — the problem. (It would be interesting to know where the links were between the colonial administrative order and the people responsible for the task of building maintenance; was it some third- or fourth-level official, whose perspective was never fully shared and whose voice would never reach the ears of the architects of African statehood?)

The point is that in Europe the necessary development of these intelligence networks had occurred over centuries as western societies accommodated to new methods and inventions. In contrast, there were no indigenous traditions of this kind in Africa, so they would have had to be imported and then absorbed. This is another important aspect of real-world intelligence networks, which, due to space constraints as well as my lack of knowledge, I will not go into here.

In some ways modern African societies resemble hybrid organisms. It now appears that in the living world such creatures can sometimes give rise to new lines of organisms, but only after a period of reshaping and in some cases reducing the genome. Although it doesn't happen often, in these cases a new species may arise that is better adapted to a certain environment than either of the parent species. Whether or not this will happen in Africa is as yet unclear, although in some places such as southern Nigeria there are hopeful signs.

Nursing in the United Kingdom

About twelve years ago an article appeared in the British magazine *Prospect* whose topic was the current state of nursing in the UK.[2] It was based on personal experience; the author had been a patient in a hospital in the UK and so the situation described was her own. It was headed by these lines[3*]:

> "The care during my recent two-week stay in a famous London hospital was appalling. What's happened to British nursing?"

The author began with an account of the situation she had found herself in:

> "I have had ten years' experience as "the patient" — a patient with a complex autoimmune disease — and consider myself an expert on hospitals. But in London I couldn't work out which nurse was responsible for me, who was in charge of the other nurses, who could give intravenous (IV) medication and who could only take blood pressure. ... People would come in ... to dump pills on my table, yet no one bothered to ask me if I was vomiting up those pills — as I was. Instead, I was repeatedly asked the same inane question, "how bad is the pain, from one to ten?"
>
> "One night nurse's actions summed up the experience. He twice brought me the wrong medication, couldn't work the IV pump ("don't you know how to use it?") and didn't know to flush my vein with saline before administrating medication; the vein, of course, collapsed. So no, I don't like British nursing. ..."

The author's diagnosis of the problem was far-reaching and included major changes in attitudes within society; in particular, the now-predominant values of self-assertion and self-esteem are in flat contradiction to the essence of nursing, which involves self-abnegation. (Another possibly relevant factor, not discussed by Magnet, is the unionization of the profession in the 1970s.) But along with this, as shown by the incidents recounted above, came a loss of competence due to the undermining of habits and traditions that supported good practice and ensured its continuance. And all this was done with the best of intentions. This has to mean that the people responsible for inaugurating these far-reaching changes to the profession had little or no understanding of how the system, i.e. the intelligence networks that supported work in different hospitals, actually worked.

Since this article was written, other articles have appeared with similar stories.[4] These authors confirm Magnet's observations of nursing incompetence as well as indifference to patient suffering. However, some of these articles as well as reader comments suggest that there are considerable differences among hospitals. In this regard, one has the impression that the more highly rated hospitals (like the one that Magnet stayed in) may be the worst offenders!

According to Magnet, an early and important influence was a report published in 1966, called *Report of the Committee on Senior Nursing Staff*

Structure, often called the "Salmon Report" after the head of the committee, Lord Salmon. In her words,[5]

> "His report … smashed the hierarchical ward system and drove nurses away from the bedside. Salmon turned the sister into the "ward manager"; the nurse's focus was henceforth on the organisation, not the patient.
>
> "You could hear Salmon in the language of modern nursing and you could see Salmon on my ward. The "ward manager" was almost inaccessible behind the nurses' desk, where she sat all day, typing figures into a computer. When I needed my IV drip, it was up to me to get out of bed and find her …"
>
> "Too often the NHS ward structure functions so that, as a nurse gains experience, she is drawn away from her patients into bureaucracy and form-filling. The result is that the healthcare assistants without nursing qualifications and students are left to do much of the hands-on nursing. A senior nurse told me: "They're doing the real work. When I *started in the 1970s* the nurses did the proper work." (emphasis added)

Now, one must always be careful in deciding actual causal relations on the basis of a journalistic essay, where these relations are stated baldly, as if surface plausibility were sufficient to establish the truth of the matter — or the author's knowledge was beyond question. So I don't know for sure whether the Salmon Report had all the effects that Magnet attributes to it.[6*] Curiously, given what Magnet observed, the Salmon Report gives the impression that confusion about roles and responsibilities already existed, which their recommendations were intended to reduce. This is reflected in the following passage:

> "There is also confusion about the functions of nurse administrators in the hospital organisation, least for the Ward Sister, more for the Matron and most for nurses of intermediate grades. As in industry and commerce where the belief survives that ability to manage is not learned but innate, nursing administration is still in the process of development. Matrons tend, for example, to hold on to tasks in which they are interested, tasks which could be carried out by other nurses or even a well-trained clerk. Few matrons appear to practice the technique of delegation. Nor do they seem to aim at decentralisation, that is, arranging that decisions of the appropriate level are taken as near as possible to the scene of the activities where these decisions are required. The Assistant Matron is often treated exactly like an assistant, not as a person between the Matron and the Ward Sister, and to whom the right to command the Ward Sister (structural authority) is delegated by the Matron. The

> Ward Sister feels she is responsible to the Matron, a remote person in a big hospital, and not to the Assistant or Deputy."[7]

In fact, what this seems to describe is not confusion so much as lack of delegation, perhaps a reflection of the hierarchical structure that Magnet referred to.

Far from reducing (or "smashing") the hierarchy, the Report lays out a fairly elaborate hierarchy (see Fig. 1 on p. 7 and Chapter 4, which goes into staffing structure). In fact, it even seems to be attempting to strengthen and clarify the hierarchy of responsibilities. In addition, among the recommendations regarding the Ward Sister, the head nurse on a ward, there is an emphasis on reduction in administrative work. Thus,

> "There are a number of tasks of which many Ward Sisters could well be relieved and so enabled to *give more direct care to the patient*. No more time should be spent on administrative work than is really necessary."[8] (emphasis added)

So I don't see how the Salmon Report could in itself have had much to do with the spectacle of a Ward Manager sitting behind a computer screen all day instead of tending to patients.

My overall impression is that the Salmon Report did not in itself initiate radical changes in the character of nursing care (note also that the nurse quoted above said that she "started in the 1970s"). Nor does it seem to have been responsible for failing to make people responsible for key tasks. In this connection, it is worth noting that all of the articles that I have found that discuss these problems were published in this century, beginning in 2003. On this basis, I suspect that the really drastic changes in nursing took place toward the end of the twentieth century.

Perhaps more inimical was a program called Project 2000, which actually started in 1988. This involved a wholesale shift from traditional methods of training to university-based instruction. Again, from Magnet's article:

> "... by 1995 all the traditional nursing schools had closed. The less academic state-enrolled nurses were phased out — either downgraded to healthcare assistants or made to sit an exam and turned into state-registered nurses. The rationale was that a degree would make nurses autonomous practitioners, the equals of doctors, ready

> to meet the challenges of the changing health service and 21st-century medicine. The reality was that nursing had become embedded in a power struggle against the doctors, the NHS, even the patients — should the patients ask nurses to do anything that undermined their status."
>
> "So what are the courses? The pure distillate of PC humbug, the usual mix of victimology, identity politics and class struggle. At King's College London's ironically titled Florence Nightingale school of nursing and midwifery, students are required to study, for instance, "the social context of health and healthcare, which considers the relevance of sociology and health policy to healthcare. Integral to this course is exploration of key sociological issues, which influence health care such a poverty, gender, social class, ethnicity, and race ... At the end of the course you will be able to begin to recognize the importance of practicing in an anti-discriminatory way.""[9]

In other words, people who go into the nursing profession today are being indoctrinated in ways that make it much more difficult to come to terms with the actual job and its responsibilities, let alone to perform the required tasks with a high degree of competence. Moreover, the increased concern with status and the like may be behind the avoidance of participation in actual patient care by accredited nurses, so that this responsibility devolves upon students and healthcare assistants — with the results witnessed by Magnet and others. Although even this does not fully account for the kind of disconnect from the responsibilities of the job that allows people to walk off their shifts without taking care that vital tasks involving patient care have been performed. Or does it explain this episode, recounted in one of M. Phillips' articles on the subject:

> "I knew things were going wrong when I was admitted to hospital for a hysterectomy in 1989. Some days after my operation I was due to have my drip removed — I was on my way to the WC and had to pass the nurses' desk. The nurse there at the time was in the middle of a private call (laughing, gossiping) but beckoned me over and proceeded to remove the needle from my arm with the hand that wasn't on the phone.
>
> Was she surprised when the blood pumped out of my arm? Who knows? She put the phone on the desk while she found a plaster and then just carried on talking."[10]

In this case, the date is interesting. This suggests that developments leading to the situation on the wards in the 21st century were already under way even before the Project 2000 initiative. Also, this episode did not involve an untrained student nurse.

At any rate, it is clear that, whatever the actual pattern of causation, high-level decisions were involved in the destruction of the intelligence networks upon which nursing care is based. In other words, the people making policy for the nursing profession did not understand the intelligence networks underlying nursing care well enough to see that the solutions proffered were in fact inimical to their continued existence. And this occurred despite almost continuous commentary in books on nursing and in nursing journals throughout the last decades of the 20th century. In fact, in reading over this material I was struck by the gap between this commentary, most of which seems thoughtful and sensible, and the direct observations by Magnet and others of how nursing in hospital wards was being carried out.

It is also worth noting that the earlier management structure was itself based on a series of innovations, going back to the mid-19th century.[11] But this raises another question: why did these innovations lead to a system that was clearly much more effective than the one observed and reported on in the early 21st century?

In this example we also have a telling demonstration of the fact that intelligence is not a property of a single individual acting alone — taken out of a viable intelligence network, individual nurses can behave in a totally incompetent manner. Also, this network or complex of networks was never represented in, shall we say, a coherent declarative form. But then we really don't know how the 'declarative' and the 'procedural' forms of 'knowledge' actually fit together to form an intelligence networks such as the one embodied in the older British nursing tradition.

Following these ideas a little further, can we call the destruction of an intelligence network in this case an example of declarative mindlessness (or mindless declarativeness — take your pick)? If so, this raises important questions regarding the scope and limitations of so-called declarative knowledge.

The American Savings & Loan Debacle

The third example I wish to discuss is the collapse of the American Savings & Loan industry in the 1980s.[12]

The S&L's were a rather staid part of the banking industry, which however performed a vital function in allowing people to get cheap mortgages. In the 1980's the industry went berserk and then collapsed. This led to a bailout that eventually totaled more than 200 billion US dollars. What was responsible for this sudden, remarkable turn of events?

Even more than the nursing case, the S&L debacle has many features other than those of interest in the present context. It should be appreciated, therefore, that I am focusing on one limited aspect of a very complicated situation.[13*] Nonetheless, as I hope to show in the next few pages, there is definite evidence of failures to understand various elements that helped this kind of intelligence network to function effectively — although in this case there were fundamental flaws in the original network design that created the initial problems.

To highlight the fact that a system that had functioned effectively for years was turned into one in which things tended to run amuck, I will first consider one new feature of the industry in the 1980s; call it the attack of the cowboys. During this decade a new breed of people entered the S&L business, people with entirely different backgrounds, who had no banking experience or even a genuine interest in this type of business. Martin Mayer gives a striking but not atypical example. This was an S&L called American Diversified "owned by Ranbir Sahni, an Air India pilot turned builder and banker". Sahni purchased it in June, 1983; at that time it had a "reported total assets" of $11.7 million. I will let Mayer describe it[14]:

> "His [Sahni's] S&L did no consumer business and never wrote a home-mortgage loan. There were no teller windows, no street-level bank — just a single "savings office" nine flights up in a building in Irvine, California ... The money came in through "money brokers," who charged S&Ls a commission for finding them depositors."
>
> "Between June 1983 and December 1985, when ... [the] California S&L commissioner issued a cease-and-desist order prohibiting Sahni from taking any more brokered deposits, American Diversified grew from $11.7 million to $1.1 *billion.* The FSLIC was on the hook for all of it."
>
> "The Bank Board couldn't shut it down because the insurance fund didn't have the money to pay off the depositors ... Finally, in 1987, Congress agreed to "recapitalize" the FSLIC and in 1988 the Bank Board formally declared American Diversified insolvent, paid off the depositors, and took possession of the assets. As far as anyone has been able to figure out, the losses by then totalled $800 million."

> "the cost to the taxpayer of this one S&L, which nobody ever heard of … was roughly as much as the federal government had at risk in the much-debated bailouts of New York City, Lockheed, and Chrysler *put together*." (italics in original)

There were also numerous examples of out-and-out criminality.[15] Usually this took the form of one of a few standard schemes, the most popular of which was land flips. In this scheme, one participant, the buyer, takes a loan from the S&L and uses it to buy a property at its market value, say one million dollars. The second participant, the original seller, then takes out a loan and buys the property back for two million. The original buyer pays back his loan and pockets a million dollar profit, which he splits with the other party. That other party defaults on his loan, and the property reverts to the thrift. The thrift collected fees, "from which executive bonuses could be drawn", and kept the property on its books at the inflated price.

According to one group of authors, between 40 and 80 percent of the S&L failures involved some sort of fraud. In addition, they show that fraud is the only reasonable explanation of the behavior of many thrifts, since the pattern of loans and investments made no sense under any rational business plan. This was reflected in the frequency of loans to one borrower, the inaccurate record keeping, and the degree to which thrifts (especially in Texas) invested in an already saturated real estate market. The authors' view is supported by a contemporary article in *Business Week* that contains this quote: "The flamboyant adventures of the go-go thrifts have the desperate quality of a joyride by a terminally ill patient."[16]

Cases like these stood at one end of the spectrum. Many thrifts (as S&L's are called), while not wholly caught up in outrageous speculative ventures or outright criminality, still made questionable investments that left them exposed and eventually led to their insolvency. This is indicated by a passage from Michael Lewis' *Liar's Poker*:

> "Ranieri's sales force persuaded the thrift managers to trade their bonds actively. A good salesman could transform a shy, nervous thrift president into a maniacal gambler. Formerly sleepy thrifts became some of the biggest swingers in the bond markets. … Salomon trader Mark Freed recalls a visit he paid to a larger California thrift manager who had been overexposed to Wall Street influence. Freed actually tried to convince the thrift manager to calm down, to take fewer outright gambles

on the market, to reduce the size of his positions, and instead hedge his bets in the bond market "You know what he told me," says Freed, "he said hedging was for sissies."''[17]

So how did all this come about? It can be safely said that the vital decisions that led to the debacle were all done with the best of intentions. And like most disasters of this sort, it happened in stages.

It is important to understand that the government's initial actions in the early 1980s were in response to a real and growing problem. During the 1970s two trends emerged that threatened the whole S&L industry. First, inflation had risen rapidly in the latter part of the decade; as a result, S&Ls began to lose money on their fixed-rate mortgages. As one author put it, "In effect, they were paying people to borrow".[18] Secondly, the rise in interest rates in the late 70s created a mismatch between the cost of short-term funds and the return on long-term fixed-rate mortgages.

In addition, the mandated cap on interest rates on deposits of 5.5% began to act as a disincentive. During this period, new modes of investment were becoming available, in particular money market mutual funds (introduced in 1972),[19] which were being marketed aggressively and which had considerable appeal for people who wanted more income on their investments or who were worried about keeping up with inflation. As a result "more and more savers deserted depositories for money market funds and other relatively safe but higher-yielding investments".[20]

Prior to this the thrift industry had been a profitable, low-risk business. They provided depositors with interest, and allowed them to withdraw cash at the window. They sold mortgages. If they needed to borrow money, they could do this from a district Federal Home Loan Bank. They also sold existing mortgages to insurance companies and savings banks. Glimpses of the intelligence networks that underpinned the industry can be found here and there in the literature, as in this passage from Mayer:

"S&Ls did little but write mortgage loans on one- to four-family housing, sometimes because their charters required it, sometimes because holding within those restrictions got them wonderful benefits under the Internal Revenue code. And until the 1970s, the housing market was a sitting duck. It was a local business: The S&L in town had a huge advantage over outsiders in judging the value of the property, the strength of the neighbourhood, and even the qualifications of the borrower.

For federally chartered S&Ls, the legislation initially permitted only loans on the collateral of residential property located within fifty miles of the home office."[21]

Much of the intelligence in the industry rested upon regulations that provided a strict system of incentives and restraints.

> "Under the Home Owners Equity Act (H.O.E.A.) of 1933, Savings and Loans were restricted to use their funds in providing home mortgages. Specifically, the Savings and Loans were only allowed to invest in fixed-rate mortgages with maturities of at least twenty years. The purposes of these restrictions were to discourage risky investments and to ensure a sufficient supply of funds for housing mortgages."[22]

In addition, loans could only be made within a 50-mile radius of the lending institution. A large number of shareholders was also required: 400, 125 of which had to live in the community.[23]

The situation began to change in the 1960s. Prior to 1966, people who had deposits in an S&L were essentially shareholders. They could withdraw money, but they could not write checks. Nor was their deposit insured by the Federal Savings and Loan Insurance Corporation (FSLIC). In 1966, after the government had to bail out an important California S&L, the law was changed. People were no longer shareholders, and their deposits were covered by the FSLIC up to $40,000. In addition, interest rates were subject to a "differential" which set them a fraction of a percent above the interest that regular banks could give.

The 1960s also saw a relaxation in the regulations that set limits on how the thrifts could make money. For the first time they were allowed to make student loans, to buy property in urban renewal areas, and to buy government securities.[24] However, it is not clear that these innovations had any immediate effect on how S&Ls did business. In addition, the limit on lending location was relaxed from 50 to 100 miles from the home office.[25]

As already noted, economic developments in the late 1970s put the thrifts in an unaccustomed and dangerous situation. At this time, in order to raise funds thrifts increasingly turned to secondary markets that traded in "bonds and certificates collateralized by individual mortgages". At the same time, new Bank Board regulations (Mayer calls them "remarkable") were put in place that encouraged such activity. And because of the ever-increasing complexity of these investment vehicles (following a succession of innovations devised by academics and Wall Street investment banks), thrifts were soon operating well outside their range of competence.[26]

These activities were abetted by two major pieces of federal legislation passed in 1980 and 1982. The 1980 Depository Institutions Deregulation and Monetary Control Act removed (usually state-initiated) interest rate ceilings on mortgage loans, allowed S&Ls to open branches throughout a state, and allowed thrifts to "put up to 20 percent of their assets in commercial loans and corporate-debt instruments".[27] It also raised the amount of a deposit that was insured from $40,000 to $100,000. (This later led to money being passed from the federal government to big institutional investors including foreign entities after a thrift had failed.) The 1982 Garn-St. Germain Depository Institutions Act removed all restrictions on the amount an S&L could lend a developer in relation to the appraised value of the project; at the same time "the Bank Board was permitting developers to buy S&Ls".[28] It legalized an idea devised earlier by the Bank Board, called the "Net Worth Certificate program" by which a thrift could exchange notes with the federal deposit insurance agency, which both could then carry on their books as assets — creating equity "out of thin air" as one of its critics said. It also validated other dubious practices that the Bank Board had recommended such as trading of hedges and selling mortgages "with recourse", which was "an arrangement whereby the buyer can return the loan and get his money back if the mortgage goes sour". This allowed the S&L to keep the risk but to "book the transaction as a completed sale and take the profits".[29]

In brief, according to Mayer, "What happened ... was that the government, confronted with a difficult problem, found a false solution that made the problem worse".[30]

A key player in all of this was Richard Pratt, Chairman of the Federal Home Loan Bank Board from 1981 to 1983.[31*]

> "A professor at the University of Utah, Pratt was ... a doctrinaire free-marketer, withal a nice fellow and (unfortunately) by far the most intelligent man ever to hold that job. The combination would make him ... the angel of death for the thrift industry."[32]

"He wrote the worst of the regs, and more than any other single person he wrote the Garn-St. Germain bill of 1982 that codified the perverse incentives the government gave the industry."[33]

In 1981, Pratt removed a seemingly arcane rule:

"joint-stock S&L that wanted federal deposit insurance had to show at least 400 shareholders, with at least 125 of them from the local community … Pratt reduced the required number of stockholders to one."[34]

According to Pratt, "It seemed like a bizarre requirement". "You didn't have to have four hundred stockholders to get deposit insurance if you were a bank". But with this action, Pratt unwittingly invited "the guys who want to hit home runs"[35] to enter this once staid industry. This included Ranbir Sahni and others like him. Thus, to cite one of the most egregious examples,

"In the four years after the passage of Garn-St. Germain, Texas S&Ls grew from $36.3 billion in assets to $97.3 billion, and less than half that growth was in the single-family home mortgages they understood."[36]

Basically, what Pratt and others did served to set up a system of perverse incentives. Incentives (perverse or otherwise) in a situation like this have two kinds of effects:

- Effects on individual actions — this happens because contingencies affect individual behavior (à la B. F. Skinner), including the decisions that individual will make
- Effects on the social organization — this happens because selective pressures at the social level favor certain people over others with respect to access and influence

As a result of the second influence, when perverse incentives are put in place, people are selected who are less capable of making sound judgments. And, of course, such influences also bring in the cowboys and the crooks. (An interesting question is whether these two qualities are related.)

These effects led to further unfortunate developments: corrupt practices among accountants, once-great law firms prostituting themselves to protect scoundrels, and a general denial of what was happening among government officials unwilling to confront a burgeoning problem. But all these varied effects were ramifications of policy decisions made in the early 1980s that eventually upturned the industry.

In this book I do not discuss the issue of self-maintenance of intelligence networks, although it is a critical one, especially in the case of human networks that emerge historically. (In the biological realm, one can fall back on adaptationist arguments in accounting for viability.) Obviously, this is a critical issue as shown by this and the previous case study.

*

More than seventy years ago James Burnham published a book called *The Managerial Revolution*.[37] In it he laid out a vision of the immediate future in which high-level managers would come to dominate societies including those that were once capitalistic or once authoritarian in the classical manner of a single dictator or oligarchy. While the book seems dated now, especially since some of the emerging managerial states that Burnham described, namely the Nazi state and the Soviet Union, have since fallen away, the overall thesis of the book certainly seems consistent with trends that can be observed in contemporary society, especially the rise of a dense network of scientific, political and business elites.

One of the things overlooked in this vision was that, while such managers would be in a position to influence society via high-level policies, they would not necessarily be in a position to fully understand the systems they were influencing. As a result, their policies might very well lead to the kind of disasters described in the case studies outlined in this chapter.

This point is, of course, similar in some respects to the arguments of F. A. Hayek and others concerning the distribution of knowledge in an economic system.[38] However, Hayek's point concerned immediate factual knowledge about economic conditions. The point I am making is that nobody necessarily understands a given intelligence network that has emerged over the years in response to a given need. Hence, when policy decisions are made, they are made more or less blindly — in a deeper sense than not knowing specific, although essential facts about the immediate working of the network.

This may be construed, at least in part, as a problem of mapping, namely between concepts used by managers and the actual working of intelligence networks. In this respect, the problem may fall under the general heading of discourse and argumentation. Another likely factor is that people don't think in terms of intelligence-as-nodes-in-a-network.

Especially in the case of the S&L disaster, there is also the character of the 'moral failure' to consider. This is discussed at some length by several of the authors: Mayer, Black, Calavita et al. and Pizzo et al. As Mayer put it,

> "Educational historians will look at the failure of our schools to teach citizens, politicians, or businessmen the most fundamental of economic rules — that rewards are necessarily, over time, correlated with risk. Lack of this rudimentary understanding lies behind the unwise legislation and perverse regulation, behind the dishonest accounting practices condoned by that profession, behind the ease, even eagerness, with which politicians, lawyers, and journalists repeatedly accepted each prosperous con man's pretensions to legitimacy."[39]

I want to look at this aspect of the problem from a somewhat different angle. Could it not have been due to the fact that a situation was created where such failure would be almost inevitable? Consider, for example, the behavior of the accountants; normally, they would not be faced with a situation like this, where it would have taken much stronger men to face the facts. In other words, morality depends in part on support from the environment, so that the moral failings themselves may have been another result of the general unraveling of this intelligence network.

Another factor that may be critical is the simple capacity to perceive or take in facts. Consider the case of Ed Gray, the head of the Federal Home Loan Bank Board during a critical time in the 1980s, who was one of the first to act to forestall the impending disaster.[37] He faced the facts, while others did not. Was this the basis of the extraordinary difference in the morality of their actions?

Let me reemphasize the point of view being taken here with regard to these case studies. I am not interested in the moral or criminal aspects of them (although whether these can really be untied from the issues of intelligence networks is an interesting question). My concern is with the light they shed on intelligence networks as well as our general insensitivity to this crucial aspect of human society and human progress.

Endnotes

1. Paul Theroux, *Dark Star Safari*, London: Penguin, 2003, p. 213.
2. J. Magnet, "What's wrong with nursing?", *Prospect*, December 2003, pp. 40–45. Quotations are on p. 40. The article is well worth reading, a testimony to the intellectual blight that has spread through Western societies during the past few decades.
3. Although these lines appear in the version found on the Web, a different standfirst passage is found in the original print version.
4. R. Johnson, "The harsh truth? We nurses have just forgotten how to care", *Mail Online*, August 28, 2009 (and comments); M. Phillips, "How feminism made so many nurses too grand to care", *Daily Mail*, October 17, 2011 and "The moral crisis in nursing: voices from the wards". *Daily Mail*, October 21, 2011; C. Patterson, "A crisis in nursing" *Independent*, April 10, 2012 (and five other articles that appeared in the same publication on successive days). (All these were downloaded from the Web.)
5. Magnet, op. cit., p. 42.
6. At this point it looks to me as if Magnet's invocation of the Salmon Report may be an example of mythical causation. In saying this I am not impugning the veracity of the author, nor am I trying to diminish the value of the article. (In fact, among the various articles on this topic that I read, this was the most substantial.) It is just that, when one makes assertions about causal relations, these must be critically examined. And an examination of this sort is not really within the demesne of journalism.
7. B. Salmon *et al.*, *Report of the Committee on Senior Nursing Staff Structure*, London: Her Majesty's Stationary Office, 1966, p. 4.
8. *Ibid.*, Chapter 4, p. 34.
9. Magnet, *op. cit.*, pp. 43–44.
10. M. Phillips, "The moral crisis in nursing: voices from the wards", *Daily Mail*, 21 October, 2011.
11. R. Dingwall, A. M. Rafferty & C. Webster. *An Introduction to the Social History of Nursing*. London: Routledge, 1988.
12. The account given here is largely drawn from Martin Mayer's classic account, *The Greatest Ever Bank Robbery*, New York: Scribner's, 1990. I have also drawn from the following sources: S. Pizzo, M. Fricker & P. Muolo, *Inside Job: The Looting of America's Savings and Loans*, New York: McGraw-Hill, 1989; R. J. Cebula & C.-S. Hung, *The Savings and Loan Crisis*, Dubuque, IA: Kendall/Hunt, 1992 ;J. R. Barth, S. Trimbath & G. Yago, *The Savings and Loan Crisis: Lessons from a Regulatory Failure*, Santa Monica, CA: Milken Institute, 2004; W. K. Black, *The Best Way to Rob a Bank is to Own One*, Austin: University of Texas, 2005.

13. Complicating factors include trends in the building industry and in home ownership as well as changes in the financial sector, especially the introduction of money market accounts in the 1980s.
14. These selections are found on pp. 5–8 of Mayer.
15. Pizzo et al. and Black, op. cit. and K. Calavita, H. N. Pontell and R. H. Tillman. *Big Money Crime. Fraud and Politics in the Savings and Loan Crisis*. Berkeley: University of California, 1997.
16. *Business Week*. The casino society, September 16, 1985, pp. 78–90. Cited by Calavita *et al.*, p. 35.
17. Michael Lewis. *Liar's Poker*, London: Hodder & Stoughton, 2006 (orig. 1989), p. 134.
18. N. Eichler, Homebuilding in the 1980s: Crisis or transition? *Annals of the American Academy of Political and Social Science*,1983, 465, 35–44. Quote on pp. 37–8.
19. R. J. Cebula and C.-S. Hung, *op. cit.*, p. 21.
20. F. S. Redburn. The deeper structure of the savings and loan disaster, *Political Science and Politics*, 1991, 24(3), 436–441. Quote on p. 436. According to Cebula and Hung, between 1978 and 1982 deposits countrywide fell by 10 billion dollars (p. 40).
21. Mayer, *op. cit.*, p. 33.
22. Cebula & Hung, *op. cit.*, p. 20.
23. Mayer, *op. cit.*; Cebula & Hung, *op. cit.*
24. Cebula & Hung, *op. cit.*, p. 20–21.
25. *Ibid.*, p. 25.
26. Mayer, *op. cit.*, p. 41.
27. *Ibid.*, p. 93.
28. *Ibid.*, p. 98.
29. *Ibid.*, p. 102.
30. *Ibid.*, p. 27.
31. The Federal Home Loan Bank Board (FHLBB) was a federal agency that oversaw the 11 regional Federal Home Loan Banks, that in turn provided liquidity for the S&L's.
32. Mayer, *op. cit.,* p. 23.
33. *Ibid.*, p. 61.
34. This and the following quote from Pratt are from Mayer, *op. cit.*, p. 63.
35. Mayer, *op. cit.*, quoting Keith Russell, p. 63.
36. *Ibid.*, p. 227.
37. James Burnham, *The Managerial Revolution*, Westport, CT: Greenwood, 1941.
38. F. A. Hayek, "The use of knowledge in society", *American Economic Review*, 1945, 35: 519–530.
39. Mayer *op. cit.*, p. 3.

12

A New Kind of AI Challenge

Among other things, the present volume is an effort at 'consciousness raising'. The goal is to engender a greater awareness of intelligence networks, more specifically, to encourage people to think about intelligence as necessarily functioning within such networks rather than being a feature of individual, isolated agents. The examples of the last chapter, I think, serve to show the importance of this endeavor. They also show that this is not something that people do naturally; instead, the failure to take such networks into account seems to be one of those mental lapses or 'constraints' that bedevil human cognition, similar in some ways to the biases or limitations of judgment touted by Tversky, Kahnemann and others.

Those examples also suggest that such lapses have to do with the 'declarative' characterization of situations. This may have to do with more general questions of adaptation: are we better adapted to handle situations that involve immediate perception than those that require more abstract analysis? I.e. are we better at seeing than thinking? This, of course, is an old AI theme.

Of course, it is not quite correct to characterize the difference as one between perception and thought. People for instance use language in the course of carrying out everyday activities, and they are exceedingly adroit in this. For example, if one listens carefully to a hotel receptionist dealing with a succession of customers who come to the desk as well as incoming phone calls, one quickly appreciates how adroit people are when it comes to solving problems that involve language and 'practical intelligence'. But the same people — or their 'betters' — seem often to fail miserably when it comes to abstract characterizations of a situation and developing prescriptive policies that actually solve problems rather than making them worse.

One can identify specific types of problems that arise in these contexts. One involves the problem of rhetorical strategies, i.e. the use of language to influence behavior rather than to produce accurate descriptions. Examples such as making false equivalences, taking facts out of context (especially statistics of various sorts), and general ad hominem references are all too characteristic of public discourse and even infect more serious forms of debate.

Another problem that perhaps is even more insidious is the use of plausible reasoning. This involves arguments that have a 'surface plausibility', i.e. an internal coherence that is often in accord with basic assumptions about a situation, and which turns out to be misleading, because the assumptions are dead wrong. (Some nice examples of plausible reasoning will be presented later in this chapter in the course of describing the first case study.)

*

I now want to lay out some proposals, all of which have to do with discourse and argumentation. The major proposal is meant to be a challenge for researchers in artificial intelligence: to build systems capable of managing and monitoring (and perhaps regulating) significant areas of discourse and argumentation.

In real-world discourse, deficiencies in the formal features of argumentation are rarely the major issue.[1*] Instead, the biggest problems have to do with the way that evidence is handled. Some obvious topics here are:

- Omissions of facts
    - Selective omissions
- Shortcomings in evidence
    - Slanted descriptions of facts
    - Measurement problems
- Shortcomings in formal analysis
    - Misuse of conceptual structures
    - Misuse of statistics

One general approach to overcoming these deficiencies is to use the Web to seek out corroborating or conflicting information. (In fact, evaluating information on the Web is a problem in itself, one that is closely related to the topic at hand.)

Another general approach to the overall problem involves creating discourse and argumentation frameworks. This means setting up requirements that participants must follow when they enter data or arguments.

It is, of course, also possible to detect logical deficiencies in arguments, in particular, certain forms of questionable reasoning. This builds upon a long tradition in logic of characterizing and analyzing sound and unsound arguments.[2]

*

To flesh out these ideas I will describe two case studies. Both involve intellectual controversies; hence discourse and argumentation are central aspects. One of the useful features of the first case study is that the controversy, which involved one-time future events, is now over. This means that the arguments are now 'frozen in time', so that they can be studied with full knowledge of the actual state of affairs that ensued. (Unfortunately, the situation is not as straightforward as one would like, since the prescriptive value of certain actions that were taken is arguable and remains a point of contention.) The second controversy is still ongoing.

In addition, (as just indicated) in the first case study, part of the argument concerned actions to be taken. The second, on the other hand, is more strictly intellectual in character. Here, it is a matter of maintaining (or raising) certain standards of intellectual discourse — although here, too, there are definite implications to the position one holds, in this case pertaining to how one construes certain aspects of literary and social history.

The first case to be considered is the controversy over the Y2K or millennium bug that took place in the 1990s and was more-or-less settled upon the arrival of the year 2000. In this case the problem was caused by inadequacies in the representation of the year in many early programs so that they could not distinguish between the years 2000 and 1900. The controversy was over the degree of disruption that would result on reaching the year 2000: expectations ranged from dismissal of the problem as trivial to claims that it would have a catastrophic effect on the functioning of modern industrial systems.

The second case is usually called the Shakespeare Authorship Question or the Shakespeare Authorship Controversy. It involves two related questions: (i) Did a man from Stratford, who lived from 1564 to 1616 and whose name was William Shakespeare (or whose name was similar — this is part of the controversy), actually write the plays and poems that are usually attributed to the author of that name? (ii) If he did not, then who was the real author?

In and of itself, the SAQ might be considered a little off-topic as a case study in intelligence networks. However, it does deal — in fascinating ways, as I hope to show — with problems of discourse and argumentation, which in many cases seem to be at the heart of contemporary problems with intelligence networks. In addition, handling the SAQ is a formidable intellectual challenge, one that may even be worth considering as a grand AI challenge.

The Millennium Bug

The Y2K problem seems almost comical when stated. In the early days of computer data processing, it was common to designate years by the final two digits. For example, "1951" would be stored in computer memory as "51". Since the "19" could be assumed, it wasn't necessary to store those digits. If the date needed to be printed out, or calculations made on it, then the "19" could be added at that time using a program instruction. But with such a system, what happens when the year 2000 is reached? In this case, the number stored is "00", and a program will print out "1900" or in other contexts it will use this year instead of the correct one in its calculations, producing incorrect results. In a nutshell, this was the problem.

Now, obviously, programs of this sort will make errors under these conditions. The important question was, what impact would this have? Here the scenarios varied wildly — and this is reflected in the writing of the time. Most of this writing is from the years 1998 and 1999, when, naturally, the sense of crisis reached its peak. (Although one or two writers raised concerns as far back as the 1980s, the issue received little attention until the run-up to the year 2000, beginning about 1997.)

One of the things that makes this an interesting testbed for AI is that the problem has passed, and the case is more or less closed. This means we can look back over the arguments that were made in support of one scenario or another and evaluate them in relation to what actually happened when the year 2000 was reached.

To give a flavor of the more extreme predictions, here is a passage from an academic article published in 1999, in a section called "The potential scale of the year 2000 problem":

> "The scale of the problem is enormous, but the time available to fix it is running out, and the huge financial and human resources needed are often not available. There are also extremely difficult logistical constraints in testing and installing the new systems. It has been predicted that many patients will die (it was estimated that half of the equipment in NHS hospitals could not cope with the date change!). Traffic will grind to a halt because some traffic lights and air traffic control systems will fail. A breakdown of essential services would quickly be followed by a breakdown in public order (The Week, 1998). The UK government is already drawing-up plans to prevent the Millennium nightmare in which the start of the Year 2000 is marked by power failures, flight problems and hospital disasters triggered by mass computer malfunction. Some experts predicted that there would be a 60-70% chance of a 1930s style depression in the world economy!"[3]

Forecasts of catastrophe like these were based on the fact that by the 1990s computers or control elements that used computer circuitry had become a critical part of the infrastructure of all major industries and public institutions. As a result, it was thought that errors could crop up almost anywhere, with potentially serious results. So various authors and commentators suggested that electrical grids might become imbalanced and then shut down because their embedded systems would malfunction, that factory floors might shut down, that ATMs might fail to operate, that telephone lines might go dead, and so forth. In many cases, they admitted that none of this was certain, but most agreed that all these dire events were in the realm of possibility.

In some cases, various authorities were cited to back up these claims, as in this passage by the author Michael Hyatt, whose books on the "millennium bug" became bestsellers. Here, he discusses the issue of embedded systems that could be at risk. First, he considers the question of how many systems there actually are:

> "The standard estimate for the number of embedded chips is 25 billion worldwide. In his testimony before Congress, David Hall, a recognized expert on embedded systems, estimated that there were likely 40 billion. Datamation magazine, a leading trade publication for computer professionals, put the number at 70 billion."[4]

Then he goes on to cite estimates of how many of these might be at risk.

> "The good news is not many of them are date sensitive. Exactly how many? That's anyone's guess. For example:
>
> - Peter de Jager, one of the first to sound the alarm on Y2K, suggests that the number is less than 0.1 percent
> - Datamation estimates that on average about 7 percent are date sensitive
> - David Hall states that "in tests accomplished so far, anywhere from 1 percent to 10 percent of an enterprise's systems and equipment items exhibit Year 2000 impacts... these impacts range from minor to catastrophic."
> - Action 2000, the British government's official Y2K awareness agency, states, "According to research conducted over the past year, around 5 percent of simple embedded systems failed Millennium Bug tests. For more sophisticated embedded systems, failure rates of between 50 and 80 percent have been reported. In manufacturing environments, the overall failure rate is around 15 percent.""[5]

In the run-up to the new millennium, as time progressed it became clear that many systems would not be "Y2K compliant" before January 1 of the year 2000. Even well into 1999, many businesses and government agencies reported that they had not yet developed a plan of action. This added to the drama.

On the other hand, a few writers did publish works saying that the whole thing was overblown. One author gave refutations to practically every claim about serious consequences:

> "... there have been bugs before. Have you ever heard of a company going out of business because of program bugs. They fix them or figure a way to work around them. ... If you have a problem you work around it as best you can."[6]

> "Many if not most of the problems have begun already and are being addressed routinely without outward trauma. Expiration dates on credit cards, driver's licenses, subscriptions are already past 2000. As the problems hit, they were addressed one at a time."[7]
>
> "There are many alarmists out there claiming that the world will come crashing down because of critical systems stopping. There's no mainframe system that I know that can't be overridden or have a bug worked around."[8]
>
> "A lot is being made of embedded PLC chips. Most PLCs embedded in devices are not date sensitive or date critical. The consultants have however made a huge project for themselves investigating all the devices to ascertain whether there is or isn't a problem. Since almost all devices with embedded chips are fairly recent creations, the likelihood that there is a date problem with the year 2000 is very small. But, given the millions of devices with computer chips embedded, you can see how much money is involved in these projects."[9]

As we now know, none of the dire predictions that had been made actually came to pass. Moreover, countries that had not done anything to prepare for the Y2K event fared no worse than the United States where billions had been spent to upgrade systems and make them ready for the Great Transition. So by and large the skeptics were right.

Let us imagine that at the time of the Y2K controversy, AI systems were in place to monitor and correct the discourse. How might they have carried out this task? More generally, how could an AI system be used to assess the various arguments and arrive at reasonable conclusions — or at least flag vague spots and contradictions? This is the challenge being posed in this chapter.

One of the interesting facets of this problem is that many of the arguments that were put forth in favor of the disastrous Y2K scenarios are quite plausible on the surface. Moreover, in many cases (and this includes Michael Hyatt), they are suitably couched in terms of likelihood. In other words, someone as sophisticated as Hyatt didn't say, "This will happen"; instead, he said, "This is what I think will happen, based on these sources". Then he unloaded a raft of references, seemingly from authoritative sources, to buttress his argument.

It will therefore require a program of considerable sophistication to assess the arguments, for it to come to the conclusion that the whole thing is overblown. A key is being able to drill down into details, a capacity that intelligent human beings have, but one that has not as far as I know received a great deal of attention in AI itself.

However, rather than a direct assault on the problem by 'artificial intelligence', indirect approaches — in keeping with ideas of intelligence presented here — may be more feasible and just as effective. Simply communicating skepticism may be very beneficial. Moreover, by comparing different lines of argument, it may be possible for a software system to 'piggyback' on human intelligence. Obviously, the Web infrastructure is well suited for such tasks.

The Shakespeare Authorship Question

The Shakespeare Authorship Question, or SAQ, concerns the problematic features of the standard or orthodox story of the life of the author who wrote the works attributed to Shakespeare. Even as early as the 1590's and early 1600's, when the name "Shakespeare" (or "Shake-Speare") first appeared in print, there were writers who intimated that the name was actually a pseudonym. And after the original collection of Shakespeare's plays (the *First Folio*) was printed in 1623, which gave great thrust to the standard story,[10*] there were still occasional expressions of doubt, as in some of the dedicatory material in the edition of the collected sonnets and poems of Shakespeare published in 1640. However, the standard story — that William Shakespeare was a yeoman's son from Stratford who went to London and became a playwright — only became established in the late 17th, early 18th century.[11] It has, of course, remained the dominant position to this day. In fact, as recently as ten years ago a leading Shakespeare scholar could say:

> "I do not myself know of a single Professor of English in the 1300-member Shakespeare Association of America who questions the identity of Shakespeare."[12]

At the same time, a tradition of doubt has also established itself. Beginning in the mid-nineteenth century there was a resurgence of 'doubters' of the Stratford story, including Joseph Hart in 1848 and, more prominently, Delia Bacon in 1856-7.[13] Over the next few decades this turned into a steady stream of works questioning the orthodox account.

Figure 12.1. Figures often put forward as candidates for the authorship of Shakespeare's plays.

If the man from Stratford was not the real Shakespeare, then someone else must be found to fill the role. In fact, there is a long list of candidates who have been proposed as the real poet-playwright, beginning with Francis Bacon; in addition various forms of group authorship have been suggested. Currently the leading contender is a nobleman named Edward De Vere, the 17th Earl of Oxford, although there are groups promoting the candidacy of Francis Bacon, Christopher Marlow, William Stanley, and others. Figure 12.1, taken from Wikipedia,[14] shows several of the leading 'contenders'.

In addition, in the 1880's an agnostic ("anti-Stratfordian") tradition began with a book by Appleton Morgan called "The Shakespeare Myth", and this tradition continues to this day with books like those by Diana Price (2001) and A. J. Pointon (2011). These authors adduce arguments against the Stratfordian account without advocating for any particular individual.[15]

That all this is not mere foolishness on the part of anti-Stratfordians can be shown quite easily. There are dozens of anomalies, discrepancies and startling omissions in the evidence which should give any unbiased cogitator cause for reflection. Here are a few[16]:

- The only verified writing we have by the Stratford man are six signatures with different spellings and which may be by different hands. (We also have good evidence that neither his parents, nor his wife, nor his two daughters could read or write.) In other words, the man from Stratford may have been illiterate.
- After trolling through millions of documents, scholars have come up with 70–80 records that probably refer to the man from Stratford. As Diana Price noted, not one of them connects the man with any form of literary activity. (In contrast, according to Price we have twelve documents for a minor Elizabethan dramatist named John Webster, and seven of them refer to literary activities.)
- The First Folio, the famous collection of the plays of Shakespeare, was published in 1623. There are a number of anomalies in the front matter, beginning with the portrait on the title page (shown below).

A number of Stratfordians have commented negatively about this figure; here are a few examples[17]:

> "expression of countenance, which is very crudely rendered, is neither distinctive nor lifelike"
>
> S. Lee, 1898

> "the Droeshout frontispiece … is nothing but a clumsy engraving derived from it [the monument]"
>
> J. D. Wilson, 1932

> "Droeshout's deficiencies are, alas, only too gross. The huge head on a plate of ruff surmounts a disproportionately small tunic."
>
> S. Schoenbaum, 1975

In 1911 an anonymous article appeared in a trade magazine, The Gentleman's Tailor, in which the author made these comments:

> "It is passing strange that something like three centuries should have been allowed to elapse before the tailor's handiwork should have been appealed to in this particular manner. The special point is that in what is known as the authentic portrait of William Shakespeare, which appears in the celebrated First Folio edition, published in 1623, a remarkable sartorial puzzle is apparent. The tunic, coat, or whatever the

Figure 12.2. The Droeshout engraving on the title page of the First Folio, the first collection of Shakespeare's plays.

garment may have been called at the time, is so strangely illustrated that the right-hand side of the forepart is obviously the left-hand side of the back part; and so gives a harlequin appearance to the figure, which it is not unnatural to assume was intentional, and done with express object and purpose."

These observations have been discussed and elaborated on more recently by John Rollett.[18] He draws attention to the stitching on both sides of the figure (cf. Figure 12.3), which has been carefully adjusted in order to make it appear as if there is a single garment. This can be contrasted with the figure shown in Figure 12.4 who is wearing a similar garment, with normal left and right shoulders; in this case the stitching is obviously symmetric.

Rollet also shows an example of the usual title page portrait (Figure 12.5). The portrait is much smaller than the one in the First Folio, and the adornments surrounding it are typical of the time. The figure is also properly proportioned, and it has a sense of individuality that the First Folio portrait lacks.

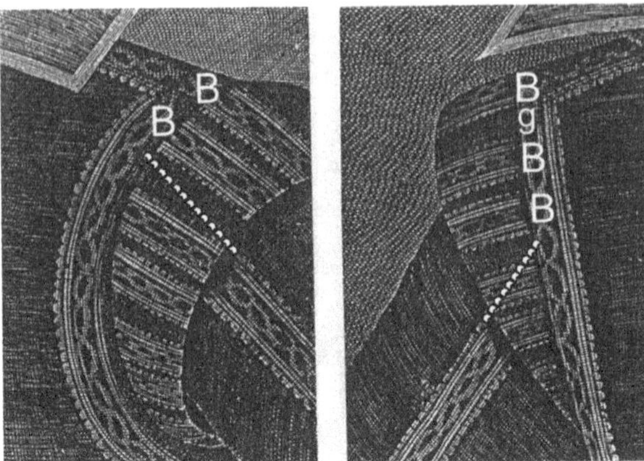

Figure 12.3. Details of the garment worn by the figure in the Droeshout engraving showing the discrepancy between the patterns on the left and right shoulders of the doublet. B is for band, g is for gap. (reprinted from Rollett, 2010, Figure 4, courtesy of the Shakespeare Oxford Fellowship).

Figure 12.4. Early 17th century portrait of an English gentleman wearing the same doublet as the figure in the Droeshout engraving. Note the symmetry of the stiching in this case.

Figure 12.5. Frontispiece of The Civile Wares by Samuel Daniels, published in 1609.

There are other anomalies in the *First Folio*, such as the Dedication to the Reader, which was probably written by Ben Jonson and not the signatories (Hemminge and Condell, two players in the King's Men, who are usually said to be the editors). It begins as follows:

"To the great Variety of Readers.

From the most able, to him that can but spell: there you are number'd. We had rather you were weighed; especially, when the fate of all bookes depends upon your capacities and not of your heads alone, but of your purses. Well! It is now publique, & you wil stand for your priviledges wee know: to read, and censure. Do so, but buy it first. That doth best commend a Booke, the Stationer saies. Then, how

> odde soever your braines be, or your wisedomes, make your licence the same, and spare not. Judge your six-pen'orth, your shillings worth, your five shillings worth at a time, or higher, so you rise to the just rates, and welcome. But, whatever you do, Buy."

I, for one, do not see how one can read this without realizing that it is tongue-in-cheek. Therefore, I will go out on a limb and say that there is a strong suggestion in all of this that more is going on in the dedicatory material of this volume than the straightforward celebration of a recently deceased author.

- Research culminating in the work of Roe (2011) shows that the author Shakespeare was familiar with many specific locales in Italy, details of which are inserted into several plays. There is no evidence that the Stratford man ever left England.[19]
- The nobleman and litterateur Fulke Greville and the poet Michael Drayton lived in Warwickshire during the time of Shakespeare. Neither ever mentions their supposed illustrious neighbour. Nor has any reference to William Shakespeare ever been discovered in the letters or documents of the estate of the Earl of Southampton, supposedly Shakespeare's great patron.[20]

There are also an extraordinary variety of arguments of varying quality on many specific issues. On the part of the Stratfordians these sometimes take the form of assertions made as if they rested on solid ground ("We know that Shakespeare wrote The Tempest in 1611"), when in fact they are balanced on top of a rickety staircase of inferences.[21] On the part of the anti-Stratfordians there are various hypotheses about the true author that are of questionable worth, the most notorious (the "Prince Tudor hypothesis") being that De Vere and Queen Elizabeth had a bastard child who was raised as the Third Earl of Southampton, and who is also the "fair youth" of the Sonnets.[22] In addition, there is the idea that the Stratford man acted as a front man for the real author - but the only evidence consists of interpretions of certain satirical passages of obscure intent from various poems and plays. (In this instance it is the lack of hard evidence that is the most telling fact.)

As a result of all this, there are a variety of basic theses, not all of which can be correct, with many, many subordinate hypotheses of varying credibility. The discussion involves numerous specialized topics, such as Elizabethan education, Italian society and culture in the 16th century, Shakespeare's knowledge of law, publishing and printing in England in the Elizabethan and Jacobean periods, etc., etc. So there is enormous scope for applying AI techniques to basic problems in discourse and argumentation.

*

In both situations, the challenge is quite different from building a super-intelligent agent, like Deep Blue or Watson. Instead, the goal is to enhance the pertinent intelligence network itself — in ways that have not been done before (since, of course, any number of improvements can and have been made to intelligence networks already through various kinds of software). In this case, this would come down to improving the level of discourse through assessment of arguments, credibility of evidence, etc. Perhaps this would involve special kinds of administrative agents which act as 'umpires' or impartial judges.

The underlying aim of these projects is to raise standards in ordinary discourse and argumentation. It also involves a view of AI as operating in a way that is medicinal or prophylactic. Instead of building intelligent agents, we would be creating frameworks for greater intelligence, i.e. building up intelligence infrastructures.

It seems to me that the SAQ in particular is singularly appropriate for this end. For one thing, there is ample room for improvement, as implied by the examples given above. Arguing more forcibly, I would say that in this area of discourse the orthodox account is to my mind preposterous. At the same time, in part perhaps because of this, views that contradict the dominant one have been marginalized. If all this is true, then clearly there are standards of discourse that have not been met — and of course they should be.

There is one other aspect of the proposed endeavors, which can be stated as follows. Technology has been successful in making us more effective, and this includes making us more intelligent. Perhaps it can also be used to help us realize our better selves.

Endnotes

1. A recent development in AI is the formal analysis of arguments in terms of their graph structure. This analysis relies on the fact that arguments always follow a pattern of attack and counter-attack (much like adversarial games). However in this work no attention is paid to the content of the arguments; hence, it has very little bearing on the problems considered in this chapter.
2. A classical reference is I. M. Copi, *Introduction to Logic,* 2nd edition, New York: Macmillan, 1961.
3. F. Li, H. Williams and M. Bogle. "The 'Millennium Bug': its origin, potential impact and possible solutions", *International Journal of Information Management*, 1999, 19, 3–15, p. 6.
4. M. S. Hyatt, *The Y2K Personal Survival Guide*, Washington, DC: Regnery, 1999, p. 272.
5. *Ibid.*, pp. 272–273.
6. A. Wallach, *The Year 2000 Hoax*, East Canaan, CT: Safe Goods, 1998, p. 46.
7. *Ibid.*, p. 42.
8. *Ibid.*, p. 46.
9. *Ibid.*, p. 42.
10. The earliest references to "Mr. William Shakespeare" or "William Shakespeare, gentleman" appear in the early 17th century a little before 1610. Before 1598, references to "Shakespeare" were strictly to the author of the poems *Venus and Adonis* and *Lucrece*. The plays began to appear in printed versions in 1594, but until 1598 they were published anonymously. In 1598, Frances Meres in his *Palladis Tamia* (*Wits Treasury*) was the first to identify Shakespeare as the author of both comedies and tragedies. This was also the first year when a printed play (*Romeo and Juliet*) appeared with the name William Shakespeare on the title page. But at this time there was no reference to the status of the author.
11. A short account appears in Aubrey's *Brief Lives* around 1681. A somewhat fuller account, written by Nicholas Rowe, appeared in the first post-folio edition of the plays, which he edited, in 1709.
12. Alan Nelson, 2004, quoted in W. Leahy, editor, *Shakespeare and His Authors. Critical Perspectives on the Authorship Question*, London: Continuum, 2010, p. 44.
13. Much of this is recounted in W. Hope & K. Holston, *The Shakespeare Controversy*, Jefferson, NC: McFarland, 2009.
14. Wikipedia, "Shakespeare Authorship Question".
15. J. A. Morgan, *The Shakespeare Myth: William Shakespeare and Circumstantial Evidence*, 3rd edition, Cincinnati, OH: R. Clark, 1888 (reprinted by Ulan Press); D. Price, *Shakespeare's Unorthodox Biography*, Westport, CT: Greenwood, 2001; A. J. Pointon, *The Man Who Was Never Shakespeare*, Turnbridge Wells: Parapress, 2011. See also J. M. Shahan & A. Waugh, *Shakespeare Beyond Doubt? Exposing an Industry in Denial*, Tamarac, FL: Llumina, 2013.

16. The basis for these assertions can be found in the references listed in footnote 15.
17. S. Lee, *A Life of William Shakespeare*, 2nd edition, London: Smith, Elder, 1898, p. 287; J. D. Wilson, *The Essential Shakespeare, a Biographical Adventure*, Cambridge: Cambridge University, 1932, p. 4; S. Schoenbaum, *William Shakespeare: A Documentary Life*, Oxford: Oxford University, 1975, p. 258.
18. J. M. Rollett, "Shakespeare's impossible doublet: Droeshout's engraving anatomized", *Brief Chronicles*, 2010, 2(9). See also: J. M. Rollett, *William Stanley as Shakespeare*, Jefferson, NC: McFarland, 2015.
19. R. P. Roe, *The Shakespeare Guide to Italy*, New York: Harper, 2011. See also the earlier work by an Italian literary scholar, E. Grillo, *Shakespeare and Italy*, Glasgow: Robert Maclehose, 1949.
20. R. Jiménez, "Shakespeare in Stratford and London: Ten witnesses who saw nothing", Shakespeare Oxford Society 50th Anniversary Anthology, 2008.
21. For the problematical character of the dating of the Tempest, see R. A. Stritmatter & L. Kositsky, *On the Date, Sources and Design of Shakespeare's The Tempest*, Jefferson, NC: McFarland, 2013.
22. Striking examples of this sort of thinking can be found in M. A'Dair, *Four Essays on the Shakespeare Authorship Question*, Willits, CA: Verisimilitude, 2012.

Part V

Where Are We Now?

13

Final Thoughts

As the reader will probably have realized, this is essentially a scruffy book. In part this reflects the author's limitations, but it is also well suited to the topic at hand. This is because the problem that this book grapples with is one of definition or characterization. In this case it is the characterization of intelligence — and with it artificial intelligence.

This book has two general themes. The first is that intelligence in the form of intelligent acts is always the product of an intelligence network. An important implication of this is that the superintelligence scare, or enthusiasm, is ill-conceived since it is based on a fundamental misunderstanding of what intelligence is.

Can our instruments actually wander off the plantation? Is the idea that they can leave their platforms really something we need to worry about? And if not, what is AI that it should dwell on such fantasies?

In fact, the entire brouhaha over superintelligence seems to me to be something of a sleight-of-hand, even a 'con game'. Basically, the smarty-pants types are busy creating artifacts that can perform tasks previously done by human beings, and eventually this will put people out of work. At the same time, they are pointing to these artifacts as if they are the potential cause of the social and economic dislocations that will almost inevitably arise as a result of their introduction into the market place and everyday life.

Artificial intelligence has therefore become a scapegoat as well as the product of a research endeavor leading to new advances in technology. Whether conscious or no, the intent seems to be to divert attention from the interests of the intelligence-class, which conflict with the interests of much of the rest of society.[1*] Under the circumstances, it is worth bearing in mind that these are *their* Martian machines.

In addition, the superintelligence fantasy may be, in part at least, an act of self-aggrandizement. (Is this why the present book is so different from the usual discussions of AI and the future of intelligence? Because it doesn't have the same partisan 'agenda'? Because it doesn't involve the same form of ego-extension? These are questions that are worth pursuing further.)

A secondary objective of this book is to convince the reader that, in spite of all its excesses and limitations, AI is indeed a serious business. This is another issue that must be approached in a somewhat scruffy manner. Consider again the two systems discussed in Chapters 2 and 4: Deep Blue and Watson. One might question the seriousness of a field in which a major goal is to build a system that can compete in Jeopardy! For reference, we can compare this endeavor with attempts to build maintainable operating systems or efficient database systems. From this perspective, one might even consider AI a kind of recreational computer science. And one might also raise the question: in years to come will AI be viewed as a sideshow that took place during the formative period of the computer revolution?

I hope that the discussions in Chapters 3 and 4 are sufficient to show that AI is much more than this. Because what it has shown is that various complex endeavors including games like chess have an underlying structure, a 'logic', that can be analyzed and then used effectively in 'real-world' situations (in this case, actual contests or tournaments). The chess competitions and the human-machine encounters with all their razzamatazz have served as concrete, real-world, in-your-face demonstrations of this fundamental fact; and in doing so they are to my mind of inestimable value.

Nonetheless, as I have tried to show in this book, by its nature AI involves a kind of conceptual illusion. It is more than an amusing footnote that its ancestry includes machines like the Mechanical Turk that played acceptable chess because a human being was hiding inside the machine. The thesis of this book is that all AI artifacts have this characteristic — by necessity they all have a human being 'inside'.

Looking ahead again, it may turn out that with the development of systems like Watson and AlphaGo, we have reached a point of transition. Perhaps their most important function is to have cleared away some of the remaining cobwebs from the field of cognitive science. They are forcing people to realize that some supposed 'mysteries' of cognition, in particular "intuition", which enable people to perform feats of intelligence such as grandmaster chess, are to some degree ignis fatui rather than genuine mysteries. Especially insofar as they are capacities that appear to set people apart from the physical world.

This is not to say that there are no puzzles remaining, maybe even mysteries. Another implication of the discussion in Chapters 2–5 is that these systems operate in a fashion that is much different than the way that human intelligence operates. In particular, in part because of the sheer power of the underlying hardware, these systems are able to deal with extraordinary numbers of possibilities at any given moment, in a way that is far beyond the abilities of human beings. Therefore, their capacities are of a different order than those of human beings. So there are still fundamental unanswered questions regarding intelligence, and we are still at an early stage of understanding major cognitive capacities.

After unpacking these systems and realizing the vast computing resources that lie behind their achievements, one begins to realize that the most intriguing thing about these human-machine encounters is that human beings — with their slow nervous systems and their unorganized information stores[2*] — were sometimes able to perform at the same level as these behemoths.

Nonetheless, the proof is in the pudding, and these systems have managed to perform brilliantly in areas that were once held to be the sole preserve of human intelligence.

Perhaps the follies that are peculiar to this field of computer science have to be accepted as an occupational hazard — related to the combination of a particular problem and certain basic human infirmities. (It should be kept in mind that such follies cannot be blamed on the artificial intelligence itself.) A more thorough, dispassionate examination of this aspect of the field would be valuable.

It should also be noted that there is no question that AI has spawned scientific work of undoubted seriousness. This includes advances in logic and the development of models and techniques for solving certain problems in combinatorial optimization. It has even been responsible for the discovery of basic data structures such as stacks that are used throughout the field of computer science.

This brings us to another consideration. At the end of the day, is there any difference between AI and computer science? Or are AI and computer science co-extensive?

Perhaps eventually, AI will be folded into the general field of combinatorial analysis in association with certain general ideas concerning computation. Even if this transpires, I think that AI will continue to exist as a particular perspective on computation and computer science as a whole.

Moreover, the present perspective on the subject suggests that, while it made sense for AI to diverge from cognitive psychology and cognitive science in the 1980s and 90s and evolve according to its own logic, at some point it will probably need to re-establish connections with these other research streams, perhaps under the general rubric of cognitive science. How these areas, in turn, will be related to the fields of computation and combinatorics is not yet clear.

The concept of intelligence networks begins to explain why a system like Deep Blue has had so little influence. And why AI systems viewed in isolation appear to be a new kind of idiot savant. And why this is not as devastating an observation as one might have thought. In fact, AI can be viewed as a novel development in the long history of cosmogenesis on this planet.

From this perspective, could it be argued that the present conception is just a restatement of cultural evolution? But if so, then why hasn't the argument been made before? The two are obviously related, but this is another topic that needs to be explored further. In particular, I don't see any previous hook-up of notions of intelligence with those of cultural evolution. Moreover, the latter clearly involves more than the evolution of intelligence, as in for example the development of odd customs and taboos.

Aside from this issue, it does seem to me that the present arguments concerning intelligence constitute another demonstration of the critical importance of historical thinking in considering systems of any complexity.

A basic error of Penrose and others is to construe the problem of intelligence in idealistic terms, so that "insight" is viewed as a property of some sort, having a kind of Platonic existence. It could be argued that the whole history of AI shows that this perspective is false and misleading.

*

The second theme of this book has to do with the shortcomings and frailties of human intelligence. Stated baldly, one implication of this thesis is that unaided human intelligence is not good enough for the Space Age, which we are now entering. In particular, it is too often subject to vagaries and even downright delusions. And, not surprisingly, this can lead to difficulties and even disasters — when collective delusions run up against the world as it actually is. The solution to this deep and abiding problem, I believe, must involve artifacts that will enable us to surmount our own limitations, much as the various prosthetic devices that we have developed in the past have enabled us to overcome all manner of physical, social, and political limitations. In short, we need solutions in the form of artificial intelligence to enhance our own circumscribed human intelligence — so we can fly right for a change (especially through declarative spaces).

For various reasons, people in modern society often undermine collective intelligence, sometimes even rubbishing the networks that embody collective wisdom. Perhaps the first person to discern this problem and to discuss it in print was Edmund Burke, notably in his criticism of the excesses of the French Revolution. Now, one does not have to yearn for the old authoritarian order to accept the force of such arguments. Instead, they should be a wake-up call: that with the passing of the old order in which much intelligence evolved without individuals really taking cognizance of it or expressing it in declarative forms, there is a critical need for new kinds of organization, new constraints if you will, so that intelligence can be preserved as well as extended.[3*]

We can be a bit more specific about what is needed in this respect. All the cases discussed in Chapters 11 and 12 (here, the reference is to the Y2K affair) were discourse-driven failures or discourse-driven disasters (DDDs). There is a need to incorporate AI into human discourse when it concerns basic knowledge or decisions springing from such knowledge. I believe that AI has the potential to free discourse from being too heavily influenced by particular human participants — and to raise standards in general. In this capacity, it can serve as a tool for avoiding DDDs, and more generally to avoid collective delusions that human beings seem prone to.

Another goal should be to make it less easy to manipulate people. But I think this can be folded into the general goals just outlined.

What I am suggesting is that AI should be inserted into human discourse, as a kind of mentor/monitor. One could think of such systems as AI umpires. We need to bootstrap our existing intelligence just as we have done in the past when we set up systems of law and government. We need truly impartial observers. And the only way I can see to have such observers is to build them ourselves.[4*]

Instead of trying to build machines that are ultra-intelligent, which the present work suggests is to pursue an ignis fatuus, researchers and practitioners should be trying to create systems that will allow (or force) people to be less stupid. (It would be nice if this included those currently fluting on about superintelligence.) Or to put it another way, the aim is to improve the general situation, not by replacing human beings with machines, but by inserting machines into the processes of everyday social existence.

In short, the idea is to use (A)AI to save us from ourselves.[5*]

Note that this constitutes a kind of 'AI vision', one that is not restricted to computer programs or 'superintelligent' artifacts. Moreover, it should begin with modest goals rather than "grand challenges". I, for one, think this would be a refreshing change.

For future observers, perhaps the greatest achievement of AI will have been taking the final step away from the sophistry and confabulation that have been the hallmark of human existence perhaps from the time we were able to communicate using natural language. A prior step in this ambitious enterprise was the scientific method itself.

Like the exponents of superintelligence, with these ideas in hand we can also invoke some frightening future scenarios — in which human beings are finally forced to grow up. But who can doubt that this may entail some accompanying benefits and even some ultimate good?

In contrast to some of the authors cited in these pages, my concern is that we are entering an age of superficial intelligence, attended by super-vulgarity and super-frivolity. This is a time when intelligence networks are dismantled almost heedlessly, deep knowledge of the world is being lost, and partly as a consequence the centrifugal forces that exist within mass society are manifesting themselves to an ever-greater extent. And while all this is happening, AI researchers and their camp followers occupy their minds with expansive visions of a mechanized future. The aim of this book has been to show that our situation is much different than the one usually depicted, and that AI may be necessary to forestall the inevitable dénouement if these all-too-*human* tendencies are allowed to proceed unchecked.

Endnotes

1. All this suggests that there is a use for people who like Karl Marx can identify differences in social self-interest that inevitably arise in mass society, but which aren't recognized for what they really are. We just don't need Marx's penchant for millenarian fantasy, and even more, his capacity for commandeering social conflicts through gimcrack analysis and rhetorical excess for the benefit of himself and his followers.
2. Clearly, there must be some sort of organization; otherwise people wouldn't be able to perform efficiently at these tasks. Nonetheless, it's unlikely that there is anything like the precise and intricate structures found in either Deep Blue or Watson, tailored for the particular task at hand.
3. Here I am thinking of the kinds of constraints that are achieved in constitutional systems, systems of checks and balances, etc.
4. An important question is, who will control the AI? But since I don't have anything particularly insightful to say about this, I leave it for "future research". In fact, it should be possible to diffuse control, especially if systems are built from 'first principles' that everyone can agree on.
5. William Blake inveighed against what he called "mind-forged manacles". From the present perspective, this is exactly what we need.